School Business Administration:
A Planning Approach
Fourth Edition

I. CARL CANDOLI
Deputy Commissioner, Emeritus
Texas Education Agency

WALTER G. HACK
The Ohio State University

JOHN R. RAY
University of Tennessee at Knoxville

ALLYN AND BACON
Boston   London   Toronto   Sydney   Tokyo   Singapore

To our wives—Barbara, Joan, and Nancy

Copyright © 1992, 1984, 1978, 1973 by Allyn and Bacon
A Division of Simon & Schuster, Inc.
160 Gould Street
Needham Heights, Massachusetts 02194

Library of Congress Cataloging-in-Publication Data

Candoli, I. Carl
    School business administration : a planning approach / I. Carl Candoli,
Walter G. Hack, John R. Ray. — 4th ed.
      p.   cm.
    Rev. ed. of: School business administration. c1984.
    Includes bibliographical references and index.
    ISBN 0-205-13139-5
    1. Public schools—United States—Business management. 2. Public
schools—United States—Finance. I. Hack, Walter G. II. Ray,
John R. III. Title.
LB2823.5.S37   1991
371.2'00973—dc20   91-3031
                                         CIP

Printed in the United States of America

10 9 8 7 6 5 4 3 2 1   95 94 93 92 91

BRIEF CONTENTS

1 School Business Administration: 1
   Function, Context, and Practices

2 A Legislative and Judicial Context for   19
   School Business Administration

3 The Revenue and Fiscal Context   35

4 A Management Concept   51

5 An Information Systems Context   85

6 Planning and Budgeting   111

7 Accounting, Auditing, and Reporting   140

8. Personnel and Payroll Administration   167

9 Purchasing, Warehousing, and Distribution   194

10 Maintenance and Operation   219

11 Capital Asset Planning and Management   248

12 Cash Management   279

13 Risk Management and Insurance   294

14 Auxiliary Services   317

15 School Business Administration Perspectives   342

GLOSSARY   357

INDEX   371

CONTENTS

Preface   **xi**

1   School Business Administration: **1**
    Function, Contexts, and Practices
    The Organizational Context of the Superintendency Team   4
    Conceptualizing a School Business Administration Function   6
    Emerging Challenges to School Business Administration   10
    Planning as Strategy and Process   13
    An Alternative View of Educational Planning   15
    Summary   16
    Suggested Activities   17
    Suggested Readings   17

2   A Legislative and Judicial Context for   **19**
    School Business Administration
    Legislative-Judicial Origins of School Business Administration   21
    Legislative and Judicial Concepts Useful in School
    Business Administration   24
    Compliance Responsibilities and Practices   31
    Summary   32
    Suggested Activities   33
    Suggested Readings   33

3   The Revenue and Fiscal Context   **35**
    Taxation   36
    Planning for Local Revenues   43
    The Interactive Nature of State-Local Funding   44
    Planning for State Revenues   45
    Summary and Implications for School Business Administration   48

Suggested Activities   49
Suggested Readings   49

4   A Management Concept   **51**

The Nature of Management Concepts   51
Private versus Public Sector Management   57
School Business Administration as a Subset of Generic Management   58
Management Applications   58
Summary   81
Suggested Activities   81
Suggested Readings   83

5   An Information Systems Context   **85**

The Linguistics of Information Systems   85
Role and Scope of Information Flow as Related to Data-Based
Management—MIS Concept   88
Selection Process   94
Utilization   99
Types of Equipment   102
The Future of Educational Data Processing   108
Summary   108
Suggested Activities   109
Suggested Readings   109

6   Planning and Budgeting   **111**

The Statutory Bases for School System Budgeting   112
Concepts of Budgeting   112
Site-Based Budgeting   114
Evolution of the Planning, Programming, Budgeting,
Evaluation System   126
Zero-Based Budgeting   130
Concepts of Budget Development   133
The Budget Process   136
Summary   138
Suggested Activities   139
Suggested Readings   139
Notes   139

7   Accounting, Auditing, and Reporting   **140**

School Accounting   141

School Fund Accounting and Operation   148

School Accounting in Contemporary Practice   152

Auditing   160

Reporting   161

Summary   165

Suggested Activities   165

Suggested Readings   166

Notes   166

8   Personnel and Payroll Administration   **167**

Challenges of Personnel Administration   167

Personnel Planning and Recruitment   171

Orientation, Training, Development, and Motivation   173

Personnel Supervision   176

Professional Negotiations   182

Personnel Budgeting   189

Summary   191

Suggested Activities   191

Suggested Readings   192

9   Purchasing, Warehousing, and Distribution   **194**

Purchasing   194

Inventory Control and Warehousing   211

Educational Materials en Route—Distribution   214

Evaluation of Purchasing, Inventory, and
Distribution Systems   216

Summary   216

Suggested Activities   217

Suggested Readings   218

10   Maintenance and Operation   **219**

Maintenance   221

Plant Operation   230

Summary   246

Suggested Activities   246

Suggested Readings   246

11   Capital Asset Planning and Management   **248**
Comprehensive Strategic Planning   248
Procurement of Furniture and Equipment   269
Orientation and Training Programs   270
Additional Planning Considerations   271
Summary   276
Suggested Activities   277
Suggested Readings   277

12   Cash Management   **279**
The Nature of Cash for Investment   279
Cash Flow   280
Investment Considerations   282
Summary   292
Suggested Activities   293
Suggested Readings   293

13   Risk Management and Insurance   **294**
The Role of Insurance   296
Planning Insurance Acquisition   298
Insurance Contracts   300
Types of Insurance Options   302
Alternative Financing for Risk Management   311
Insurance Records, Maintenance, and Protection   311
Personnel and Contractor Concerns of Risk Management   312
Vehicle Insurance   313
Occupational Safety and Health Act   314
Summary   314
Suggested Activities   315
Suggested Readings   315

14   Auxiliary Services   **317**
Transportation Services   318
Food Services   327
Security Services   335
Other Auxiliary Services   338
Summary   339

Suggested Activities   340
Suggested Readings   340

15 School Business Administration Perspectives   **342**
Fiscal and Economic Perspectives   343
The Centralization/Decentralization Dichotomy   345
Site-Based Management   348
Personal Skills for School Business Administrators in the 1990s   350
Summary   355
Suggested Activities   355
Suggested Readings   356

GLOSSARY   **357**

INDEX   **371**

PREFACE

ONE OF THE MORE useful clichés suggests that the only constant is change. This is quite appropriate when considering the present and immediate future of school business administration. Powerful external forces have altered the nature and character of school business administration. The conventional control function had long dominated the field. Until a few years ago budgets were developed to provide orderly revenue-generation and expenditure plans. Purchasing procedures made certain that statutory mandates were followed, and accounting practices provided documentation for these kinds of controls. Other conventional school business functions reflected a similar mind set.

During the past few years the practice of school business has been subjected to pervasive social forces. Changing demographics have resulted in declining enrollments. Tax revolts have swept the country. Economic downturns, tax deficits, the change from smokestack industry to high technology, the shift of economic activity from the Frostbelt to the Sunbelt, and international competition all contribute to today's school finance dislocation and in many instances fiscal crises. Conventional tax sources and revenue patterns have proven to be inadequate. School funds are more difficult to acquire. Nearly all school systems have gone through "belt-tightening," if not absolute budget and expenditure cuts. Some school systems are bankrupt and have been placed under state trusteeship, which imposes stringent management controls. As a result of these fiscal crises, there is widespread recognition that productivity of the limited financial resources must be enhanced to better meet educational needs. Cries for more efficient use of scarce dollars come from professional as well as lay communities. Cries to reduce real or perceived waste are heard in nearly all budgeting meetings.

In addition to these concerns, the cries for educational reform have intensified public apprehension. Charges that schools are not effective, that American education is not competitive with our international neighbors, and that schools are not responsive to the needs of individuals and neighborhoods all have heightened the demand for change. Today school business administration feels the effects of this disequilibrium.

In general, the social changes and demands for educational reform have been focused on instruction, curriculum, finance, and teaching conditions. The specific reform demands on school business administration have been limited to carrying out conventional business administration tasks—but only faster, better, or cheaper. Seldom is there a call for restructuring school business administration; rather, the demand is for rigorous fiscal accountability, participatory management, or decentralized budgeting. These are essentially reactive remedies. What is conspicuous by its absence in both the literature and in the public practice of school business administration is an alternative or a reconceptualized role or function of school business administration, along with a description of the implications for an implementing process and for practice.

In the following chapters the authors develop a rationale for the function of school business administration and describe the concepts and practices that implement that function. We hold that the function of school business administration is to contribute to instructional effectiveness by assisting key decision makers in using financial resources in ways to maximize the achievement of educational goals. We contend that instructional decisions have business implications and that business decisions have instructional implications. Thus, school business administrators and instructional and support personnel must collaborate in both kinds of decisions. Site-based management is one strategy that may be used to demonstrate this collaboration.

Over nearly two decades both the agenda and procedures of school business administration have been impacted by numerous and often conflicting demands and requirements. Demands for improved educational quality translated into demands for increased cost-effectiveness in the business office. Getting more and better instruction will require business administrators to develop and present to policy makers new options and new sets of priorities for budgeting and expending school revenue.

Politically, school effectiveness movements often have been linked with school restructuring. Again, the school business administrator has been charged with the responsibility of operationalizing many of the logistics of the concept. How does a school system get "more bang for the buck" in order to meet new demands without substantially increasing school revenue?

The impact of school reform in the 1980s and early 1990s has been felt largely through the federal government's initiation and endorsement, with implementation responsibility and funding at the state and local levels. Most states have enacted modest reform legislation. Others have initiated massive reforms, such as in California, Texas, Kentucky, and West Virginia. In all cases, school business administration has not been in a "business as usual" mode, but it has tended to react in conventional ways. However, there is some evidence of school business administrators taking initiatives not only to maintain efficient and appropriate practices but also to adopt a proactive posture, joining with policy makers and educational professionals to respond to educational and social demands in such a way as to make instruction as effective as possible.

One of the most significant reforms within the education profession is generally labeled *teacher empowerment*. Granted, some impetus for the movement was provided by external bodies that advocated the movement of many instructional decisions from high administrative levels to teachers, who, after all, had the expertise to best make those decisions. However, it has only been when teachers and principals accept this responsibility that we move from rhetoric to action. The concept of site-based management captures the notions of teachers empowered and the policies to enable them to exercise the power.

The new conceptualization of the business administrative function is a potentially powerful mechanism to implement the goal of teacher empowerment. Empowerment is an empty concept unless teachers are able to make decisions in their areas of responsibility and expertise and then take action to see that they are implemented. If teachers are empowered to make instructional decisions, then it follows that they should also make key business decisions to implement the instructional decisions. If a given instructional strategy is selected, then the teacher should be able to decide what supplies, services, and materials are needed to optimize the achievement of the goals related to the instructional decision. Thus, parts of the business administration function will be carried out by teaching personnel.

The call for more effective instructional leadership has prompted principals to also call for more autonomy so that empowered teachers may better respond to the unique needs of the individual school. Principals and school business administrators are joining in a cooperative effort to decentralize many school business administration functions to the individual building. This effort dramatically illustrates how the school business administration function, at least in part, can be delegated to the building principal and his/her staff.

Given this new perspective, the field of school business administration must recognize the possibility and reality of increased complexity and workloads. The information revolution threatened to inundate and eventually immobilize administrative offices. To change this liability to an asset, school administrators must rapidly acquire a new sophistication in the creation and management of crucial information. Help has been sought and received from both business and educators for this burgeoning medium.

An example of this response is the recognition of outstanding school business practices by the Association of School Business Officials (ASBO). The ASBO not only provides national visibility for individuals and school systems for excellence in practice, but also disseminates the specifics to its members.

A related and significant change is characterized by the movement to professionalize further school business administration functions. Community demands, as well as state and federal mandates, for educational and fiscal accountability have provided impetus for adding and upgrading the positions of school business administrators. More states are now providing administrative certificates for these positions. Standards are becoming more rigorous, and more in-service education in school business administration functions is being provided not only to school business administrators but also to superintendents, other administrators, and school board members.

The new function of school business administration is both more intensive and more extensive. Many new demands are included in the function, and more recognition is given to how crucial it is. The old or conventional distinction between instruction versus business has given way to the recognition of the symbiotic relationship between them. New and emerging conditions have forced us to recognize the instructional implications of business decisions, and likewise the business implications of instructional decisions. A persuasive body of evidence suggests that school business administration has now moved out of the school's business office and that there are clear and discernible business administration functions in all operations of the school.

The authors have developed this fourth edition of *School Business Administration: A Planning Approach* in the context of the changing function of school business administration. We have discussed the presence of the forces causing changes, as well as the changes themselves. Most importantly, we have described how educational professionals can view the contemporary school business administration functions and how these can be addressed.

The authors' debts of gratitude have grown over the more than eighteen years since the first edition of the book. We appreciate the valuable critiques by students who have used the book, the frank and insightful evaluations by peer reviewers, and the helpful day-to-day conversations with colleagues in our universities, in the public schools, and from our professional organizations. An especial acknowledgment must be made to David Baits and Carl Tabb, who provided invaluable assistance in researching and assembling the manuscript. To all of these good friends we are most grateful.

I.C.C.
W.G.H.
J.R.R.

1

School Business Administration: Function, Contexts, and Practices

SCHOOL BUSINESS ADMINISTRATION as a discrete function of professional school administration is a relatively recent phenomenon. Historically, the business aspects of the local school system were handled by a board of education. Because large multi-unit school systems are of recent vintage, the school system business office is also a relative newcomer on the education scene. Actually, the business function of school systems antedates the superintendency. In early prototype superintendencies such as Buffalo, New York (1837), Louisville, Kentucky (1839), and Cleveland, Ohio (1841), these positions were largely "superintendence of instruction." Traditions of local control, Jacksonian democracy, and skepticism toward professionals effectively separated educational program considerations from school finance and business functions.

In the earliest superintendency, business and fiscal affairs were typically handled by school committees, board members, or chief fiscal officers (usually laypersons), reporting directly to boards of education. This precedent, set in New Jersey, Pennsylvania, and Ohio, was adopted in varying degrees by many other states. As a result the concept of multiple control was well accepted in school business administration in the latter part of the nineteenth century. Vestiges of it are still apparent. Multiple control means that more than one administrator reports directly to the policy-making body. For example, when both the superintendent and the business official report to the board of education, the board itself must reconcile and coordinate educational programs with fiscal and business programs.

The concept of unit control is in direct contrast to that of multiple control. In a situation of unit control, a single administrator has responsibility for the implementation of educational policy as well as fiscal and business policy. A board can then evaluate the performance of the total administrative effort without having to sort out where responsibility is to be fixed between (or among) the administrators reporting to it.

American society has always been changing and dynamic. Social demands have stimulated social innovation and invention. As the American population grew and prospered, heavy demands were placed on the simplistic educational system originally designed for the frontier and agrarian society. Industrialization and concommitant urbanization concentrated the population, increased the variety and specialization of skills demanded for job entry, and required schools to assume broader community and social services functions. The waves of immigrants arriving on American shores during the second half of the nineteenth century forced the schools into new roles. Increasing educational requirements and the modest knowledge explosions of the day broadened and deepened school programs. All these changes in the nature of education resulted in vast increases in the revenues and expenditures required for public education. Complexity replaced simplicity in the system.

Because of the rapid expansion and the changing character of the educational program, many of the finance and business functions of the school board were gradually delegated to the superintendent of schools. However, vestiges of lay control of fiscal and business affairs remain today in the forms of fiscal officers, treasurers, and comptrollers reporting directly to the boards. Often these positions carry with them state-mandated duties, e.g., approving purchases or contracts, encumbering funds to satisfy these obligations, accounting for school district receipts and expenditures to state officials, and so forth.

Frederick W. Hill, in his Special Committee Report to the Association of School Business Officials, identified several milestones in the history of school business administrators.[1] The nearly complete lay control of school business affairs was challenged in 1841 when the Cleveland city council appointed an "Acting Manager" of schools with responsibilities in several business areas. Other cities followed suit, establishing these positions even before city superintendents were appointed.

By the end of the nineteenth century, professionally trained business administrators were employed by boards of education. These were frequently business-oriented administrators who served in a multiple control organization.

In the early 1900s considerable interest was generated in "professionalizing" this area of administration. Professor N. L. Englehart, Sr., of Teachers College, Columbia University, was influential in identifying school business administration as a specialized area of general school administration and in designing preparation programs for it.

Professionalization among school business administrators has had a second side. As early as 1910 the National Association of Public School Business Officials was formed; later it became the Association of School Business Officials of the United States and Canada (ASBO). This organization is devoted to upgrading the performance and professionalism of school business officials. It embraces both education-oriented and business-oriented professionals in the field.

Laws regarding certification for school business administrators remain unclear in most states. Since historical precedent provided that laypersons rather than professionally trained administrators serve as fiscal and business administrators, most states have not designed specific training or experience requirements for such individuals. In a presentation at the fifty-fourth annual meeting of the ASBO, William E. Endicott reviewed progress on state certification for these administrators.[2] In 1965 six states had such certificates. By 1968 three additional states had established certification. Several other states provided (but did not require) certification or were in the process of studying such provisions.

During the decade of the 1970s, a number of states added certification requirements so that by 1982 the number of states and provinces requiring certification was eleven

(Delaware, Illinois, Kentucky, Maryland, Massachusetts, New Hampshire, New Jersey, New York, Wisconsin, West Virginia, and Ontario). Additionally, eight states and provinces had developed a plan for permissive certification (Arkansas, Maryland, Minnesota, New Mexico, Ohio, South Dakota, Alberta, and Manitoba).[3]

As observed earlier, the school business administration function is an integral part of the superintendency. However, because of the varying sizes of school systems, the complexity of educational programs, historical precedent, and state law, there is considerable variation in the nature of the position that includes the business administration function. In relatively large cities the position is frequently designated as assistant superintendent in charge of business. Other titles are director of business affairs, associate superintendent for business services, director of administrative services, and administrative assistant.

As there is variation in titles, there is also variation in tasks performed. Tasks that generally fall in the domain of school business administration are frequently distributed among the superintendent, the school business administrator, and often a state-mandated fiscal officer appointed by the school board. Thus, surveys in the field are not particularly helpful in determining what business administrators do or should do. Ample evidence has been cited to substantiate the varied and dynamic character of the school business administrator's position. Responsibilities that accrue to this person reflect the same features. These variations are related to the maturation and acceptance of the role as a professional position in school systems. That is, the levels of role maturation seem to follow Katz's taxonomy of the skills of an effective administrator.[4] Katz developed the idea that the tasks of an administrator could be analyzed in terms of technical, human, and conceptual skills.[5]

The initial level of skill required in the school business administrator is technical in nature. The school business administrator performs in skill areas of budget development, purchasing, accounting, warehousing, building maintenance and operation, facility planning and construction, transportation, and food services. At this role level a relatively discrete function is performed. The administrator applies specialized knowledge to responsibilities and problems assigned by the superintendent.

In the technically oriented role level, the school business administrator serves as a second set of hands for the superintendent. He/she acts for the superintendent in business affairs and exercises influence over others in the system as a delegate of authority.

The second level of skills reflecting the increased professional status of the position is that of human relations. At this level the school business administrator is a specialist among specialists. The task is not only technical; it is also to relate responsibilities and skills to others in the system. At this level the administrator is no longer exclusively the agent of the superintendent but is instead a coordinate administrator who directly relates his/her function to that of the other administrators.

At this level the school business administrator spells out the business implications of group and individual proposals and decisions. The business administrator advises the board, the superintendent, the central office, and the principals.

The third and highest level of maturation of the role of the school business administrator is reflected in what Katz identifies as conceptual skill. The dominant feature of this role level is participation in planning and policy development and execution. It is important to note the necessity of planning to achieve appropriate policy development and execution. Without ultimate policy goals, planning is an empty concept. Such responsibilities clearly demand well-developed conceptual skills.

At the conceptual level the business administrator provides more than consultant help to other administrators. He/she becomes an active planning member of the superintendency team. As a planner the business administrator lends creativity and expertise to the team by creating, structuring, leading, and participating in planning the school business administration function and by relating this planning to the several other structures developed by fellow administrators. He/she becomes a planner among planners. As a result of this relationship, the school business administrator is involved in long-range curriculum planning and is not merely informed of technical responsibilities accruing from each new program. The business administrator is involved in long-range staff personnel development programs rather than, for example, being instructed to develop alternatives to increase the personnel budget by thirty percent over a three-year negotiated contract. He/she is involved in planning long-range pupil personnel programs rather than, for example, being given responsibility for setting up shuttle bus service among the several school sites during the school day.

The Organizational Context of the Superintendency Team

The notion of the superintendency team probably was well established in practice before it attained much visibility in the literature. As implied in the preceding discussion, teams may be drawn together on many different bases. A superintendent who assumes primary or nearly complete responsibility for planning might surround himself/herself with competent and dedicated technicians. The organization will then appear to be "lean, efficient, and well-directed." In one sense this is analogous to the relationship of a general with an army, a quarterback with a team, and so forth. The point is to look beyond the mere existence of the team. The organizational context within which the team operates must be considered.

The conventional structure of the superintendency team has been in recent years modified by two concepts. Site-based management was introduced as a means of bringing the focus of management back to pupil, teaching, and learning outcomes. Thus, key decisions related to these outcomes are made at the site and by persons most directly influenced by them. A second, and complementary concept, is that of the recognition of school business administration decisions as an order of decisions to be made or influenced in part by professionals at the school site, especially teachers and principals.

Given these concepts, the nature of the superintendency team incorporates a decentralized function wherein central office administrators act as support personnel to teachers and principals as well as line officers in terms of the functions that are centralized.

Role of the School Business Administrator on the Team

In one sense all the preceding discussion of this chapter has been prologue to a description of the role of the school business administrator in a planning context. The major dimensions of that role include the school business administrator as (a) a general administrator, (b) an administrative specialist, (c) a member of the superintendency team, and (d) a planner on that team.

As a general administrator the school business administrator employs processes that have long been associated with and are common to the role—planning, deciding, programming, stimulating, coordinating, and appraising. The position of school business administrator calls for expertise in the specific area of business affairs in the administration of schools. Therefore, these common processes are employed and applied to specific tasks within the general area of business affairs. These tasks include budgeting, purchasing, plant planning and construction, school–community relations, personnel management, plant operation and maintenance, transportation, food services, accounting and reporting, investing and asset management, and office management.

The overall objective of school business administration is to contribute to the development and implementation of general policies and administrative decisions that provide the most effective, efficient management of business affairs and optimize reaching educational goals. The objective is clearly implementative—that is, maximum utilization of fiscal and physical resources to attain educational goals.

The school business administrator does not work in isolation. He/she must relate to many individuals, offices, and groups in order to attain educational goals through the appropriate administration of the school system's business affairs. The structure of these relationships is best provided by the superintendency team. It is important that the business administrator relate unique skills and responsibilities to administrative problems and policy questions that are identified and defined by the broadly based administrative team. The business administrator must advise the team of the business implications of policies and decisions and is in turn advised of their effect on other task areas.

The school business administrator should have a close working relationship with building principals. The superintendency team approach calls for both line and staff relationships with field administrators. The business administrator performs as a line officer, in that principals are directly responsible to him/her for business affairs conducted in the individual school units. The business administrator serves as an advisor to principals as they carry out their responsibilities in the business affairs area.

Role of the School Business Administrator Under
Site-Based Management

The site-based management theme, which will be a common thread throughout this book, is introduced here and will be expanded and amplified in subsequent chapters. Special treatment will be provided when discussing the budgeting function (Chapter 6) and when dealing with perspectives on school business administration (Chapter 15).

The business administrator–principal relationship has increased in visibility and importance with the recent advent of demands for principal accountability for program and educational outcomes. If principals are to be held accountable for results, it follows that authority for some measure of program decision making must be delegated to them. Consequently, some states have mandated that principals prepare or participate in the preparation of budgets and be given the authority to administer them. Clearly, such mandates require a close and effective working relationship between principals and business administrators as "building" or "site" budgeting is inaugurated and operated. They also require that the principal have close working relationships with administrators of staff personnel, pupil personnel, instruction personnel, and all other cabinet officers who play a support role.

The school business administration functions performed by principals who have moved toward autonomy in developing and being accountable for programs in the building under their supervision are similar to the functions appropriate to the school district as a whole. Budgeting is a key responsibility. At the building level this usually includes budget categories related to current expenses or instructional funds and accounts. (Different terminology is used in the several states for these items.) Instructional supplies, materials, equipment, texts, library books, and the like are frequently budgeted at the building level. Some decentralized systems also provide individual building personnel budgets for teachers, aides, and custodians. Most school districts that have moved to site-based budgeting have retained certain centralized and district-level budgeting for capital outlay, maintenance and administration, and other funds and accounts that are districtwide rather than individual school building functions.

In situations in which considerable budgeting autonomy is granted to the principal, considerable school business administration responsibility follows. The principal must develop and maintain a purchasing subsystem that coordinates with that of the school district. The functions of recruiting, selecting, orienting, and appraising personnel need to be accomplished within the general personnel policies of the school system. When fiscal autonomy is exercised, an accounting system must provide the principal with fiscal information needed to make reasonable decisions. Principals who make purchases from their own budgeted funds must adopt procedures that assure the school and staff of the most suitable materials at the best possible price. The school business administrator's role of providing staff development in business affairs to both principal and staff in each building is a necessary and effective practice in the development of building-level budgeting.

The business administration function affects the principal, as well as members of the superintendency team. Consequently, a close relationship between the principal and the school business administration is crucial. The administrator helps the principal to carry out systemwide policy in business affairs and advises the principal with regard to decisions involving personnel, purchasing, and the like.

The planning approach is an important concept that permeates the role of the school business administrator. The business decisions of a school system touch pupils, teachers, principals, the administrative team, the superintendent, the board of education, and the community as well as the school business administrator. The individual best able to provide the planning point of view and the planning structure for business affairs is the school business administrator.

The school business office must continue to exercise the monitoring and control functions regardless of the organizational thrust of the system. Indeed, the control function becomes even more crucial and demanding under the site-based management concept since it creates many additional budget centers and activities that must be controlled and monitored. The business office, as the single most important support staff of the school system, has a major role in the planning needed to develop the concept.

Conceptualizing a School Business Administration Function

Given the emerging character of school business administration, the specific tasks usually attached to it, and the generic roles for school business administrators, one might ask, "What is the essential function that underlies these practices, tasks, and roles?" An answer to this question relates school business administration to general school system administration as well as to school boards and other policy-making bodies.

It is generally accepted that the primary implementing function of schools is that of creating and extending teaching and learning.[6] It follows then that the general function of educational administration is related to stimulating, developing or organizing, and implementing systems that deliver effective teaching and learning. School business administration as a subsystem of educational administration in turn embodies activities that enable teachers, administrators, and policy makers to make the ''best'' educational decisions that have business implications. School business administration may not only provide the most economical purchase of textbooks; it does so in terms of the most effective textbooks given the purposes of those who make these kinds of instructional decisions. Thus, instructional or educational specifications are an integral part of the business decision. Textbook selection also has business implications because if dollars are spent on a given textbook series, those dollars cannot be spent on other goods or services.

Given a finite amount of dollars available at a given time, it is important to consider economy, efficiency, and effectiveness. School business administration contributes to teaching and learning by providing information and services that speak to questions such as:

1. What are educational needs that have business implications?
2. What are the nature and cost of each feasible alternative to meet a given educational need?
3. What is the most efficient means to provide each alternative?
4. What is the cost-effectiveness of each alternative (to what extent does each alternative meet the educational need, and how does this equate to the expenditure involved)?
5. What is the relative priority of each expenditure decision to all of the other expenditure decisions in the school system?

In simple form a concept of the function of school business administration might be described as providing the most effective and efficient business operations for the most effective and efficient educational programs and services in the school system. An operational description of this function is that the school business administration provides and/or supports:

1. A structure in which qualified educational personnel identify and specify program needs
2. Alternative program specifications, services, and materials for these needs
3. Cost-utility or cost-effectiveness analyses of these alternatives, supplying these data to the program decision makers
4. A process for procuring or providing appropriate personnel, material, and equipment to implement the selected programs as specified, providing these at the least cost
5. Appropriate performance and cost data for evaluation of the selected programs
6. Recommendations for the modification of present programs and policies or proposals for new policies

This concept of the function of school business administration implies that educational decisions have two important perspectives: Program decisions have business implications, and school business decisions have program implications. If a leak in the gymnasium roof threatens to buckle the floor and funds need to be transferred from the textbook account to the maintenance account, this business decision has implications for instruction. Likewise, if an extra field trip has been approved, this instructional decision has business implications since a bus driver must be hired and extra operating costs are incurred.

The concept also implies that nearly all persons in the school system make certain decisions that contribute to the school business administration function. The function is not the exclusive domain of boards, superintendents, and school business administrators. Teachers, custodians, central office staff members, clerks, and school district fiscal officers also make decisions that have business implications. If their decisions are to approach the optimum, the decision makers should relate their choices to both business and instructional implications.

Contextual Perspectives

School business administration does not occur in a stable environment or a closed system. Instead, it is contextual—it responds to and is a product of many, and often conflicting, forces. There is wide variance among the pupils, families, schools, and school systems throughout each of the fifty states. Thus, the function of school business administration is influenced by the unique context within which it occurs. The contexts that appear to be most relevant to school business administration are described in chapters 2 through 5. They are the constitutional, statutory, and political; the resource and financial; management and systems; and the information systems.

The constitutional, statutory, and political context describes the nature of fundamental rights of citizens to public education and the roles and responsibilities of government to provide and protect these rights. In this context one can observe the nature and range of authority of school system personnel to make school business–related decisions and the mandated and permissive processes to do so.

The resource and financial context is important, as programmatic decisions and the school business decisions implementing them are limited by resources and the available financing structures. This context brings together considerations such as: To what extent does a community choose to meet all of the educational needs; for any proposed education program, how should costs be shared among local, state, and federal resources; how should revenue from various sources be raised (i.e., type and level of tax); and so forth. It is within this context that budget decisions are related to tax and resource decisions.

The context of management and systems relates to the ways in which complex decisions are made in the larger system. Many of the illustrations and considerations used in the preceding sections are examples of relating several factors in order to arrive at an optimum or satisfactory answer or solution. Thus, the manner of organizational decision making influences the way in which school business administration is conducted.

Closely related to the context of management and systems is the nature of data or information that flows through the organization and provides the basis for organizational decisions. In simple organizations with few variables to consider, information systems can be simple and direct. However, as complexity and interdependence become the norm, it is crucial to generate, validate, order, analyze, interpret, and disseminate data. Data flow tends to be cyclical, so many or continuous repetitions are necessary, each with updated information.

In describing school business administration it is necessary not only to consider its function but also to consider the contexts within which it takes place. The specific tasks and practices of school business administration are influenced by these considerations, and so a wide range of practices is the norm.

Perspectives of Conventional Practice

The practices of school business administration are the most obvious manifestations of the functions of this field. When a budget is formulated and implemented, it is evident that choices have been made among alternative goals and expenditures for their achievement.

The nature of practices is greatly influenced by the context or setting of a given school system at a given time. When new technologies are introduced, some school systems are early adopters and the new practices are reflected as changes in the practice of school business administration. The computer and microchip breakthrough altered the practices of data processing not only by the introduction of the hardware that speeded up the processing of information but also by the introduction of new software that extended the capability of using information. However, the level of use—and hence the nature of practices—is not uniform among all school systems. Some large and sophisticated systems have computer centers with both internal and external links so computers can "talk to each other" within the school system and to some extent with agencies outside such as state departments of education, finance, auditing, and the like. Other systems are much simpler.

Recognizing this caveat, however, it is apparent that there are some common areas of practices that are reflected in summaries of duties, tasks, and responsibilities. The ASBO has identified major areas of responsibility for school business administrators, and these appear to be representative of those positions entailing the business administration function in schools. The responsibilities are:

1. Budgeting and financial planning
2. Purchasing and supply management
3. Plant planning and construction
4. School–community relations
5. Personnel management
6. In-service training
7. Operation and maintenance of plant
8. Transportation
9. Food services
10. Accounting and reporting
11. Data processing
12. Grantsmanship
13. Office management
14. Educational resources management[7]

Beyond the specific responsibilities such as those cited by the ASBO, persons involved in the school business administration function demonstrate other practices, tasks, and interrelationships. Some of the generic tasks have been broken into several more specific tasks. For example, pupil transportation responsibilities have been divided into areas of routing and scheduling, school bus housing, maintenance and repairs, and transportation personnel (which may include recruiting, assignment, staff development, and so forth). Accounting and reporting responsibilities have been subdivided into many separate but related tasks. Payroll divisions use accounting, budgeting, and appropriation data but often are separate given the size and crucial nature of the task.

New and situationally unique tasks have always expanded the conventional responsibilities. Large urban school systems usually organize and staff a division of security personnel. Today nearly all medium-sized school systems have employed such personnel or contracted with private firms for such services. In many instances electronic devices are used rather than the typical nightguard, but responsibility for this form of security is frequently assigned to the school business office.

Purchasing and supply management as a task has expanded into specialized tasks. Full-time persons or separate offices are responsible for purchase planning (development of educational specifications) and the purchasing agent functions, warehousing, product testing and evaluation, inventory and control, and so on.

Emerging Challenges to School Business Administration

In viewing public schools in the present and near term, it is obvious that there are many challenges to conventional thinking about the function and practice of school business administration. The intensity of demands placed on public education in general and school business administration in particular has escalated rapidly. Just a few examples will illuminate the point.

Public interest and acceptance of the "educational reform movement" from the 1980s into the 1990s drew much of its initial impetus from *A Nation at Risk*.[8] Major recommendations reflected many "improvements" that were to lead to excellence as sought by different advocates over a long period. These included strengthening high school curricula, adopting more rigorous and measurable standards, requiring more time be devoted to the "New Basics," improving the preparation of teachers and making teaching a more rewarding profession, and, lastly, ". . . holding educators and elected officials responsible for providing leadership necessary to achieve these reforms, and that citizens provide the fiscal support and stability required to bring about the reforms we propose."[9]

The final process recommendation carries awesome implications for all educational administrators and certainly for school business administrators. Achievement of excellence requires not only moral commitment but also a firm and reliable infrastructure to support it on a broad and universal scope. This concept has been well articulated and demonstrated by the flurry (or perhaps the blizzard) of reports, recommendations, and state and local legislation reflecting the major points of *A Nation at Risk*. For example, individual school systems and several states designed and implemented career ladders wherein able and productive teachers could increase their levels of professional status and salaries. "Teacher empowerment" policies have been enacted to broaden the locus of teacher decision making.

A second and nearly universal theme running through the school reform reports of the 1980s was effectiveness. Again, this was manifested in differing recommendations or proposals. Analysts urged making school organizations and the management of schools more effective. Since teachers and teaching are at the heart of the teaching-learning process, reformers have called for empowerment of teachers, reduction of administrative bureaucracy, and designation of principals as instructional leaders. Other proposals call for breaking the monopoly of the educational establishment by initiating and empowering relationships with business and industry.

Much of the effective schools movement is reform oriented, with impetus provided by the early work of Ron Edmonds.[10] This movement is significant when considered along with the excellence movement of *A Nation at Risk,* especially as it juxtaposes an equity theme.

> *In short, the Effective Schools Movement has an equity dimension, the Excellence Movement apparently does not. In a world of finite resources, schools may have to make some choices about how to best use their resources for the good of communities and society. For example policy makers may have to decide whether to spend school resources on helping all primary grade students master reading skills, or to allocate those resources to ensure that outstanding older students have the opportunities to become national or world leaders in science and mathematics. The debate penetrates to the very heart of the nation's fundamental vision of public education.*[11]

A third contemporary demand placed on schools today and for the immediate future, then, is that of reforming schools to provide greater equity. Edmonds's concepts of equity have been broadened and extended. One example with far-reaching implications is the comprehensive statewide reform program proposed for West Virginia. As a result of a class action suit against the education agency on the basis of educational and financial inequities, the remedy called for a comprehensive reform of the educational system and the school finance program. The costs for full implementation would have resulted in massive increases in state taxes, and so at this date the remedy has not been implemented.

The fourth theme that has been woven into the fabric of educational reform is that of liberty, or, more specifically, the concept of parent choice. "Choice" has become a buzz word for varied agendas using a common term. One of its earliest forms was articulated by Milton Friedman, an economist at the University of Chicago.[12] Under his proposal, parents would receive vouchers that could be "spent" at a school of their choice. It is assumed that parents as rational consumers would select the school that would best fit their children's needs. The better schools would thrive; the poorest schools would be driven out of business unless they improved. Thus, free market competition would provide choice for parents, and the resulting competition would motivate school improvement.

Many permutations of the two elemental concepts, choice and competition among schools, have been incorporated in various reform concepts over the years. The Alum Rock[13] experiment and a proposed California initiative[14] are examples of specific reform proposals of this genre.

Any discussion of the educational reform movement must include at least an acknowledgement of a countervailing or alternative movement: restructuring the educational system. The basic thesis of this alternative view is that patching or fixing the existing system is inadequate given the major changes and/or dislocations in our population, economy, social institutions, national and international political life, and environment. Such a perspective was perhaps best articulated by Lewis J. Perlman. "This grim view of the future of American education and the American economy is not the product of some speculative future cataclysm. Changes are occurring in the real world, and the educational system must respond to these changes or become as obsolete and irrelevant as an abandoned U.S. steel mill."[15]

The driving premise behind Perlman's restructuring proposal is that a fundamental shift in our philosophy of learning must take place. We must shift to mastery learning rather than learning attributed to time in classes, courses passed, or degrees or diplomas awarded. Such a philosophical shift would reverse "the tendency (which reached a watershed in the late 1980s) to 'micromanage' the education process by regulating schools, teachers, the curriculum, and virtually every minute of classroom practice. Instead the states . . .(will concentrate) on . . .defining specific objectives for basic educational performance and ways of measuring and certifying students' achievement of them."[16]

Perlman spells out considerations that should guide such a restructuring. Several of these are particularly relevant to the school business administration function:

- *The productivity of the learning industry must be increased—through serving more effectively the individual consumer's needs for learning and development.*
- *Better measures of educational costs and effectiveness are needed. . . .*
- *Technology is creating opportunities for cost-effective learning. . . .*
- *Innovation in any component of the system almost invariably requires modification of the whole system. . . .*
- *To achieve productive innovations in the schools, educational deregulation and decentralization are urgently needed. State and local policies must grant greater freedom and accountability for decision making to school districts and individual schools. . . .*
- *Large scale technological change in education requires an environment of choice and competition to provide the payoff for productive innovation that a monopolistic bureaucracy inevitably lacks.*
- *Evaluation can lead to more successful implementation through better policy decisions and program management. But evaluation must be balanced to allow room for the flowering of imagination and creativity. . . .*[17]

The possibilities of some kind or kinds of school reform, whether related to excellence, effectiveness, equity, liberty, or restructuring, suggest some implications for the function and practice of school business administration. It is implied that school business administration should:

1. Provide expanded applications of benefit/cost analysis within the present function to determine present levels of both program and cost effectiveness.
2. Assist in the design and operation of accountability systems for decentralized structures. This involves describing and evaluating the areas of responsibilities and the extent to which these are met.
3. Develop cooperative relationships with empowered teachers, principals, staff, and others who assume authority and responsibility in the school business administration function. These newly empowered persons may be making decisions in areas of budgeting, purchasing, personnel administration, and related tasks.
4. Assist in the development of a cost-effectiveness rationale for increased expenditure or shifting priorities to accommodate proposed reforms that require financial outlay.
5. Assist in the description of the business implications of implementing alternative educational goals that compete for scarce resources.
6. Advise policy makers on the adaptations that are necessary to implement as a reform measure is enacted.
7. Design a system to describe and present fiscal accountability to the public, the governing and administrative agencies, and the education community. Open and mean-

ingful records are provided to reflect the way in which school boards and administrations exercise their fiduciary responsibilities.

The challenges of a rapidly changing environment, the new demands on schools, and the possibility of an altered school business administration function all suggest that school business administration will not be "business as usual." Regardless of which type of reform is enacted, regardless of the specific environmental changes that impact on the school system, and regardless of the perception of the school business administration function, a strong case may be made for developing a strategy and a process of planning in order to carry out a reconceptualized business administration function.

Planning as Strategy and Process

The continuing evolution of educational systems from small, fragmented, ineffective organizations numbering over 100,000 nationally to much larger, centrally controlled, but inefficient overlapping bureaucracies has forced a recognition of the business administration function as an integral part of the operation of the modern educational system. At the same time as the consolidation of thousands of small units was taking place, new expanded school systems were beginning to recognize the difficulty and enormity of the business function. The growth of the central business office has been an attempt to respond to the pressures for adequate business procedure application to the administration of the educational enterprise. This educational enterprise often commands the largest single budget in a community. Indeed, the expenditures for public education in the United States have grown to an estimated one hundred billion dollars annually, and projections indicate continued growth.

From the early development of school business administration through the very recent past, the focus of the business office has been largely on day-to-day operations of the school system. True, there have been attempts to perform planning activities, but these have been largely short-range efforts and have all too often been virtually extracurricular attempts by concerned individuals to determine directions and implications of certain actions. There is little in the literature or in field practice to suggest that any great effort has been expended on the orderly, systematic, coordinated creation of alternative plans for school districts to use as guidelines for future actions. This paucity of planning is best reflected in the manner in which many school systems have had to adopt "crash" programs to achieve certain goals and in the way accumulated pressures have led to several dislocations in educational programs.

The planning void in the utilization of modern technology has been particularly acute. The technological explosion has created, in effect, a technological gap in that second-, third-, and even fourth-generation computers have been developed while educational organizations are still trying to master the first-generation equipment. The increasing tempo of development has forced an awareness of the need for planning.

Technological progress has provided the tools to mechanize the business function in our educational system and has forced an awakening to the need to develop planning procedures. The gathering, sorting, storing, and interpreting of data that once required inordinate amounts of energy, time, and resources have now become almost a by-product of the sophisticated business equipment and procedures utilized by most educational systems. The time is already at hand when organizations are in danger of being overwhelmed by the deluge of data, most of which are irrelevant or at least unusable by the system. This is not because these data are inaccurate but because there is a lack of sophistication in the application of planning procedures. Most school systems now have the means to generate tons of statistical summaries, ranging from demographic to financial to student to personnel information. The difficulty arises when school system personnel attempt to utilize these data for long-range planning or specific task assignments. Quite often, because of the naiveté with which most tasks are approached, the data become worthless. One often hears the phrase ''garbage in, garbage out'' to describe the use of exotic machines for the production of answers to irrelevant questions. It seems that most educational systems are suffering from a technological gap resulting from the wide disparity between the capacity of machines to perform routine, mechanizable tasks and the ability of people to assimilate for the betterment of the system this sometimes awesome capacity. We are attempting to steer a horse and buggy suddenly moving at the speed of sound. It is terrifying, yet we cannot let go of the reins for fear of certain death.

As a result of the many pressures impinging on the educational system, the planning function is rapidly assuming a top priority with school administrators. Our world has moved from a state of sporadic and infrequent change to one of continuous change. Where school business administration could once predict future expenditures on the basis of past experience, it now becomes necessary to identify and project the effect of many variables when attempting to identify long-range needs. Solutions that were once unilateral have become multilateral, with planning efforts directed toward the provisions of a series of alternatives that recognize as many variables as can be identified. The school business administrator has become a most important member of the chief school administrator's planning team. He/she not only must be concerned with the day-to-day fiscal and management operations of the school system, but must energetically pursue long- and short-term planning efforts. In addition to ordinary tasks the business administrator must also cultivate expertise in areas such as demography, city planning, economic cycles and trends, communications, and negotiations. It is safe to suggest that in the larger systems the school business administrator should spend the greatest portion of time developing long- and short-range plans. This does not mean that the day-to-day tasks of school operation are not important; they remain a prime responsibility. It does mean that those tasks can and should be delegated to permit a channeling of time and energy into the more creative activity of planning.

The rapidly changing behavior patterns of school boards, personnel, students, and patrons strongly suggest a real change in the role of the school business administrator. Although the control function will always be an important and crucial component of the office, decisions as to priority will involve many other people.

The emerging role of the school business administrator will include planning activities such as the development of alternative strategies for identifying resources that will permit totally different kinds of educational programs to operate in the future. The school business administrator must be able to project the impact of societal change that leads to educational modifications. Predictions of the composition of the school clientele must be utilized to develop alternative schemes for meeting educational needs. Present resources have to be analyzed and means devised for gathering and allocating new resources in the future. A comprehensive knowledge of the economic forces at work, along with an ability to predict accurately future economic potential, will be most important.

The era of planning will demand far greater capacity to conceive, to conceptualize, to negotiate, and to compromise on the part of the school business administrator. At the same time it will provide a great opportunity to create, to affect, and to participate in a uniquely American invention—our public school system.

An Alternative View of Educational Planning

Educational planning is a relatively new concept being utilized in many of the more sophisticated school systems of the country. Originally introduced as a result of planning experiences and models in the military, the planning role is rapidly being developed to resolve educational problems with a set of tools unique to education. For example, the Planning Programming Budgeting System has been refined to the Planning Programming Budgeting Evaluation System, or PPBES. Continuing efforts by selected school systems and the Association of School Business Officials are aimed at providing a viable, pertinent, understandable PPBES approach to education.

The development of an educational model to carry on the planning function must rest on the validity of several assumptions, which are:

1. The comprehensive planning role must be separated from the operational planning roles so that resources are available to carry out the planning task. Those charged with comprehensive planning obligations cannot in addition devote the time and energy needed for the operational duties of the system. (This idea will be expanded upon in subsequent sections.)
2. Planning encompasses the total system and its needs, not only the planning of facilities or any other segment.
3. The diversity of skills needed to mount a planning function mandates a team effort, not a one-person show.
4. Resources needed for planning are crucial to its success and are a continuing part of any budget.

Ideally, then, the educational system should create a planning cadre that addresses itself to the planning function. This staff should undertake all planning activities for the system, including the establishment of educational goals, the development of educational programs reflecting the goals, the identification of resources needed to implement programs, the allocation of physical and human resources in implementations, and, finally, the evaluation process so necessary to continued plan development. At the very least the superintendent of schools should be readily available to the planning staff for consultation and direction. Preferably, the superintendent should be the chief planner and actively participate in the planning, particularly at the decision-making level. Key members of any planning team should include the financial planner, the curriculum planner, the facilities planner, and the evaluations specialist. Decisions as to programs, facilities, organization, resources, and time should be the task of the planning team. The school system should operate its educational programs on the basis of desired outcomes as identified and codified by the planning effort. Changes, modifications, alternatives, and evaluation of program effectiveness should all be the responsibility of the planning staff. Decisions as to continuation of programs, shifts in emphasis, initiation of new and different programs, priorities in the application of resources, and allocations should be planning tasks.

Because the foregoing implies a staff of such size that it is not realistically possible for the many smaller school systems, alternatives must be devised. One alternative, again dependent on the size of the system, is to establish a one-person planning office with the main task of generalized planning and coordinating total systems planning. This office would draw on specialized personnel in other divisions of the school system for input into the development of a total plan. Persons in various components of the school system—e.g., the business office, the curriculum office, and so forth—would have to be provided with sufficient resources to enable them to channel some time and effort into the planning process.

Another alternative presently utilized by many systems, particularly in the development of facility plans, is to contract either private consulting firms or university planning teams to develop educational plans. While this method of planning does provide a school system with a set of master plans for implementation, it is not without some danger. First, while the objectivity used by the outside consultant is a real strength, lack of complete knowledge of a school system can be a weakness. Second, although the outside agency has expertise in the planning process, the increased capacity of the local school system must be a main objective to ensure continued success. Third, there is great danger in accepting a master plan based on present data and then following it blindly without giving consideration to changing variables and their effects on the plan.

A third alternative, just beginning to be explored, is for groups of districts to pool their planning resources and to share the services of a planning staff. This not only provides smaller districts with planning services, but also tends to encourage cooperative efforts in certain curriculum areas not feasible for the very small district.

In the opinion of the authors, some combination of the preceding alternatives is most desirable. The educational system must develop a planning capacity of its own and should call on specialists from the field to supplement and complement its own staff. In this way, expert advice on particular problems can be made available, while at the same time local personnel can give continuity to the planning process.

Of course, the least desirable way of carrying on the planning function is to expect existing staff to attempt to plan while at the same time resolving all existent operational decisions entrusted to them. While this is most common, it is not the most efficient or productive use of human resources.

Recognizing that the pressures of time and limited resources often determine the scope of the planning effort, the authors urge that a firm commitment be made to the planning function in every system.

Summary

School business functions and tasks antedate the superintendency. In their earliest manifestation they were largely control functions to see that public monies were spent for their intended purposes. School business administration was separated from the instructional function in both structure and process. Only when public education became larger and more complex and cries for reform of local and municipal government were finally heeded did school business administration become integrated into the superintendency.

The function of school business administration has traditionally been defined in terms of tasks such as budgeting, accounting, purchasing, maintaining and operating buildings, and providing similar services to support the instructional program. It has been seen as a part of the superintendency with the school business administrator as a member of the superintendency team.

In recent years the emergence of the concept of site-based management and the educational reform movement have given an impetus to a reconceptualization of school business administration. Rather than functioning as a subunit of the superintendency that provides a service to instruction, school business administration can be viewed as a function exercised by many persons in the school organization. Superintendents, central office personnel, principals, and teachers are involved in making educational decisions. Instructional decisions have business implications and business decisions have instructional implications. Thus, the school business administration function permeates the whole school system. This suggests that collaboration of all decision makers in the system with the school business administrator is imperative if these decisions are to be cost effective. That is, educational goal achievement should be maximized with the lowest possible cost. Persons with educational expertise should make the decision as to where the tradeoff point between goals and cost is to be fixed.

Present or conventional practices inherent to school business administration were described in terms of specific tasks and responsibilities of the school business administrator. Within this context, current challenges of the educational reform movement are juxtaposed with the school business administration function. Given these challenges, it appears that the proposed reconceptualization of the school business administration function can support or enhance school reform.

Suggested Activities

1. Identify a major decision related to school business administration in a system, and then trace the planning activities (or lack of them) that went into the decision. Try to identify and describe the several planning activities.
2. Interview administrators in small, medium, and large school systems. Identify where and with whom most of the responsibility for school business administration lies. Try to draw generalizations as to the comparative structures.
3. Discuss the pros and cons of restricting school business administrator positions to those who have taught and have had appropriate educational administrative positions.
4. Identify a major instructional decision and trace the development or evolution of the decision. Point out at each step the presence or absence of inclusions of school business implications.

Suggested Readings

Campbell, Roald F., Luvern L. Cunningham, Raphael O. Nystrand, and Michael D. Usdan. *The Organization and Control of American Schools,* 6th ed. Columbus, OH: Merrill, 1990.
Donnelly, James H., et al. *Fundamentals of Management.* Georgetown, Ontario: Dorsey, 1981.

Hill, F. W. *The School Business Administrator.* Reston, VA: Association of School Business Officials, 1982.

McGuffey, C. W. *Competencies Needed by Chief School Business Administrators.* Park Ridge, IL: Association of School Business Officials, 1980.

Naisbett, John. *Megatrends.* New York: Warner Books, 1982.

Tanner, C. Kenneth, and Earl J. Williams. *Educational Planning and Decision Making.* Lexington, MA: Heath Lexington Books, 1981.

Notes

1. Frederick W. Hill, *The School Business Administrator* (Chicago: Association of School Business Officials, 1970), 8–10.

2. Association of School Business Officials of the United States and Canada, *Proceedings, Fifty-fourth Annual Meeting* (Evanston, IL: ASBO, 1968), 243–49.

3. Association of School Business Officials of the United States and Canada, Unpublished report, *Survey of States and Provinces on Professional Certification of School Business Officials,* 1982.

4. Robert L. Katz, "Skills of an Effective Administrator," *Harvard Business Review 33,* 1 (January-February 1955):33–42.

5. Ibid., 33–42.

6. The present discussion is limited to the *implementive* function. The varied philosophical bases or functions of schools—e.g., enabling children to develop to their fullest potential, preparing youth for democratic living, or perpetuating American society—are acknowledged but will not be debated.

7. Hill, *The School Business Administrator,* 18–21.

8. The National Commission on Excellence in Education, *A Nation at Risk: The Imperative for Educational Reform* (Washington, DC: U.S. Department of Education, April 1983).

9. Ibid., 32.

10. R. R. Edmonds, "Effective Schools for the Urban Poor," *Educational Leadership 37,* 1979, 15–27.

11. Betty Mace-Matluck, *The Effective Schools Movement: Its History and Context* (Austin, TX: Southwest Educational Development Laboratory, 1987), 15–16.

12. Milton Friedman, *Capitalism and Freedom* (Chicago: The University of Chicago Press, 1962).

13. James A. Micklenberg and Richard W. Hostrop, *Educational Vouchers: From Theory to Alum Rock* (Homewood, IL: ETC Publications, 1972).

14. John E. Coons and Stephen D. Sugarman, *Education by Choice: The Case for Family Control* (Berkeley: University of California Press, 1978).

15. Lewis J. Perlman, "Restructuring the System Is the Solution," *Phi Delta Kappan 70,* 1, September 1988, 20–24.

16. Ibid., 22.

17. Ibid., 23–24.

2

A Legislative and Judicial Context for School Business Administration

IN BOTH THE LITERATURE and practice of school business administration, it is accepted that business administrators must possess and act from a knowledge of law as applied to their professional field of activity. However, in the past the context of this action has often appeared to be "know school law sufficiently well to keep out of trouble." The authors maintain that this limited concept of school law is inadequate for business administrators, as they play a key role in determining how a school system addresses today's unique educational challenges.

The school business administrator's role and responsibilities must be carried out with the knowledge of legal constraints as well as legal authority and powers. In the past much attention was given to the former. Frequently, business administrators were noted for their ability to know and cite scores of laws, opinions, findings, and cases, which they used to convince superintendents, principals, and teachers that requests could not be met or were clearly illegal. Many boards and superintendents depended on the business administrator to keep the system out of trouble by knowing and respecting the constraints.

At the same time, however, school systems and their administrators possess or have access to considerable legitimate authority and power that can be used to achieve the goals of the educational program. In the past these powers were not always fully exercised, and so school systems and their administrators tended to be confirming and reactive. In today's context an understanding of law can assist administrators in finding new and creative approaches to carry out their functions.

With the growing intensity and complexity of social and economic problems in the 1990s, the call for effective performance and accountability is loud and clear. Major social and hence educational changes have redefined legal responsibility and authority in the public schools. School personnel are no longer exempted from lawsuits as *in loco parentis* protection crumbles. School systems have been challenged in court for ineffective instruction.[1] Fiscal accountability legislation has been enacted to hold superintendents liable for miscalculating estimated available revenues and expenditures.[2] Courts have granted or recognized new powers in professional negotiations for teachers' organizations. At the same time, legislatures have extended the power of school systems in areas of fiscal management such as investing active and inactive funds, interfund transfer and borrowing, purchasing and leasing authority, and the like.

However, only planning for and reacting to the present is inadequate. Given the nature of changes in the environment, planning for the future today is essentially planning for tomorrow's present. The analogy of "shooting at a moving target" is appropriate. Examples from the recent past suggest how changing environments create changes in the legislative and judicial context. There is a strong likelihood of additional and unique legislation and litigation in several areas.

The civil rights of school system employees and students are constantly being redefined in both state and federal courts. The extent of the rights of privacy related to a student's locker is balanced with the responsibility and authority of school officials to protect other students from drug traffickers. The rights of an individual teacher or student carrying the AIDS virus or HIV are balanced with the responsibility of the school systems to provide a safe environment for students and staff.

Challenges to the constitutionality of a state's school finance system continue to be heard. Litigation has been heard in Minnesota, West Virginia, Kentucky, Louisiana, and New Jersey. State intervention in local school district management has been initiated in several states where financial mismanagement and/or "educational bankruptcy" has been charged. The bases for the fiscal decisions in these cases are likely to set case law precedents that will be considered in future cases of similar genre.

The Asbestos Hazard Emergency Response Act (1986) required school systems to inspect buildings for friable asbestos and then submit management plans for its removal. The acute shortage of certified technicians has made it impossible to meet the original deadlines. It is likely that enforcement problems not only will persist but also will eventually result in some form of adjudication and possible liability.

The rights of freedom of choice by parents in issues related to educational vouchers and tuition tax credits have surfaced in the recent past and are likely to reappear in the future. At the federal level the Moynihan proposal (1979)[3] would have provided a tax credit to parents who paid tuition to send their children to private or independent schools. In essence, part of the tuition cost would have been offset by the tax credit. Knotty issues such as the separation of church and state, the relative advantages provided for wealthy families versus poor families, and the effect of the tax credit on tuition levels were implied but never joined as the proposal was not reported out of committee. However, several states including Minnesota[4] have implemented such a plan, which has withstood the state's constitutionality test.

Voucher proposals have been raised at the state level. To date the only one implemented was the Alum Rock experiment,[5] funded by the Office of Economic Opportunity in 1972 under the Nixon administration. For three years the program provided parents a choice among elementary schools in the Alum Rock (California) school system. Each school had its own program—some were traditional, some were unique. Cohen and Farrar concluded there was relatively little change from "long established and accepted practice."[6]

An elaborate proposal was the topic of an initiative referendum in California based on the work of John E. Coons and Stephen D. Sugarman.[7] The proposed system was complex and broadly based, with public, parochial, and independent schools eligible to accept vouchers issued to parents by the state. The number of signatures on the petition was insufficient to have the issue placed on the State of California ballot, and so legislation was not introduced and subject to a constitutional test. However, the issue is a recurring one that probably will resurface, with concomitant implications for litigation.

There appear to be three levels of understanding regarding legal authority and powers.

First, the administrator must know the legal setting in terms of legal constraints, fiscal controls, and legal procedures.

Second, the school business administrator must recognize his/her own limitations in interpreting the law and should utilize legal counsel. In some states the city attorney has the responsibility of providing legal counsel to the city school district. Many states have enacted permissive legislation to enable boards to obtain legal opinions on specialized functions such as issuing school bonds or entering into construction contracts. The administrator should also use the offices of the state's attorney or attorney general to obtain current opinion on knotty legal questions within the state.

A third area where legislative and judicial concepts apply in the planning function of the school business administrator is that of acquiring a legal orientation as to the powers and authority exerted within the several levels of government and the relationships among these levels. In a simplistic model we can accept the notion that authority should accompany responsibility and that authority is implemented through the exercise of power. Thus, knowing where responsibility lies, the administrator can begin to ascertain where and what kind of authority and exercise of power is appropriate. Such an orientation provides the administrator with a base for concluding legal generalities. Thus, he/she is not solely dependent on specific statutory law or the state education code but instead has a legal ''gestalt'' into which the specific laws and legal problems fit.

Legislative-Judicial Origins of School Business Administration

Fundamental principles guiding the development of school business administration practices spring from concepts of government rather than concepts of business or administration. Because public education is a function of government and school business administration is an implementing device, one must initially look to the allocation of responsibility and authority by government to determine how school business affairs are to be administered. A wealth of professional literature provides a comprehensive description of the allocation of responsibility, authority, and power among levels of government in regard to public education.[8] However, only a brief summary of generalizations from that body of knowledge will follow in order to provide an orientation for the legal setting of school business administration.

The allocation of control in education, through law, is expressed by the term *jurisdiction*. This term means authority that is legitimated through law. The exercise of power without legal authority is unlawful; hence the concept of jurisdiction is central to distinguishing between lawful and lawless acts of school administrators. In our system the hierarchy of legal jurisdiction is determined in two ways: (1) by the source or level of law and (2) by the authority of different government agencies. Since school law is an outgrowth of the basic scheme of the entire legal system, its place in that system must be understood in terms of universal principles that determine legal jurisdiction.[9]

Valente identified four sources and levels of law:

1. *Written Constitutions.* These are charters that establish the basic structures and powers of state and federal governments. Courts provide interpretations of constitutional intent over long periods of time and changing social conditions.

2. *Statutes.* The second echelon of law is provided in legislation. Statutes develop the specifics of organization and policy. They are developed over time, and thus new legislation frequently replaces or amends earlier enactments. Courts rule on the constitutionality and the interpretation of statutes.

3. *Judge-made Law.* Since legislative enactments apply to the entire citizenry, courts rule on disputes between citizens under the universal law. In so doing, judges interpret the law and apply it to specific cases. Frequently, they develop general principles to supplement the law but within the law's intent.

4. *Administrative Law.* In terms of sheer volume the largest body of law is that developed by administrative agencies created by statute. In education, administrative law is created by state boards of education, state departments of education, county boards of education, local boards of education, administrative units of the previously mentioned bodies, and similar entities.[10]

Bases of Federal Responsibility and Authority

The American scheme of government is a type of federalism, since there is a division of powers between the central government and the several constituent states. Through the instrument of the U.S. Constitution, a federal government was created by virtue of the states delegating powers to the central government. As a result the federal government has only those powers that the states either expressly or by implication delegated to it; all other powers are reserved to the states.

Since no specific reference is made to education in the Constitution, federal government powers in education must be derived from implied powers. To date, the general welfare clause has been the primary source for federal government involvement in public education. The federal government has used two discrete premises to penetrate educational legislation and litigation. The *civil liberties premise* is developed under federal constitutional law and statutes that prohibit the abridgment of civil liberties. These include guarantees of freedom of speech, press, association, and religious exercise, as well as the guarantee of freedom from discrimination on the basis of race, sex, and physical impairment.

The *curriculum or program premise* is based on the importance of certain educational programs to the achievement of other federal government goals. Thus, to promote the national defense the National Defense Education Act of 1958 spent federal dollars to improve the teaching of the sciences and related programs. The Vocational Education Act of 1963 sought to improve vocational education programs in order to reduce unemployment and increase productivity, and the Elementary and Secondary Education Act of 1965 sought to develop improved educational programs to help stamp out poverty. The Education Consolidation and Improvement Act was passed in 1981 to reduce administrative burdens and consolidate other ESEA titles along with parts of the National Science Foundation Act and the Higher Education Act.

Bases of State Responsibility and Authority

Since authority over matters of public education was not delegated to the federal government, it was reserved to the states. States have plenary power in these matters—subject, of course, to the limitations mentioned previously in connection with the federal authority.

School districts, as creatures of the state, have no original powers but only those delegated to them by the state.[11] The state (usually through legislative action) has the authority to modify or abolish school districts and change the powers delegated to them. It has been held that "school districts are state organizations: their school personnel are state employees, and their school buildings are state property."[12]

Responsibility for public education in a state may be thought to originate in the legislature. It is here that basic educational policy is created and financial systems, appropriations, and controls are enacted. However, with education growing in complexity and magnitude, many legislatures have created state boards of education and charged them with the responsibility of developing specific education policy complementary to the basic policy enacted by the state legislature.

In most states the executive responsibility in matters of education is delegated to a state superintendent for public schools or a comparable officer. This official is frequently appointed by the state board of education, although in some states he/she is appointed by the governor or the legislature or is elected. The superintendent and his/her staff—usually termed the state department of education—have the responsibility of implementing the policies developed by the legislature and the state board of education.

The judicial function in public education at the state level is split. State school legislation is subject to interpretation by the state court system, but the state board of education holds quasi-judicial power insofar as it maintains an evaluative function over the whole state school system.

This structure of educational governance at the state level exerts a unique influence on the school business official in the local school districts. He/she is a state official, the incumbent in a position approved (and often certificated) by a state agency. The local school business official must work within general and specific educational policies created by the legislature and the state board of education and administered, supervised, and evaluated by a state superintendent and state department of education. As a result the business administrator must know the character of these policies and regulations; must monitor their development, modification, and interpretation; and, perhaps more importantly, must know and appreciate the processes employed in order to intervene effectively in their genesis and development. This requires a state leadership role for the local school district business administrator. He/she must assume the responsibility of providing expertise in state policy formulation. The rationale for this is the principle that those who are affected by a policy should have a voice in its development. Planning for involvement is crucial if this approach is to be taken.

A second type of state-level influence on the school business administrator is that exerted by agencies of general rather than educational governance. Although educational appropriations and the mechanisms for allocation are specifically designed for the public schools of a state, frequently they are administered, monitored, and evaluated by general government offices. Thus, school business administrators must be familiar with state government accounting and auditing procedures and requirements. Certain state-level procedures for purchasing, issuing bonds, employing civil service personnel, and so forth must be followed in public school systems because they are state agencies.

In judicial matters the school business administrator of the local school system is bound by rulings of the state courts. However, he/she must also be familiar with the opinions of the state's attorney or attorney general, as these constitute valuable (but not infallible) directions of possible subsequent court action.

State Responsibility and Authority Delegated to Local School Districts

In all states (with the exception of Hawaii) considerable responsibility and authority in the conduct of public education are delegated by the state to local school systems. In general, states create the educational programs and local school districts operate them. These processes are predicated on the concept that the state is plenary—it delegates to school districts of its own creation the authority to operate these programs.

It is imperative that all school administrators know the process and the substance of delegated responsibility and authority within their own states and localities. This important legal knowledge is necessary for developing and expanding the planning role.

Local School District Responsibility and Authority

From the foregoing it is apparent that the nature of local school district responsibility and authority is essentially implementative. The tradition of local control of education has been retained over the years. However, only recently have states vigorously exercised their authority. States have enacted much permissive legislation, and many local districts (especially those with sufficient school revenue) have often gone far beyond the mandatory programs spelled out by the state.

The most important exercise of local district authority is found in the local policies developed to carry out state policies. The local district executes the state policy as a quasi corporation of the state. However, to implement the policy fully, administrative machinery must often be established.

Legislative and Judicial Concepts Useful in School Business Administration

Legislation, judicial decisions, and administrative procedures evolving from the three levels of government provide specific legal concepts that may or must be used by the school business administrator. The previous section contained exhortations for a thorough understanding of these ideas. In the following chapters pertaining to the task areas of school business administration, further reference will be made to specific legal aspects of each area. The purpose of the present section is to provide an overview of some of the most important legal concepts, which are general in nature and apply to many if not most of the several task areas.

Minutes of the Board of Education

State statutes determine whether it is obligatory for a board of education to maintain records and if so what must be included in the records. However, the official records of the board are ordinarily *prima facie* evidence of its actions. Minutes of a board may be corrected and supplemented.

Contractual Authority

Since school districts are agencies of the state charged with carrying out state functions, it follows that they must be provided authority to do so. State statutes provide limited contractual authority to school districts.

Contracts

Although patterns of limitations vary among states, restrictions usually include requirements that contracts be made by designated agents at legal board meetings, that contracts be written to include specified data, that contracts exceeding a given amount be awarded after competitive bidding, and that a specified indebtedness ceiling be respected.

Common essential elements in all contracts include considerations of: the legal capacities of the parties; the legality of the substance of the contract; proper offers with mutual consent to terms; and an enforceable agreement.[13]

Competitive Bids

Although states do not uniformly require competitive bidding, nearly all school districts use this procedure in some form. Boards may use competitive bidding at their own discretion if it is not mandated by law. If a board so elects, it is then obligated to clearly state in any advertisement that bids are to be competitive and thus bind itself to accept the lowest responsible bid. If the advertisement merely invites bids, the board is not obligated to accept any of the bids; if in its advertisement a board offers to accept the lowest bid, it must do so unless substantial reasons are given for the rejection.

If competitive bidding is used, it is necessary to provide "a common standard" on which the bids are to be based. Failure to do so eliminates the basis of real competitive bidding. Thus, rather definitive plans and specifications must be provided to prospective bidders in order to enable them to ascertain a precise bid on a specifically designated job. This practice incorporates an enlightened business principle as well as a legal requirement.

Boards of education may solicit bids on essentially the same work. In essence, several bids are requested, and the board exercises its discretion in selecting the lowest responsible bidder on the best alternative. Contractors are free to submit bids on any or all of the separate alternatives and thus compete freely.

Many states require competitive bidding and further specify that the contract be awarded to "the lowest responsible bidder." It has been held that this does not require the board to accept the lowest dollar bid. Instead, the board can exercise its discretion in determining which bidder is most responsible and how this is equated with the dollar bids. In exercising this discretion, boards must act in good faith, must not act capriciously, and must conduct appropriate investigation to enable them to make a decision based on substantial facts.

Often a board in its advertisement for competitive bids declares its intention to award the contract to the lowest responsible bidder but subsequently finds none of the bids acceptable. It has been held that despite the original declaration, a board may reject all bids, but in doing so the board must indicate substantial reasons for its action. This is another illustration of the board's exercise of discretion with justification.

When the board accepts the bid of a contractor, it has been held (1) that the contractor must be notified, (2) that a definite offer must be submitted, and (3) that there must be a definite acceptance. This is contrary to the popular belief that the board merely has to extend a contract to the contractor.

The law protects contractors who, in the process of submitting bids, make errors in their bids. The general principle is that of not permitting one of the parties to profit by the mistake of another. Thus, the contractor may withdraw an erroneous bid and is not obligated to enter into a contract with the school district.

In like fashion, boards of education may make slight or superficial alterations in specifications once a contract is let. The degree of change, however, must be such that it does not substantially alter the character of the building or item and thus destroy the equity of competitive bidding on the original specifications.

School Monies

A considerable portion of the responsibility borne by the school business administrator is devoted to money management. Fiscal matters in the business administrator's office include gathering, holding, investing, and expending monies.

School monies themselves are classified in several ways. The most generic classification is by function. Income monies are designated as revenue or nonrevenue. *Nonrevenue monies* are those that do not add to the assets of the school system. These are typically monies derived from bond issues (which must be eventually repaid), monies derived from the sale of school property (and so the form of the asset is changed but not increased), or monies derived from loans (which must be repaid). *Revenue monies* are those that add to the assets of the school system; they include taxes, transfer payments or subventions, gifts, fines, fees, tuitions, and the like. Chapters 3 and 12 deal more extensively with revenue and investment.

Control Systems for School Fiscal Policy

The discretionary power of local school boards, and hence of the school business administrator, is severely limited. As indicated in the first section of this chapter, the state, through the exercise of its plenary power, specifies general policies, then delegates to school districts those powers that must be exercised at the local level to implement the state's educational program. In terms of fiscal policy the state usually specifies the nature of local taxes, procedures that local school boards may use to levy taxes, and quantitative limitations. The state also specifies other sources of revenue that may be obtained and used, as well as how these revenues may be expended.

The budgetary function in school systems is a crucial one, and it lies at the heart of state fiscal policy for schools. As will be seen in the later chapter on budgeting, this process is used to determine not only the amount to be expended in a given area or account but also the total amount of revenue needed to support the program. Because of the crucial nature of the latter decision, states usually set up precise procedures to ensure adequate decision making at appropriate levels. Budgeting authority dichotomizes school systems into two groups:

1. *Fiscally Dependent Systems:* those in which school boards must get budgets approved by another local governmental body, e.g., a city council.
2. *Fiscally Independent Systems:* those in which the board can act (within state controls) without approval from other local bodies.

Administrator responsibility in accounting, auditing, and reporting is also limited. Usually a state-specified accounting system is mandated to provide uniform reporting and controls. Common definitions of revenue and expenditure areas are mandated. Frequently, state-specified or administered auditing procedures are employed to monitor the accounting function in the state's school systems.

State law frequently spells out control procedures with regard to transferring monies within and between state-specified funds. Most states have some explicit provision for carrying balances from the end of one fiscal year to the beginning of the next.

Several areas of fiscal policy and money management seem to make headlines nearly every year in one part of the country or another. One of the most visible problem areas is the gathering and use of ''extracurricular'' monies. Some years ago most states considered the administration of such monies as beyond the jurisdiction of legislatures. However, in more recent years, states have required school boards and administrators to abide by fiscal control procedures when handling extracurricular monies as well as when handling monies generated from school taxes.

Given the economic and fiscal stringencies of recent years, there is increased evidence of fiscal accountability[14] legislation at the state level affecting practices at the school district level. States impose ceilings on taxes levied by the district. Voter controls are also used. Budgeting procedures and levels are imposed on school systems by restrictions on proportions of increase, budget approval procedures, and the like. Some states have established actual expenditure ceilings on much the same basis. The latter fiscal controls have been initiated either in the legislature or by initiative of the state's voters.

Tort and Tort Liability

The legal posture of school districts on the question of tort liability has changed dramatically over the past several decades. The concept of sovereign immunity (''the king can do no wrong'') has been breached in many states, and now school districts stand liable, in varying degrees, for torts.

> . . . [A] tort is a civil wrong for which a court will award damages. A tort may be committed against either a person or his property and may range from direct physical injury to a person (assault or battery) to damage to an intangible asset such as a person's reputation (libel or slander).
>   . . . [A] civil action for a tort is brought by the injured person for the purpose of obtaining from the wrongdoer compensation for the damage he has suffered.[15]

In general, tort liability has been derived from common (judge-made) law. Fault is a primary consideration. Tort liability occurs when a person causes injury due to intention or negligence. Key questions must be answered to establish tort liability:

> *What duty of care does the law require of individuals in particular situations? When is the duty of care lawfully met or breached? If breached, was it a sufficient cause of the claimed injury? What special defenses, privileges and immunities may limit or defeat an otherwise valid tort claim? Finally, what role do judges and juries play in answering the foregoing questions and in assessing the amount of damages to be paid to the injured party?*[16]

It is imperative that the school business administrator know the state statutes, as well as case law and legal opinion on the nature and extent of tort liability in the state. This knowledge provides some guidelines regarding legality and amount of insurance coverage, as well as substantive advice to school personnel in matters of reducing their vulnerability to tort suits. School district financial resources are clearly in jeopardy if the district is sued for the contributory negligence of one of its employees, as in the case of a school bus driver in Illinois.[17]

Conflict of Interest

Common law has long held that a school board member, as a public official, cannot consummate a contract that results in a conflict between his/her personal or pecuniary interests and the interests of the school system. Frequently board members are (or are related to) potential school system vendors or contractors. Questions are raised as to whether these simultaneous interests are in conflict, and, if so, in what way and in what degree.

The general principle of conflict of interest is easily understood, but difficulty arises in applying the concept to specific situations. Courts in different states have handed down almost diametrically opposed rulings on essentially similar cases. Differences center on two major considerations:

1. *What constitutes personal interest?* Some courts find conflict of interest only in cases of direct and pecuniary interest, whereas others find on the basis of any personal interest, even indirect.
2. *What is the degree of taint of contract?* Some state courts have held that contracts in their entirety are invalidated if any part bears conflict of interest. Courts in other states have declared that such contracts are void only under certain circumstances.

Similar patterns of variation are found in rulings on questions related to contracts with board member spouses and in cases of nepotism, the employment of relatives by the board of education.

Given this checkered pattern of judge-made law, it is incumbent on the school business administrator to be familiar with the posture of the courts in his/her state on the question of conflict of interest. It is important to ascertain the nature and consistency of state court rulings on the various kinds of conflict of interest cases. Opinions of attorneys general are also enlightening, although they do not stand as case law.

Race and Sex Discrimination

The school business administrator finds legislation and judicial opinion that both restrict and direct certain personnel decisions. Decisions with regard to noninstructional or classified employees in most school systems are conditioned by compliance with the Civil Rights Act of 1964.

> *This legislation empowered the Department of Health, Education, and Welfare to withhold federal funds from school districts that continued to discriminate against blacks and gave the attorney general authority to file desegregation suits on the complaint of private citizens. 42 UCS 2000 c-6, d-I (1970).*[18]

This legislation and the compliance directives also point up the important role of the school business administrator in monitoring all the programs of financial assistance in order to determine their compliance. If there is a possibility of noncompliance, the funds may be withdrawn, which would precipitate major budgeting problems.

A similar pattern of constraints obtains in matters of sex discrimination. Title IX—Prohibition of Sex Discrimination in the Education Amendments of 1972, Public Law 92–318 sets the parameters of this antidiscrimination legislation.

> *Sec. 901 (a) No person in the United States shall, on the basis of sex, be excluded from participation in, be denied the benefits of, or be subject to discrimination under any educational program or activity assistance. . . .*

Interpretation of specific institutional and program restrictions has varied among the cases heard. Litigation of the most visible kinds of cases, such as whether girls must be given opportunities to play on boys' baseball teams, has not clarified the legal mandate. However, it is obvious that the school business administrator, who has some responsibility for budgeting educational and support programs, must know the points of vulnerability of specific programs.

The impact of Title IX is yet to be determined. Campbell and associates suggest that it might foreshadow major federal intervention in the operation of public schools.

> *Federal control is implicit not only in the language of the act itself but also in the detailed nature of the regulations. At this point, it seems pertinent to note the place of administrative law, in this case at the federal level, in the control of schools. Unless challenged and reversed in the courts, the stipulations of a federal agency force compliance as truly as the statutes themselves.*[19]

The concern of Campbell and his colleagues has lent impetus to the recent movement to decrease the power and authority of the federal government in creating and implementing educational policy. School business administrators will have to monitor carefully the actions of the courts as they address Title IX issues. These decisions will spell out specific compliance requirements and will also foreshadow the direction of forthcoming trends.

Due Process

With the advent of wide and comprehensive civil rights legislation and litigation, due process has become highly visible in the public schools. Teachers and others in the school system have *substantive rights,* which cannot be abridged, conferred on them by federal and state constitutions. These include federal constitutional and statutory rights (e.g., freedom of speech, religion, association) as well as those secured in the state constitution and laws. However, unique rights and privileges not specified in the federal constitution are protected only by the states conferring them. States will often enact *statutory due process* procedures to ensure the provisions of these rights.

Procedural due process is derived from the due process clause of the federal Constitution's Fourteenth Amendment. The amendment confers the substantive rights just mentioned and also provides procedural protection against illegal deprivation of these rights.

Due process has no simple definition. It varies with the circumstances involved. Factors that must be considered include the nature of the right, the danger of the denial of the right, and the nature of remediation. Two major questions must be addressed:

> *Application of this prohibition requires the familiar two stage analysis: we must first ask whether the asserted individual interests are encompassed within the Fourteenth Amendment's protection of "life, liberty or property"; if protected interests are implicated, we then must decide what procedures constitute "due process of law."* [20]

Few school-related circumstances jeopardize life, but allegations of the denial of liberty-related rights without due process have become rather frequent. An example is the denial of the right of seeking a livelihood by citing negative work habits[21] (thereby jeopardizing opportunity for future employment).

The denial of property-related rights includes denial of employment as ensured by some legal entitlement under laws, regulations, contracts, and the like. Most of these allegations relate to property interest in continued employment and state statutes specifying processes required for termination of employment.

The second stage of the analysis suggests that if protected interests are encompassed, then courts must decide what constitutes due process. Valente cites the following procedures:

1. *The affected party must be given fair and reasonable* notice *of the charges.*
2. *The affected party must be accorded a hearing.*
3. *The hearing should be set promptly but sufficiently in advance to afford a fair opportunity to prepare for the hearing.*
4. *The party is accorded the right to be represented by legal* counsel.
5. *The party is permitted to present oral and written evidence at the hearing.*
6. *The party and his or her counsel is allowed to confront and challenge all evidence against him or her, including written documents and testimony of adverse witnesses.*
7. *The hearing must be conducted by an impartial tribunal.*
8. *The party is entitled to have an official record, usually by stenographic transcript, of the hearing.*
9. *The party should be allowed* appeal *to higher legal authority, including access to courts to redress legal errors.*[22]

School business administrators most frequently have personnel responsibilities with classified and noncertificated personnel. Consequently, due process–related problems and responsibilities fall in the areas of employee evaluations, promotions, transfers, and dismissals. State statutes and school system policy must be carefully checked to determine what procedural rights are conferred. Naturally, substantive rights of these employees must be honored, but the incidence of denial of federal constitutional rights is relatively low. All administrators in school systems are well advised to make certain the board of education has incorporated due process procedures in its policy and that it conforms to the constitutions and statutes of the federal and state government.

Compliance Responsibilities and Practices

The present chapter has dealt with those school business functions that the legislature and courts have said the schools must do, must not do, or may do. Another important consideration is related to *compliance:* the degree to which the mandatory and permissive functions accepted by the school system are actually carried out. On occasion, school systems, communities, and even state legislatures have refused to comply with legitimate but unpopular legislative or court mandates.

> *The courts depend heavily upon the assistance from the legislative and executive branches of government as well as general public support to promote compliance with their decisions. Where such assistance and support is lacking, decisions may go unheeded. . . . For example, President Andrew Jackson reportedly responded to a Supreme Court decision which was sympathetic to Indian claims by saying, "John Marshall has made his decision; now let him enforce it."*[23]

School business administrators may be placed in demanding and even sharp role conflict situations when certain questions of compliance are raised.

Acceptance of Compliance Responsibilities

Compliance is an integral part of legislative and judicial mandates. Governmental agencies and their officers and agents have the inherent responsibility to implement the authoritative policies and carry out the directives of their units. Frequently, oaths of office include explicit language concerning this obligation. Problems of compliance arise when communities or administrators are guilty of malfeasance or nonfeasance.

Fixing Compliance Responsibility

Compliance responsibilities exclusively fixed with school business administrators are relatively few. Most school-related compliance responsibilities are fixed at the state and the local board of education level. These bodies have the responsibility to see that they carry out federal mandates in such actions as the Civil Rights Act of 1964, federal court desegregation orders, the Education for the Handicapped Act, and school prayer decisions. State legislatures and local boards of education usually delegate the responsibility for implementation to subordinate agencies or administrators. Thus, responsibility becomes blurred or confused, and noncompliance becomes a major problem.

Noncompliance might occur because the administrator chooses not to comply or is inept in understanding the mandate or in carrying it out. Another reason for noncompliance is that the policy-making body or superordinate responsible for the administrator chooses not to comply or is inept in understanding the mandate.

The authors choose not to catalog all the possible compliance responsibilities to be assumed by the school business administrator. Rather, let us use a few typical responsibilities to examine ways in which they may be carried out.

Federal programs invariably carry compliance requirements. Public Law 94-142, concerning education for the handicapped, requires school systems to provide programs and services to specified handicapped students. School business administrators have considerable responsibility for appropriate budgeting, purchasing, accounting, and reporting mandates contained in the legislation. In districts utilizing the federal school lunch programs, legislation mandates eligibility criteria, revenue sources and guidelines, nutritional specifications, and accounting procedures.

State compliance requirements are demonstrated in pupil transportation policies. States frequently specify pupil eligibility for the state transportation subsidy. In addition, the district, in order to obtain the subsidy, must comply with requirements in the areas of vehicle specifications, driver qualifications, routing specifications, and vehicle purchase and maintenance procedures.

Perhaps the area of the most important stringent state compliance requirements is that of fiscal management. States frequently require school systems to use standardized budgeting, purchasing, accounting, auditing, and reporting systems. Procedures, calendars, and forms for these aspects of management are mandated by the state agencies involved.

At the local school system level, the school business administration function often assumes responsibility for compliance with local policy mandates. Consistent and uniform application of local board policy in the areas of the master contract with the teachers' negotiation body is perhaps the largest monetary responsibility in many systems. Business administrators assume compliance responsibility for the board of education in contracts with vendors. When boards contract for use or rental of school facilities by outside individuals or groups, business administrators have compliance responsibilities thrust on them.

Monitoring Compliance

Since legislative and judicial mandates have compliance requirements that fall into the areas of responsibility of other administrators besides the school business administrator, it is important that a comprehensive systemwide monitoring program be developed. In the example of Public Law 94-142, the superintendency team should be involved in monitoring the several aspects of student eligibility, staffing requirements, program specifications, facility requirements, and other obligations as well as those responsibilities accruing to the school business administrator. Since lack of compliance might result in the withdrawal of funding, the role of the school business administrator is twice impacted by the mandates—in terms of overall school system planning as well as specific 94-142 responsibilities.

The monitoring function implies an additional and generic responsibility for the school business administrator: spelling out the nature of school business–related legislative and judicial mandates to the superintendency team. These are aggregated with additional mandates identified by other members of the team and are transmitted by the superintendent to the board of education with (1) implications for program and funding and (2) the consequences for compliance or noncompliance.

Summary

Because schools are agencies of the state, a school business administrator must be knowledgeable in legislative and judicial matters that involve public education. He/she must have a generalized knowledge and appreciation of the legal bases in order to see the ''gestalt'' and thereby relate specific legal principles to the total legal concept. The derivation of legal power to enact educational policy, the exercise of plenary power by the states, and the delegation of power by the state to local school boards are among the fundamental legal concepts underlying the governance of public schools.

Since school business administrators are typically given the responsibility for executing local school district policies, it is necessary for them to know the policy-making structure and how they can relate administrative procedures to such policy. The chapter covers several specific concepts that the school business administrator uses. These include the minutes of the board of education—the legal voice of the board; contractual authority—the power and constraints on contractual obligations; competitive bids—the procedures and principles necessary to protect the school system and satisfy the law; school monies—to protect the resources of the school system and use them as intended; control systems for school fiscal policy—those fiscal controls designed to provide fiscal accountability; torts—civil wrongs for which a court will award damages; conflicts of interest—contracts which result in conflicts between interests of school system personnel and the interests of the school system itself; race and sex discrimination—where there is denial of rights provided under federal statute or administrative law; due process—where there is denial of rights provided under the Fourteenth Amendment of the Constitution or a comparable provision in a state constitution; and compliance.

The authors contend that these legal and judicial concepts underlie nearly every action of the school business administrator, who is obligated to know many of them specifically (e.g., what size purchase requires a competitive bid?). He/she must also be generally aware of others in order to know when to obtain legal assistance (e.g., what kind of investments can be made with the proceeds of a bond issue?).

Suggested Activities

1. Obtain a copy of your state's school code (codification of state law pertaining to schools) and determine the specific legal requirements in matters of board of education minutes, contractual authority, competitive bidding, accounting, investment of funds, budgeting, and related business functions.
2. Review the policy handbook of a school system and determine the legal bases of the school business administration–related policies that have been established.
3. Interview a school superintendent or school business official in order to identify and discuss examples that have influenced school business administration in your state of:
   a. Legislation (both state and federal)
   b. Case law (both state and federal)
   c. Judicial opinion (opinions of the state's attorney general or state's attorney)

Suggested Readings

Alexander, Kern. *School Law*. St. Paul, MN: West, 1980.

Bolmeier, Edward C. *The School in the Legal Structure*. Cincinnati, OH: Anderson, 1968.

Campbell, Roald F., Luvern L. Cunningham, Raphael O. Nystrand, and Michael D. Usdan. *The Organization and Control of American Schools*. Columbus, OH: Merrill, 1990.

Data Research, Inc., *Deskbook Encyclopedia of American School Law.* Rosemont, MN: Data Research, Inc., 1989.

Gee, E. Gordon, and David J. Sperry. *Educational Law and the Public Schools: A Compendium.* Boston: Allyn and Bacon, 1978.

Goldstein, Stephen R., and E. Gordon Gee. *Law and Public Education,* 2nd ed. Indianapolis, IN: Bobbs-Merrill, 1980.

Kirp, David L., and Mark G. Yudof. *Educational Policy and the Law.* Berkeley, CA: McCutchan, 1974.

McDaniel, Jesse L. *Law Governing Acquisition of School Property.* Cincinnati, OH: Anderson, 1966.

Peterson, Leroy J., Richard A. Rossmiller, and Martin M. Volz. *The Law and Public School Operation.* New York: Harper & Row, 1978.

Reutter, E. Edmund, and Robert R. Hamilton. *The Law of Public Education.* New York: Foundation Press, 1976.

Strahan, Richard D., and L. Charles Turner. *The Courts and the Schools.* New York: Longman, 1987.

Valente, William D. *Law in the Schools.* Columbus, OH: Merrill, 1987.

Notes

1. *Peter W.* v. *San Francisco Unified School District,* 131 Cal. Rptr. 854 (1976).
2. Ohio Revised Code, Section 5705.412.
3. James Catterall, *Tuition Tax Credits for Schools: A Federal Priority for the 1980's* (Palo Alto, CA.: Institute for Research on Educational Finance and Governance, Stanford University, 1981).
4. *Mueller* v. *Allen,* 463 U.S. 388 (1983).
5. David K. Cohen and Eleanor Farrar, "Power to the Parents? The Story of Education Vouchers," *Public Interest,* 48 (Summer 1977), 72–97.
6. Ibid.
7. John E. Coons and Stephen D. Sugarman, *Education By Choice: The Case for Family Control* (Berkeley, CA: The University of California Press, 1978).
8. William Valente, *Law in the Schools* (Columbus, OH: Merrill, 1980).
9. Ibid., 6.
10. Ibid., 6–12.
11. Ibid., 24.
12. Robert J. Simpson, *Education and the Law in Ohio* (Cincinnati, OH: Anderson, 1968), 1.
13. Valente, *Law in the Schools,* 417.
14. Walter G. Hack, Carla Edlefson, and Rodney Ogawa, "Fiscal Accountability: The Challenge of Formulating Responsive Policy," in Forbis Jordan and Nelda Cambron, eds., *Perspectives in State School Support Programs* (Gainesville, FL.: American Education Finance Association, 1981).
15. LeRoy J. Peterson, Richard A. Rossmiller, and Marlin M. Volz, *The Law and Public School Operation* (New York: Harper & Row, 1969), 200.
16. Valente, *Law in the Schools,* 349.
17. *Molitor* v. *Kaneland Community,* Unit District No. 302, 163 N.E. 2d 89 (111, 1959).
18. David L. Kirp and Mark G. Yudof, *Educational Policy and the Law* (Berkeley, CA: McCutchan, 1974), 321.
19. Roald Campbell, Luvern L. Cunningham, Raphael O. Nystrand, and Michael D. Usdan, *The Organization and Control of American Schools* (Columbus, OH: Merrill, 1990), 48.
20. *Ingram* v. *Wright,* 430 U.S. 651, 672 (1977).
21. *Coen* v. *Boulder Valley School District,* 402F Supp 1335 (D. Colo 1975).
22. Valente, *Law in the Schools,* 194.
23. Campbell et al., *The Organization and Control of American Schools,* 172.

3

The Revenue and Fiscal Context

"IF THERE WERE ONLY MORE MONEY!" is the oft-heard lament of school business administrators. Despite the cliché of their being tight-fisted guardians of the exchequer, most of these administrators recognize that many legitimate requests must go unfunded. Given the scarcity of resources and the function of school business administration described in Chapter 1, it can be concluded that the traditional role of only husbanding the available resources should be expanded. It is necessary to propose policies and actions to increase financial support to meet present and future needs at levels called for by governing boards and/or instructional personnel.

Accepting the role of a policy advocate places the school administrator in a dilemma: Should one advocate policies that maximize revenues only for the school system of her/his employment, or should this advocacy advance policies for the welfare of the state or nation as a whole? In practice one can find school administrators lobbying for legislation to increase appropriations for their own systems in the state. This raises questions of equity, of representing the narrow interests of one's employer, and of the nature of the relationship between the state and the local school system. For these questions there is no prescriptive answer; school administrators must wrestle with them and develop their own personal positions on them. But, clearly, there are possibilities that policies that increase the revenue for one's school system might well not increase the revenue for other school systems in the same way. In like fashion the ultimate effect of such revenue increases may place disproportionate burdens on other school systems or other kinds of public services. The implications of increasing school system revenue are many and complex.

Budget development is the focal point for fiscal and revenue planning in the local school system. Chapter 7 is devoted to budget development, but much of the specific context for this task is described in the present chapter as well as Chapter 2. A fundamental concept of school system budgeting is that it has three interrelated components: the educational plan, the expenditure plan, and the revenue plan. Obviously, if there is a revenue shortfall, expenditures will be reduced (either immediately or eventually), and thus the educational program is restricted.

A proactive posture to improve revenue reliability and adequacy demands an understanding of the various sources of revenue, the bases from which they are drawn, the mechanisms (policies and administrative procedures) necessary to tap potential sources, the relationship of school system revenue generation to revenue generation practices of other competing governmental agencies, and the public perceptions of the relative merit of using public revenue for schools as opposed to use for other public purposes. If the school business administrator is to advise policy makers, it is imperative that he/she not only understand sources of revenue, but also what factors determine the flow of revenue and how policy and economic changes affect it.

Resource and fiscal decisions in public schools are embedded in constitutional, statutory, and political contexts as described in Chapter 2. Schools in the United States are financed as governmental agencies which are empowered by such provisions. Revenues flow to school systems from all three levels of government—federal, state, and local.

The authoritative bases for fiscal provisions both empower and restrict the financing roles for each level of government. The federal role is primarily based on the general welfare clause. So-called federal aid is almost exclusively categorical aid targeted for specified programs and pupils. This intervention has as its rationale the improvement of the general welfare rather than aid to general education programs.

The state as plenary body has the ultimate responsibility for providing and funding public education. In all states except Hawaii, state legislatures have created school districts as agencies of the state to actually operate the educational programs to implement the state's education policies. Thus, in most states there is state-local partnership as states grant permissive power to school districts to provide financing and to operate programs above the minimum standards required by state policy.

Revenues flowing from the federal and most state governments are derived from monies appropriated from general fund budgets. That is, most revenue comes from non-earmarked funds. The key decisions as to the amount and purpose of federal and state educational funding are essentially budgetary and appropriation decisions. Education funding considerations compete with other federal and state functions for a "slice" of a revenue pie of a relatively fixed size.

Revenue flowing into these general funds reflects the taxation policy of the federal government and each of the individual states. Both levels of government use a variety of tax and revenue sources, so one cannot identify the specific source and amount of revenue coming from a federal or state appropriation.

At the local level this generalization is less true. In many states local property taxes for schools are the only or the largest single source of revenue. Frequently, school districts are granted taxing authority, subject to various limitations.

Patterns of distribution of federal-state-local revenue among school systems are influenced by the positions that these policy bodies take on issues of equity, adequacy, equality, efficiency and liberty.

The predominant policy mechanism used by government to provide revenue for schools is that of taxation. The following section incorporates key considerations of these policies.

Taxation

A tax has been defined as ". . . a compulsory contribution from the person to the government to defray the expenses incurred in the common interests of all without reference to the special benefits conferred.''[1] It is useful to analyze the definition in terms of its component parts.

- *A compulsory contribution:* Taxes are compulsory; they are excluded from discretionary expenditures.
- *From the person:* Taxes are eventually paid by individuals, not necessarily by the individuals or agencies upon whom they may originally be levied or from whom they might originally be collected.
- *To the government to defray the expenses incurred in the common interests of all:* Taxes are purposive in terms of policies related to the common welfare; thus, one needs to examine taxation policy as it relates to specific goals of government.
- *Without reference to the special benefits conferred:* Taxes for the common welfare should not be viewed as means to obtain specific benefits for a given individual. Thus, taxes for education differ from a city's special assessment on property owners in order to install a sidewalk on the owner's lot.

Theories of Taxation

The theoretical bases for determining how the burdens of taxation are to be distributed among the taxpayers have been identified as (a) the benefit theory and (b) the ability to pay theory.

The *benefit theory* states that, as much as possible, taxes should be assessed in terms of the benefits received from those governmental services being supported by the tax. A benefit-based tax is one that uses a measure of benefit received by the taxpayer as the basis for paying taxes. The greater the relative benefits received, the greater the amount of the tax paid. Measures of benefit must be determined, and a tax rate is levied against that measure. A state gasoline tax uses the number of gallons of gasoline purchased as a measure of the benefits received from using state highways.

In contrast, the advocates of the *ability to pay theory* of taxation take the position that most governmental services are for the common good, that they are consumed by the community or society as a whole, and that it is impossible to attribute accurately individual benefits. Thus, these services should be supported on the basis of individual taxpaying ability.

An ability-based tax obviously has the inherent problem of establishing a justifiable measure of ability. Alternative measures have included income, property, and expenditures. A personal income tax uses the amount of income as the measure of ability, a real property tax uses the value of property as a proxy measure of ability to pay (the greater the value of property possessed, the greater the ability to pay taxes), and the retail sales tax uses the amount of a sale as a measure (the greater the volume of expenditure, the greater the ability to pay taxes).

Shifting

One of the most sensitive points in any tax policy or program is that of who ultimately bears the burden of the tax. It is an accepted fact that not all taxes levied increase the burden of the person or entity on which they were initially levied. Taxes levied on corporations or landlords are considered costs of doing business and are often passed on to consumers or tenants. Thus, it is important to know the extent to which taxes are shifted, and to whom, in order to ascertain the burden of a tax.

The point at which the tax is imposed is termed *tax impact*. When the burden of the tax is assumed by the person or entity on which it is levied, no shifting occurs. This presumably happens when a property tax is levied on an owner-occupied residence. Personal income taxes are not shifted, because as a result of the tax the personal income is reduced by the amount of the tax. When some person or entity other than the one on whom the tax was originally levied bears the burden of the tax, then *tax shifting* has occurred.[2] After a tax (or a part of the tax) has been shifted, the place where the burden has been finally assumed is the point of *tax incidence*.

When taxes are levied, shifting can take place in two directions. All or part of the tax can be *forward shifted* to customers, tenants, and such. In time, the burdens shifted in this fashion become costs of doing business and thus may be further shifted to the ultimate consumer. However, part of the burden may remain at any point in the form of reduced profits or income, and so the tax is only partially shifted.

A business or industry deals not only with customers and consumers but also with suppliers, employees, and stockholders. Thus, there is the possibility of a tax that is *backward shifted*. If a new tax is levied on a business or industry, imposing an additional cost of doing business, some options facing that business or industry are to negotiate a lower price on the supplies it uses, reduce wages of employees, or reduce profits and thus dividends to the stockholders. If these were to occur, the burden of the additional tax would not be borne by the ultimate consumers of the product but instead by the suppliers, employees, or stockholders.

Distributive Aspects

The distribution of burdens of taxation is a major consideration in the development of tax policy. The benefit theory and the ability to pay theory each speak to certain fundamental burden aspects but do not detail principles guiding decisions as to how tax burdens are distributed among taxpayers and how these burdens are measured.

The distribution of tax burden can be described in terms of the effect of taxes. Conventional descriptions relate taxation to income and variations in levels of income. These relationships are classified by John F. Due as:

- *A progressive relationship:* The percentage of income paid in taxes increases with increases in income.
- *A proportional relationship:* The ratio of tax to income remains the same throughout, regardless of the size of the increase.
- *A regressive relationship:* The ratio of the tax to income is lower with larger incomes than with small.[3]

Elasticity

Students of public finance policy are aware of the desirability of both stability and flexibility attributes in a tax system. One needs stability of revenue yield for some assurance of continuity, and one needs flexibility to accommodate change. The concept of elasticity embraces elements of both stability and flexibility.

In a volatile economy characterized by either growth and expansion or by abnormally high levels of inflation, it is highly desirable that a tax system has the attribute of elasticity. *Tax elasticity* can be defined as a condition in which tax revenues expand at least as fast as does the economy itself. Alternative measures of economic expansion have been used to determine elasticity. Gross national product, national income, and personal income are the most frequently used measures. Economists concerned with the responsiveness of tax yield to changes in income have developed the concept of *income elasticity of yield*. It is expressed as the ratio

$$\text{Elasticity} = \frac{\text{percent change in tax yield}}{\text{percent change in national (regional) income}}$$

If the percent change in the tax yield is exactly the same as the percent change in income, the elasticity ratio is 1.00. A highly elastic tax is one that has a ratio greatly exceeding 1.00 since its percent change in tax yield is much larger than its percent change in income. Conversely, an inelastic tax is one where the percent change in tax yield is smaller than the percent change in income. The Advisory Commission on Intergovernmental Relations (ACIR) has estimated the ranges of income elasticities of major state taxes.[4] One is struck by the range of elasticities among the fifty states regarding their state tax systems. On balance, most state tax systems are somewhat elastic, but a substantial minority are inelastic.

Criteria of Taxation

For as long as there have been taxes, people have been evaluating them. Many patterns of criteria for taxation have been developed, based on varying perspectives. Given our perspective of school fiscal policy, it appears that four general criteria are the most useful. These relate to equity, economic effects, revenue effects, and administrative feasibility.

Equity

A tax to support a public service such as public education should be fair in the imposition of burdens on the taxpayers. Equity, the ultimate goal, can be defined as equal treatment of equals and unequal treatment of unequals. Problems arise as one attempts an operational definition. If one uses the benefit principle of taxation, equity can be attained by charging the same tax for identical units of benefit. However, if the ability to pay principle is embraced, then equity is determined on the basis of income or some other comparable measure of ability. Taxpayers of equal ability or income pay the same tax.

A major difficulty is encountered when one attempts to design a system that provides for equity among unequals. If the benefit principle is employed, unequals will continue to pay taxes according to the units of benefit derived. However, if the ability principle is embraced, then taxation burdens will vary among the range of unequals, and some rational system must be developed to differentiate burdens.[5]

The nature of public education, with its difficult-to-separate blend of individual and social benefits, suggests that ability principle taxes are more compatible with its purposes than are benefit principle taxes. Thus, equity will be discussed in the context of ability to pay taxes.

Equity raises specific criterion questions. Does the tax fall equally on all taxpayers who are similarly situated? This suggests the necessity of horizontal equity—e.g., do all households of $30,000 taxable income pay the same amount in taxes?

A second series of questions is raised as to whether the tax differentiates fairly and systematically among those who have unequal ability. This suggests the necessity of vertical equity: Do households of varying taxable income pay varying amounts of tax according to increments of relative ability? Are there varying amounts systematically related to taxable income in a progressive, proportional, or regressive mode?

In order to determine actual tax burden, one must ask: To what extent is the tax shifted from the point at which it is levied and collected (impact) to its ultimate bearer (incidence)? What are the direction and magnitude of the shifting? Who ultimately bears the burden of the tax, and how does this relate to that person's or household's ability (income)?

Economic Effects

The imposition of a tax or an increase in an existing tax must by definition have an economic effect. Taxes by their very nature reduce income, and thus economic changes ensue. The issue becomes one of what kind and magnitude of economic effects are brought about by change in tax policy. By asking several questions we can explore several major economic effects.

How does the tax influence economic incentives? To what extent does the tax discourage workers to become or remain fully employed? Does it discourage the investment of new capital? Does it reduce levels of production? Does it cause harmful distortions in economic decisions? Answers to these questions can reveal qualitative economic effects as the change of taxation is imposed.

How does the tax influence economic growth? Does the tax have a significant dampening effect on the economy? If a tax increase slows down a sluggish economy or one that is in equilibrium, the tax will have deleterious effects. If the economy is ebullient or "overheated," the tax might well have very wholesome effects. Answers to these questions can reveal quantitative economic effects as the change of taxation is imposed.

What is the effect of the tax in terms of economic neutrality? A good tax should be neutral, or have no effect on the allocation of resources or consumer spending and saving or investment patterns. When a tax is imposed, economic resources are diverted from private sector savings or consumption to the public sector. Taxes may be added to product prices and treated as costs of doing business, with consequent increases in prices and ultimately reduced production. The extent to which such dislocations result from a tax increase should be considered as the "price to pay" for the increased benefits derived from expanded public school expenditures. Is the advantage of the increased tax sufficient to offset the dislocation of economic neutrality that it creates?

Revenue Effects

Revenue effects might be related to or be a subset of economic effects. Here we are interested in evaluating the magnitude and nature of the revenue generated by the tax.

An initial criterion measure of a tax is that of adequacy. Is the revenue derived from the tax adequate to meet its purpose—does the tax have the potential to provide adequate revenue? Consideration must be given to the nature of the tax base—is it sufficiently broad to cover many households to generate adequate revenue for a service such as public education? Is the tax rate established in such a way that the tax potential can be tapped to the extent needed to generate adequate revenue?

This criterion therefore considers *adequacy* in terms of (1) the role of the revenue source if there are multiple sources for funding a public service such as public education, and (2) the adequacy of this revenue, or the potential the tax has for meeting the level of adequacy.

A second criterion for revenue effects deals with relative degrees of stability and flexibility. From these contrasting concepts, a third, elasticity, has been developed; this was discussed earlier in this chapter.

A "good" tax should have the attribute of *stability* as opposed to volatility. This is of major import as related to continuity and reliability in school finance policy. The local property tax with all its faults has been retained, among other reasons, because of its stability. It has a base (property) that is visible and does not go away. The tax system encourages payment of property tax even in economic depression through the threat of foreclosures, tax sales, and the like. During periods of high unemployment personal income taxes markedly decline. Property taxes during the same period may be paid from capital rather than income. Even if tax delinquency increases, eventually the property taxes will be paid when properties are sold since payment of delinquent taxes is usually a required part of the transfer of title of the property.

Revenue sources should be amenable to planning—certainly short-range and probably mid-range. The multitude of variables and their interaction have forced a posture of considerable modesty on most long-range fiscal policy planners.

Stability does not imply, however, a static condition. No fiscal life is like that. Instead, stability is interpreted more as a dynamic equilibrium wherein changing conditions are due to known and measurable variables. Therefore, reasonably accurate projections can be made. Thus, a stable tax is one that can be relied on to generate a given amount of revenue, and if the amount changes, it is for known and explicit causes.

The converse and complement to stability is that of *flexibility*. A static tax source is not much better than a volatile one. So, the attribute of flexibility is important. Since economic and political conditions are fluid, revenue sources should be able to accommodate changes.

Elasticity as a concept flows from flexibility but applies the notion to changes in the economy. Elasticity of yield calls for a responsiveness of yield to changing economic conditions. Thus, tax revenues should grow as the economy grows. Revenues should also be responsive to fiscal policy changes (e.g., changing the rate of taxation or expanding the base). Also, in a long-term inflationary spiral it is desirable that public school tax revenue expands to the extent that revenue inflation approximates consumer and wage earner inflation.

As is the case with stability, tax revenues should be elastic to the extent that changes in the generation of revenue follow rather reliably the explicit and measurable variables that make them predictable, at least in the short run.

Revenue effects can be characterized by a third criterion measure, *balanced and diversified* revenue sources. Our increasingly complex and dynamic economy makes it impossible to depend on only one, or even a few, taxes to support governmental services. As a result balance and diversification are appropriate to the total and interrelated tax system.

Criteria for such an evaluation should suggest questions as: Is there a balance between taxes with the attributes of stability and those having the attributes of flexibility and elasticity? Are taxes with regressive effects balanced with those having progressive effects? Is there balance between business taxes and nonbusiness taxes?

Frederick Stocker spoke to the question of balance and diversification as he considered reform of present tax systems:

> There is merit in a balanced and diversified tax structure. A good tax, if overworked, can create more problems at the margin (inequities, adverse economic effects, administrative problems) than an inherently inferior tax that is used relatively lightly. Judgment must therefore be focused on applying the criteria . . . to marginal (incremental) changes in each of the various taxes.[6]

Administrative Feasibility

Because different taxes affect different persons or households in different ways, administrative procedures must be developed to put the taxation policy into operation. To ensure equity or any of the other criteria or tax principles, elaborate administrative machinery is often developed to ensure adherence to the letter of the tax law as well as to meet the spirit of the policy. Clearly, if a tax is imposed to generate revenue, it is important to consider the net amount collected after administrative or overhead costs have been met. Taxes that are costly to administer are not desirable. A tax such as the federal personal income tax has low administrative costs as most individuals simply declare their personal income, find their tax liability from a tax table, relate this to their taxes withheld, and then either claim a refund or send a check to cover their tax liability.

On the other hand, property taxes have high administrative costs. Most states have an elaborate mechanism wherein property is assessed according to complex scales of value according to multiple property classes; where such assessments are subject to frequent review or updates (demanded especially in periods of rapidly inflating property values); where assessments are subject to appeals and adjustments; and where property tax rebates, rollbacks, "circuit-breakers," and other forms of property tax relief have been enacted. One must determine the point, however, where additional administration expenditures do not provide the additional benefits to justify them.

Another cost that affects the feasibility of a tax is that of compliance. Since taxes reduce disposable income or increase the cost of doing business, there is a tendency to avoid or even evade them. Thus, government must make reasonable efforts to ensure compliance. Tax systems incorporate monitoring and auditing procedures to see that taxable property, sales, wealth, and income are reported and taxed at appropriate levels. Property taxes appear to have relatively low compliance costs, as one merely receives one's tax bill and pays it. Personal income taxes tend to have high compliance costs, however. Large governmental bureaucracies have been set up to oversee the administration of federal personal income taxes. Many other costs are absorbed by employers and the taxpayers themselves in gathering and processing data in order to comply with the tax code's provisions.

Charles Benson[7] equates administrative feasibility with the match-up of a tax with given characteristics to a given governmental unit with its unique tax administration capabilities.

> We thus see that the reliance of different levels of government on different types of taxes—progressive income taxes at the federal, sales and excise at the state, and property at the local—is

grounded in consideration of administrative feasibility. A tax is administratively feasible when the given level of government can employ staff of sufficient competence to deal with technicalities and can control taxpayer mobility to reduce tax avoidance to a tolerable level. A good tax, then, is a tax that is administratively feasible for the level of government that needs to use it.[8]

Planning for Local Revenues

All states except Hawaii have built a state-local partnership for funding public education. The long tradition of local control of education with concomitant development of local taxing mechanisms dominates present state financing systems. In a comprehensive study of state financing systems,[9] it was found that all states except Hawaii use some kind of property tax for the local contribution to the partnership. Among these forty-nine states there is wide variety in the local proportion and the specific mechanisms for determining the revenue yield. Even states considered as having "full state-funded" status (California, Hawaii, New Mexico, and Washington) still have (with the exception of Hawaii) some local property taxation flowing into their revenue plans.

Also, the large majority of states require local contributions to the state-local partnership, and in nearly all instances these are based on the local property tax.[10] Since property tax yield is a function of rate times base, both of these variables must be considered in developing the local revenue plan. The plan is developed concurrently with the educational plan and the expenditure plan. As described earlier, these three plans are fundamental elements of a budget, so the budgeting process becomes a focal point for the development of the revenue plan as well as the education and financing plans.

In states using the property tax a typical scenario for local revenue planning is initiated by a sequence of state-mandated steps for budget development and administration. Revenue or expenditure figures from the previous year(s) often serve as baseline data. Estimates of revenues and expenditures are forecast for the upcoming year. These in turn are based on the estimated taxable value of the taxable property in the school system (the tax base) and the tax rate that will be levied on the taxable property for the upcoming year. The base times rate yields the estimated tax revenue.

It is recognized that the latter two variables are complex. Economic conditions may change the amount and value of taxable property. Policy changes may alter the assessment ratios of taxable property or the effective tax rates through mandated tax relief measures and the like. Market forces that increase or decrease the demand for property cause volatility in property values. And, most obviously, taxpayer support or resistance to increased property tax rates influences the revenue forecasts. All of this suggests an important role for the school business administrator in identifying, gathering, and processing data to provide forecasts or assisting those who do the forecasting.

The same general concepts are applicable in revenue forecasting if nonproperty taxes may be available. Some states utilize other local taxes (e.g., income, local sales) as part of the tax base for school systems. These too have unique variables that complicate forecasting.

The mechanics of property tax forecasting reflect the legislated structure of the tax. The tax base may change because of additions (new property on the tax rolls), changes in tax classification (e.g., agricultural to residential or industrial), and property reappraisal or reassessment. Thus, tax base data must be updated each year.

The tax rate may change because of voted or board-mandated increases, voted or board-mandated decreases, legislated tax relief measures, or other events. Business administrators and boards need to be cognizant of anticipated tax delinquencies and of tax abatements either initiated or phased out. Levying taxes does not ensure that the extended amount will actually be collected. In general, tax rates are usually established to generate sufficient revenue (along with other sources of revenue) to fund the established educational program for the anticipated group of students (the educational plan). So, the revenue forecast should provide an answer to the question: Is there sufficient revenue to meet the educational program requirements? If there is not, either additional revenue must be generated—usually by increasing the local tax or by reducing expenditures in the educational plan.

The administrator's dilemma in tax policy advocacy, as posed at the beginning of this chapter, is illustrated in a state where a school district personal income tax may be levied in addition to a real property tax. Given this alternative, consideration must be given to not only rates and yields but also to the concepts of taxation discussed earlier. For each alternative one must answer questions such as:

- Who will bear the tax burden?
- What will be the nature of tax equity?
- What will be the likely revenue effects? What are prospects for elasticity?
- What will be the likely economic effects?
- What aspects of stability and flexibility are likely to be present?

In states with a state-local partnership for school financing, local revenue potential is frequently used as a proxy for calculating the fiscal ability of a given school system. In thirty states, state revenue is distributed at least in part on the equalization principle that state aid is inversely related to local school system fiscal ability.[11] Thus, it is prudent for local policy makers to know how much "local effort" must be expended in order to optimize the state aid provision. They must recognize the volatility of these measures and plan accordingly to accommodate changing local effort requirements.

The Interactive Nature of State-Local Funding

Salmon and others[12] found that nearly all states used local property tax bases as a means of measuring school district fiscal capacity. Additionally, a given property tax rate or tax yield is usually required in order to qualify the district for state aid and is an important variable in influencing the relative proportion of state revenue available to local school districts. Local taxation and state revenue are interrelated and interactive. Several models, to be discussed in the next section, illustrate the interrelationships.

In states with foundation programs and percentage equalized programs, a school system must levy a local tax sufficient to qualify for state revenue. In states with a guaranteed tax yield or guaranteed tax base program, the local school district is rewarded for local tax effort—usually the greater the local effort (tax rate), the greater the state revenue. Thus, school boards and administrators must interrelate and eventually reconcile concerns regarding levels of program needs and expenditures, local revenue (and taxation) levels, and amounts and proportion of state revenue that are available. Considerations may revolve around the question: How high a local tax levy is necessary to qualify for the amount of state aid needed as a supplement to fund the educational program we need in our school system? The interrelations become even more complex when one introduces the questions of cost-effectiveness as described in Chapter 1—e.g., At what level of expenditure do we get ''most bang for the buck''? and What is the best option to generate the needed revenue?

Planning for State Revenues

Given the principle of states having plenary power in matters of public education, state legislatures have the responsibility for developing funding plans for the financial support of these schools. In the very early years of the nation, much of this responsibility was delegated to the local school systems. However, since the turn of the century, states have become active partners in school funding. By 1986–87 local sources of revenue provided 44.1 percent, state sources constituted 49.6 percent, and federal revenues accounted for 6.3 percent of total public school revenue.[13] There is, of course, considerable variation in these proportions both within and between states, as well as some variation from year to year. The overall trend has been for the state to assume the senior partner role.

The mechanisms that states use to distribute state revenue to individual school systems also vary a great deal. Hawaii is essentially a one school district state; nearly all public school revenue is generated at the state level and is distributed to all of the 226 regular schools throughout the state.[14] Hawaii is the only state organized without local boards of education, local property taxes, and the conventional state-local partnership. In the following discussion most of our references will relate to the remaining forty-nine states. It must be noted that the Hawaii model has influenced other states, and its essential feature is recognized in the full state-funded model, which will be described below.

As the state-local partnership has evolved over the years, several models for the distribution of state revenue to local school systems have emerged. Salmon and colleagues[15] classified major state aid programs in the general models listed in Figure 3-1.

Foundation programs typically establish a dollar value for each pupil or weighted pupil and a mandated local effort (usually a property tax rate). A school system receives the difference between the mandated effort times the system's fiscal capacity (usually assessed valuation) and the dollar value for pupil times the number of pupils in the school system. The amount of state aid tends to be inversely related to fiscal capacity or wealth; low-capacity districts receive relatively large amounts of state aid per pupil while high-capacity districts receive lesser amounts or none. In most but not all states there is a local effort mandate.

Percentage-equalization models likewise vary in terms of whether local fiscal effort is required. The fiscal capacity of the individual school district divided by the fiscal capacity of the state as a whole yields the percent of the cost constant (or foundation level) selected by the state. As of 1986–87 two states required a given level of local effort, whereas three states using a percentage equalization model did not.

The *guaranteed tax yield or guaranteed tax base model* guarantees all school districts a given tax yield or the taxing power of a given tax base times a given tax effort. Thus, variations in tax base are in effect neutralized among all districts in the state. States vary in terms of the range in tax rates that may be applied to the guaranteed tax base.

Flat grant programs allocate state revenues on a per unit basis (pupils, teachers, approved programs, and the like) without regard to the district tax base. In some states a

FIGURE 3-1   Classification of State Public School Finance Programs, 1986–87

The fifty state public school finance programs employed in 1986–87 were classified into the following: *Equalization Programs, Flat Grant Programs,* and *Full State Funded.* State aid programs classified as Equalization were sub-classified as Foundation (Required Local Effort and No Required Local Effort), Percentage-Equalization (Required Local Effort and No Required Local Effort), and Guaranteed Tax Base Yield. Neither the Flat Grant nor Full State Funded programs required sub-classification. Preceding the classification tables are abbreviated definitions of the respective classifications.

Equalization programs

• Foundation programs—Commonly referred to as Strayer-Haig Programs. . . . the foundation formula is as follows:

$$S_i = P_i F - rV_i$$

   where:

   S_i = state equalization aid to $_i$th district
   P_i = pupils, ADA, ADM, or FTE weighted for costs of program, in $_i$th district
   F = foundation program dollar value
   r = mandated fiscal effort
   V_i = fiscal capacity of the $_i$th district

   While a local required effort technically is required for proper classification as a foundation program, for lack of a more appropriate classification, several states with foundation-type programs without a required local effort, were so classified. A review. . . . will show that a total of 30 states, or 60%, employed the foundation program formula in 1986–87. Twenty-two states, or 44%, mandated a minimum fiscal effort by their local school districts, while seven, or 14%, did not.

• Percentage-Equalization—Two types of percentage-equalization programs were employed by several states in 1986–87; one type specified a certain level of fiscal effort by their local school districts, while the other type did not. Both types, however, employed a variation of the following formula:

$$\text{State Aid Ratio (SAR}_i) = 1 - V_iS \times k$$

   where:

   V_i = per unit fiscal capacity of $_i$th district
   S = per unit fiscal capacity of the state
   k = constant selected by state

   The SAR_i was applied to a per unit expenditure multiplied by the number of units of the $_i$th district in order to derive the state allocation. If the per unit expenditure were mandated by the state, the percentage-equalization formula had the characteristics of the foundation program described earlier. If the local school districts had the power to select the per unit expenditure levels, the percentage-equalization program can be described as *District-Power Equalization* (DPE) and assumed the characteristics of *Guaranteed Tax Yield/Base Programs* (GTY/GTB) to be described later. . . . five states . . . employed percentage-equalization programs in 1986–87. Two states, or 4%, mandated a specific fiscal effort by their local school districts and three states, or 6%, did not.

• Guaranteed Tax Yield/Base—While technically different, Guaranteed Tax Yield and Guaranteed Tax Base (GTY/GTB) programs are conceptually similar, and the states that employed such programs were so classified. States that used GTY/GTB programs assured (guaranteed) all school districts a certain tax yield or tax base per unit for each unit of local fiscal effort. In essence, the states fiscally neutralized the effects created by the variance in wealth or fiscal capacity among their school districts. Commonly, the GTY/GTB programs were restrained by state-imposed limitations on the levels of local fiscal effort assured by the states. An example of a GTY program formula is as follows:

   The state will guarantee $100 per pupil in Average Daily Membership (ADM) for each mill levied up to a maximum of 35 mills.

. . . six states, or 12%, . . . used GTY/GTB programs as their major fiscal equalization programs in 1986–87. However, as noted in the discussion pursuant to percentage-equalization programs, three states classified as percentage equalization did not specify local levels of fiscal effort and assumed the characteristics of GTY/GTB programs. If the six states that used the GTY/GTB programs are addd to the three states that employed the percentage-equalization formula without a state-mandated fiscal effort, a total of nine states, or 18%, have implemented either conceptually similar DPE or GTY/GTB programs.

Flat Grant Programs

By definition, Flat Grant programs do not take into consideration the fiscal capacities of the individual school districts to support public elementary and secondary education. A fixed amount of state revenue is allocated on a per-unit basis to all local school districts. Several states relied primarily upon flat grant programs for the allocation of state aid to local school districts. . . . six states, or 12%, . . . employed flat grant programs as their primary allocation systems in 1986–87.

Full State Funded

Traditionally, only Hawaii with its governance structure of a single state-administered school district has been classified as a full state-funded system of public elementary and secondary education. However, as the trend toward greater state assumption for funding public elementary and secondary education has continued, additional states have approached full state-funded programs and were so classified. If the state government provided a high level of total revenue receipts (over two-thirds) coupled with fiscal equalization programs that deducted much of the remaining local revenue from the state allocations, the states employing such programs were classified as full state funded. . . . four states, or 8%, . . . have implemented programs classified as full state funded in 1986–87.

Source: Richard Salmon, Christina Dawson, Steven Lawton, and Thomas Johns (Eds.), *1986–1987 Public School Finance Programs of the United States and Canada.* Blacksburg, VA: American Education Finance Association and Virginia Polytechnic Institute and State University, 1988, pp. 2–5.

minimum tax effort is required in order to qualify for the grant(s). Flat grant programs do not have an equalization effect.

As was mentioned earlier, the only state with a pure form of the full state-funded model is Hawaii. However, in recent years several states (California, New Mexico, Washington) have approached full state funding.

The mechanics of state revenue forecasting incorporate some of the variables used to forecast local revenue. These variables are specified in the given state aid program model, but often other calculations are necessary to derive them.

In foundation program models it is necessary to forecast enrollment categories by age or grade, nature of program (vocational, special, and the like) or other factors (tuition, nonpublic, etcetera). School administrators have the responsibility for providing current and reliable data not only to ensure that appropriate program planning decisions can be made, but also so pupils can be classified to meet the intent of the law. Enrollments in specified categories are multiplied by the dollar value of the allocation units used in the formula to calculate the cost of the foundation program of the given school district.

The mandated local school district contribution to meeting the cost of the program is calculated by multiplying the fiscal capacity (usually the assessed valuation[16] of real property) times the mandated tax rate. This product is considered the local district contribution. It is subtracted from the cost of the foundation program. The remainder is the projected amount of state aid the district should receive.

Percentage-equalization models incorporate the concept that state aid is based on a proportion of school district expenditure per pupil. There may or may not be a state-mandated minimum expenditure per pupil. The formula is spelled out in Figure 3-1.

The mechanics of forecasting state revenues derived from a percentage-equalization model include the determination of fiscal capacity. This procedure is identical to that described in the foundation program model. The per unit fiscal capacity of the state is usually calculated by a state agency and is the only figure used. The constant is in essence the level of funding guaranteed by the state. If it is a state-mandated minimum (e.g., $2500 per pupil) and the fiscal capacity of the district is $50,000 per pupil and the fiscal capacity of the state is $100,000, then the state aid would be

$$1 - \frac{\$50,000}{\$100,000} \times \$2500 \text{ or } \$1250 \text{ per pupil.}$$

If there is no state minimum, then each school board can select the level of expenditure it chooses. For example, if the fiscal capacity of both the local district and the state as a whole were the same as the previous example and the school board decided on a $3000 per pupil expenditure, the constant becomes $3000. State aid in this case would be

$$1 - \frac{\$50,000}{\$100,000} \times \$3000 \text{ or } \$1500 \text{ per pupil.}$$

In the mandated expenditure version, forecasting must be done to ascertain the fiscal capacity. If it increases in proportion to the state fiscal capacity, the school district will receive a proportionally small amount. Thus, if the school board wishes to expend more than the constant (minimum amount per pupil), school administrators must project additional amounts of local revenue needed to reach the derived level of expenditure.

If the model does not include a mandated expenditure, the school board sets the desired level, determines the percent of state aid, then calculates the local tax levy necessary to meet the local percentage required. In practice a series of calculations is needed to determine the desirable balance between the benefit of state subsidies and the burden of local taxes required.

Summary and Implications for School Business Administration

Even though most school fiscal policy decisions are made a long way from the local school system, school business administrators who choose to be proactive and influential in policy development can be informed by understanding the fiscal context, including taxation. If a proposed modification in state tax policy would have deleterious effects on the school system (or state education system), they might well lobby against the proposed change. Being armed with relevant taxation concepts and data along with analysis and interpretation, school business administrators can contribute to rational decision making and consequently improve educational programming.

An understanding of taxation concepts provides for improved analysis and interpretation of revenue history and projection used in the budget development process. In school systems with changing demographics and economic conditions, the tax base also changes in nature and magnitude. Consequently, simple linear projections are ineffective. Instead, new variables deduced from taxation concepts are useful in developing more accurate revenue estimates.

Suggested Activities

1. Review the financial reports of a school system over a five-year period. Determine the amount of revenue from each discrete source in the general operating fund (exclude other special funds such as capital outlay, debt service, and rotating funds). Develop an explanation as to why the amounts and proportions of revenue for each source have changed over the period.
2. Describe the characteristics of local taxes levied for school purposes in a given school system. Analyze the tax structure in terms of the characteristics of a tax. Do the same for state taxes that provide for the state aid or subsidy the system receives.
3. Describe how local tax rates are set in your state. Review how these have been implemented in your school system.
4. Using the Salmon classification, identify the state school funding model used in your state.

Suggested Readings

Gurwitz, Aaron S. *The Economics of Public School Finance*. Cambridge, MA: Ballinger, 1982.

Guthrie, James W., Walter I. Garms, and Lawrence C. Pierce. *School Finance and Education Policy,* 2nd ed. Englewood Cliffs, NJ: Prentice-Hall, 1988.

Jones, Thomas H. *Introduction to School Finance: Technique and Social Policy*. New York: Macmillan, 1985.

McMahon, Walter W., and Terry G. Geske (Eds.). *Financing Education: Overcoming Inefficiency and Inequity*. Urbana, IL: University of Illinois Press, 1982.

Monk, David H. *Educational Finance: An Economic Approach*. New York: McGraw-Hill, 1990.

Mueller, Van D., and Mary P. McKeown (Eds.). *The Fiscal, Legal, and Political Aspects of State Reform of Elementary and Secondary Education*. Cambridge, MA: Ballinger, 1985.

Underwood, Julie K., and Deborah A. Verstegen (Eds.). *The Impacts of Litigation and Legislation on Public School Finance: Adequacy, Equity, and Excellence*. New York: Harper & Row, 1990.

Webb, L. D., Martha M. McCarthy, and Stephen B. Thomas. *Financing Elementary and Secondary Education*. Columbus, OH: Merrill, 1988.

Webb, L. D., and Van D. Mueller (Eds.). *Managing Limited Resources: New Demands on Public School Management*. Cambridge, MA: Ballinger, 1984.

Notes

1. E. R. A. Seligman, *Essays in Taxation,* 10th ed. (New York: Macmillan, 1955), 432.

2. For a fuller discussion see Walter G. Hack and Francis O. Woodward, *Economic Dimensions of Public School Finance: Concepts and Cases* (New York: McGraw-Hill, 1971), 151–155.

3. John F. Due, "Principles of Taxation," in Charles S. Benson (Ed.), *Perspectives on the Economics of Education* (Boston: Houghton-Mifflin, 1963), 170–171.

4. Advisory Commission on Intergovernmental Relations (ACIR), *Significant Features of Fiscal Federalism, 1976–77* (Washington, DC: ACIR, 1977), 50.

5. For a full discussion of treatment of unequals, see Charles J. Benson, *The Economics of Public Education,* 3rd ed. (Boston: Houghton-Mifflin, 1978), 271–74.

6. Frederick D. Stocker, *Financing Ohio's Schools and Other Public Services* (Washington, DC: National Education Association, 1980), 40.

7. Charles S. Benson, *The Economics of Public Education,* 3rd ed. (Boston: Houghton-Mifflin, 1978) 276–77.

8. Ibid., 277.

9. Richard Salmon, Christina Dawson, Steven Lawton, and Thomas Johns (Eds.), *Public School Finance Programs of the United States and Canada* (Blacksburg, VA: American Education Finance Association and Virginia Polytechnic Institute and State University, 1988).

10. Ibid., 2–7.

11. Ibid., 2–5.

12. Ibid.

13. ACIR, *Significant Features of Fiscal Federalism,* 44–45.

14. Salmon et al., *Public School Finance Programs of the United States and Canada,* 9.

15. Ibid., 2.

16. The mechanics are identical to that of projecting the local property base described on page 43 in the section, "Planning for Local Revenues."

4

A Management Concept

The Nature of Management Concepts

While a number of theories and notions about management are currently being articulated and espoused, there seems to be a growing momentum for the development of a set of central core or generic domains, augmented by job-specific skills needed in particular task areas. These core or generic administrative skills are common to all management assignments and must be exhibited by all, no matter what their particular job obligations are. In addition, the job-specific skills are being identified by a number of groups and organizations across the country.

Organizations like the American Association of School Administrators (AASA) and the National Association of Secondary School Principals (NASSP) have provided leadership in the development of administrator assessment models predicated on expectations of particular positions. As early as 1982, AASA identified the following seven performance goals for school leaders.

School Leaders of Tomorrow Must:

1. *Establish and maintain a positive and open learning environment to bring about the motivation and social integration of students and staff.*
2. *Build strong local, state, and national support for education.*
3. *Develop and deliver an effective curriculum which expands the definitions of literacy, competency, and cultural integration to include advanced technologies, problem solving, critical thinking and communication skills, and cultural enrichment for all students.*
4. *Develop and implement effective models/modes of instructional delivery that makes the best use of time, staff, advanced technologies, community resources, and financial means to maximize student outcomes.*
5. *Create programs of continuous improvement, including evaluation of both staff and program effectiveness as keys to student learning and development.*
6. *Skillfully manage school system operations and facilities to enhance student learning.*
7. *Conduct and make use of significant research as a basis for problem solving and program planning of all kinds.*[1]

Since the 1982 publication, AASA expanded its efforts. By 1988 several pilot assessment sites had been identified and work was proceeding in the development of specific indicators for evaluation. One such site is the University of Texas, where a massive effort is underway to devise an exemplary administrator preparation program and an evaluation system to assist individuals in understanding where they are with respect to the needed knowledge. The University of Texas development emphasizes the use of multiple sources of assistance in the training of educational administrators. They have recognized the following leadership domains for inclusion in the preparation programs:

1. Liberal education
2. Instructional leadership
3. General administration leadership
4. Human relations leadership
5. Personal capabilities

These domains are an outgrowth of the work of the National Commission on Excellence in Educational Administration sponsored by the University Council for Educational Administration. In 1987 the commission published a report, *Leaders for America's Schools,*[2] that stated that the various complex demands on educational leadership require attention to the following five strands for preparation:

1. Study of administration
2. Study of the technical core of educational administration and the acquisition of vital administrative skills
3. Application of research findings and methods to problems
4. Supervised practice
5. Demonstration of competence

During the same period (1986–1988) the Texas Education Agency, acting under a legislative mandate, developed an in-service core or generic program for practicing administrators. This program—which is in addition to instructional leadership training, evaluation preparation, and certification (job-specific) requirements—includes the following domains:

1. Administrative skills
2. Conceptual skills
3. Interpersonal skills
4. Resource skills

Prospective administrators must qualify for the administrator's certificate by completing the required courses and by passing the Examination for the Certification of Educators in Texas (EXCET) exam for the particular certificate desired. Once employed, the administrator must complete a 40-hour curriculum in instructional leadership training and a 40-hour course in teacher evaluation. The state requires ongoing development of administrative skills based on individual needs assessments that indicate participants must complete a 40-hour curriculum in instructional leadership training and a 40-hour course in teacher evaluation. Also required are administrative skills based on individual needs, especially in the core or generic areas. Now under development is an administrator evaluation instrument predicated on the common core, job-specific requirements, and instructional management. It is projected that the evaluation system will be operational by the 1991–92 academic year.

These developments are paralleled in many of the states, with California providing leadership in administrator development as a result of state-mandated administrator academics. The funding of Leadership in Educational Administration Development (LEAD) in each state has also served to give a boost to the movement to improve leadership development.

It behooves the school business administrator to become totally immersed in the variety of opportunities emerging as a result of the recognition of the importance of highly qualified and competent educational leaders. The core of generic skills is, indeed, the basis for all administrative assignments. The successful business administrator has these skills in addition to the job-specific attributes required in the performance of his/her duties.

The Evolution of Management Theory

Hoy and Miskel define theory in educational administration thusly: "Theory is a set of interrelated concepts, assumptions, and generalizations that systematically describes and explains regularities in behavior in educational administration."[3]

Management theory has as its foundation the work of Frederick Taylor, known as the father of the scientific management movement. There are three distinct phases of development of administrative science as presented by Hoy and Miskel. These are identified as the classical organization phase, starting roughly in 1900 and pioneered by Taylor, Fayol, Gulick, and Urwick; the human relations phase, starting in 1930 with Follett, Mayo, and Roethlisberger as early advocates; and the behavioral science phase, starting in 1950 with Barnard and Simon as leaders in its development.

The Classical Approach

The basic features of the traditional or classical administrative models are as follows:

- *Time and Motion Studies:* The task is carried out in a way that minimizes time and effort.
- *Division of Labor and Specialization:* Efficiency can be attained by subdividing any operation into its basic components to ensure workers' performance.
- *Standardization of Tasks:* Breaking tasks into component parts allows for routinized performance.
- *Unity of Command:* To coordinate the organization, decision making is centralized, with responsibility flowing from top to bottom.
- *Span of Control:* Unity of command and coordination are possible only if each superior at any level has a limited number of subordinates (five to ten) to direct.
- *Uniqueness of Function:* One department of an organization should not duplicate the functions performed by another.
- *Formal Organization:* The focus of analysis is on the official organizational blueprint; semiformal and informal structure created by the dynamic interaction of people within the formal organization are not analyzed.[4]

As events of the past forty or fifty years have borne out, the classical model suffers from organizational rigidity and its refusal to recognize the impact of events external to the organization and events that are poorly coordinated internally.

The Human Relations Phase

The human relations approach evolved as a reaction to the rigidity of the classical model. Mary Parker Follett, who wrote a series of papers dealing with the human side of administration,[5] believed that the fundamental problem in all organizations was developing and maintaining dynamic and harmonious relationships.

The studies that stimulated the human relations phase of management theory were those done in the Hawthorne plant of the Western Electric Company in New Jersey. These three studies, although inconclusive as to results, prompted a great deal of research. The Hawthorne studies suggested that workers react positively to attention given them by management. Further, workers can endure any amount of discomfort if they are involved in the decision process.

Hoy and Miskel summarize the Hawthorne studies as follows:[6]

1. Economic incentive is not the only significant motivator. In fact, noneconomic social sanctions limit the effectiveness of economic incentives.
2. Workers respond to management as members of an informal group, not as individuals.
3. Production levels are limited more by the social norms of the informal organization than by its physiological capacities.
4. Specialization does not necessarily create the most efficient organization of the work group.
5. Workers use informal organization to protect themselves against arbitrary management decisions.
6. Informal social organizations interact with management.
7. A narrow span of control is not a prerequisite to effective management.
8. Informal leaders are often as important as formal supervisors.
9. Individuals are active human beings, not passive cogs in a machine.

The Behavioral Science Phase

The work of Chester I. Barnard and Herbert Simon originated much of the behavioral science methodology. Barnard and Simon drew on the work of Max Weber, particularly the view that organizations are social systems that interact with and are dependent on their environments.

Historically, organizations have been seen as closed systems with a set of interdependent elements forming an organized whole. By the early 1960s behavioral scientists began to focus attention on the fact that organizations are not only influenced by their environments but also dependent on them. The open system definition has now become the norm, so that today few, if any, organizational theorists accept the premise that organizations can be understood in isolation from external events.

Three competing systems perspectives have emerged and continue today, each with its share of advocates. W. Richard Scott calls them the rational systems, the natural systems, and the open systems perspectives.[7] These three views are relatively distinct, yet they are partially overlapping, partially complementary, as well as partially conflicting.

Rational Systems   Stemming from the early classical organizational thought of scientific management theorists, rational systems view the behavior of organizations as purposeful, disciplined, and rational. The concerns and concepts of rational systems theorists are conveyed by such terms as *information, efficiency, effectiveness, optimization, implementation, rationality,* and *design.*[8]

Rational systems are best described by their emphasis on goal specificity and on formalization. Examples of technical tools used by managers to facilitate rational decision making are management by objective (MBO); planning, programming, and budgeting systems (PPBS); and performance evaluation and review techniques (PERT).

Natural Systems   In contrast to the rational system perspective, the natural systems view springs from the human relations approach of the 1930s. While natural systems proponents agree that goal specificity and formalization are characteristics of organizations, they argue that other attributes such as similarities among social groups and survival are of far greater importance.

The natural systems adherents stress the individual over structure. Later theorists added the impact of the environment as an important consideration for organization health.

Open Systems   The open systems theory holds that it is unrealistic to assume that organizational behavior can be isolated from external forces. Indeed, the open systems model views organizations as not only influenced by environments but also dependent on them. For example, schools are social systems that take resources such as labor, students, and community directions from the environment, and subject these inputs to an educational transformation process to produce literate and educated students and graduates.

Open systems tend to move toward a state of equilibrium by exporting and importing energy from the environment. Open systems are able to adapt to changing environments by responding to demands with a variety of means and mechanisms. Thus, the open system is better able to survive because its structure is not fixed and it can change roles and relationships to meet changing environments.

While each of the three models has its supporters and advocates, the authors of this text believe that open systems theory is an appropriate framework for the school business administrator to use in developing an understanding of and an appreciation for the complexity of the educational organization. Unlike business, educational organizations are unique in that they deal with the provision of certain services to people. These services are not definable by any product or quantity or goods, yet education is a labor-intensive industry. Therefore, while it is appropriate to examine business, commercial, and industrial management models, the uniqueness of the endeavor demands appropriate adjustments and accommodations.

The Establishment of Management Sciences

Peters and Waterman in their classic work *In Search of Excellence* present a schematic showing the four stages in the development of management sciences and the leading theorists in each stage.[9]

	Closed System	*Open System*
Rational Actor	I. 1900–1930 Weber, Taylor	III. 1960–1970 Chandler, Lawrence, Lorsch
Social Actor	II. 1930–1960 Mayo, et. al., McGregor, Barnard, Selznick	IV. 1970– Welch, March

Each of the stages or eras in the development of management science contributed a set of major premises to the field. The period of 1900 to 1930 is the closed system–rational actor era. The two main proponents were Max Weber, a German sociologist, and Frederick Taylor, an American who put Weber's theories to the test with time and motion studies. They attempted to formulate a finite set of rules and techniques to be learned and mastered about maximum span of control and about matching authority and responsibility leading to the solution of problems of managing large groups of people.

The next era, that of the closed system–social actor, spanned the period from 1930 to 1960. Among the chief spokespersons for this era were Elton Mayo, Douglas McGregor, Chester Barnard, and Philip Selznick. Mayo was the father of the Hawthorne experiments that suggested that by giving personal attention to individuals and groups, production can be increased. McGregor is known chiefly for his development of Theory X and Theory Y. Theory X holds that people have an inherent dislike for work and they must be coerced, controlled, directed, and threatened to work toward an organization's goals, while Theory Y holds that humans like work, that commitment to objectives is satisfying to the ego and is the direct product of efforts directed to an organization's purposes, and that the capacity to exercise a relatively high degree of imagination, ingenuity, and creativity is widely distributed in the population.

Barnard and Selznick focused on the role of the CEO as the shaper and manager of shared values in an organization. They stressed managing the whole enterprise and emphasized the nature of the organization as a set of social interactions.

Stage three, the open system–rational actor era, lasted from 1960 to 1970 and was dominated by names like Alfred Chandler, Paul Lawrence, and Jay Lorsch. They viewed a company as part of a competitive marketplace, shaped and molded by forces outside itself. They were the first to notice that in fast developing businesses a more decentralized form of organization enabled quick responses to emerging situations.

Stage four, starting in 1970 and continuing today, is described as open system–social actor. In the view of today's theorists, everything is in flux—ends, means, and the storm of external change. Leading theorists are Karl Weick and James March. The dominant theme of this era is informality, individual entrepreneurship, and evolution. Weick is convinced that military metaphors are a bad choice when it comes to managing a commercial enterprise because someone always wins and/or loses in the military scenario. Additionally, the military metaphor limits the solutions to a problem and the ways of organizing for delivery of services.

Peters and Waterman suggest four elements of the new theory[10] to be: (1) people's need for meaning; (2) people's need for a medium of control; (3) people's need for positive reinforcement, to think of themselves as winners in some sense; and (4) the degree to which actions and behaviors shape attitudes and beliefs rather than vice versa. They also stress the notion of companies as distinctive cultures and the emergence of the successful company through purposeful but specifically unpredictable evolution.

Since school organizations have primarily used the military metaphor to conceptualize and develop organizational schemata, the emerging era gives pause for contemplation and reflection. Paralleling this emerging thought is the issue of site-based management or decentralization, or cultural understanding and differences between and among campuses and districts, and of the need to quickly change plans and delivery to accommodate specific students.

Educational leaders must be knowledgeable of the changing organizational theory and adapt it to their own organizations.

Private Versus Public Sector Management

Perhaps the biggest adjustment between private and public sector management is the realization that public sector is just that—public—and all the issues, decisions, and deliberations are made in the full view of the public. Open meetings laws of various types and the heightened interest and focus of the media also contribute to the involvement of the citizens of a community in the school organizations.

Also contributing to the interest of the citizenry is the awareness of the educational reforms of the late 1980s and the cruciality of the educational system to the general well-being of a town, city, and state. In addition to being a city's largest employer and often having the largest budget of any organization, the school system holds the keys to success and/or failure for the young people of a community.

However, it is the view of the authors that, in terms of organization and operation, the educational organization is more alike than different from any other organization. It is labor-intensive like many business and commercial organizations, is a provider of services like many organizations, is a multi-building, multi-unit organization like many other organizations, and is diverse and serves a varied clientele like other organizations. While it is not possible to measure by counting the number of "widgets" manufactured, individual and group academic growth is capable of and worthy of being measured.

Whereas the business, commercial, or industrial organization is organized to produce the greatest profit and the military organization is organized to produce the strongest and most effective army, the educational organization must produce the greatest academic growth possible on a cost-effective basis. The business administrator, particularly, is crucial to the application of cost-effectiveness techniques to the educational enterprise.

The application of management theory to educational institutions is appropriate and necessary. Organizational similarities are much more prevalent than are differences in comparing public and private institutions. Any number of authors and researchers have studied the applicability of the various theories to educational institutions, and they have confirmed the appropriateness of the theoretical applications.

While it is much more difficult to generate profit and loss statements in the educational enterprise, it is possible to generate progress toward academic objectives and to indicate the cost-effectiveness of the organization in meeting those objectives. Comparative data between similar districts and between units within districts can be used to tell the full story.

The significant difference, of course, is that every citizen of the community is a stockholder in the organization and deserves the full report of progress or lack thereof.

School Business Administration as a Subset of Generic Management

The practice of school business administration encompasses the totality of generic leadership domains as identified in emerging literature. For example, the use of general administrative skills, human relations competencies, and personal capabilities, in addition to the job-specific skills in finance, is consistent with expectations of the good business administrator.

The capable school business administrator must possess knowledge and understanding of administrative skills, conceptual skills, interpersonal skills, and resource skills in order to succeed. These ''generic'' abilities and skills are really prerequisites for the development of specific job-related capacities. The application of theory—e.g., open versus closed systems, human relations versus scientific management—allows the school business administrator to examine a situation under a number of different circumstances before selecting the appropriate solution to a problem.

Management Applications

In the following sections a number of technical options are offered as management tools for school business administrators. Each is provided as a sample of the myriad ways available to school business administrators as they go about their daily tasks. The items are neither exhaustive nor encompassing but rather are samples of what is available to school business administrators in the pursuit of their duties.

Network Analysis

Network models are extremely useful in planning and controlling both simple and complex projects. Actually, network models are as old as scientific management. The reader may recall the Gantt chart, a contribution of Henry Gantt and the classical management school. While network models are more sophisticated, they are based on the same philosophy. The two basic and most common types of network models are program evaluation and review technique (PERT) and critical path method (CPM). PERT is a method of planning and controlling nonrepetitive projects—projects that have not been done before and will not be done again in the same exact manner (for example, the space shuttle). CPM is a planning and control technique used in projects for which some past cost data are available. Network models are normative in purpose and contain probabilistic variables.

CPM and PERT

CPM was used by DuPont in 1959 to schedule plant-maintenance shutdowns during changeover. Subsequently, it was used to plan building construction and other large projects. In CPM the primary analytical emphasis is to determine the programming strategy that will satisfy schedule requirements at minimum cost. The analyst will trace through the paths of the diagram (see Figure 4-1) and estimate the shortest time in which each job can

FIGURE 4-1 A Critical Path Network

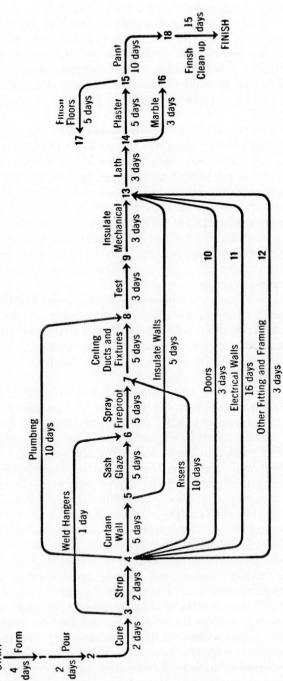

be accomplished (minimum time) and what it would cost under this condition (maximum cost). With ranges of time and cost established, the critical path and the cost of reducing the time can be determined. CPM has been very effective in areas relating to planning, scheduling, and coordinating of total developmental projects.

PERT is based on critical path scheduling. However, there is a fundamental difference between it and CPM. The PERT technique is applicable where there is no established system for doing the task and therefore no exact basis for estimating the required time to complete each task. Critical path scheduling, on the other hand, usually is applied to jobs that are established or have been done before and where it is possible to predict performance accurately. Consequently, more sophisticated mathematical models must be used in the PERT technique.

During the past few years the techniques of CPM and PERT have been refined and other variations have been added. The first developments were concerned principally with a description of a total task, the relationship among various elements, and the cost of performing various segments of the operation. More recent variations of CPM and PERT have added features of minimax theory (determining the range between the minimal and maximal solutions to a given problem) in determining the optimum way to complete the job.

Another variation of CPM and PERT is least cost estimating and scheduling (LESS), which designates what time and hour each job should be done so as to complete the project at a minimum cost or in a specified time. This technique can be very useful for larger school systems with extensive maintenance crews. Some that are equipped to do minor construction might utilize this technique.

Resource allocation and multi-project scheduling (RAMPS) considers restrictions such as quantity of resources available, priorities, resource team composition, additional staff, subcontracting to another educational agency, and inefficient staff utilization rates. Other related factors may be incorporated in the procedure. Considering these restrictions and requirements, RAMPS develops a schedule that satisfies various criteria including minimum costs.

There are numerous other variations, many of which at the present do not have applications in education. It is safe to say that most are basically the same and only the acronyms differ. Inasmuch as PERT was one of the first, and also the most widely accepted, we will use it to illustrate networking and give illustrated uses in school business management.

The PERT technique can be used in planning and developing internal and external audits; moving from a line- to program-type budget; switching from a manual to machine record system; planning and controlling the budgetary process; planning mergers or consolidations of school systems; organizing and determining priorities for school construction and acquisition of capital equipment; timing and selling bond issues; scheduling unusual school operations; closing out a school plant and opening another; installing and integrating a new organization structure; planning student, staff, and educational resource flow; planning and implementing maintenance programs; studying the educational process; planning acquisition programs; and planning and scheduling transportation programs, especially when alternatives are available but of a complex nature.

The PERT network is **the working model** of the technique. It illustrates by diagram, the sequential relationships among the tasks that must be completed to accomplish the project. PERT treats planning and scheduling separately. First the plan is developed, and then the limitations are added to the problem. The first step in developing the PERT network is to gather a list of all the activities needed to complete the project; the people associated with project activities have the best knowledge of detailed tasks. Next, the network is constructed to show the sequential relationships among the activities.

Figure 4-2 is an example of a simplified PERT network. Each event is lettered for identification; activity *A/H* is the activity that takes place between events lettered *A* and *H*. It is possible to start the diagram from the completion of the project and work backward, or from the beginning and work toward completion. Lengths of arrows do not denote time span but logical sequence. Activities *B/F* and *C/F* must be completed before activity *F/H* or *F/J* can begin. Event *F* signifies the completion of activities *H/F* and *C/F* and the starting point for the next related activities.

Once the flow network has been determined for the system, the next step is to obtain an estimate of the elapsed time (in time module) required by each individual responsible to accomplish each element of work. As shown in Figure 4-3, this time forecast consists of three individual estimates: the most likely estimate (*x*), the optimistic estimate (*a*), and the pessimistic estimate (*y*).

The flow network, with its coded events, can be programmed for a computer. The elapsed-time estimates can likewise be used as input to the computer processing. The computer solves the mathematical problems (calculation of each estimate) and, by adding the calculated expected times for each activity, computes the expected time for each event.

Example of a PERT Analysis

Let us now use PERT to analyze a common educational activity such as census taking. Steps to be taken include:

1. Listing activities
2. Charting activities
3. Developing a time estimate for each activity
4. Scheduling activities on a calendar
5. Analyzing the structure, sequence, and timing of activities

FIGURE 4-2 A Network Example of PERT

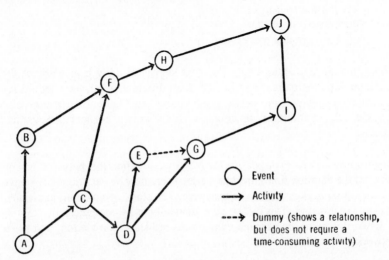

FIGURE 4-3   Estimating the Time Distribution

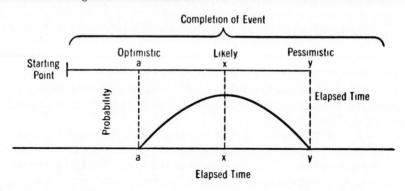

Listing Activities   There is no simple or correct list of activities. Each administrator might approach the list differently. Activities should be listed as they come to mind. No order should be followed at this time. The list might contain the following activities:

> Determine number of workers needed
> Order forms
> Publicity
> Computer analysis of census data
> Determine information needed
> Take census
> Write final report
> Employ workers
> Design forms
> Instructional meetings with workers
> Printing forms
> Arrange publicity
> Determine census grids
> Punching of census data
> Arrange computer processing

Charting the List of Activities   The next step is to draw a network of these activities. Different administrators might handle them differently, but they should follow a logical sequence and relationship between activities. See Figure 4-4 for a possible network of activities. Some additions, deletions, or revision may be necessary as the network progresses.

Developing a Time Estimate for Each Activity   After the network is completed, estimates of the duration times must be made. There may be variations between administrators depending on background and experience. The start, completion, and slack time for each activity is estimated. This can be done manually or by computer.

   At this point the user may wish to record start, completion, and slack times on the network.

FIGURE 4-4 PERT Diagram

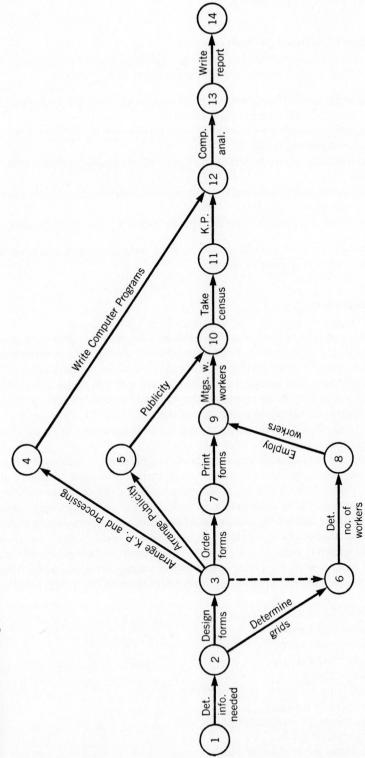

Source: Ralph A. Van Dusseldorp, Duane E. Richardson, and Walter J. Foley, *Educational Decision-Making Through Operations Research* (Boston: Allyn and Bacon, 1971), p. 64.

Advantages of Network Analysis

In summary, network analysis is a useful managerial technique for planning, organizing, and evaluating. The advantages of PERT can be summarized as follows:

- The sequence and relationship network of all significant events in planning how the end objective will be achieved is identified.
- The relative uncertainty in meeting or accomplishing all activities in the plan is measured and evaluated.
- The relatively critical condition in areas of effort required is shown to the administrator.
- Slack areas, where some delay will not preclude the meeting of end objectives on time, are shown.
- The current probability of meeting schedule events is provided for the administrator.

Network analysis is useful; however, when the system to be described is complex, the use of computers is almost a necessity.

Linear Programming

One of the most widely used allocation models is the linear programming model. Linear programming expresses the objective to be achieved in the form of a mathematical function, the value of which is to be maximized (for example, profits) or minimized (for example, costs). Constraints are introduced that reduce the number of feasible alternatives. A powerful linear programming procedure known as the *simplex method* searches the feasible alternatives in order to find the particular one that maximizes or minimizes the value of the objective function. The linear programming model is normative in purpose and contains deterministic variables.

Educators have been slow to adopt linear programming. For many it was not a part of their training programs. Another problem has been the inability or reluctance of educators to express the goals of educational programs in terms that can be measured objectively and to relate these goals to contributing factors. Because of the growing scarcity of the educational dollar, linear programming will be used increasingly to allocate scarce resources among competing activities within given constraints in order to attain certain objectives. Previously written (''canned'') computer programs exist, so the business administrator can avoid the tedious work of solving mathematical programming problems. The following educational examples are amenable to optimization through linear programming.

Maximize
- Student achievement
- Teacher experience
- Teacher training
- Time for instruction
- Availability of instructional materials
- Utilization of facilities
- Opportunity for extracurricular activities
- Subject offerings
- Nutritional value of school lunches

Minimize

- Cost of

    — Total education
    — School lunches
    — Facilities
    — Transportation
    — Interest or bonds
    — Equipment and supplies

- Pupil–teacher ratio
- Transportation time
- Dropouts
- Distance students must travel to school
- Distance student must travel between classes
- Class size
- Underachievers

Some examples in these lists are more easily related to contributing factors than are others. Unless a rather precise statement can be made about factors contributing to a goal, linear programming is probably not the appropriate tool. When formulating a linear programming model, the following steps must be considered:

1. Recognition of the problem
2. Formulation of the mathematical model
    a. Identification of the decision variables
    b. Choice of a measure of effectiveness
    c. Symbolic representation of the objective function
    d. Identification of the constraints
    e. Algebraic representation of the constraints
3. Estimation of the parameters of the model

Once these steps have been completed, the problem is easily solved with linear programming.

The linear program deals with allocating limited resources among a variety of activities in the best possible (optimal), manner. Linear programming can be applied to a great variety of activities within the school setting. Generally, these have their basis in the competition among groups or units for certain scarce resources.

Linear programming uses a mathematical model to describe an area of need. The one major restriction of linear programming work is that all the mathematical functions must be linear (i.e., not second order or curvilinear or the like).

Cost-Effectiveness Analysis

The purpose of cost-effectiveness analysis is to help the decision maker choose among feasible alternatives on the basis of least cost and greatest effectiveness. While cost-benefit is a preprogramming process, cost-effectiveness should be considered a tool for microanalysis. Information generated by this analysis will be of great value to the educational administrator. The technique should answer such questions as: How effective has our program been? How could it be better? What were our failures? Some suggested ratios for educational programs are:

1. Effective Ratio $= \dfrac{\text{Actual Output/Time Period}}{\text{Planned Output/Time Period}}$

This formula will show clearly whether or not targets were reached. It is commonly agreed that program effectiveness should be determined by analysis of outputs achieved compared with planned outputs.

2. Effectiveness Ratio $= \dfrac{\text{Standard Cost/Unit of Output}}{\text{Actual Cost/Unit of Output}}$

If we are to engage in reasonably intelligent planning, we must consider variances. This ratio is an expression of overall variance.

Most of the preceding analytic process has concentrated on the cost of education—earnings foregone as well as potential higher incomes gained. Consideration of dollar amounts is the primary factor in such analysis. It is relatively easy to obtain the input costs of education, the tax load, the bonds sold, and contributions from the public and industry. Also, it is easy to determine the short- and long-term financial results or gains made possible by education. The difficulty is to measure personal and social outcomes, effective domain development, and benefits to society as a whole.

Management Information Systems

Management information systems (MIS) have the basic purpose of generating, storing, retrieving, computing, and disseminating information to decision makers. Traditionally, the technology for performing these tasks consists of filing systems, typewriters, and copying equipment. However, the MIS of the 1990s will increasingly use the advanced technologies of (1) text or word processing, comprising automatic text-editing devices, dictation systems, and computer graphics; (2) automated data processing, which has been made possible through the integrated circuit technology of microcomputers and microprocessors; and (3) telecommunication using digital transmission systems, software controlled systems, and satellite communications. These technological advances are not now widely in use, yet the compelling need to increase productivity will stimulate their use in private and public sector organizations. The present rapid drop in costs will expedite their utilization.

Apart from the implications of these technologies for more efficient and effective management of information, other results can be anticipated. For example, the jobs of clerical workers will evolve from the performance of routine, relatively simple tasks toward broader and more stimulating ones. Schools must employ better educated, higher-salaried personnel as support persons. The total office machinery mix will change drastically. Office personnel training courses in the public schools must shift curricula.

Middle managers as well should find the application of advanced technologies more to their liking. In traditional offices they spend considerable amounts of time communicating, coordinating, and monitoring, rather than making decisions. Their routine and time-consuming tasks will be automated, freeing time for more challenging problems.

At the system level the new technology will no doubt result in the centralization of certain aspects of MIS. Storage and computational processes will be undertaken in centralized units; the enormous capacity of computers would be underutilized with a decentralized arrangement. However, access to the information and data stored in the computer will be available throughout the organization. Through the use of site-based terminals, all centrally stored information can be made available for planning and solving site-based problems.

Analytical Prerequisites

Information, like inventory, must be of the proper variety and type, stored and made available for use in proper locations at the required times and frequencies. Too much information is as costly as too little is damaging. Information also must be protected from use by unauthorized persons and from physical loss from fire, flood, or power failure. The components of an information system consist of input, processing, control, and output. A flowchart is a shorthand method for representing an overview or logic of an information system. See Figure 4-5 for a flow chart of a management information system.

Developing an Information System

One of the first steps in developing an information system is a feasibility study. There are four major phases of the feasibility study: (1) organizing for the study, (2) searching for alternative solutions, (3) analyzing the relative merits of feasible alternatives, and (4) selecting an alternative. The following information should be provided for each alternative: (1) resources required, both developmental and recurring, including equipment, personnel and space; (2) anticipated consequences, including organizational and informational changes and anticipated problems; (3) limitations; (4) benefits, stated in a variety of terms,

FIGURE 4-5   Functions of a Management Information Center

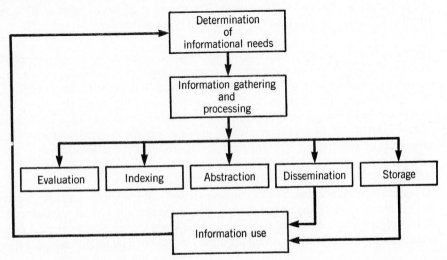

including economic, organization, and so forth; and (5) the time schedule, including the priority reassignment of other jobs if applicable.

Having determined the gross specifications from the user's point of view, it is now necessary to specify the details of the design from the construction of the system. Conceptually, this follows the previous design with one exception. In the actual design of the system, the major responsibility lies with the information systems analyst. The steps required for this activity include (1) determining operations procedures for the handling of information; (2) determining hardware requirements; (3) designing input and output forms; and (4) determining programming needs (some canned programs are available), personnel needs, and procedures for testing.

Information Required for Different Types of Management Decisions

The types as well as sources of information will vary by level in the organization. We shall use the classifications of planning information, control information, and operational information.

Planning Information   Planning information relates to the top-management tasks of formulating objectives for the organization, the amounts and kinds of resources necessary to attain the objectives, and the policies that govern their use. Much of this information will come from external sources and will relate to such factors as the present and predicted state of the economy, availability of resources (nonhuman as well as human resources), and the political and regulatory environment. This information forms the input to the nonprogrammed types of decisions made at this level in the organization.

Control Information   Control information aids managers to make decisions that are consistent with the achievement of organizational objectives as well as to see how efficiently resources are being used. It enables middle managers to determine if actual results are meeting planned-for results (objectives). It relies heavily on internal sources of information (often interdepartmental) and involves such problems as developing budgets and measuring the performance of teachers and students. The nature of problems faced at this level may result in either programmed or nonprogrammed types of decisions.

Operational Information   Operational information relates to the day-to-day activities of the organization. It includes routine and necessary types of information such as financial accounting, inventory control, and student scheduling. It is generated internally and, since it usually relates to specific tasks, it often comes from one designated department. First-line supervisors and principals are the primary users of this information. Since decision making at this level in the organization usually involves structured types of problems, many problems at the operations level can be stated as mathematical relationships.

Administrators' Attitudes toward Information Generation

Many school personnel believe that computer-based information systems are objective and neutral means of gathering and producing data. However, any system is influenced by the values of the person designing the system. Since computers handle numerical data better than other data, information systems are biased in favor of quantifiable data. Most systems are developed on the premise that managers need more information. However, management often suffers from an overabundance of irrelevant information. Criteria dealing with quality may be superseded by criteria dealing with quantity. Give managers the information they need and their decisions will improve.

Impact of Computer-Based Information Systems

Computer-based information systems bring about fundamental changes in the way an organization conducts its business, and educational organizations are no exception. Three areas are affected.

1. One area deals with the educational organizations where computer-based information handling appears to be more cost-effective. Computer-based information systems affect the behavior of educational managers.

2. Management skills must change to utilize a data-based organizational environment. Information systems development is more likely to take place in educational units where speed and manipulation of data are crucial factors in the decision-making process.

3. Academic managers in educational organizations need greater technical skills than their predecessors. Clearly, there is a high positive relationship between educational administrators and their models, systems, and computer technology, just as there is between surgeons and their support systems.

Demographic Forecasting

Educational planning relies heavily on demographic forecasting, without knowing exactly the number of pupils to be served now and in the future. Planning is the continuous, systematic, step-by-step process of changing present organizational goals to fit emerging needs. In general, the kinds and number of assumptions made in projecting populations depend on three factors:

1. The level of detail required
2. The time span between present and past projections
3. The degree of accuracy desired.

Use of Assumptions in Forecasting

To project populations for a defined period, it is necessary to assume that some variables will remain in the future as they were in the past and that if they do change, it will be in a predictable manner.

Six basic assumptions that are generally made in demographic forecasting are:

1. There will be no change in mortality rate for any age group, or the rate of change will be predictable.
2. There will be no dramatic change in birth rate; any change will be predictable.
3. Local economic conditions will remain stable or change at a predictable rate.
4. There will be no boundary changes, or such changes will be included in analysis.
5. Administrative policy will not change during time period, or change will be predictable.
6. No major catastrophe will occur.

Using Enrollment-Based Data

Enrollment histories can be used as a base for predicting enrollment if demographic indications are relatively stable. The three major factors affecting school populations are births, migration, and holding power. The *cohort survival ratio method* is widely accepted as the best means of projecting school membership. This method accommodates the following factors:

- Increase or decrease in births
- Student deaths
- Net in-migration or out-migration
- Nonpromotions
- Increase or decrease in holding powers of the secondary schools
- Increase or decrease in private school membership

The cohort survival ratio method can be used to project the number of elementary students for five years and the number of junior and high school students for ten years. Like many systems for making projections, the process is more reliable for short-range rather than long-range predictions; consequently, the projections should be updated each year.

Using Census-Based Data

The census-based approach to school enrollments is similar to the method used to project population changes for states and nations. Census data are gathered from each household and organized by geographical area. The following data are available by household: age of each child, race, length of residence, type of dwelling unit, age of dwelling unit, and occupation of household.

By proper manipulation of data a yield factor can be determined for each age group by race and by type of dwelling. From this, future populations may be projected.

Evaluation Models

The school business administrator needs to be able to measure educational outcomes (e.g., cost-benefit analysis, cost-effectiveness analysis, cost-alternative programs). Evaluation models are helpful in planning for the measurement of educational outcomes. Factors contributing to the present emphasis on evaluation include rising cost of education, declining student performance, high dropout statistics, and a general public demand for accountability.

CIPP Model

The CIPP model for evaluation originated with Daniel S. Stufflebeam of Ohio State University. It provides evaluative information on which decisions can be made and identifies points at which decisions are needed. The model is geared for use at local, state, and national levels, with information being collected at the local level and fed to state and national programs in a feedback cycle. The acronym CIPP is from the labels that Stufflebeam has used for the four kinds of evaluation activity—Context, Input, Process, and Product. The strategies of the CIPP evaluation model are shown in Figure 4-6.

FIGURE 4-6 The CIPP Evaluation Model: A Classification Scheme of Strategies for Evaluational Change

	OBJECTIVE	METHOD	DECISION-MAKING RELATION
CONTEXT EVALUATION	To define the operation context, to identify and assess needs in the context, and to identify and delineate problems underlying the needs.	By describing individually and in relevant perspectives the major subsystems of the context; by comparing actual and intended inputs and outputs of the subsystems; and by analyzing possible causes of discrepancies between actualities and intentions.	For deciding upon the setting to be served, the goals associated with meeting needs and the objectives associated with solving problems, i.e., for planning needed changes.
INPUT EVALUATION	To identify and assess system capabilities, available input strategies, and designs for implementing strategies.	By describing and analyzing available human and material resources, solution strategies, and procedural designs for relevance, feasibility and economy in the course of action taken.	For selecting sources of support, solution strategies, and procedural designs, i.e., for program changing activities.
PROCESS EVALUATION	To identify or predict, in process, defects in the procedural design or its implementation, and to maintain a record of procedural events and activities.	By monitoring the activity's potential procedural barriers and remaining alert to unanticipated ones.	For implementing and refining the program design and procedure, i.e., for effective process control.
PRODUCT EVALUATION	To relate outcome information to objectives and to context, input, and process information.	By defining operationally and measuring criteria associated with the objectives, by comparing these measurements with pre-determined standards or comparative bases, and by interpreting the outcome in terms of recorded input and process information.	For deciding to continue, terminate, modify or refocus a change activity, and for linking the activity to other phases of the change process, i.e., for evolving change activities.

Source: Daniel S. Stufflebeam, ''The Use and Abuse of Evaluation in Title III,'' *Theory into Practice, 6,* 3 (June 1967), 130.

Context Evaluation   Context evaluation is conducted first as a basis for planning and focusing on the problem—to enable the user to make decisions about problem identification, emphasis, and priority.

Input Evaluation   Input evaluation is for the purpose of deciding how best to solve the problems identified during context evaluation. This includes examining strategies and designs as alternatives and deciding on the appropriate ones to meet the needs. Objectives must be specified so that procedural determinations can be made. Available and potentially available resources must be evaluated and decisions made on their use as the result of input evaluation.

Process Evaluation   Process evaluation is a monitoring of the project to provide information for making decisions or adjustments to improve the project during implementation. In process evaluation the evaluator monitors the project so corrective measures can be taken immediately (rather than after the project ends). The feedback of evaluative information to the project administrator allows him/her to control, refine, and redirect or otherwise adjust during the project's operational life. Daily, weekly, and monthly reports and analyses are potential products of process evaluation. Stufflebeam equates process evaluation with contingency evaluation, where actions are based on contingencies that are not predictable.

Product Evaluation   Product evaluation is used to make decisions about the effectiveness of the project after its completion. Product evaluation is conducted by comparing measured outcomes with the criteria and standards previously determined and analyzing and interpreting the results. The feedback of information into a recycling is the basis for a decision on whether or not to continue, modify, or terminate the project. Dissemination of information to others is appropriate after the evaluative cycle is completed.

The Administrator and Evaluation

In summary, evaluation models are necessary if school systems are going to be successful in planning. The school business administrator will be deeply involved because he/she must furnish appropriate data for costing programs.

Management by Objective

Management by objective (MBO) is far more than just an appraisal approach. It is usually part of an overall motivational program, planning technique, or organizational change and development program. However, the idea of MBO will be introduced here as a performance appraisal method. An MBO performance appraisal program focuses on what the employee achieves. The key features of a typical MBO program are as follows:

1. The supervisor and subordinate meet to discuss and jointly set objectives for the subordinate for a specified period of time (e.g., six months or one year).
2. Both the supervisor and the subordinate attempt to establish objectives that are realistic, challenging, clear, and comprehensive. The objective should be related to the needs of both the organization and the subordinate.

3. The standards for measuring and evaluating the objectives are agreed upon.
4. The supervisor and the subordinate establish some intermediate review dates when the objectives will be reexamined.
5. The supervisor plays more of a coaching, counseling, and supportive role and less of a judgmental role.
6. The entire process focuses on results and on the counseling of the subordinate, and not on activities, mistakes, and organizational requirements.

Mission

The primary problem with the utilization of MBO is the lack of clear, concise mission statements by many organizations. For MBO to function effectively, the total organization must have an overall mission statement. If MBO is to be implemented at the site level, a site-level mission statement is needed. Other problems that have been linked to MBO programs include improper implementation, lack of top-management commitment, too much emphasis on paperwork, failing to use an MBO system that best fits the needs of the organization and the employees, and inadequate preparation for employees who are asked to establish objectives.

Primary Goals

The primary goals should be the goals of the overall organization as to teaching, research and scholarship, and public service. These should come from the mission statement, goals, and objectives of the total organization, which should provide the overall parameters within which the site-based group can develop its goal statement. Each site should have specific goals that reflect the individualized programs for that particular setting. Then each faculty/staff member develops his/her MBO that gives direction to the individual's work plan.

Support Goals

All the divisions within the system that lend support to the faculty develop MBO statements that reflect both the support and operational goals of the organization. This can be very helpful to groups such as school business administrators in continually remembering that theirs is a support function and not an end in itself.

Staff Evaluation

Five possible parties may serve as appraisers:

1. The supervisor or supervisors of the appraised
2. Organizational peers
3. The appraised
4. Subordinates of the appraised
5. Individuals outside the work environment

In most situations, the appraiser is the immediate supervisor and is assumed to be most familiar with the employee's performance. In addition, many organizations regard performance appraisal as an integral part of the immediate supervisor's job. The supervisor's appraisals are often reviewed by higher management, thereby maintaining managerial control over the appraisals. The major claims in support of this approach are that it improves the employee's understanding of job performance, it increases the personal commitment of employees because of their participation in the performance appraisal process, and it reduces the hostility between superior and subordinates over ratings.

There is some support for increased use of multiple appraisers. The major advantage of using superior, peer, and self-rating is that this provides a great deal of information about the appraised. In making decisions about promotion, training and staff development, and career planning, as much information as possible is needed to suggest the best alternative courses of action for the employer.

Reward through MBO—A Limiting Factor

Many systems tie MBO appraisal to salary increases. This puts too much pressure on the MBO system. This is not to say that financial reward cannot be tied to MBO, but when a direct objective/cause–salary/effect relationship is maintained, it puts the primary emphasis on the wrong phase of employee improvement.

The Delphi Process

Delphi was developed by Olaf Helmer and his colleagues at the Rand Corporation in the early 1950s.[11] Delphi process has become an excellent tool for administrative planning. It is a process for working toward consensus on issues. Individuals can be involved in the development of the original list of objectives. The participant can take part and see the objectives being prioritized according to some predetermined scale. Seeing the total process in operation increases the probability of the individual's working toward achievement of objectives on implementation.

Assumptions of the Inductive Delphi Process

Since we are devoting our attention to the organizational-process approach of educational planning, there are several assumptions that may deviate from those in the current literature on Delphi. According to Tanner and Williams, seven general assumptions emerge through working with a total organization. These are as follows:

1. *The inductive Delphi process will yield normative results in large groups.*
2. *Because the total organization is utilized, there will be a large number of representative experts.*
3. *Participants within certain interest areas may stay outside the range of consensus. For example, in a college of education where there may be a heavy concentration of generalists, it may be difficult to get consensus on the use of computers in management. This is especially true if the objectives related to technology tend to threaten certain jobs.*
4. *Most participants will remain in the Delphi study if they are able to identify their input and if they understand the purpose of the study. Furthermore, the semantic analysis of round 1 is important, and care should be taken to keep original statements close to the intent of the contributor.*
5. *Narrative manipulation of feedback from probe 1 will be minimized through the elimination of ambiguity of statements. Thus, participants will remain in the study when face validity is maximized.*

6. *The planners in charge of the Delphi analysis will not manipulate statistical feedback to support their own biases. It would be tragic to develop objectives that were outside the mission of an organization if they focused on destroying vital organizational components; therefore, it is important to note that if a ''bogus'' objective is included, this objective must be highly scrutinized.*

7. *All responders will receive feedback on all probes and remain in the study. Whether they participate throughout the entire study is of concern, but on rounds where individuals fail to participate, it can be assumed that their perceptions were within the domain of the responders.*[12]

According to Tanner and Williams, five general assumptions concerning procedure are important for the administration planners who conduct Delphi studies in the context of an organization. One chief assumption is that the planners must remain unbiased. Other assumptions are:

1. Each participant must understand the purposes of the Delphi process. In a large organization ample time must be taken to advertise the importance of developing objectives as well as the necessity of remaining in the study until its completion. Here the importance of the results should be stressed over the characteristics of the Delphi process itself.

2. In the inductive process the initial probe is opened. Objectives by nature are futuristic in that they provide direction; consequently, a statement such as ''In the decade ahead this organization should concentrate its energies and resources on . . .'' is appropriate.

3. The judgmental approach in analyzing probe 1 yields better semantic similarity than does the analytic approach. For example, Rubenstein has reported that the judgment approaches (scaling, sorting, and substituting) have generally been found to have a rank correlation of .92 between groups judging semantic similarity, while analytical approaches (verbal context, association, semantic generalization, and thesaurus information) produced correlations of .85 or less.

4. Consensus is reached on any objective when stability between two probes occurs, and unanimity is achieved when more than 50 percent of the respondents are found to be within predetermined limits.

5. Responders participating in a Delphi study can be manipulated to produce significant changes in their responses.[13]

Utilizing Delphi in Establishing Objectives

In our example let us assume that we are developing objectives for a site-based program. We might involve building faculty, support personnel, students, former students, central office personnel working with the particular site, and persons from the community. Objectives for the overall educational system should be furnished each participant. The purpose of the study will be to establish and prioritize site objectives. When this is completed, the group can work toward time and cost estimates for each objective in order that the implementation and operation phases might begin.

The initial probe will seek a list of objectives that apply to this particular site-based program. This must be done within the parameter of the overall system objectives. When the total list is obtained, a committee must peruse the list to make certain each suggested objective is a single statement and to see that these objectives do not conflict with the system's overall objectives. Finally, each objective should be stated as nearly as possible in the original language of the suggestor.

The second probe will be for the purpose of prioritizing the objectives. It may take one or more additional probes to reach relative consensus. Once relative consensus is attained, the time and cost estimates should be reached. The school business officials may need to help in making time and cost estimates. Within time and cost constraints, the objectives may be implemented. This process usually leads to a high degree of understanding and support of the site-based programs.

Human Interaction Concepts

In addition to the technical skills previously enumerated, certain interaction concepts can be applied as management tools. Administrators are practitioners more than theoreticians, conceptualizers, creators of knowledge, or philosophers, although they are also all of these. They have a unique responsibility to know, to understand, and to do. In the past, administrators were given information about technological development to help them be better doers, but their professional needs have changed. Decision making is now more of a political process than an accounting procedure. The negotiation process is replacing authoritative leadership. Coordination is more acceptable than supervision. Participation has affected the process of evaluation. Consistent with this changing focus of administrative practice is the need for administrators, and those who prepare administrators, to behave authentically and with consideration for human beings.

Principles of Human Relations

We must accept the view that the administrator's task is organizing, integrating, motivating, and supervising the activities of people in such a way that the system's objectives are achieved economically and efficiently. In most cases, administrators do not do; they get others to do.

A corollary to this generalization is that the job of the personnel department is to provide expert advice and assistance to line administrators. The personnel department may administer a limited number of functions directly, but it is becoming clear that these functions must indeed be limited in scope and number. A good illustration is employment. Among progressive school systems today the employment department does not itself actually recommend anyone for employment. Its function is to recruit and screen applicants who are then recommended or rejected by the appropriate line officer. Even the process of induction, traditionally a personnel department function, is truly effective when it is directly administered by the line staff.

School administrators generally resent the rapid increase in governmental restrictions and limitations on freedom of action. Many of these have been directly connected with personnel administration. However, it is important to consider that government intervention in such matters is due to public pressure, which in turn is a direct (although often delayed) consequence of management's own failure to assume a necessary responsibility. The only way to reverse the current trend is for management to assume such responsibility individually and widely. The only alternative to increasingly centralized governmental control lies in the acceptance of responsibility for human relations and human welfare. As in all aspects of living in society, the price of freedom from central control is personal responsibility.

Administrators must recognize that neither fear nor gratitude is an effective motivational principle. They must recognize that fear, because it is frustrating, leads inevitably to aggressive reactions, restriction of output, featherbedding, obstructive contract clauses, militant and hostile unionism, and other more subtle consequences that tend to defeat organizational objectives. Administrators must create conditions that will generate active and willing collaboration among all members of the organization and will lead people to want to direct their efforts toward the objectives of the system. It is interesting that this problem of getting employee collaboration is identical with the problem we face in attempting to reverse the trend toward more centralized government control. Just as we require a high level of management responsibility to solve the latter problems, we require a high level of responsibility to solve the former. In both instances we require greater understanding, more self-discipline, more consciousness of the needs of others, and more willingness to take long views.

Application of Human Relations to School Business Administration

The individual is important; let us make no mistake about that. But individual human beings have strong social needs. Wherever they are found, they congregate and form intricate and complex social structures. Many such groupings are informal in the sense that they are not part of the organizational chart. They are, however, powerful in the influence they exert over their members. The school administrator must recognize this phenomenon and act accordingly.

School administrators are acquiring increasing understanding of human motivation and human behavior as a result of their greater concern with the problems of human relations. They recognize that rewards and benefits that provide satisfaction outside of work are not enough, that work itself must be satisfying and meaningful, and that administrative practices that produce technical efficiency are not effective unless they take into account people as human beings.

Communication Concepts

The public schools belong to the public. For years, little has been done to help administrators communicate effectively with the community, staff, and students. With taxes continuing to go up, taxpayers are demanding to know what the schools are doing with their money. Administrators face crisis after crisis—many of them easily traced to poor communication somewhere along the line. These crises are eroding the once solid confidence the public had in public education. Too many administrators have attempted to hide problems, hoping they would disappear before the public discovered them. This approach might have worked in the days when people believed that school officials possessed a special sort of omniscience. It isn't working in most places today. It won't work anywhere tomorrow. Citizens, feeling they are shareholders in the schools, are seeking a piece of the action. They have entrusted their two most prized possessions—their children and their money—to school officials, and they want to know what's being done with them. The administrator who does not think of communication when he/she considers accountability, bond issues, student riots, teacher demands, complaints at board meetings, and community group pressures isn't prepared for today's challenges.

Principles of Communication

Good communication is not the same as selling. A school district's communication designed to sell something is not communication at all.

Communication has to be honest, thorough, and valid. An innovation should not be announced with fanfare and glowing generalities in September and completely ignored after a spring evaluation indicates the need for either a major overhaul of the program or its abandonment.

Good communication should be a two-way system. Not only do school officials inform, but they are kept informed. Not only do they state opinions and express needs, but they listen to the opinions and desires of others.

The communication system is for all people. The audience is not just teachers, not just parents, not just community leaders. The audience is everybody, including students.

The communication system is continuous. The good school communication system does not operate only before tax levies, only in quarterly newsletters, only when the news media will print articles about the system. District officials should be consciously operating their two-way communication system every day, even though the same things do not necessarily happen every day.

A good communication system is not only system-oriented. A proper system includes site-based communication.

Processes of Communication

An effective way to start a communication program is to have an advisory or study group look at existing communication efforts. Students, staff members, and residents can determine communication needs. Once commitment to a communication program is made, school officials should put the communication goals in writing. A policy should be prepared and a job description written. The job description should specify the title of the position. If funds are not available to appoint a full-time communications specialist, alternatives exist. These include:

- A teacher with a background in communications or public relations
- An administrator with a communications or public relations background
- Someone in the community—especially a retired person—with the proper skills
- A school public relations practitioner from another district who can work part-time for the system
- A reporter who can work on a part-time basis
- A consulting firm

Ask school administrators or board members about their schools' communication efforts, and chances are you'll hear about news releases and newsletters or other written, one-way communication tools. Seldom will school officials talk about the ways they get feedback—the methods of determining what the public is thinking about the school. Don't wait until after a crisis to find out what went wrong. Don't take a survey after a bond issue defeat to determine areas of possible misunderstanding. Build into your system's ongoing communications program a constant two-way flow of information, questions, constructive criticism, and suggestions. Your district will be better for it.

Some specific suggestions for obtaining feedback follow:

1. *Establish advisory committees.* Have one committee from each audience. For instance, set up an advisory committee of students, one of faculty, and another of lay citizens. Committee members, by feeling they are an integral part of the school, will be quick to apprise you of their group's thinking on a possible problem. The groups also serve as sounding boards for ideas. Properly selected groups, if representative of the community, can provide a constant source of information about what the community at large is thinking about the schools.

2. *Select key communicators.* These are the people at the top of the communications pyramid in a community. Some may be professional people. Others may be bartenders, beauticians, barbers—people who talk with many other people. Others might be retired people who want to remain active in the community and therefore spend time talking with others about community topics.

Invite these people in groups of six to twelve to meet with the chief school administrator. It helps if he/she takes the time to make the calls personally. When people agree to serve as key communicators, they will be quick to let the superintendent know if the community is rumbling about some school concern. It is a good feeling for a barber, when asked a question about the schools, to say: ''I'll call the superintendent and find out; I had lunch with him the other day.'' This kind of group spreads a feeling of ''the schools are ours'' that gains community support for the schools.

This group must be kept informed at all times of problems as well as of successes. One school district, Central Bucks, in Doylestown, Pennsylvania, prepares a special publication, ''Facts,'' to distribute to this group when a rumor is spreading.

3. *Invite taxpayers to lunch.* Each principal might invite groups of six or eight taxpayers to lunch twice a week. In an informal atmosphere, eating cafeteria food, the taxpayers can discuss school matters. This encourages those who met with the principal to call him/her the next time a question arises rather than spread misinformation that could lead to severe problems.

4. *Listen to what's said at meetings of service groups.* People who belong to these organizations often talk with many others in the community. It is a good idea to have a school administrator join these groups, if for no other reason than to know what the groups' concerns about the schools are.

5. *Distribute wallet-size calendars to residents.* In addition to key school dates and general information about the schools, include a phone number to be called for information or to check a rumor. This number should be answered twenty-four hours a day and on holidays by an answering service. An administrator (perhaps on a rotating basis) should be available when necessary to respond to crisis calls.

6. *Get people's ideas on tape.* Provide tape recorders throughout school buildings during events such as parent conferences and back-to-school night and school activities such as basketball games and plays. Their availability and use should be explained, encouraging people to make suggestions for the improvement of the school. Questions might also be asked this way by people who do not feel comfortable with the written word. It also guarantees anonymity for those who desire it.

7. *Listen to local radio call-in shows.* Often one crank call will not mean much, but a series of calls showing concern about a topic will alert the administrator that some explanation or action is required.

8. *Include a question session at public meetings.* By formally establishing such a procedure, the administrator will demonstrate that he/she encourages questions and suggestions. At the same time this will communicate a climate that says: ''We want to do a better job; if you have an idea, share it.''

   9. *Offer guidance and administrative services at night occasionally.* Some people who would lose a day's work if they came during the day will appreciate the opportunity to talk with you at their convenience. Even if only a few people use the service, this approach indicates that the school is trying to serve the public.

   10. *Establish a community resource file.* By bringing people to the schools to speak to classes or assemblies, you involve them in ''their school.'' They will be quick to let officials know about a festering problem if they feel the school cares about them enough to ask them to share their talents. Maintaining such a file is helpful to teachers at all grade levels.

   11. *Have the switchboard operator keep a list of common questions.* If a large number of people call about one topic, it's time to do a story on that topic for the media or for the newsletter.

   12. *Read church bulletins and work with the local clergy.* They can frequently identify community concerns before they surface. Keep these people well informed at all times.

   13. *Establish a speakers' bureau.* By offering free speakers as a service, the district engenders solid rapport with local organizations. Speakers can be encouraged to report questions to the administration for answering.

   14. *Include questionnaires in newsletters sent to the public.* Even though many people will not return the questionnaires, the ones who do will provide another insight into what some people are thinking.

   15. *Note questions asked by reporters at news conferences and after board meetings.* These questions represent the thinking not only of the reporters but of community residents.

   16. *Be candid with town officials and civic leaders.* In turn, these people will express what is concerning them and their groups. This kind of information can be extremely valuable.

   17. *Distribute golden-age cards to residents over sixty or sixty-five.* These cards allow residents to attend free such school activities as sports events and plays. When giving each person the card, the school official might discuss the concerns the senior has about the schools and encourage him/her to call the schools with questions.

   18. *Have an open forum once a month.* Invite students, parents, administrators, teachers, and taxpayers. Encourage people to come up with questions that will lead to answers that make the schools better. Set the groundrules clearly and in writing so the meetings don't become ax-grinding arenas for special-interest groups seeking to gain publicity. You might start this program with just students. Then, if feasible, expand it. Be ready for criticism; if you can't stand someone telling you that the school isn't doing its job in some area, don't try this. Make sure all suggestions are properly noted and that the person making the suggestion is told officially what happened to it.

Application of Communication Concepts

The school business administrator is deeply involved in most communication processes. Any issue involving finance or other technical phases of school administration seriously concerns the school business administrator. Getting people to vote for higher taxes poses a challenge for the business administrator. Voter support forms a basis for sound educational programs in school districts requiring budget and building approval at the polls.

The effective communicator must realize that the school's communications program should be a year-round undertaking. Too often, educators expect a short, intense, hard-hitting public relations campaign to ensure victory at the polls. Then they forget about the public until two weeks before the next school election. This approach leads to a credibility gap, one that creates doubt about the district's educational leadership. The "man on the street" wonders how he can be told for fifty weeks that the schools are doing an excellent job and then be informed suddenly that disaster looms if voter approval is not forthcoming.

By building confidence in the schools through clear communication about problems as well as successes, the educator establishes rapport with taxpayers, rapport that is needed for voter support.

Whether you are seeking approval of a tax levy, a bond issue, or an innovation, remember to focus on the reason for the schools' existence—students. Point out how the needed change will improve the education of Johnny and Jane. Too many school publications and educational presentations dwell on bricks, blocks, and bathrooms, often forgetting to mention children. As one expert puts it, "You're dealing with the taxpayer's two prized possessions—his children and his money; you should be able to communicate easily with the public."

Summary

This chapter reviews management tools that can be of particular use to the school business administrator. Some techniques vary in applicability according to the size of the school system. Some techniques require the utilization of computers and appropriate software. Other tools require a familiarity with symbolic language and mathematical concepts. Many tools are in the developmental stage, and utilization will increase as ingenious school business administrators work with the techniques.

This review of the use of management tools for planning is only illustrative, not exhaustive. For a more detailed and basic approach to the utilization of management tools, see one of the general texts listed in the Suggested Readings.

Suggested Activities

1. Consider the PERT system flow plan in Figure 4-7. Assume that the time required (in weeks) for each activity is a predictable constant and that it is given by the number along the corresponding branch. Find the earliest possible time, the latest possible time, and slack time for each event. Also identify the critical path (CPM).
2. A superintendent is making plans for a bond issue referendum. He/she received the services of six volunteer workers for precinct work and wishes to assign them to precincts in such a way as to maximize their effectiveness. The superintendent feels that it would be inefficient to assign a worker to more than one precinct but is willing to assign no workers to some of the precincts if they can accomplish more in other precincts.

FIGURE 4-7 A PERT System Flow Plan

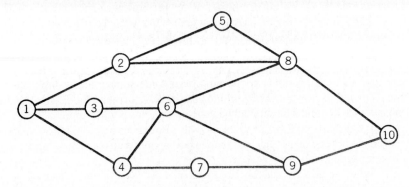

Table 4-1 gives the estimated increase in the plurality (positive or negative) of the bond referendum in each precinct if it were allocated various numbers of workers. Develop a plan for assigning the workers.

TABLE 4-1 Flow Network

Number of Workers	Precinct			
	1	*2*	*3*	*4*
0	0	0	0	0
1	25	21	32	15
2	42	38	41	25
3	58	55	48	33
4	62	64	52	40
5	68	72	54	46
6	73	81	55	51

3. A single crew is provided for unloading or loading each truck that arrives at the loading dock of the school system's warehouse. These trucks arrive at a mean rate of one per hour. The time required by the school warehouse crew to unload or load a truck has an exponential distribution (regardless of the warehouse crew size). The expected time required by a one-person crew would be two hours.

   The cost of providing each additional member of the crew is $6 per hour. The cost that is attributable to having a truck not in use (i.e., a truck standing at the dock) is estimated to be $25 per hour.

   a. Assume that the mean service rate of the crew is proportional to its size. What should the size be in order to minimize the expected total cost per hour?

   b. Assume that the mean service rate of the warehouse crew is proportional to the square root of its size. What should the size be in order to minimize expected total cost per hour?

4. Suppose the demand for a product from the school's carpenter shop is fifty units per month and the items are withdrawn uniformly. The setup cost each time a production run is made is $30. The production cost is $5 per item, and the inventory holding cost is $1 per month.

a. Assuming shortages are not allowed, determine how often to make a production run, and what size it should be.

b. If shortages cost $5 per item per month, determine how often to make a production run, and what size it should be.

Suggested Readings

Banghart, Frank W. *Educational Systems Analysis*. Toronto: Macmillan, 1969.

Catanese, Anthony J., and Alan M. Steiss. *Systematic Planning: Theory Application*. Lexington, MA: Heath, 1970.

Churchman, C. West. *The Systems Approach*. New York: Delacorte Press, 1968.

Cleveland, David I., and Willlam R. King. *Systems, Organizations, Analysis, Management: A Book of Readings*. New York: McGraw-Hill, 1969.

Cooper, Constance C., Nancy L. Knapp, and Cornelius Patterson. *Public Education toward Equality, Equity and Excellence*. Dubuque, IA: Kendall/Hunt, 1981.

Correa, Hector. *Quantitative Methods of Educational Planning*. Scranton, PA: International Textbook Company, 1969.

Donnelly, James H., James L. Gibson, and John M. Ivancevich. *Fundamentals of Management*. Georgetown, Ontario: Dorsey, 1981.

Hall, Douglas T., Donald D. Bowen, Roy J. Lewicki, and Francine Hall. *Experiences in Management and Organizational Behavior*. Chicago: St. Clair Press, 1978.

Hartley, Harry J. *Educational Planning-Programming-Budgeting: A Systems Approach*. Englewood Cliffs, NJ: Prentice-Hall, 1968.

Hentschke, Guilbert C. *Management Operations in Education*. Berkeley, CA: McCutchen, 1975.

Hillier, Frederick S., and Gerald J. Lieberman. *Introduction to Operation Research*. San Francisco: Holden-Day, 1967.

Hoy, Wayne K., and Cecil G. Miskel. *Educational Administration*. New York: Random House, 1987.

Kelley, Edgar A. *Improving School Climate*. Reston, VA: National Association of Secondary School Principals, 1981.

Knezevich, Stephen J., and Glen G. Eye, Eds. *Instructional Technology and the School Administrators*. Washington, DC: American Association of School Administrators, 1970.

Laughery, John W. *Man-Machine Systems in Education*. New York: Harper & Row, 1966.

Lewis, James, Jr. *Long-Range and Short-Range Planning for Educational Administrators*. Boston: Allyn and Bacon, 1983.

Martin, Francis F. *Computer Modeling and Simulation*. New York: Wiley, 1968.

Peters, Thomas J., and Robert H. Waterman, Jr. *In Search of Excellence*. New York: Harper & Row, 1982.

Sergiovanni, Thomas J., Martin Burlingame, Fred S. Coombs, and Paul W. Thurston. *Educational Governance and Administration*. Englewood Cliffs, NJ: Prentice-Hall, 1987.

Tanner, C. Kenneth, and Earl J. Williams. *Educational Planning and Decision Making*. Lexington, MA: Heath Lexington Books, 1981.

Van Dusseldorp, Ralph A., Duane E. Richardson, and Walter J. Foley. *Educational Decision-Making through Operations Research*. Boston: Allyn and Bacon, 1971.

Waterman, Robert H., Jr. *The Renewal Factor*. New York: Bantam Books, 1987.

Notes

1. *Guidelines for the Preparation of School Administrators,* (Arlington, VA: American Association of School Administrators, 1982), 6.

2. National Commission on Excellence in Educational Administration, *Leaders for America's Schools* (Tempe, AZ: University Council for Educational Administration, 1987).

3. Wayne K. Hoy and Cecil G. Miskel, *Educational Administration Theory, Research, and Practice,* 3rd ed. (New York: Random House, 1987), 2.

4. Ibid., 11.

5. Mary Parker Follett, *Dynamic Administration: The Collected Papers of Mary Parker Follett,* Henry C. Metcalf and Lyndall F. Urwick (Eds.) (New York: Harper, 1941).

6. Hoy and Miskel, *Educational Administration: Theory, Research, and Practice,* 15.

7. W. Richard Scott, *Organizations: Rational, Natural and Open Systems* (Englewood Cliffs, NJ: Prentice-Hall, 1981).

8. Hoy and Miskel, *Educational Administration: Theory, Research, and Practice,* 17.

9. Thomas J. Peters and Robert H. Waterman, Jr., *In Search of Excellence* (New York: Harper & Row, 1982), 93.

10. Ibid., 102,

11. Olaf Helmer, *Analysis of the Future: The Delphi Method* (Santa Monica, CA: Rand Corporation, 1967), 7–36.

12. C. Kenneth Tanner and Earl J. Williams, *Educational Planning and Decision Making* (Lexington, MA: Heath, 1981), 115–16.

13. Ibid.

5

An Information Systems Context

THE EXPLOSION OF DATA and information continues at a rate that makes both its management and use difficult and yet mandatory for school personnel—especially educational decision makers. Specifically, the need to reduce vast quantities of data and evaluate volumes of information to make critical decisions is of continuing concern to all administrators and certainly to school business administration. *Data* is defined as any representation of a fact or an idea that can be manipulated and to which meaning can be assigned. *Information* is defined as the meaning that a human assigns to data by means of known conventions used in the data representation.[1] A *data-based management system* is an organized collection of related data.[2] Specifically, a data base is a collection of data files tied together by keys or identifying names. This eliminates the need to store redundant data in several files or sets. Data sets represent an organized collection of data items. Reduced enrollments and shrinking funds in a period of decline increase the importance of managerial decisions and the data on which they are based.

When little up-to-date data or information were available, decisions were based on experience, intuition, or some other less-than-exact system. Today, decision makers are inundated with data. Computer printouts, graphs, charts, cost projections, demographic profiles, and columns of governmental and private statistics are available for minimal cost. The problem then becomes one of managing these vast resources of data and information.

The Linguistics of Information Systems

One of the key elements of the information systems context is the ability of varied audiences within the system to utilize the data base and retrieve the information needed to perform the tasks desired. The search strategy used by the system developer has a major impact on the usability of the system.

The real concern of any information system designer is how to employ the words and phrases of individual users while maintaining the general nature of a system that may be used by many people. The use of key-word-in-context strategies or table look-up information may be useful ideas for consideration. For example, the school business administrator's need in the area of budgeting and accounting requires the use of certain terms and parameters that will influence the way the system is built and accessed. The user must recognize the special needs required in construction of the system to accommodate multiple users, but the system designer needs to provide a "user friendly" scheme for each user.

All information system applications should be accompanied by thorough, well-written, easily understood documentation. The three general types of documentations include tutorials, user's manuals, and reference manuals. *Tutorials* lead the new user through examples of the program's capabilities and usually involve demonstration programs. A *user's manual* documents the systems features and functions in a systematic and comprehensive manner. The *reference manual* provides in-depth, technical descriptions of the program's capabilities and functions. High-quality documentation is crucial for the successful implementation of any software package.

Users also need procedures for operation's activities. These concern the use and maintenance of system components including the setting up of hardware, installation of programs and data files, and instructions for performing basic equipment maintenance. Procedures should also describe how to manage data files and how to maintain security of the system.

The Concept of Systems

David Kroenke, in a recent book titled *Management Information Systems,* states: "MIS is the development and use of effective information systems in organizations."[3] Clearly the key to the effectiveness of an information system context for the school business administrator is the manner in which usage occurs. Organizational professionals generally use three levels of analysis: the individual, the group or department, and the total organization.[4]

The school business administrator is a key individual in the MIS context of a school district or system. School business administrator usage is related to departments (or groups) throughout the district including instructional personnel, all support departments, and units such as the superintendent's office or the board. Responsibilities to the total organization—from parents and pupils to board members and fiscal/political support groups—affect the MIS context for the school business administrator.

Planning, organizing, and controlling within the MIS context are the driving forces for the school business administrator. The integration of the three elements of individual, group, and total usage into the MIS context is the likely determinate of the school business administrator's success. To manage the use of information (i.e., knowledge coming from data) through the structure of the system (a group of components, individuals, or the total system) is the major role of the school business administrator.

All aspects of information—accuracy, timeliness, pertinency—are moot if the system structure for management is not in place *and* utilized. A system's being in place is not sufficient—the system must be used, reviewed, and modified as needed. The school business administrator, in the role of supporting the key instructional goals of the system, must utilize information in its upward and downward flow for the success of various groups and the total system.

A good information system strategy for many school business administrators working with superintendents and other key central office administrators as well as site-based administrators is stated in these objectives:

1. Bring all users closer to required information.
2. Overcome and manage the burdens of information requests on both central administration and school site personnel.
3. Provide faster, better technologies to serve all users.

Clearly, the central administration of a school system is concerned with the management of its resources. This umbrella concept of management includes both a process and people to implement that process. Generally, a plan for management must first be established. Then a structure through which implementation can occur must be developed. Staff must be selected and resources allocated. Finally, overall direction and control must be established. Site-based managers are vitally concerned with the successful implementation of a data-based management system. The need for local data is of primary importance at each building.

The business functions of a complex organization such as a school system are of course an integral part of a data-based management system. The capability to store and retrieve data on a variety of personnel, facility, equipment, and supply expenditures is essential to efficient and effective budget planning. Raw data and derived elements produced over a five-year period (ranging from individual salary figures to total costs for glass replacement) allow decisions to be based on hard information.

Today even the smallest school district can have access to some type of computer system. Several manufacturers provide electronic equipment with monthly rental prices that fit within the budgets of any school district. Additionally, manufacturers, data processing or leasing companies, and software houses have developed remote data-processing capabilities to such a degree that they are available for relatively small monthly expenditures. The recent introduction of low-cost minicomputers and microcomputers has added yet another dimension to data processing. Development activities are continuing at a rapid rate in all areas of computing. The emergence of extensive competition is reducing the total cost for many facets of computer systems. Hardware costs are reduced each year, and performance increases. Software development has proceeded at a rapid rate. Generally, software for any business or administrative function is available from a large number of sources. Hardware manufacturers, user groups, and software houses all provide programs for specific machines. Costs range from zero to thousands of dollars.

Clearly, the amount of hardware available determines appropriate applications and thus software selection. These considerations will be discussed in a later section.

Thus, the relationship between a data-based management system and business functions allows raw data gathered from multiple sources to provide meaningful information to a wide variety of users. This information is then available to be used in making decisions on significant issues.

Failure Recovery

All information systems fail at one time or another, and components likewise can fail. The hardware can malfunction, programs can have errors, data can be lost, procedures can be misunderstood and misapplied, and people make mistakes. The time to consider such possibilities is before the failure. Users must know what to do when the system fails and how to proceed when the system is restarted.

First, users must know how to detect that a failure has occurred and know what is normal and abnormal behavior for the system. When a failure does occur, users need to know how to bring their activity to a halt. Then, the users need a procedure stipulating how to proceed. This may involve calling for assistance or initiating file recovery for themselves. Secondly, users need to know how to proceed to identify and fix the problem. Furthermore, users need to know what are possible costs in terms of time and money for each response.

Even when their systems are performing well, users should anticipate failure. Periodic backups of the data need to be made. Additionally, some form of the workload processed since the backup must be kept so that during recovery the files can be restored from the backup data. Procedures must exist not only for making the backup copies, but also for executing the recovery. During a failure, time is the most critical factor.

Role and Scope of Information Flow as Related to Data-Based Management—MIS Concept

For the purposes of this text, MIS will be defined as a computer-based system that provides management with useful information for decision making within the appropriate time frame. Additionally, the MIS should process day-to-day business, personnel, and educational data generated by the system in an effective and efficient manner.[5] An MIS generally provides regular reports of school issues (e.g., payrolls), special reports (e.g., number of teachers certified in Latin), and summary reports (e.g., pupil population projections). These reports need to be timely, relevant, and complete. To be effective, an MIS must operate from a sound data base. The selection of data-base items (e.g., age, race, certification, IQ, immunization records) is the key to report production. Information cannot be derived from incomplete or inaccurate data.

The means of collecting data are as varied as their applications. One of the concerns facing school business administrators is what type of collection procedures to use. The options vary from the traditional written report that must be keyed into a system to direct terminal input at remote sites. Additionally, grade sheets and student tests can easily be scored by high-speed equipment such as optical character recognition machines.

Since data are the raw materials used in decision making, the determination of hardware and software to be used in processing is of major importance to the school system. Communication links with the ability to "talk" from one terminal to another are another feature of current computer systems.

As site-based management becomes more widespread, the need for an effective MIS becomes paramount for building-level administrators and school business administrators. As noted in other chapters, the necessity of maintaining relationships between centralized management functions and site-based management functions becomes critical for the day-to-day operations of an instructional program. The periodic reports necessary at both levels require access to data and adequate processing capabilities. Purchasing and inventory control represent two areas where an MIS would be of major importance. Since selected items are purchased at the user site and others are purchased at the system level, an automated inventory and accounting control makes purchase, warehousing, and payment decisions easier and more accurate. The merging of accounts administered at the system level and those administered at the site level is accomplished more easily and with a greater degree of accuracy through up-to-date, correct data from an MIS.

Since school business administrators—as well as all other system and site-based administrators—are users of information and data-base services, "linkage" among these users and access to the various data sources becomes critical. As is noted in the section on types of hardware, the ability for local sites and the central office to be connected through the use of a terminal or microcomputer is a simple, relatively inexpensive operation with the current hardware available.

The ability to access data-base information dealing with fiscal and/or instructional applications allows for rapid, accurate flow of vital information for decision making and the sharing of alternative planning strategies. When all involved parties are working from the latest set of information, the possibility of error and miscommunication is certainly lessened if not removed. By having on-line presentations and interactions, proposal modifications can be tested, evaluated, and then either integrated or discarded as the result dictates.

Linkages also allow a flow of information and directories from the central office to local sites and from local sites to the central office. Additionally, school-to-school linkage allows the flow of student records and appropriate faculty and staff records information.

Unique Role of the School Business Administrator

The school business administrator has a unique role in hardware/software selection and use. This person will be involved in the bid process and in evaluation of specifications and proposals from vendors. School business administrators must understand the concept of MIS/data flow and its relation to decision making. The long-range potential and the current concerns of data security and budget constraints are real considerations of the school business administrator.

A part of the support effort of most school districts relative to computer utilization is training of a person to serve as a backup for the school business administrator. Expending only the time and resources necessary to train one person (the school business administrator) is a mistake. Illness, accident, or a sudden departure of the school business administrator poses a potentially devastating situation for a district with any extensive computer involvement.

A recent edition of *Electronic Learning* included a list of "8 Things Most Superintendents Don't Know about Computers." The eight items are:

1. Where the on/off switch is
2. That most important element of an effective computer program is neither hardware nor software, but skilled and willing teachers
3. The need for a plan and leadership
4. That elementary students can benefit from using computers as much as high school students
5. How to use them! (see #3)
6. Everything
7. That you have to buy software and support personnel, not just hardware
8. How to plan for effective use of computers[6]

These items center around planning, top-level leadership, and staff development. All are key items, considering that the school business administrator must often work with superintendents with this little knowledge about a very important and expensive aspect of today's schools.

Effect on Staff System

The installation of computer equipment in a school district may require several changes, such as the moving, retraining, or replacing of certain currently employed personnel. Also, additional personnel are often needed for specific positions generated by the installation of new equipment.

Several situations must be considered when computers are brought into a school district. Among the key considerations is staff morale. A new level of personnel is likely to be needed—the technical employee. These employees will not fit into the current structure of administrator, teacher, or clerk and will present a series of unique personnel problems. Pay scales are likely to be altered drastically, and usual lines of authority may need to be changed. The type of employee associated with general machine operations will be a new breed for most school districts. His/her requirements for space, clerical and technical assistance, and working conditions will be significantly different from those of other employees. Physical facilities may have to be altered, and equipment and materials used by the new employees will be expensive, new, and perhaps threatening to many people within the current administrative structure.

It is possible that certain staff members may be retrained to work with the new equipment, but to expect that all positions can be filled by reshuffling current personnel is beyond reason.

A key reason for introducing these concerns at this point is that activities under the direction of the school business administrator are among the first tasks for the machine. As such, the automation of payroll, purchasing, inventory control, and similar functions will be closely observed by all administrative and instructional units within the school district.

Distributed processing at local sites should be coordinated through the school business administrator. This facilitates initial purchase arrangements for hardware and continuing costs for software, consumable supplies, and maintenance as well as allowing the necessary linkage to appropriate central data-processing facilities.

Effect on Administrators

Conflicts may arise within the central office when a central data-processing facility is established in a school district. Inadequate thought is often given to the placement of the data-processing center, which in turn leads to future problems. The fact that a data-processing facility is to serve the entire school system is often overlooked at installation time. The school business administrator should resist having the data-processing operation placed under him/her and push for a placement within the district where the computer can serve all areas of the program. Two possible top-level organizational schemes are shown in Figure 5-1 and Figure 5-2.

The use of microcomputers at a local school site will have a limited effect on a large central facility's operation. However, as remote processing and the use of remote terminal

FIGURE 5-1   Organizational Scheme I

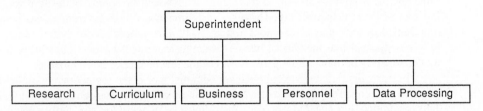

FIGURE 5-2   Organizational Scheme II

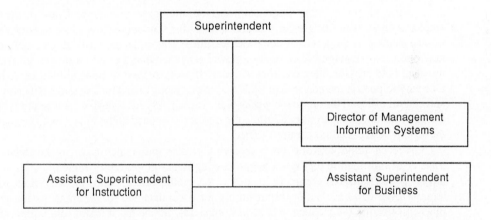

input increase, the use and control of the main computer might become a shared problem. This problem centers on the distribution of resources necessary to serve all possible users effectively. It is at this point that scheduling and prioritization of job selection become major concerns.

Either of the organizational patterns shown in figures 5-1 and 5-2 allows the flexibility necessary to provide service to all areas of a school district with a minimum of conflict among departments concerning control and allocation of funds. Both types of organization will provide a structure for distribution to the proper location within the organization without some of the problems of clearing data sources with various groups throughout the central staff.

The need to get necessary information and data into proper hands within the district cannot be overemphasized. The flow of information and data to various areas of the district is the only logical base for decision makers to use in working through key problem areas. As will be discussed later, the computer can serve as a key provider of planning information when correctly applied within any school district.

The business administrator and other key administrators within the district must consider the concepts of data processing in terms of systemwide use. A full understanding of the uses of data processing systemwide is a major step toward its proper utilization. A continual search for more and better uses of the data-processing system is an objective for all concerned. The business system must be consulted as scarce resources are allocated.

Problems associated with the placement of a computing or data-processing facility often revolve around fiscal control. It is natural to associate the control of the hardware with the area of fiscal responsibility. However, it is imperative that the tremendous resource represented by an "electronic school system" will have proper access to the hardware. It is to be expected that the school business administrator will have responsibility for the implementation of many of the general uses of the machine once it is available.

In many districts the school business administrator is the logical person to head the advance planning group for the district, and he/she should be on the committee in all cases. This committee, or one similarly constituted, must be in operation well before installation time and should continue as an integral part of the system's organization. Generally, the time frame of an academic year is best since many nontraditional activities often occur during the summer period.

With the increasingly large emphasis on site-based management and a parallel emphasis on the usage of greater volumes of data, the school business administrator's role in management of the district's computer facilities takes on an increased degree of importance. Since more and more computing power is available to the site-based administrator, the need is to provide the most effective and efficient method of transmitting these data. One very important method is to provide diskettes (floppy disks) for exchange between site and central office. This approach works well, is relatively inexpensive, and requires only enough machine compatibility to allow the diskette produced at the local site to be read at the school business administrator's office.

A recent trend, and one that is receiving greater and greater usage, is the electronic transfer of information through a teleprocessing hook-up between "remote" sites and a larger, general-purpose computer located at the central office. Since the school business administrator will have major responsibility for fiscal data and for the transmission of all other information (attendance, test scores, etcetera), he/she has a major role in the establishment of the network for transmission of these data.

The local site machines will probably be stand-alone microcomputers with the capability to have a separate workload. These machines support the three major functions needed by administrators—spreadsheet, database, and word processing. The capability of a microcomputer to perform stand-alone functions as well as to serve as a terminal for transmission *and* receipt of data and/or other information is critical.

Recruitment/Selection

The recruitment of sufficient personnel for work in a data-processing system may well be an expensive and laborious task for school districts. The selection of proper staff in systems where the need for members is small requires that the data-processing/computer staff have varied skills, including competence with hardware and the interpersonal skills to work with a large variety of people. The school business administrator may be charged with the initial selection and recommendation for hiring of the entire computer center staff. This will include the operators, programmers, and management personnel necessary to develop a smooth and well-functioning organization. Again, the size of the computer center operation is crucial. In an organization serving small school systems, perhaps only one or two people are needed. In larger systems the staff needs will be magnified. A small staff may need more flexibility to do more things with more people, especially in relation to contacting individuals, as opposed to those organizations where large numbers of people can be employed and only selected professionals need to talk with other members of the school administrative and teaching staffs.

Retention of any staff member in the data-processing center should reflect the staff retention policies applicable across the entire district. While unusual hiring practices may have to be used when securing data-processing professionals, the policies for retention of these professionals should in no way violate established school board policies relative to promotion and retention of any staff member.

As with any group of employees, attention must be given to union/nonunion personnel problems. General contract situations will cover most issues, but specific language may be needed to protect the sensitive records or critical operations facets of a computer center.

Staff Training

The threat of educational data processing is very real to certified and noncertified personnel in many school districts. The idea of a machine taking over in areas where people previously worked, the question of data privacy, and the fear of discharge or major job shift are problems faced by many school personnel. The school business administrator and other key staff members have a major responsibility to reduce these fears.

A significant factor in the installation of a data-processing system of any type is staff training. A well-planned staff renewal program involving all levels of staff affected by the computer will increase the acceptance of the hardware and the new staff roles. An open discussion of what the machine can and cannot do and of the important role people play in the successful use of computers is a valuable part of staff training. Another method of reducing fears is to have staff members at various levels in other districts with data-processing systems visit with the local system's personnel. These face-to-face visits will do much to dispel fears.

Discussion of data security, privacy of information, and the multitude of factors of operation and management are all key factors to incorporate into staff training programs. The problem of security occurs for information produced, personnel records, and hardware. The establishment of realistic goals and objectives for the data-processing unit, built with the involvement of local personnel and consultants, will provide direction. Proper procedures for the review and rewriting of goals and objectives, as well as for a review of the operating procedures, are vital for effective implementation of a data-processing system.

The more fully the staff understands the implementation of the computer system, the more they will cooperate. Finally, the new functions required of each staff member should be thoroughly understood by both conversion team members and other staff members.

Legal Aspects

Data-processing records-keeping systems and use must provide for the level of security required by federal privacy laws and freedom of information act requirements. Therefore, the requirements for privacy of information in tape files, disk files, or card files is no different in structure from that used in other records-keeping systems within the district. For example, the security necessary to determine who has access to computer files is a primary concern when persons have access to on-line data files or to stored files including information on individual students. Thus, it is very important that passwording sequences, security clearances, number identifications, and the like be made a part of any system in which files are addressed through the use of terminals or accessed with programs. The information stored in personnel files and that stored in student files must be protected in the same manner. All data of a privileged nature must be afforded the security required of a paper document. Thus, machine-readable files, such as tapes and disks, should be protected and accessible only to qualified and authorized personnel within the district and only to authorized agents outside the district. Additionally, the distribution of printed information, whether student records or personnel records, from computer files must be carefully screened and only appropriate information provided. It is imperative that the same procedures for data security be applicable for all records within the district.

Passwords

One of the most widely used and effective measures for providing computer security is passwords. A password is a secret word or number or combination of letters and numbers that must be typed in on the keyboard before the system will allow any activity to take place. What normally occurs in passwording is that the computer user or group of users having access to a particular data file (such as student test records or individual fiscal information) must provide a certain predetermined code before that file can be unlocked. When that password is implemented, it then allows access to any authorized user. Most computer systems work so that the password entered at the keyboard does not appear on the screen or on typed copy anywhere. This is to avoid unauthorized distribution of the password and to prevent any unauthorized casual observation of a particular password used by an individual. Passwords become even more effective when they are changed on a regular basis and when the individual users remember to not share their password with unauthorized persons. One of the problems with passwords is obvious—if a person is authorized to use the file but does not have access to the password, then the file remains locked.

Selection Process

Since hardware/software selection will lead to a major expenditure, whether on a lease, purchase, or some combination plan, care must be exercised from the beginning. Appropriate persons from the central office, local building sites, the community, and other areas need to have input. This approach presents a potentially difficult situation. The committee must establish a time frame for decision making and adhere to it. ''Lobbying'' by staff or others for a specific brand of hardware is another potential problem. The identification of all educational needs of the district must be made prior to final selection. Appropriate funds should be budgeted for the selection process.

Need

Without question, a need must be established before a data-processing facility is introduced into a public school system. There are numerous instances in which computer facilities have been opened in a district long before the proper cost-utilization studies have been made. The result of such premature installation is exactly what could be expected—disaster. Often the center does not function in an efficient manner, and the hardware is removed. The real loser in this instance is the school district. Once hardware has been removed, whatever the cause, replacement or reinstallation is a difficult process. In fact, it is often much more difficult than the initial effort to secure equipment.

This reinforces the need to verify the qualifications for data-processing facilities in a particular school district. The needs of each district vary, and unique applications should be expected for most situations.

Need for data-processing equipment should be established on a day-to-day basis, for several years in advance, and in close cooperation with representatives of all phases of the school program. The services will be offered across several, if not all, aspects of the school program—business, instruction, and research—and should involve representatives from these areas in the planning phase. As stated before, it is necessary to start planning early, and it is not unusual to plan in detail for at least three years, and in one or two five-year blocks after that. These plans provide the director of data processing with current as well as long-range systemwide goals to consider.

A hierarchical arrangement of services needed should be established by representatives of each of the groups. It is to be expected that one of the functions associated with school business administration (payroll, inventory, budgeting) will be among the first identified and the first selected for implementation. Cost figures should be computed, as should time commitments and data security for each identified need. Needs cannot always be computed in cost terms because it is not always possible to know the value of rapid turnaround of information if none has been available in the past. Detailed cost figures for machine utilization, software development, personnel expenditures, and supplies should be maintained for the various facets of the school program. Data security should receive high priority in order to maintain the privacy of the individual student and staff member and to ensure the maintenance of correct and accurate data.

Visits to similar and somewhat larger school districts are generally profitable. Those within the same state are best because they operate in the same governmental framework. The same state reports are required, and the same rules and regulations govern items from transportation to cafeterias. Care should be taken to discuss problems of implementation, user education, staff acceptance, and machine selection with all affected levels of personnel within the organization. Systems people and supervisors are often more valuable to those seeking technical information than are central office level personnel.

Selection Factors

It is impossible to give a formula for machine selection. The variables involved in this decision are many and complex. As has been previously noted, visits to other school districts, regional facilities, and university centers have merit. Discussion of need with data-processing consultants is another valuable source of information. Vendors' information can be used profitably when solutions for the same problems are offered by several companies. These solutions should be based on hardware configurations. Another source of information are the varied technical reports researched by reputable firms or national data-processing organizations.

An alternative arrangement to sole ownership or rental, and one that has been used across the country, is time sharing. With the current 386 systems and the upcoming 486 systems having excellent networking capabilities, rental on a time-sharing system may be a local alternative for a short- or medium-range period.[7] Terminals (typewriters, card reader-printers, visual display systems) are used by the local system and are tied to a large central processor at some remote location. This may be the most economical way for some districts to secure data-processing services.

A third arrangement is the service-center concept for data-processing. The use of a service center generally involves the packaging of material at the local district and the physical movement of that material to a remote location for processing. The cost of processing is then set as per the function performed and the number of students served. For example, school scheduling is often performed for a fixed amount plus a charge for each student scheduled, assuming a standard computer scheduling program can be used. If special processing must be done, additional costs are involved. Priority of work is always a concern in dealing with a service center. Front-end agreements need to be negotiated to accommodate special needs such as payroll processing, grade reports, and time-dependent reports.

Backup provisions for hardware utilization are important for all types of data processing. A related concern with backup systems is security of data and output.

The actual selection of a computer system, time-sharing service, or service center is a laborious and time-consuming task. The discussions of core size, computer speed, cycle time, compiler languages, satellite devices, new personnel, expensive physical facilities, and the thousands of other details that must be examined to produce the best possible recommendation for board action are complex and onerous. Decisions as to what features can be cut without hampering proposed operations are difficult to make. Service and software (program) support are especially difficult to evaluate. Some maintenance plans include a certain number of service calls, others provide for unlimited calls, and some require a fee for each call. Figure 5-3 shows a typical computer system.

Costs of machines are low enough to warrant serious consideration of initial purchase, at least for some components. The place of micros in a line purchase plan must also be considered. Lease/purchase plans are still important when growth potential cannot be predicted for a five-year period. If major changes will occur in less than five years, costs of replacement may outweigh the difference in purchase versus lease arrangements.

Cooperative Efforts in Data Processing

Most school districts in this nation are not large enough to maintain extensive educational data-processing systems, thus the necessity to group together in consortiums, intermediate units, boards of cooperative educational services, and other types of cooperative arrangements to provide the basic data-processing services of instruction, administration, and research application. In order to bring the technology of the twentieth century to focus on education, it is necessary to have access to large machines, with the capabilities of time sharing, simulation, gaming, data-base management, instructional activities, and other applications previously thought to be useful only to the largest school districts or research agencies. Since few school districts have the resources to maintain such a broad-based system, cooperative ventures are necessary.

FIGURE 5-3   A Sample Computer Configuration
The popular Apple® Macintosh® SE computer is now available in three configurations: the entry-level model with two 800K disk drives, the standard model with 1MB of RAM and a 20MB hard disk, and the advanced model with 2MB of RAM and a 40MB hard disk.

Cooperative data-processing centers are in use across the country, as are cooperative efforts in purchasing and other activities. The determination of who is to produce what, and who is to pay for what, must be a cooperative one in which the role and scope of individual school systems are maintained. Proper assurances of data security under the Family Rights and Privacy Act must be maintained. Yet an adequate flow of information must be obtainable for planning purposes. Access to the system must be regulated, and various input and output security procedures must be established for utilization by all members of the consortium. The success of groups in which resources have been shared needs to be expanded. It is imperative that students not be penalized in terms of accessibility to machines, programming, and good decisions simply because they are in small districts that cannot afford massive computing resources.

Security

As has been noted, the computer center or data-processing center is generally under the direction of the school business administrator. Thus, the issue of computer and software security is yet another responsibility/concern of this person.

Basic consideration for hardware security includes the physical protection of the machines and environment in which the hardware is located. Special locks, security codes for workers, and limited access are general, well-known means of protecting computer centers. Cameras and/or sound monitoring may also be used. Additionally, potential losses from disasters such as fires, floods, earthquakes, and tornadoes must be considered in locating a computer center within a district and in selecting accessibility and limiting ease of ingress and egress. The installation of prior detections systems and fire extinguishing systems as well as burglar alarm systems is a must. The threat of vandalism and purposeful destruction of computer data systems must always be the concern of the school business administrator.

Software and data file protection include all of these measures plus some special efforts. Basic features of data protection include the age-old but extremely successful practice of making backup copies of sensitive data files and archival type of information that is then stored at other sites. Also, where appropriate, copies of key software should be physically secured as the hardware is protected. One of the best methods of protecting software on the local site is, of course, to make copies and locate them in fire-proof containers within the building.

Physical Protection

Trainor and Krasnewick provide a list of physical controls to secure computer systems in their book *Computers*. The suggestions are extremely useful for school business administrators to consider as they work through protection of hardware and software. The suggested physical controls to secure computer systems are:

1. Place computer equipment in areas of limited access from the outside.
2. Physically secure equipment to floors and tables.
3. Place identification numbers on all equipment, manuals, and software.
4. Restrict physical access to authorized people.
5. Build computer centers to withstand natural disasters.
6. Provide smoke detectors and fire suppression systems that do not harm electronic equipment.
7. Place unused storage media in secure library.
8. Copy-protect software.
9. Use data encryption when storing data and software on storage media.[8]

Computer Viruses

While not currently the problem for school systems that it is for governmental and industrial settings, the issue of a computer virus is still a very real consideration. A computer virus is really a tiny program purposefully introduced by a computer programmer (commonly called a ''hacker''). This program is designed to break into computers by looking for flaws in the password system or through other methods of gaining entry. Once inside the computer, the program is designed to spread throughout the system, multiply itself, and/or make visual displays at terminals. A virus can be told to attack certain things (e.g., remove names of all teachers making $1,200 or more), modify items (e.g., add $5,000 to each salary figure) or just create a nuisance (e.g., flash a message).

School sites and school districts have not been heavily attacked by viruses, but they are vulnerable. One of the most effective measures for protecting against a virus attack continues to be a good password security system, changed often and creatively developed. Second, and perhaps more important, is the need to backup files on a daily basis. There are infection detection programs and also infection prevention programs. No program will find or cure all viruses, but many can be of help to the school business administrator in the fight to maintain secure, usable files. Finally, remember that there is no single fix for all viruses and that constant vigilance is a key part of avoiding severe damage.

Utilization

The need to utilize properly the vast potential of the MIS system is of major importance. Decisions as to what functions are to be automated, how data will be collected, how persons will obtain information, how information will be protected, and what areas have the greatest need are all part of proper utilization of the MIS. The concerns of the various publics and the real considerations of costs are important areas of attention.

Development of Suitable Software

The previous section indicates that while there are problems with machine selection, solutions are available that will allow these problems to be attacked by the district with the likelihood of success. The larger problem for study in the area of school business administration is the development of suitable software.[9]

After the rather routine functions have been programmed, the real value of a complex computer facility will be found in the area of management decision making. The function of management decision making, in which alternatives are explored based on sufficient data, is generally lacking in the public schools. No programs for securing necessary data or projections have been available to general school administrators, and this deficiency has contributed to errors in selection of building sites, program planning, personnel selection, and long-range growth projections.

The simple data-processing system is a transaction-oriented system designed for the express purpose of producing reports from a set of data. These reports include the attendance, grade reporting, and general bookkeeping functions associated with the area of school business management and student personnel work. The value of an integrated data-processing system is to go beyond these transactions, use the collected data on many facets of the school program, pose questions of a sophisticated data base, and utilize these data to discover alternative courses of action.

No area of computer data-processing applications is in more flux than that of software applications packages. Thousands of software packages are available in financial planning, word processing, graphics, insurance, computer-aided instruction (CAI), and hundreds of other specialized areas. However, some few dozen have emerged as industry standards for use with each type of machine. A major problem for school business administrators and other education professionals is to realize that a distinction must be made between applications software packages that provide solutions and those that provide users with tools to solve problems. Unlike most statistical applications, most business applications are complex, without an accepted method for solution. These procedures may even vary from building to building. Thus, the selection of an applications package may only be the beginning of work for the school business administrator. The idea of a perfect fit for specific software applications is probably a myth. Many software professionals agree that if a package does 70 to 80 percent of what is desired, it is worth serious examination.

Proper documentation of any program and training in its use is essential for error-free operation at a new site. Any modification of purchased, free, or locally developed software will require some programming staff. Even with packaged programs, many systems have specific needs that require software modification or development. These needs affect staff costs and support costs.

Software Purchase

A study by Conners and Valesky in *AS&U*, February 1988, indicates ten rules to be used in the purchasing of software for use in educational environments. The antecedent reason for having a set of rules is that technological advantages of the last few years have indicated that a tremendous amount of software is available, and that while this amount has gone up, the difficulty of determining quality and, more importantly, usability in the appropriate setting has become more and more difficult. The Conners/Valesky rules include:

1. *Know exactly what you want.*
2. *Standardize the use of microcomputer software as much as possible.*
3. *Purchase the most advanced version of the software available.*
4. *Never purchase off-beat or no-name brand software.*
5. *Check with state-level or controlling agencies to see if they are moving toward any specific type or brand of software.*
6. *Generally, avoid custom-written or custom-designed software.*
7. *Discount software houses rarely provide any support services.*
8. *If you have no in-house expert to get the system up and running and to train users, include support service in the purchase agreement.*
9. *Once you receive the software, begin to use it immediately.*
10. *Almost every major software manufacturer provides some kind of educational discount.*[10]

Standardization and Maintenance Procedures

The determination of computer program needs as a part of the overall program of systems analysis for a school district is but the initial step in a series of steps. The programs necessary for the total operation must be part of an integrated system that meets the total requirements of a district. Without some standardization of programming efforts, replacement of personnel is difficult, and the maintenance of the system through hardware changes is virtually impossible.

Figure 5-4 gives a picture of a scheme for converting a problem into results. Each step is detailed, but each is a part of the overall plan.

Single-shot, special-purpose programs should be avoided if at all possible. This approach tends to be wasteful of scarce resources and produces a type of unstructured working environment not conducive to efficient operation. The areas where this general rule

FIGURE 5-4 Direct Conversion of Problem to Machine Program

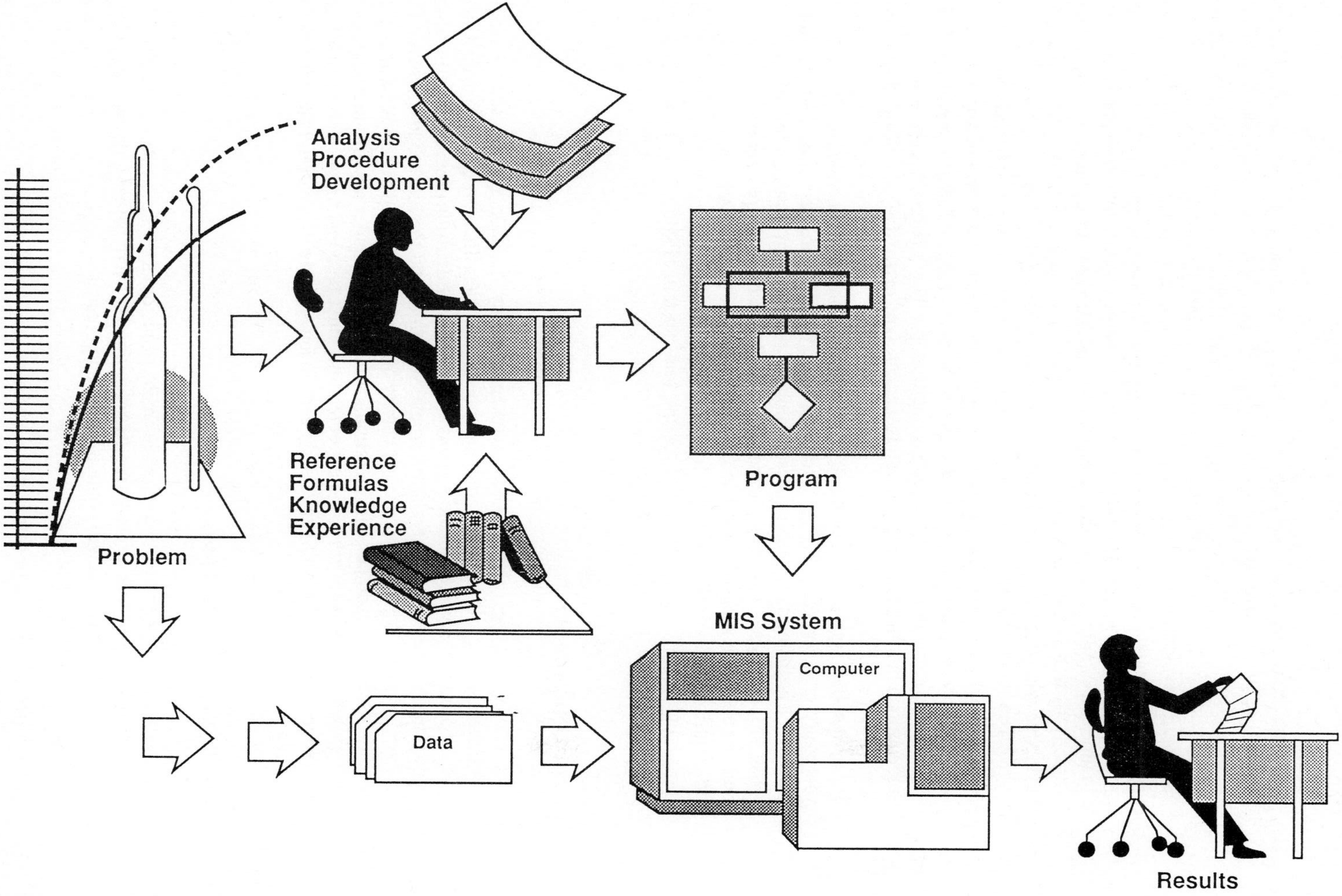

Analysis
Procedure
Development

Program

Reference
Formulas
Knowledge
Experience

Problem

Data

MIS System

Computer

Results

may not hold are in the activities of research and instruction sections. The needs for processing in these two areas are variable and will, on occasion, require special applications.

Software formats should be standardized across all units of a district. For example, if a reporting format for costs in transportation can be used by food services, the costs of software development and maintenance can be kept to a minimum. Reporting formats should be standardized where possible and used on both output and input documents. Some printed reports can become "turnaround" documents for divisions and thus create savings in time and supplies. Self-mailer forms for grades and attendance can be printed and mailed directly from the data-processing center or from a site using desktop publishing options available with many microcomputers. Numerous other applications are also possible.

The standardizing of terminology used in all system and site reports is a major feature of an efficient, effective MIS. Consistent use of such terms as *per-pupil costs, average daily membership, assessed valuation per pupil, achievement,* and *instructional level* allows effective communication to all school audiences. The standardization also allows for reduction in number of forms and in unnecessary (and expensive) alteration of software for use with the MIS.

Another argument favoring strict standardization and maintenance procedures is the necessity of a control process. Without strict control of programming and machine use records, it is difficult for the business administrator to get an accurate picture of costs. These costs are, of course, invaluable to the business administrator for projecting areas of growth and the attendant growth costs. The minute details required for each subset of the operation to contribute successfully to the total scheme are evident, as is the need for proper documentation of each subset and for the total system. Figure 5-5 shows some of the characteristics of a pupil record file.

Types of Equipment

The choice of types of equipment represents a key decision for the school business administrator and other system staff members. The identification of the district's needs, growth potential, and cost considerations are input for the decision process. Whether to lease or purchase, types of peripherals, personnel selection, and the like are all involved in the decision process. Again, input from a variety of sources is needed to provide a sound basis for final selection. Another consideration is that most computer systems are modular and that growth and change are to be expected and must be considered. The decision must serve the central office and site-based needs in a multitude of areas and for wide ranging applications.

Digital Computing Systems

Generally, a *computer* can be defined as an electronic device able to manipulate data under the control of a program or programs stored within it. There is really no typical computer system, but most systems will contain these components:

- Central processor
- Input/output devices (not including printer)

FIGURE 5-5   Pupil Record File

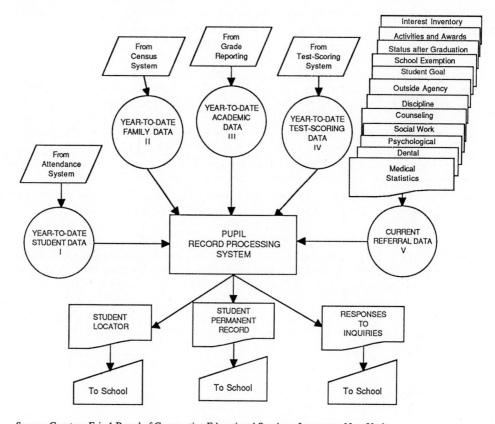

Source: Courtesy Erie 1 Board of Cooperative Educational Services, Lancaster, New York.

- Storage unit
- Control devices
- Printer

Figure 5-6 shows the relationship of the functions of a computer system.

Mainframes

Mainframes are large, expensive computers that offer extensive problem-solving capabilities and require a large staff for operations. Mainframes can have memory capacities measured in billions of characters. The largest mainframes can process several million instructions each second, and their operating systems allow time-sharing applications and multi-processing efforts. Data storage is often on hard disks, with wide use of tapes. Mainframes are used as the basic instructional for an entire system of computers, with minicomputers and microcomputers linked to the mainframe as part of a distributed processing system.

FIGURE 5-6 Relationship of Functions of a Computer System

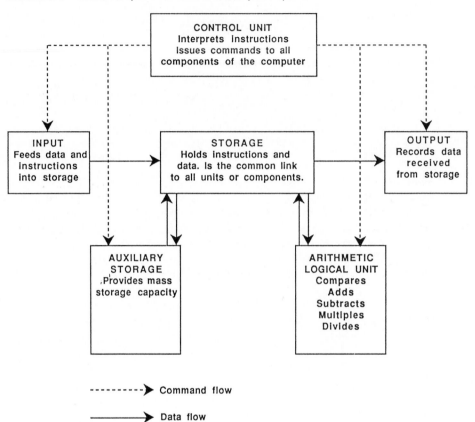

Minicomputers

The minicomputer is a smaller version of the mainframe computer. The processing power and cost of minicomputers are smaller, yet minicomputers have larger memory sizes and faster processing speeds than microcomputers. These machines are well suited to the needs of small- and medium-sized schools/organizations. Minicomputer prices range from about $10,000 to several hundred thousand dollars, but have memory capacities measured in millions of characters. Minis have fast processing speeds and operating systems with multiprogramming capabilities while generally using hard disks. They can be equipped with drives for "floppy" disks and tapes.

With minicomputers, more than just large organizations have access to computer problem-solving power. Data and information held in minicomputers are invaluable to researchers who need to locate pertinent facts quickly and easily. Minicomputers can be used as a part of a distributed processing system with the advantage that all processing power is not dependent on a single machine.

Microcomputers

Recent computer technology has not only brought machines into the workplace but also into homes. Called "home" computers, "personal" computers, "microcomputers," or "micros," these machines are powerful, yet user-friendly. They are capable of performing a multitude of tasks once handled only by large computers. Purchase prices for micros range from $100 for home units to $5,000 or more for professional models. A typical microcomputer memory unit stores from 128,000 to 1 million characters of data.

Table 5-1 presents a summary look at selected features of several important computer system components.

Maintenance

With many computer centers and individual sites using hardware from a number of vendors, the determination of the cause of a problem is often difficult for data-processing managers. The interface among different machines and component parts (including telephone connections) often creates mechanical difficulties that are hard to pinpoint. Controller units, telephone connections, and remote entry devices are especially vulnerable.

Maintenance contracts are most often written in two forms—contract option and per-call basis. Contract-option agreements are sold in blocks (usually eight hours, although after the initial block smaller segments may be offered), with a general starting time of 8 A.M.

The per-call client pays for service on the basis of need and is billed for service time including travel to and from the site. Per-call clients are generally serviced after contract option calls, regardless of when the contract-option call is received—i.e., contract-option customers are serviced even if a per-call client has logged a request previously. Basic package upgrade can occur under most agreements. This allows for service calls to be completed once started.

TABLE 5-1 Illustrative Category, Size, Cost, and Selected Examples of Computers

Category of Computers	Memory Size*	Cost**	Illustrative Manufacturer
Micro	4K–256K	$2K–10K	Apple, TRS 80, Xerox 820, HP 125
Mini	256K–1 meg	$15K and up	HP 2000, HP 3000, DEC PDPII
Large	1 meg–16 million	$200K and up	IBM 370, Amdahl V6, Honeywell 6600, DEC 20

*Core size is described in terms of 1000 positions or Ks (i.e., 5K = 5000 positions, meg = 1 million)

**Cost is approximate and determined by such items as software and peripherals. (Special attention should be given to the high cost of graphics, terminals, printers, and plotters.)

Another concern for all customers is to determine what levels of maintenance support are available—for example, local office to regional office to national office. Established companies will have several levels of personnel support and, equally important, an adequate supply of spare parts. Recommendations for services from satisfied users are a good way to determine local locations providing acceptable services.

Other Equipment Needs

The installation of a computer system in a school district affects the selection of peripheral equipment and the disposition of equipment that may be currently in use in the school district. As is evident from previous discussion, supporting devices are necessary for any computing system.

A complete review of equipment requirements within a district provides an opportunity to look critically at how monies are spent on equipment of this type and at how efficiently it is being used to further the overall scheme of district operations. Therefore, some machines may be sold or turned back to the company because of cost-effectiveness considerations.

Disaster Recovery

There is a clear need for a comprehensive disaster recovery plan for computer centers and local site machines in today's operating environment. The increasing dependence on automated systems and technological activities in most school districts mandate this protection. Certainly, the possibilities for disaster, including natural calamities such as earthquakes and floods, human errors, and purposeful destructions such as the introduction of a computer virus make all educational computer systems vulnerable. Because many of these events cannot be prevented, it is imperative to devise a strategy that can be utilized in the event of a disaster of any sort.

The most important initial activity for a school system to develop is a comprehensive, consistent statement of all actions to be taken before, during, and after a disaster occurs. The plan should include documented and tested procedures that will ensure the availability of critical resources and guarantee that facilities maintain operations at some acceptable level. Such a plan must provide for minimal disruption to operations in the event of major problems and/or interruptions, ensure organizational stability, and provide an orderly plan for recovery.

Clearly, a several-phase plan is important. The first step is to obtain the support and involvement of top management officials. The second step is to appoint a group that will be in charge of guiding the development of the plan, setting the scope of the plan, and developing procedures to cover business disruption, restoration plans, and what happens to microcomputers, word-processing units, and any telecommunications networks. A risk analysis that includes a range of possible disasters should be determined, and each component of the system, both hardware and software, should be analyzed against these risks. The identification and prioritization of processing applications to be recovered and reinstituted after a disaster plan must then be made. A final step in this plan is to determine the most practical backup operations for the data entry, which includes facilities most likely to be used as backup, those having a secondary backup possibility, multiple computers, data centers, vendor-supplied equipment, and so forth—in other words, all the options that are available for backup systems, both in terms of hardware and software. These procedures should be in written form and provided to all personnel with a need to know. Funding must be secured and the plan must be tested, evaluated, and, if necessary, revised.

Materials Selection

Materials selection for a computing facility is not a simple or easily accomplished task. Materials necessary for a computing facility to operate efficiently seem to be without number. They fall into the categories of consumable materials, such as paper products, cards, and ribbons, and nonconsumable materials, like desks, cabinets, tape racks, tapes, and disk packs.

Consumable Supplies

The consumable supplies needed in any computing facility certainly include paper products such as daily attendance records, checks, transfer vouchers, invoices and other billing materials, and personnel reports, charts, and graphs, as well as other administrative information. Standard computer printer paper is intended for general-purpose reports, for testing, and for production of rather limited amounts of material. Preprinted forms on which material may be printed in special blanks are widely useful. Some uses of these special forms are payroll checks, W-2 forms, monthly reports, class registers, invoices, transfer vouchers, and other material in which header information can be given routinely, lines can be drawn, and certain columns can be preprinted to save both time and money.

In addition, supplies that are not always considered in relation to computer facilities but which generate expense include rubber bands, marking pencils, batch tickets, and separator cards. All centers do not use all types of materials; but as any school administrator knows, many kinds of supplies must be available in order to make the operation run smoothly enough to justify the cost of computer installation.

Nonconsumable Supplies

Consumable supplies make up a rather large expenditure for a computing center, but expenditures for nonconsumable supplies must also be considered. When we include items such as magnetic tapes at approximately $20 per reel, or disk packs leasing for $15 to $25 per month or purchased for $200 to $500, the cost of nonconsumable supplies can rise sharply. For example, tapes must be stored in racks and must be provided with either tape seals or canisters to prevent dust accumulation, which would make them useless. A tape library of hundreds or thousands of reels is not uncommon. The disks must be stored in a relatively secure place so that there will be no damage to the actual disk pack. Special cabinets are generally used by most computing installations.

Other nonconsumable supplies needed by the computing center include breakdown and setup desks, chairs, programming desks, key punch chairs, and storage devices such as facilities used to store cards and card boxes. Failure to provide sufficient supplies (often costing thousands of dollars) would doom the computer center (often costing several thousand dollars per month) to inefficiency.

Office Procedures Operations

By the time the school business administrator has participated in the decision-making process described in the previous sections of this chapter, it is doubtful that he/she would wish to take on more reorganization or alteration projects. However, the opportunity to examine the totality of office procedures will never be better. Staff reorganization, filing processes, and record management can be logically examined at this point.

With the introduction of computer processing, many of the filing and record-keeping procedures will be automatically altered. Current records, permanent files, transfer vouchers, purchase orders, and the like can all be generated by the computer system. This causes a restructuring of filing procedures and may call for the removal of certain files, such as the on-line inventory control system. Files of computer output differ from current files and may produce more detailed records requiring more space, but they will be organized so as to facilitate data retrieval.

Security of data, including personnel and financial records, is a current concern and will remain so. If data are maintained on-line, this is especially crucial. Centralization of responsibility is a vital part of any look at the current organizational scheme. Both the "owner" and "user" of sensitive computer files have responsibilities to control access to data.

Computer-generated output, including paper and punched cards, will grow as the school system's ability to use the data-processing system grows. Remote inquiry stations may become an integral part of financial and personnel records. Storage locations for printed material are needed, and an access scheme or system for this material must be devised. Most computer system costs must be prorated to many areas within the system, and a machine program and accounting scheme must be developed to perform the task.

Output will build up rapidly, and a procedure for retention and disposition of all levels of records—nonessential, useful, important, and vital—must be established. Microfilming is a useful technique for producing more easily retrieved material. Personnel must be taught to interact with the machine and to get production as needed without becoming subjugated to the system.

The Future of Educational Data Processing

No area of school business administration and school system work in general has as much potential for improvement or change as the area of educational data processing. The regular use of computers throughout school districts has just begun. Utilization of broad-based data systems and the expanded hardware resources at the disposal of the school district provides excellent opportunities for improving services and is today's norm rather than an option.

Summary

The school business administrator's role in planning within the local district involves many applications of management tools and processes. However, no tool is of more potential assistance in decision making and management operations than the computer. Computers facilitate the storage, manipulation, and retrieval of vast amounts of data on a multitude of subjects.

There is little doubt that the availability of the computer is an asset. However, as previously noted above, the true value of the computer is in the combined use of the machine by several key staff members, including the school business administrator, and the creation of imaginative software to make proper use of the hardware. As was stated previously, personnel to do these jobs are difficult to locate, but invaluable in assisting with conceptualization and applications in a school system.

The school business administrator is one key member of the administrative team charged with properly charting the progress of the local district. This is a relatively new role for the school business manager. It requires that he/she serve in an analysis and planning role, as well as manage the day-to-day operation of the office. This new role gives the proper emphasis to the planning and initiating theme of the position.

Personnel, administrative control, hardware and software selections, and space allocations are but a few of the challenges to be faced in the operation of a computer facility. Machine activities must be monitored and evaluated on an ongoing basis throughout the system and across the various types of activities within the district. Yet, no single development can have as much impact on the district as the electronic computer.

Suggested Activities

1. How would you plan for the implementation of a management information system in a school system?
2. What is the relationship between a MIS system and the responsibility of a site administrator?
3. Discuss the role of the computer in administration, research, and teaching for elementary and secondary schools.
4. How would you determine uses of an MIS in your role as school business administrator?
5. Rank in terms of priority of need the major uses of the MIS
   a. In your school system
   b. In your administrative area
6. Design a plan for the selection and utilization of microcomputers
   a. In a school district
   b. At a local site
7. Design a plan for providing the linkage for data flow among local sites, district offices, and the state department of education.
8. What will be the role of the MIS in decision making in your school system? In your administrative area?

Suggested Readings

Bohl, Marilyn. *Information Processing,* 3rd ed. Chicago: Science Research Associates, 1980.

Chorafas, Dimitris N. *The Handbook of Data Communications and Computer Networks.* Princeton, NJ: Petrocelli Books, 1985.

Conners, Eugene, and Thomas Valesky. "How to select software." *American School and University, 60,* 6 (1988)

Daft, Richard L., and Richard M. Steers. *Organizations: A Micro/Macro Approach.* Glenview, IL: Scott Foresman, 1986.

Kroenke, David. *Management Information Systems.* Santa Cruz, CA: Mitchell Publishing Company, 1989.

Lillie, David L., Wallace H. Hannum, and Gary B. Stuck. *Computers and Effective Instruction.* New York: Longman, 1989.

"101 things you want to know about educational technology." *Electronic Learning 7,* 8 (May/June 1988), 33.

Sanders, Donald H., and Stanley J. Birkin. *Computers and Management: In a Changing Society.* New York: McGraw-Hill, 1980.

Shelly, Gary B., and Thomas J. Cashman. *Introduction to Computers and Data Processing.* Fullerton, CA: Anaheim Publishing, 1980.

Silver, Gerald A., and Myrna L. Silver. *Data Communications for Business.* Boston: Boyd and Fraser, 1987.

Trainor, Timothy N., and Diane Kransewick. *Computers.* Santa Cruz, CA: Mitchell Publishing Company, 1987.

Wasik, John F. *The Electronic Business Information Sourcebook.* New York: Wiley, 1987.

Notes

1. Marilyn Bohl, *Information Processing,* 3rd ed. (Chicago: Science Research Associates, 1980), 478–781.

2. Ibid., 373–78.

3. David Kroenke, *Management Information Systems* (Santa Cruz, CA: Mitchell Publishing, 1989), 14.

4. Richard L. Daft and Richard M. Steers, *Organizations: A Micro/Macro Approach* (Glenview, IL: Scott Foresman, 1986), 7–8.

5. Thomas J. Cashman and Gary B. Shelley, *Introduction to Computers and Data Processing* (Fullerton, CA: Anaheim Publishing, 1980), 9.5–9.10.

6. "101 things you want to know about educational technology," *Electronic Learning 7,* 8 (May/June 1988), 33.

7. Intel Corporation developed the basic microcompressor chip for these systems.

8. Timothy N. Trainor and Diane Krasnewick, *Computers* (Santa Cruz, CA: Mitchell Publishing, 1987), 364.

9. Carl Feingold, *Introduction to Data Processing,* 2nd ed. (Dubuque, IA: Brown, 1976), 235–91.

10. Eugene Conners and Thomas Valesky, "How to select software," *American School and University 60,* 6 (1988).

6
Planning and Budgeting

EDUCATIONAL PLANNING, the weighing of priorities and of alternative means to accomplish them, is the essential feature of effective budgeting in the schools

The important role of planning in the budgetary process was not always fully comprehended. Several developments have focused attention on the importance of planning. The decline in pupil population, the changing demographic patterns of enrollment, continuing inflation, increasing demand for accountability, state and federal mandated programs without appropriate funding (e.g., special education mandates, Title IX restrictions, OSHA requirements, handicapped accessibility, asbestos removal, court-mandated desegregation, affirmative action, mandated class size and education reform), economic downturns, Proposition 13–type tax cutting initiatives, and professional negotiations have all added to the need for more complex budget planning.

In short, the rate of change in the educational environment calls for periodic, intensive examinations of alternative ways to allocate school funds. Additionally, multi-year projections of budgetary needs are essential to provide needed continuity in the allocation process.

Traditional methods of budgeting have not given the school administrator adequate insight to weigh alternative plans for funding education. Past definitions of the term *budget* reflect the traditional methodology of budget development. The educational budget is the translation of educational needs into a fiscal plan that, when formally adopted, expresses the kind of educational program the community is willing to support, financially and morally, for the budget period. The school budget expresses to the citizens of a community the dollar value of the program of education provided them.

The school budget is basically an instrument of educational planning and, incidentally, an instrument of control. It reflects the organizational pattern by categorizing the elements of a total plan into sectional, campus, and departmental components, allowing costs to be more easily estimated. It then forces a coordination of these elements by reassembling costs into a whole, so that a comparison can be made with total revenues. This very process requires a kind of orderly planning that otherwise might never take place. Budgeting, then, forces the community, board, administrators, and staff to plan together what needs to be done, how it will be done, and by whom it will be done.

Some benefits of planning and budgeting are:

1. It requires a plan of action for the future.
2. It requires an appraisal of past activities in relation to planned activities.
3. It necessitates the formulation of work plans.
4. It necessitates expenditures and estimating revenues.
5. It mandates orderly planning and coordination throughout the organization.
6. It establishes a system of management controls.
7. It serves as a public information system.

The Statutory Bases for School System Budgeting

The principle is well established that each of the states is vested with plenary control over educational policy within the sphere of its jurisdiction. In a great many cases the courts have uniformly held that education is essentially and intrinsically a state function; the maintenance of public schools is, in legal theory, a matter of state and not local concern.

Subject to constitutional limitations, a state legislature has plenary power with respect to educational policy. It may determine the ends to be achieved and the means to be employed. It may determine the types of schools to be established, the means of this support, the content of their curricula, and the qualifications of their teachers. It may do all these things with or without the consent of the localities, for in education the state is the unit and there are no local rights except those safeguarded by the Constitution. Even local school board members are state officers. This plenary power allows the state to mandate that school districts develop budgets and to determine the format, calendar, procedures, and so forth for the budgeting process. The state mandates budget categories. This is also related to the state's mandated system of financial accounting, auditing, and reporting. The budgeting process is also utilized to establish tax rates. For a more detailed discussion of the legislative and judicial context, see Chapter 2.

Concepts of Budgeting

Concepts of budgeting can generally be plotted on a continuum ranging from very poor to outstanding. At the lower end of the scale are methods presently used that are rooted in the historical development of educational budgeting into a closed, authoritarian, unresponsive, negative system that shows little planning. At the upper end of the continuum are emerging concepts of budgeting that emphasize educational planning and evaluation as the basis for budget development. The discussion that follows contrasts obsolete budgeting systems with those now being utilized by the more innovative, dynamic school systems in the country.

Concepts of Budgeting Not Viable for Today's Needs

Mechanical Budget *More favored by board members*
The mechanical type of budget can be set forth on two sheets of paper—one presenting the estimated yearly receipts of an institution and the other showing how the money can

be divided in order to run the school. Under this concept, budgeting is strictly a revenue-and-expenditure operation—a bookkeeping chore—required by law, which is feverishly pored over near the end of the year and then is quickly forgotten until the end of the next year. This type of budgeting forces expenditures to fit income expectations and pays no attention to needs. Any planning done is negative, calculating what can be eliminated or what can be padded so that the budget will come out right. The main task of this type of budgeting is to keep costs at a minimum without regard for needs or educational improvements.

Yearly Budget

The yearly or periodic type of budget approach attempts to construct a school budget in a short (three- to four-week) period for presentation to the board of education and to the community. It is almost a refinement of the mechanical type, in that it forces quick decisions on expenditures and revenues and little effort is made to evaluate its impact. Decisions on staffing, salaries, programs, supplies, and services are often made without any consideration of educational needs or evolving educational opportunities. The challenge is to get the budget document completed and approved before the deadline date. Usually, this method attempts to adjust the previous year's document to include such items as pay increases, enlarged staff, and increased numbers of students but does not consider changes in program, availability of new materials, differing needs, and emerging concepts. Once completed, this type of budget becomes a straitjacket that provides little opportunity for shifts in priority.

Administration-Dominated Budget

This concept views the development of the budget as strictly a responsibility of management. No staff help is asked for or desired. The central office gives the impression that budgeting is a very complex process and that only the ''chosen few'' are sufficiently sophisticated to participate. The prevailing philosophy seems to be that if fewer people know about the budget, there will be less static and fewer questions. Often, value judgements are made without proper evaluation and with no options offered to those affected. This tight-ship approach is symptomatic of authoritarian systems and has hastened the coming of our present era of negotiations, citizen involvement, and student awareness. While still in existence, it is dying out and will not be an effective concept in the future.

Centralized Budget

The centralized concept of budgeting treats all schools in a system as if they were only one. While it is an efficient way of developing a budget, little consideration is permitted for differing needs among the various communities served. Allocations are made on a per-pupil basis, and no attention is given to existing resources or to any backlog of requests. Decisions concerning such issues as teacher-pupil ratio, supplies, materials, texts, and curriculum are made at the central office, and all schools must conform. This concept tends to treat the entire system as a homogeneous unit rather than recognize that even the smallest systems are heterogeneous, made up of diverse people with unique needs, abilities, and capacities. The trend today is toward decentralization, which permits schools to be relevant and responsive to the needs of a local area.

Concepts of Budgeting More Suited to Present and Future Educational Systems

Because of recent demands for greater involvement of principals and teachers in instructional decision making, educational efficiency and cost effectiveness, and limits on spending for only high priority programs, several new concepts of budgeting have been introduced in school systems. Site-based budgeting has been inaugurated to extend the involvement of principals and teachers. Planning, Programming, Budgeting and Evaluation Systems are being employed to relate measurable educational objectives to the cost effectiveness of alternate programs. Zero-based budgeting has been used to ensure the funding of highest priority programs before lower priority programs are incorporated in the budget.

Site-Based Budgeting

This section on site-based budgeting is based on a document titled *Building Budget and You: A Primer for School Principals*, written by I. Carl Candoli and Gary L. Wegenke for the Michigan State Department of Education.[1] One of the major dilemmas facing today's educator is providing increased fiscal flexibility at the building level in an attempt to heighten the impact of program decisions on individual student growth. This fiscal flexibility requires the staff and principal of a specific building to become more intimately involved in day-to-day budgeting and budget control processes. Historically, teacher and administrator training programs have not provided teachers and principals with the background needed to understand the nuances of budgeting and fiscal resource allocation. This section has been prepared as a basic guideline to enable principals and other educators to appreciate and understand building-level fiscal approaches associated with educational decision making and problem resolution.

A departure from traditional centralized administrative methods is possible when buildings, their staffs, and community members have the capacity to control the budget of a particular building and have the necessary expertise to match student needs with available resources. Underlying this section is the realization that pupils vary. Building principals and staffs must recognize these differences (e.g., cultural, ethnic, and socioeconomic) and serve pragmatically the varying levels of their students by utilizing strengths of staff and community and by deploying fiscal resources to meet priority issues. A carefully planned needs assessment of pupils should be conducted in the local district before building priorities are established.

Implementation of the building budget process is dependent on the principal's capacity and skill to coordinate the various planning and operational components of a total educational program. Inherent in the process is the principal's ability to work with a limited number of dollars to meet specific educational needs. This is not a simple process. It is new and different, and it will take some effort on the part of building-level administrators to redefine their traditional roles by absorbing and applying fiscal management techniques encouraged by the site budgeting process, a process that allows the building staff to be proactive rather than reactive. The process forces planning and operational educational decisions to be made at the level closest to the student—the building level. The site budgeting process also encourages imaginative principals to proceed with the development of unique educational programs. It is limited only by the professional training and capacity of principals and their staffs.

With site-based budgeting, instructional supplies, materials, equipment, texts, and library books are frequently budgeted at the building level. Some decentralized systems also provide individual building personnel budgets for teachers, aides, and custodians. Most school districts that have moved to building budgeting have retained centralized and district-level budgeting for capital outlay, maintenance, administration, and other funds and accounts that are districtwide rather than individual school building functions.

The role of the central administrative staff is also drastically changed under site-based budgeting. Central administrators become support rather than line personnel. They become facilitators to be utilized by building staffs and the community to enhance further educational concepts unique to a building's service area. Therefore, a close dialogue between community members and school staff is encouraged.

Site-Based Budget Components

School Budget Composition

Despite the mystique that has developed around the so-called intricacy of school finance and school budgets, it is possible to simplify the process. The educational system is charged with providing educational services to its clients. This is accomplished by delivering programs directly to students. The delivery process invariably involves professionally trained educators meeting with students and their parents, either in groups or individually, to accomplish this task. In addition, the process includes the provision of support services to the direct teacher-learner relationship. These support activities are defined as direct instructional support (e.g., pupil personnel, psychological, sociological) and noninstructional support (e.g., maintenance, custodial, food service, transportation).

Approximately 85 percent of a school district budget is allocated to personnel. Another 8 to 9 percent of total costs are allocated to fixed costs (such as utilities, fringe benefits, insurance, and interest) over which little control can be exercised. The remaining 6 to 7 percent of the total budget is allocated to supplies, materials, and equipment used in the system, including instructional as well as noninstructional materials.

It is important to the educational process to develop a mechanism that permits more than the limited 6 to 7 percent of resources to be used for unique student needs as identified at the building level. A growing number of educators feel this is best accomplished through a flexible system of allocating personnel and resources at the building level.

Many school districts are restricted in personnel allocations by union contracts that specify pupil–teacher ratios and determine class size. However, many union contracts permit deviation from contract language for specific educational purposes. At the least, the specific use of professional personnel as determined by the educational needs of the student body of a particular building can be approached with reasonable flexibility. The application of staff strengths to highest-priority educational needs is the most important task faced by the building principal. Similarly, the allocation of nonprofessional instructional personnel (e.g., aides, clerical) can enhance an educational program. It is appropriate that this allocation be made at the building level.

Conversely, the application of noninstructional support services, such as maintenance, transportation, data processing, food services, payroll, and purchasing, is best accomplished at districtwide or even regional/state levels because of the potential reduction in unit cost for such services.

Since the personnel portion of the school budget is so great, and since union agreements sometimes dictate size of staffs, it becomes a matter of deploying staff so program needs can be met. The building principal must have the leadership responsibility for such deployment, and it must be predicated on careful needs assessment and priority establishment.

Nonstaff Budget Components
The portion of the typical school budget allocated to nonpersonnel items is roughly 15 to 18 percent. Of this, some 8 to 9 percent is utilized to pay for fixed costs that allow for little flexibility. Minor savings can be effected in certain areas such as utilities by setting thermostats at a lower level or by cutting the number of lights in buildings. However, even with such conservation measures, the net savings are usually much less than the increased cost of energy, which has almost doubled in the past five years.

Similarly, insurance costs, interest charges, and fringe benefits are all undergoing dramatic increases, leading to the speculation that the fixed-cost portion of the school budget will continue to rise in the coming decades. Certainly, legislative mandates and contractual agreements will not lower the impact of fixed costs.

Budget Component Summary
The following outline is a summary of the components that make up the school budget. It does not follow the prescribed accounting manual; rather, it is a recognition of the three major delineations identified here.

   I. Personnel (78 to 82 percent of total budget)
      A. Instructional
         1. Professional—teachers, administrators, specialists (certificated)
         2. Classified—aides, clerical and technical personnel
      B. Noninstructional
         1. Professional—engineers, administrators, specialists, analysts, accountants
         2. Classified—custodians, skills craftspeople, cooks, bakers, clerical and warehouse personnel, drivers, technicians
  II. Fixed Costs (10 to 12 percent of total budget)
      A. Utilities
      B. Insurance
      C. Fringe Benefits
 III. Other Costs (6 to 7 percent of total budget)
      A. Supplies and Materials
      B. Equipment (new and replacement; upkeep and repair)

The foregoing emphasizes the restrictive nature of the school budget and the limits of what can be considered discretionary resources. The next section presents a model for building-level budgeting that permits flexibility in the allocation of resources.

Site-Based Building Allocation Procedures—A Model

Staff Allotments

Assuming that a school system makes a decision to share budget prerogatives with building principals, staff, and community and that after careful study it is decided that the direct delivery of educational services is appropriately the purview of the building, what then can be presented as a model for such a decision? Based on the experiences of districts that have studied the process and implemented it for a number or years, it is felt that union agreements, contract language, community expectations, staff and principal capacity, and student needs must be considered in developing a model flexible enough to serve diverse school systems. For purposes of such development the following assumptions are made:

1. That classroom teacher–pupil ratios are fixed by union contract
2. That the building is administered by a nonteaching principal
3. That a variety of noncertificated instructional personnel is part of that staff
4. That instructional specialists in art, music, physical education, and media are available on either a full- or part-time basis
5. That deployment of teaching personnel can be either through self-contained scheduling or by team/departmental/differentiated procedures

Given these parameters, how does the school system provide flexibility to principals and their staffs so they can direct their best effort toward meeting educational needs of students?

Although the number of teachers assigned to a particular building is often based on a negotiated agreement that specifies a ratio of students to teachers, the deployment of staff does not necessarily have to be entirely on the self-contained classroom concept at the elementary level or predicated on each class meeting daily for one period at the secondary level. Optimum use of teaching staff is possible when professional staff are assigned to areas of staff strength and when support personnel are used for tasks better performed by classified staff.

The model assumes such staff deployment but goes beyond it to include the potential of diverting resources according to specific needs at the building level. The following two examples illustrate the proposed model for elementary and secondary schools.

#1—Elementary Staffing

Assumptions

- Student enrollment of 600 students
- Nonteaching full-time principal
- Contract calls for funding at 1/30 teacher–pupil ratio
- Music/art/physical education/media personnel are assigned according to a district plan
- Secretarial/clerical personnel assigned on a 1/300 student ratio
- Instructional aides assigned on 1/100 student ratio

Staff Allocation Based on the Above:

- 20 classroom teachers
- Two secretary/clerks
- Six aides
- Principal
- Assorted specialist personnel in music, art, physical education, and instructional media

Additionally, all staff allocations are based on actual personnel employed or equivalent salary amounts. For example, an equivalent salary amount for teachers is the average teaching salary in the district. The average salary is $26,000 per year.

As the staff, community, and principal develop educational priorities for the school several important objectives are adopted.

Objectives

- The need for consultative assistance in teaching basic skills, i.e., reading and mathematics
- A need for programmed materials
- A priority for increasing the number of aides from six to nine

In terms of dollars, the plan calls for the following:

One reading specialist at	$26,000
Materials totaling	5,000
Three aides at $7,000 each	21,000
Total	$52,000

To generate the needed resources ($52,000), the building staff determines that it can provide basic classroom instruction with eighteen rather than twenty classroom teachers. Since the building qualifies, by contract, for the twenty teachers, the equivalent dollars, or 2 times $26,000, are allocated to the building to be used in meeting program objectives. This amount is the average teacher's salary multiplied by the number of positions not filled. The principal is then able to hire a reading specialist and three aides and provide for the programmed materials. (In the event that only one opening is available, an existing staff member could be assigned the reading specialist role and with equivalent funding for one position, accomplish the same objective.)

The potential of this example is limited only by the limits of human creativity. Several districts have, under this model, provided great program diversity to their elementary programs.

#2—Secondary Staffing

Assumptions

- Enrollment of 1,500 students
- Principal and three assistant principals

- Contract calls for maximum pupil/teacher–ratio ranging from 1/28 in English to 1/50 in physical education
- Vocational programs meet state/federal guidelines
- Clerical staff assigned on a 1/150 student ratio
- Media professionals assigned on a 1/750 student ratio

Staff Allocations Based on the Above:

- 80 teachers (including/vocational education staff)
- Six counselors
- Two instructional media (library) staff
- Four administrators
- Ten clerical staff
- Ten instructional aides

The building staff, community, and principal have established priorities as part of the educational plan for the coming academic year:

Priorities

- The establishment of four study centers, each to be staffed by a professional trained in English, math, science, and social science as well as two aides
- A program of video and audio tape materials to be initiated at a cost of $6,000/year
- Materials totaling $12,000 needed for initiation of the program

The proposed four centers can be staffed by absorbing three teaching positions, which will generate 3 times $26,000 (average salary) or $78,000 for use by the building. Using the money generated by staff reductions, the building can meet the identified priorities as follows:

Assign four center leaders from existing staff	-0-
Employ eight aides at $7,000 each	$56,000
Purchase center materials	12,000
Develop tape library	6,000
Total	$74,000

Using the Site-Based Allocation Model

Many variations of the above examples are possible. The model provides that buildings receive personnel resources according to contract, either in the form of staff or equivalent dollars based on the average teacher's salary. It is important to indicate that existing staff members are not discharged to create equivalent dollars. Only when attrition creates openings is the model usable. Given normal conditions, however, such opportunities are readily available.

Foundation Allotment

A second major item of concern to principals is the utilization of the resources allocated for supplies, materials, and equipment. The model provides for block grant allocations to buildings for these items on the basis of an amount per student. This allocation replaces the line item amounts generally found in school accounting procedures. The building principal, the staff, and the community determine the type and number of line item allocations. They determine how much will be allocated to capital outlay, how much to textbooks, how much to library books, and how much to general supplies.

Once that determination is made, the central office must be notified how the block grant has been distributed so budget control mechanisms can operate for the protection of the total system. On a periodic basis, usually weekly, building administrators receive printouts indicating the status of each of the supply, materials, and equipment accounts they have identified, the amount of encumbrances, and the current status of available budget funds. Should there be a need for shifting of funds from one account to another during the year a simple form, shown in the succeeding section, will handle that transaction. In this manner, funds are allocated equitably to all buildings in the school system on a per-pupil basis, eliminating central office judgments as to how these resources are to be expended. The central office does oversee to ensure that building totals do not exceed the amount of the block grant.

Internal shifting of resources to meet emergency needs is the purview of the building principal. The foundation allowance provides for teaching, supplies, textbooks, instructional materials, replacement of equipment, new equipment, or whatever the building educational plan calls for. Limits on foundation allowance are the same restrictions that face all school systems.

Categorical Funds

Many school systems receive categorical funds by virtue of qualifying for one or more of the various state or federal programs. These may be Title I funds, Chapter III funds, bilingual funds, or migrant funds. They are devised to meet specific kinds of needs found in school buildings and school systems. All categorical funds in the model are allocated on a per-pupil basis to buildings. The use of categorical funds must be incorporated into the total educational plan of the building. Typically, categorical funds are used to hire staff, to buy supplies and equipment, to hire specific consultative help, and the like. They are passed to individual buildings in the form of block grants earmarked according to the specific category for which the funds are received. They must be utilized for that particular kind of program, but the development of those resources either in the form of personnel or materials is strictly the purview of the building staff.

Grants

School systems apply for and receive grants from a number of agencies and foundations. In addition, many school systems have devised internal grant systems for addressing particular educational needs. Much the same as the categorical funds allocation, the grant allocation is funnelled to the building level in the form of a block allocation. The use and dispersal of these funds are dependent on the educational plan devised for that building.

A model of this type creates a need for greater fiscal management sophistication on the part of principals, who do possess this potential and have for decades been anxious to assume such leadership responsibility. It is, therefore, an evolving model that can be utilized and changed to accommodate the particular characteristics of a school system.

Site-Based Budget Control Procedures

Coordination of fiscal information between the central finance office and the buildings is a key step in the implementation of the budget process. It is the responsibility of the finance office to develop, with the cooperation of the building principals, budget control procedures. The procedures focus on: (1) an equitable method of distributing building funds (autonomous funds) on a yearly basis; (2) sufficient time for building principals, students, and parents to plan for the best use of available resources; (3) a systematic monitoring of all building funds; and (4) the establishment of a purchasing process to accommodate building budget expenditure requests.

Distributing Building Funds

Each year before the board of education accepts the school district's budget, a decision must be made as to how much money should be allotted to buildings as autonomous funds. In order to maintain equity between buildings, the amount is based on the number of students enrolled per building. Enrollment figures are projected in January for buildings and adjusted on the fourth Friday count submitted to the state for state aid monies.

Program assumptions related to dollars required also become a variable to be considered in fund allocation. A distinction between elementary, middle, junior high, and senior high fiscal needs is one method of approaching the problem. Differences may occur in the following areas:

Elementary	*Junior High*	*Senior High*
Basic Allowance Amount Initial Repairs and Maintenance Contracts	Basic Allowance Amount Initial Repairs and Maintenance Contracts	*Basic Allowance Amount* Initial Repairs and Maintenance Contracts
Total per Student	Total per Student	Total per Student

In the area of initial allowances, specialized programs requiring expensive equipment and large quantities of consumable supplies generally mandate larger allocations for junior and senior high schools when compared with elementary schools. Differences based on programmatic emphasis (e.g., an all-student requirement involving industrial arts or home economics in the junior high) will cause fiscal differences even between junior and senior high school program costs.

Another dimension to autonomous funds involves the unique use of personnel and the budget. A model for utilization of certificated personnel, presented earlier, was predicated on flexibility in staffing buildings, thereby allowing building staffs to design a variety of differentiated staffing arrangements.

Fiscal appropriations for additional supervision, clerical support, and extra personnel beyond normal classroom needs are important to consider when defining building programs. Supervision may vary from elementary lunchroom duties to ticket-taking at a senior high school basketball game. Funding decisions for these purposes must consider revenues engendered locally such as ticket sales as well as contractually determined rates of reimburse-ment. The ability to generate revenue for paying supervisors for extra assignments like ticket-taking is greater at the secondary level.

Because of size, elementary schools usually have more difficulty in meeting supervi-sory needs. A secondary school with three or four times the staff may find the task much easier. Therefore, a difference in autonomous dollars allocated for supervisory aides may vary per student from elementary to junior high to senior high. Clerical support will also vary depending on student enrollment and responsibilities unique to elementary and second-ary operations. However, the unit cost of clerical support throughout the district is defined by contract.

An internal accounting system is established at all levels of building operations. Such a system allows individual buildings additional fiscal flexibility. Class and club activities are a few areas found in the internal accounts of buildings, the larger of which are found in high schools. Therefore, principals and their staffs are charged to plan the wise use of both autonomous and internal account funds to meet student needs.

Planning the Use of Funds

In order for building principals to involve staff, parent organizations and student organiza-tions in the budget process, initial direction and ample time must be provided by the central finance office. The degree of group involvement in the budget process will vary based on the management abilities of the principal.

Projections made the previous year are the basis for original allocations. Final budget revisions are made according to the official fourth Friday enrollment of each building. Most building principals have learned to prepare for a slight gain or loss in monies by placing from 10 to 15 percent of their projected budget in a contingency account. The impact of gains or losses is felt in the contingency account and not necessarily in accounts affecting building operations.

As an example, a secondary principal and staff plan courses based on projected enrollments. If more students are actually taking a course on the fourth Friday, an adjustment is made internally to provide the instructor with extra resources. On the other hand, a decrease in a specific course's enrollment would cause a proportionate decrease in funds. This secondary building makes per-pupil adjustments not only on the fourth Friday in the fall but also on an internally designated fourth Friday in the spring semester.

Once adjustments for enrollment are made, a regular monitoring of the budget is accomplished with the aid of data provided by the finance office. (The details of the monitoring process are discussed in the next subsection.) Using detailed budget reports identifying building accounts and monies budgeted, encumbered, and expended, the prin-cipal, staff, PTA/CIC, and student organizations can begin to note trends between projected budget figures and actual expenditures. Decisions are made during the year to revise original budget projections in accordance with actual budget expenditures. The principal is held accountable by the finance office for any budget revisions made while the budget is being implemented. A few principals have delegated budget monitoring to their head secretary or treasurer.

As semesters and fiscal years pass, budget histories are established. These financial histories, based on monies budgeted and expended, are useful in providing fiscal projections for succeeding years. Building account histories coupled with finance office direction early in September provide the basic information and time needed to complete budget projections by the end of March.

Between September and March, building principals and staffs are busy with day-to-day operational matters. In order to involve staff, parents, and students in the planning of the following year's budget, a time line must be established by the building principal. The time line is determined by the data available, staff awareness of student needs, existing resources, and community expectations. Building priorities are established through extensive dialogue among the various publics and must be consistent with school district goals.

In April or early May, final decisions related to the new budget must be arrived at by all parties concerned. Although all members involved in the budget process may not agree with final allocations, they must at least understand the rationale for projecting the following year's budget. The final budget document must reflect (a) adequate time and information for determining client needs, (b) school district goals and building priorities, (c) use of past fiscal budget information (reports), and (d) a concerted effort by all parties to operate within the budget for one fiscal year.

Monitoring Building Funds

Once a building budget has been approved by building planners and revised in accordance with student enrollment, the monitoring process becomes extremely important. Fiscal accountability between a building administration and the finance office (central administration) is based on a successful, routine flow of information between both parties.

The process of aiding the fiscal information flow requires an extension of most school districts' accounting systems to include autonomous fund accounts at the building level. Secondly, a direct relationship between accounts and data processing must be established. Finally, internal auditing procedures must be established at the district and building level to make certain that expending of the autonomous budget takes place as planned.

One district uses a six-digit accounting system that supplies fiscal information to decision makers at the board of education central administration, building, and outside agency levels. Building principals report budget figures on a document that allows for a differential in excess of 250 accounts. The sizable number of accounts available to buildings for budgeting purposes permits principals and their staffs to monitor more completely their own expenditures. For example, a differentiation among monies budgeted for repairs, supplies, and equipment in a typing class can be quickly identified by looking at a building's account structure.

A biweekly budget report from the finance office is sent to each building principal. The building code number precedes the account number, followed by a brief description of the account. Monies budgeted, encumbered, and expended are itemized on the report. Close monitoring of the report allows a building's budget committee to make revisions (transfers of monies) at any time there is a need. Generally speaking, revisions are needed when planned expenditures exceed monies budgeted. The correction should be made when, for example, industrial arts-woods becomes overdrawn; the deficit should be handled from funds within the same industrial arts account structure. The managing of deficits in this manner puts part of the pressure of fiscal management on the staff member directly involved with the account.

In some instances unforeseen circumstances cause certain accounts to become quickly overdrawn. An example might be the home economics supply account. Alternatives are (1) transferring monies from another home economics account or (b) carrying the deficit over into the next fiscal year. As the reason for the deficit is discussed in budget projection meetings, the need to increase an appropriation may surface; this would cover the prior year's deficit.

Carryover is a unique feature of the autonomous fund budget process. All funds allocated to buildings but unexpended are carried over from one year to the next. This allows buildings to accumulate funds in order to purchase items that exceed any one year's allocation. For example, a $2,500 copy machine for office use may be purchased after funds in the office's equipment account have been carried over for two or three years. Principals have the option of carrying over funds in specific accounts or transferring such funds to a general building account for carryover purpose. These monies can then be reapportioned on the basis of need by the building budget committee. Without the carryover budget feature, long-range planning takes a back seat to a traditional building fiscal philosophy that implies "spend it now on anything; otherwise, you may not have another opportunity."

Establishing the Purchasing Process

After planning budget allocation, account code assignment, and record bank establishment, the building personnel begin to identify items to be purchased. Items identified are generally categorized as supply, textbook, furniture, equipment, or repair. A purchasing form is filled out at the building level. The proper account number, a brief description of the item, the vendor, and the cost are noted. Once signed by the principal, or his/her designee, the form is forwarded to the purchasing department. There a purchase order number is assigned after all other segments of the form have been checked for accuracy.

A situation occasionally exists when sudden price changes necessitate cost column revisions. If this situation occurs, building personnel are notified immediately before the order for purchase is submitted to the vendor. The total purchasing process from building to purchasing department to vendor takes from three to four days. When a situation necessitates much quicker action, a telephone transaction between the building, the purchasing department, and the vendor may take place. All telephone transactions are quickly followed up with the appropriate paperwork. Generally, equipment breakdowns requiring immediate repair are permitted as verbal transactions.

The purchasing department is an integral part of the building's fiscal planning process. Annual requisition forms identifying items commonly used by all buildings (e.g., pencils, theme paper, first aid supplies, machine oils) are sent to buildings in the spring. Although autonomous funds are used for purchases, large-quantity buying of items by the purchasing department permits buildings to receive lower costs per item. Central supply and warehousing capacity are essential for such economy of scale. In summary, the purchasing department staff serve as expediters between buildings and vendors, maintaining credibility between the school district and vendors on items requiring the bidding process. Additionally, good business procedures are maintained by developing standardized equipment, supply, and materials lists for use by all schools.

Site-Based Community and Staff Involvement in Budget Process

The budget process varies little from other sound management techniques implemented by school administrators. Management processes designed to provide useful and timely information to educational decision makers become the framework on which school districts succeed or fail. In educational programs offered by the district, activity in the areas of planning, operations, communication evaluation, and finance is continually assessed, adjusted, or discontinued based on information matching available resources (e.g., monies, staff, facilities) to current student needs. Constantly keeping abreast of existing student needs requires the district and individual school buildings to involve as many "stakeholders"[2] (e.g., parents, staff board members, community leaders, and students) as possible in decision-making processes that affect educational programs.

An administrator cannot afford the luxury of rationalizing away the need for community involvement. When the community is not involved in decision making, decisions have a tendency to be made that are not community supported. Involvement of staff, students, and community is best accomplished through organized activities. Techniques utilized to involve stakeholders will vary by situation. Some schools utilize the PTA (or PTSA) as the vehicle; others develop formalized mechanisms such as CICs (Community Involvement Committees) or CACs (Community Advisory Committees). It is crucial for the building to have such participation. The following is a brief outline of events that make a point of involving various stakeholders in the budget process:

Defining the Limits of Dollars Available

The finance office must serve as a catalyst to the other four general areas of the district by projecting expected revenues and anticipated expenditures over a period of one to three or more years. In the process, fixed factors (e.g., enrollments, staff salaries, utility rates) may be considered by groups like the board, citizen advisory committees, bargaining units, and building involvement committees (e.g., PTA, CIC). Once the big picture of financial resources related to "fixed charges" (generally 93 to 94 percent of a total budget) is communicated to stakeholders, decisions related to the other 6 to 7 percent of a budget can be made. To make the best use of the remaining portion of the projected budget, an amount must be allocated to meet overall district concerns and priorities, while the balance is distributed to buildings.

Involving Stakeholders at the Building Level

Once dollars per student or per program have been clearly defined for building administrators, they in turn can begin involving stakeholders in preparing the building's budget. Generally, the building budget committee is made up of teaching staff representatives, CIC or PTA delegates, and selected students (more common in secondary schools). The committee's charge is to plan a program budget, keeping in mind the school district's goals and student needs assessment information. As weeks of the process unfold, time is spent discussing the points of view of all stakeholders regarding the building's program priorities. Initial "dreams" requiring far more money than is appropriated to a building give way to short- and long-range allotment of funds. Negotiation skills are quickly learned by all parties. Ultimately, this budget process creates useful spin-offs for other areas of the building's decision-making process. If the budget process allows for meaningful involvement, the result is a committed group of stakeholders ready to see to the successful implementation of programs based on a budget arrived at through mutual agreement.

Monitoring an Approved Building Budget

Periodic budget reports should be available to any group of stakeholders throughout a fiscal year. Openness expressed by having a budget report at faculty meetings, student meetings, and PTA or CIC sessions is a key to seeing that the money is expended as planned. Invariably, unforeseen expenditures over a fiscal year will require revision of building budgets. A building that predicates the preparation of the budget on involving stakeholders and continues a policy of open review throughout the year will have little difficulty in explaining the need to revise initial budget priority projections. In contrast, lack of management skill on the part of the building administrator as he/she prepares and monitors the budget process generally leads toward allegations of misappropriation and misuse of public funds and ultimately a lack of trust in the administrator as a professional.

In conclusion, involvement of stakeholders in the budget process will lead toward a feeling by the community in general that they have a say in how "their" dollars are spent in educational programming. Staffs operating in buildings are no longer totally dependent on central administrators providing instructional materials, supplies, and equipment for meeting the needs of students they are teaching. And, most important, students in a building or classroom have the benefit of a planned process to identity their unique needs and to provide available financial resources to meet those needs. Two alternatives to site-based budgeting are the planning, programming, budgeting, evaluation system, and zero-based budgeting.

Evolution of the Planning, Programming, Budgeting, Evaluation System

Some of the principles of the *planning, programming, budgeting, evaluation system (PPBES)* have long been recognized in the writings of professional educators. However, often the principles were fragmented, and little attempt was made to make the total concept operational.

The essential aspects of PPBES are as follows:

1. A careful specification and a systematic analysis of objectives
2. A search for the relevant alternatives—the different ways of achieving the objectives
3. An estimate of the total cost of each alternative—direct and indirect costs, initial costs and those to which the alternatives would commit the organization for future years, and those costs that cannot be measured in dollar terms
4. An estimate of the effectiveness of each alternative—how close it comes to satisfying the objective
5. A comparison and analysis of the alternatives, seeking that combination of alternatives that promises the greatest effectiveness, for given resources, in achieving the objectives

PPBES is not a panacea. It is not a substitute for the experience, intuition, and judgment of educational planners. Its aim is to sharpen that intuition and judgment by stating problems more precisely, discovering new alternatives, and making explicit the comparison among alternatives.

Although computers may expedite PPBES, they are not the decision makers. Decisions will continue to come, as they should, from the educational planners and from the political process, influenced by value judgments and pressures from various interested parties as well as by the process of systematic analysis. PPBES, through systematic analysis, seeks to aid the educational planner by being clearer and more explicit about objectives, assumptions, and facts; by trying to distinguish relevant issues from irrelevant ones; and by tracing out the costs and consequences of the alternatives, to the extent that these are knowable.

Computers and machine-like analysis cannot, by highly abstract mathematical or economic techniques, solve the value-laden problems of educational financing. However, these persons, machines, and techniques may make important contributions to the budgeting process.

PPBES and systematic analysis are not limited to cost accounting or to economic considerations in the narrow sense. PPBES should not neglect a wide range of human factors, and it should not attempt, naively, to measure factors that are really unmeasurable. Wherever possible, relevant, quantitative estimates are to be encouraged. Good systematic analysis does not try to assign numbers to every element of a problem, does not ignore the intangible, and does not rule out subjective evaluation and the appropriate use of judgment. On the contrary, the very name PPBES reminds us that the question of who benefits and whom it costs are questions involving values as well as analysis.

The term *program budgeting* is not equivalent, in this context, to PPBES. Program accounting and program budgeting are basic conceptual elements of PPBES but are limited to accounting and budgeting systems emphasizing categorization schemes by programs.

Five major categories of data must be developed in order to estimate, evaluate, and report within the multi-year framework of PPBES. They pertain to pupils, programs, personnel, facilities, and finance.

Pupil Data

It has been pointed out that one of the major ingredients of PPBES is program evaluation. The criteria developed in each district to evaluate programs will vary and may include not only classroom test results, but other pupil statistics such as dropout rate, college entry rate, job entry rate, or return-to-school rate. The school districts implementing PPBES will find it necessary to record such statistics in a consistent format and report these statistics in specific time frames and against specific programs. The districts should also be prepared to utilize these statistics in the preparation of new programs, as well as in the evaluation of current programs, and to maintain such statistics for long periods of time to develop behavior patterns, trend reports, and long-range pupil need evaluations.

In the multi-year financial planning portions of PPBES, the districts will find it necessary to project pupil enrollment data, not only in numbers of students, but also in socioeconomic changes within the community.

Program Data

Goals, objectives, evaluation criteria, and program memoranda pertaining to each individual program operating in the school district must be recorded, stored, and reported for the successful operation of a school district PPBES. This is true for the education program (e.g., math, English, social studies), as well as the special programs (counseling, career guidance and ancillary services, transportation, maintenance, custodial).

Personnel Data

At least two major clusters of information on school district employees are required by PPBES: payroll information and assignment information. Within the PPBES framework a district may choose to distribute first-grade teachers' pay to several different first-grade programs while charging all of the kindergarten teachers' salaries to a single preschool program. If a high school Spanish teacher works two periods a day as a counselor, is also assigned as an assistant football coach three months of the school year, and teaches driver training on Saturdays, specific portions of this teacher's salary must be prorated to the Spanish program, the counseling program, the athletic program, and the driver training program. The allocation of personnel assignments and costing are a necessary part of PPBES.

Facilities Data

The expenses involved in the operation of each school district facility must be recorded in order to accommodate the reporting requirements of PPBES. This requires the development of location and sublocation codes and the assignment of these codes to such items as inventory supplies, equipment, custodial and overhead costs, maintenance projects, and construction projects in the school district.

Financial Data

In addition to program-oriented budgeting and accounting, traditional (and often state-mandated) line item budgeting and accounting should be maintained by responsible levels (school districts, subdistricts, buildings), funds, and functional areas as long as it is required. It should be emphasized that in order to preserve data comparability for state, federal, and local analysis by existing functions—such as instruction, administration, and transportation—budgets can be cast by line item within the function format and in a program format.

A caution should be inserted here to allay the fears of educators who are unfamiliar with school fiscal affairs. Accounting, enriched by cost accounting and budgeting, is crucial for the successful operation of PPBES, but it is merely a tool of the organization, not an end. Educational decision makers must guard against forming conclusions about instructional activities solely on the basis of costs. Costs must be weighed against benefits and values held by citizens for the development of their children.

Procedure of PPBES

While PPBES is not a step-by-step procedure per se, for the purpose of illustration, we shall use a step-by-step approach in further describing PPBES. The way PPBES might work is illustrated in Figure 6-1. The process is continuous and cyclical and requires feedback into all parts of the system.

FIGURE 6-1   Illustration of How a Planning, Programming, Budgeting, Evaluation System (PPBES) Might Work

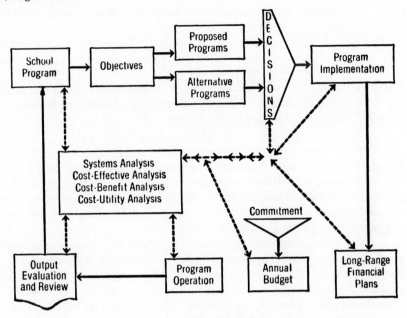

Step 1. State measurable objectives and measurable planned accomplishments for a given school with regard to direction, program, subject area, courses, and activities over a specified period of time—possibly five years.

Step 2. Assign priorities to the various objectives and planned accomplishments of the school.

Step 3. Determine alternative plans for achieving the objectives expressed in Step 1. Alternative plans would be expressed in terms of inputs and processes over a specified time span.

Examples of inputs are: staff mix and composition, including the number of paraprofessionals and professionals and their levels of preparation and experience; pupil–teacher ratio; number and types of learning facilities; learning resources; curricula; and so forth.

Examples of processes are: instructional methodology, length of periods and school day, research and development, in-service training, assignment of teachers, and so forth.

Step 4. Assign a dollar estimate to the various alternative plans based on the inputs and processes of those plans. Remember that the dollar amounts are to be expressed over a possible five-year period.

Step 5. Select within dollar constraints those alternative plans that appear to foster efficient and effective accomplishment of the predetermined objectives.

Step 6. Place the system in operation—that is, implement the inputs and processes that have been determined and budgeted.

Step 7. Analyze and evaluate the outputs of the school—directions, programs, subject areas, courses, and activities. Following evaluation it may be necessary to change the inputs and processes in order that the following year's budget can better achieve the objectives set forth.

Step 8. Review the objectives set forth in Step 1. This review could result in the changing of previously stated objectives or the continuance of previously stated objectives and their respective priorities.

Step 9. Review and continuously prepare alternative plans (inputs and processes) in search of a more efficient, effective means for achieving the stated objectives.

Step 10. Return to Step 3 and restart the cycle.

The selection of program alternatives is no less promising in its potential payoff at the school district level than it is at state and federal levels, but to date there is little application of PPBES among school districts throughout the nation. This is caused by (1) most school administrators' lack of specific knowledge of PPBES, its associated techniques, and its potential rewards and (2) the shortage of qualified analysts and other personnel to design, implement, and operate a successful PPBES.

Categorizing proposed expenditures by object or character is probably the most uninformative way the human mind can conceive to show what government agencies really propose to do with the money they hope to get from legislators. We learn nothing of the work to be undertaken from a list of proposed salaries, transportation, educational equipment and supplies, operation, maintenance, communication, or other items of expenditure. The significant thing for citizens and their school board representatives is to know what effect the listed items will have, what plans are part of the permanent program of departments, or what new plans are being undertaken for contractions or expansions of services involving such items. If a government budget is regarded as a prospectus for the sale of certain services to the public, then most jurisdictions today are playing a guessing game with the citizen taxpayers so long as they continue to show merely objects of expenditure.

Program budgeting is designed to remedy this defect by showing the public what services and benefits are being purchased. Emphasis, however, is on the performance of certain tasks rather than on the purchase of certain items with which to do the task. Administrative management comes into the direction of many activities from which it was previously absent. Budget execution follow-up ensures that departments are actually performing activities for which funds were allocated.

Zero-Based Budgeting

Arthur Burns, former chairman of the Federal Reserve Board, is generally credited with first using the term *zero-based budgeting* publicly, in 1969. The concept of zero-based budgeting (ZBB) was initiated in the private sector by Texas Instruments. It was begun as a means of answering the traditional question of how to allocate resources. Rather than conducting endless revisions of existing budgets, Texas Instruments decided to start each year from ground zero, review all activities and priorities, and from this develop a new and better blueprint of allocations for the coming budget year. In 1979, President Carter issued an executive order directing each agency head, under the direction of the Office of Management and Budgeting, to submit budget materials following the new ZBB format. Through the current taxpayer revolt, public schools are facing property tax limits, budget cuts, and program and staff reductions. Some states are adopting ZBB as a way of meeting the financial crunch.

In the hands of a competent principal, ZBB can be used to improve budget planning, control expenses, and justify funds to support various program alternatives. Some ZBB advocates promise more than they can deliver and minimize potential misuses of the concept, such as creating excessive paperwork and forms, reducing staff morale, and overemphasizing quantification in the evaluation of instructional programs.

The ZBB process can be simplified into four basic steps:

1. *Define the organization's decision units.* A decision unit is the lowest practical organizational unit that is knowledgeable about the spending request and its impact. This unit will very likely be responsible and accountable for implementing the proposal, if approved, and has some flexibility in choosing between two or more spending options. In a school district a decision unit would be, for example, a building administrator or a department chairperson. As a first step all possible decision units should be identified and the nature of their responsibilities and operation defined to prevent conflicts and ensure complete budgeting for the total educational setting.

2. *Develop decision packages for all activities.* A decision package identifies in a definitive manner a discrete function or operation that can be evaluated and compared to other functions, including:

    a. The goal to be achieved or the service to be performed
    b. Alternative means of achieving the goal
    c. Alternative levels of effort that will achieve the goal
    d. The cost and benefits of each alternative
    e. The technical and operational feasibility of each alternative
    f. The consequences of not funding a particular function

Decision packages are of two basic types: mutually exclusive packages, which identify alternative means of performing the same function, with the best alternative finally chosen and the remaining packages discarded; or incremental packages, which illustrate different levels of funding for a specific function. The incremental packages will show costs from a base level to a maximum level of cost for any one function. Normally each division package should represent one year's effort for a person, or $10,000 of expenses. Any lower figure requires too much paperwork for the possible gains.

3. *Rank the decision packages.* This process provides information necessary for the appropriate allocation of resources. The ranking should include all decision packages, in order of decreasing benefit to the organization. The initial ranking should occur at the lowest decision unit level. This permits the unit administrator to evaluate the importance of his/her own activities and to rank the decision packages affecting the unit accordingly. In the educational organization the packages would then be ranked by each succeeding administrative level and finally by the board of education.

4. *Approve and fund each activity or decision package to the level of affordability.* Inherent in this fourth area is the subjectivity of the definition of *affordability*. Taxpayers and boards have been known to disagree frequently on this word.

Advantages and Disadvantages of ZBB

Educators may have a tendency to reject zero-based budgeting because it appears to be a close relative of PPBES. It should be understood that ZBB is not simply a derivative of PPBES. PPBES has five weaknesses that are corrected by ZBB:

1. PPBES focuses on what will be done, but not on how to do it.
2. Budgeting as defined by PPBES is a cost calculation based on the decisions made in the planning and programming steps, whereas there are in reality many policy decisions and alternatives to be evaluated during the actual budget preparation.
3. PPBES does not provide any operating tool for the managers who implement the policy and program decisions.
4. PPBES does not provide a mechanism to evaluate the impact of various funding levels on each program and program element, nor does it establish priorities among the programs and varying levels of program effort.
5. PPBES focuses primarily on new programs or major increases in ongoing programs and does not force the continual evaluation of ongoing program activities and operations.

PPBES cannot perform these five tasks; the fact that these tasks are inherent in ZBB is, therefore, a distinct advantage of zero-based budgeting. The advantages of ZBB are:

1. ZBB controls staff expenses.
2. ZBB focuses management processes on analysis and decision making rather than on quibbling about incremental requests.
3. ZBB combines planning, budgeting, business proposals, and operational decision making into one process.
4. In ZBB, managers have an ongoing requirement to evaluate in detail their operations, efficiency, and cost-effectiveness.
5. With ZBB all expenditures are evaluated, and discretionary and penalty cost exposures are specifically identified.
6. ZBB offers mechanisms to trade off manpower and expenses between decision units.
7. In ZBB, top management has a follow-up tool to determine the level of achievement of each program relative to the cost and effectiveness of the program.
8. In ZBB the ranking sheet can be used to adjust the budget during the operating year.
9. ZBB identifies similar functions among different staffs for comparison and evaluation.
10. ZBB provides management training and participation in decision making.

What disadvantages or problems might occur as an organization moves from the traditional budgeting practices to a zero-based format? The most common areas of difficulty are the following:

1. ZBB is threatening.
2. Administration and communications are more complicated because more people are involved in decision making.

3. ZBB requires more time in budget preparation.
4. ZBB places emphasis on work measures and evaluative data that are often unavailable.
5. ZBB forces management to make decisions.
6. The large volume of decision packages inherent in ZBB makes ranking difficult.
7. ZBB involves the evaluation of dissimilar functions, which is not feasible.
8. Evaluation of the ''priority'' or ''required'' packages can become a political nightmare.

District Use of ZBB

There is little doubt that a systematic budgeting system such as ZBB can assist local school districts in stemming the tide of rising budgets. Furthermore, ZBB is a tool that can be used to increase management and program effectiveness.

Assuming that ZBB is a worthy tool, how does a school district move from the traditional line item budgeting to the new model? The concept is astonishingly simple, but the mechanics of implementation are considerably more complex. Three conditions are necessary to successful implementation:

1. A genuine commitment to and support of the concept by top district management.
2. Support of the concept of building-level planning and the building-level management team.
3. Adequate technical assistance for all management levels.

Assuming the acceptance of these conditions, the school district should be able to implement a ZBB approach. The prime factor, as noted earlier, is the development of the decision package. These decision packages have features identical to many aspects of PPBES; however, there are three important differences:

1. ZBB forces consideration of alternative courses of action.
2. ZBB forces identification of varying levels of effort.
3. ZBB forces the ranking of decision packages by progressive levels of management.

Zero-based budgeting, if adopted by a local school district, will force a rigorous evaluation of all programs. Once each program has been subjected to the evaluation procedures, it may be continued or begun at current or proposed funding levels, continued at current or proposed funding levels with modifications, expanded, reduced, or eliminated.

Whatever choice a district makes, it should not expect ZBB to be a panacea. Excessive expectations can be harmful. However, properly carried out, ZBB can have a significant effect on the budget.

Concepts of Budget Development

Several concepts of budgeting have evolved over the years. The functional model is based on a sequence of steps beginning with an educational plan, an expenditure plan, and ending with a revenue plan. The continuous budgeting concept is based on the several steps of the functional model but incorporates continuous evaluation and modification. The participatory budget concept involves relevant groups in decision making. A fourth concept draws on elements of the three models described above but incorporates considerations of organizational, political, and economic environments.

Functional Budget

The concept of functional budget development requires that the planners attempt to determine the educational objectives of a school district as the first step in the budget process. The educational plan is then translated into a budget and presented to the community for reaction and adoption. The outcome is usually a compromise between what people are willing to pay for and what the planners think is needed. It represents the best program of education the people of a community will buy at a particular time.

Using the functional approach the budget committee considers the educational plan first. It translates the qualitative and quantitative aspects of the educational program into planned expenditures and then communicates these to the taxpayers, who provide the resources.

Continuous Budget

The concept of continuous budget development considers budgeting an integral part of daily operation. Immediately upon adoption of a budget, work starts on the development of the next budget document. Strengths and weaknesses in the operation of the present budget are appraised, and proposed budget plans are made. Educational plans are conceived on a long-range basis. Hastily formulated educational programs are not considered. All program plans are developed in the context of proposed financing for implementation. With year-round budget development various areas of the school can be better coordinated, and the board of education can be given time to consider an addition or deletion on the basis of educational merit as well as of cost.

The continuous consideration of the budget is not an automatic operation. Certain administrative devices must be used, including: (a) scheduling discussions of the budget throughout the year at staff, teachers, and board meetings; (b) setting up ''tickler'' files around the system to stimulate people to think about and make suggestions concerning the budget; (c) establishing a calendar that distributes the various phases of budget making over a twelve-month period; and (d) requiring reports that force consideration of items that should be included in the budget.

Participatory Budget

The participatory budget concept recognizes two basic principles. First, schools, as tax-supported institutions, must consult citizens in the planning process if they expect to obtain continuing and expanding support. Second, persons who teach in schools using equipment and facilities should be given the opportunity to suggest procedures and materials that they believe are most effective.

Education is big business. If we think of it as an investment that develops our human resources, then it is one of the largest, most important undertakings in the United States. Yet school costs are small compared with some other expenditures. As an example, public education expenditures for grades kindergarten through twelve are running about 3 percent of the gross national product, and considerably less than the amount spent on autos, alcohol, and defense each year. Public education is the largest governmental unit controlled and administered at the local community level. People in the community must be convinced of the desirability of a particular educational program before they will support it. By the same token, teachers must believe in and understand a plan before they will contribute actively to its success.

The participatory concept of budget development involves and provides for the interplay of the school staff and public representatives at the various levels of budget making. A combination of formal and informal methods is used to encourage involvement in budget development.

Teachers and other staff members are asked to submit individual requests for needed supplies and equipment. In addition, staff participation on formal committees dealing with budget development is encouraged. Many schools also conduct staff hearings and in-service meetings on the budget.

Citizens are involved as members of advisory committees and study groups. The budget hearing to report committee findings is one of the best ways to keep all citizens informed. Public sentiment is, in the long run, in favor of clear, unbiased presentations of problems and honestly sought advice and suggestions.

Attempts to involve teachers, staff, and citizens often fail because of inadequate planning and a lack of role definition. Clear delineation of the advisory nature of the participants is important before any work is completed. However, all participants deserve to know the disposition of their proposals and the results of their efforts. Staff and citizen participation helps create a better understanding of education for the future and assists in giving direction and scope to budget development.

Alternative—Rational/Political/Economic Budget

There are those who insist, with some justification, that existing budget theories have a number of problems. First, these theories cannot satisfactorily explain disequilibrium and decremental decision making. Second, rational behavior is defined so narrowly by both rational and public choice theorists that evidence of inefficiency is interpreted as irrational and unresponsive behavior and, moreover, as indicative of bureaucratic pathology.[3]

In this view the notion persists that a series of conditions affect rational budget development, among them the political realities of a given situation and the need to respond to pressures and demands that are often far removed from rationality. Another impact is the set of economic conditions that ultimately affects the rational budget process. Included here are market conditions and the stability or instability of particular areas because of conditions not able to be controlled.

Still another variable that affects the rational budget process is the impact of organizational behavior when it comes to employee justice. Because education is such a labor-intensive activity, this variable can have significant impact on the budget process.

It is important that the rational/political/economic budget process seeks to incorporate the key elements of several approaches to budgeting. It is an effort to recognize the realities of emerging conditions while preserving existing budget theory.

The Budget Process

The educational plan is the starting point of the budget process. The school budget is the educational plan translated into dollars. The school budget can be conceptualized as an equilateral triangle, with the educational program as the base and expenditures and revenues as the other two legs (see Figure 6-2). If any one of the three sides is shortened, the other two must also be shortened. Only when the three sides meet is there a budget document.

For many the budget may be seen as both a needs and a working budget. In the needs budget, program costs are projected as if all educational needs are to be met. The working budget is the final document drawn according to educational priorities and will serve as the financial plan throughout the year.

Specifically, the needs budget calls for cooperatively defined educational plans, both short- and long-range. The development should involve the staff and community and be initiated at the building level under broad guidelines established by the central office administration. The educational needs must be translated into financial terms. As the community and staff gain experience in this type of activity, the level of sophistication in budget development increases. Important considerations for the development of a needs budget are:

- Special programs
- Innovations
- Staff increases
- Salary adjustments
- Operations and maintenance
- Fixed costs
- Supplies, equipment requests

FIGURE 6-2   Budget Process

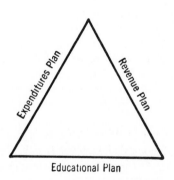

Educational Plan

A further step in the development of the needs budget is the determination of resources needed to meet the budget. The total spectrum of local, state, and federal sources must be considered. Decisions should be made as to the disposition of the budget. Plans should be made for staff and community involvement in the important step of budget appraisal.

The working budget is actually a further refinement of the needs budget. The needs budget is more idealistic, in that it lacks the realistic parameters that surround the working budget. The working budget calls for the establishment of program priorities. Again, the staff and community are involved. Costing must be developed for each priority level. Determination of the amount of support from each source must be figured. At this stage the working budget can be established. It should include appropriate documentation throughout. Approval by the board of education is absolutely necessary, and approval by the community is desired. A plan for budget appraisal should be made, such as the following (each state may have a unique fiscal year).

The Budget Calendar—Fiscal Year

Month 1	Budget year begins
Month 3	Quarterly revision—to incorporate accurate revenue and enrollment figures (present budget)
Month 4	Population (enrollment) projections Staff needs projections Program changes and addition projections Facilities needs projection
Month 5	Staff requisitions—supplies Capital outlay preliminary requests
Month 6	Budget revisions (present budget) Central staff sessions on needs Maintenance and operations requests
Month 7	Rough draft of needs budget
Month 8	Meet with staffs and principals to establish priorities Citizen committees' reports and reviews Central staff and board of education budget sessions
Month 9	Budget revision (present budget)
Month 10	Working budget draft Meet with staff and community groups to revise working budget
Month 11	Final draft of working budget
Month 12	Budget hearings and adoption of working budget

Staff Personnel

Declining enrollment and lower teacher turnover have forced many school districts to reduce the number of professional personnel employed. The difficult task of reduction in force is often guided by state statutes, the courts, and local negotiated agreements. Consequently, knowledge of how legislation and litigation relate to reduction in force for school personnel has become imperative for the development of sound school policy and management.

Accurate pupil population projections are the basis for planning staff needs. With the restrictions mentioned above it is difficult to utilize mathematical formulae for projecting staff needs. If the school system is utilizing site-based budgeting, the building staff will coordinate the deployment of staff under guidelines furnished by the central office staff. Categories that might be utilized in adjusting staffing to innovation might fit the following headings:

- Position title
- Category
- Same
- New
- Upgrade
- Downgrade
- Eliminate
- Cost

For a more detailed discussion, please refer to Chapter 8 on personnel.

Resource Allocation

Today we are facing an increasing demand for government services in many areas, including education. Government expenditures are expanding at a faster rate than the increase of the GNP. We have moved from the world's credit banker to the world's largest debtor as a nation. Our trade deficit in 1989 was over $120 billion a year. The demands on the federal budget for defense-related expenditures have shifted the burden of social services, including education, to state and local governments. Continued expansion of federal, state, and local expenditures would naturally result in an increase in tax rates or new taxes or accelerated borrowing (as has happened at the federal level). Governmental mandates, without proper support funding at the state and federal level, have greatly increased the complexity of funding at the local level.

Summary

Long-range fiscal planning and the establishment of goals for future programs are a logical outgrowth of budgeting. The natural extension of this, in turn, is the development of better educational program plans and the synthesis of these plans into broad fiscal plans. The resulting fiscal plans, because they are based on educational programs, will strengthen and unify the budget process. When these activities are accomplished, not only will school system operations be much more comprehensive, but there will be meaningful bases and systematic techniques for planning, reviewing, modifying, and carrying out educational programs. This, we think, will help both the superintendent and the school board to weigh the value and effectiveness of educational programs and to balance and decide on the essential policy alternatives available to them. It will also help interested citizens to understand and evaluate the services their school system provides.

Suggested Activities

1. Develop a budget calendar that allows involvement by community, staff, and student body but still fits the proper time sequence for each of the budget steps.
2. Develop a line item and a programmatic type of budget for some phase of the school program. How would each type of cost allocation lend itself to program cost analysis?
3. Develop a site-based budget for an elementary school. Indicate parameters on spending decided by central administration.
4. Outline a zero-based budgeting system for a high school.
5. Relate the activity of budget building to a community information program or system.

Selected Readings

Benson, Charles S. *The Economics of Public Education*. Boston: Houghton Mifflin, 1978.
Burrup, Percy E. *Financing Education in a Climate of Change*. Boston: Allyn and Bacon, 1977.
Candoli, I. Carl. *School District Administration: Strategic Planning for Site Based Management*. Lancaster, PA: Technomics Publishing, 1990.
Guthrie, James W., Ed. *School Finance Policies and Practices*. Cambridge, MA: Ballinger Publishing, 1980.
Hartman, William T. *School District Budgeting*. Englewood Cliffs, NJ: Prentice-Hall, 1988.
Hentschke, Guilbert C. *Management Operations in Education*. Berkeley, CA: McCutchan Publishing, 1975.
Johns, Roe L, Edgar L. Morphet, and Kern Alexander. *The Economics and Financing of Education*. Englewood Cliffs, NJ: Prentice-Hall, 1983.
Wagner, I. D., and S. M. Sniderman. *Budgeting School Dollars: A Guide to Spending and Saving*. Washington, DC: National School Board Association, 1984.
Wildavsky, Aaron. *Budgeting: A Comparative Theory of Budgetary Processes*. Boston: Little, Brown, 1975.

Notes

1. Carl Candoli and Gary L. Wegenke, *Building Budget and You: A Primer for School Principals*. (Lansing, Mi.: State Department of Education, 1978), 1–24.
2. Stakeholders are individuals or group representatives who share common interests in the educational process of a school or building.
3. James G. Cibulka, "Theories of Educational Budgeting: Lessons from the Management of Decline," *Education Administration Quarterly 23*, 1 (Feb. 1987), 28.

_7_ Accounting, Auditing, and Reporting

THE TASKS OF ACCOUNTING, AUDITING, AND REPORTING have been associated with school business administration since its inception. In the past few years, however, the function of these tasks has changed considerably. In the initial period of development, accounting tasks were oriented to control; i.e., the public monies had to be accounted for to assure the school district's patrons that tax dollars were being spent in the proper amounts and for the proper purposes.

More recently, accounting tasks have been expanded to incorporate the contemporary concept of accountability. With this orientation, accounting, auditing, and reporting are used to provide necessary data and interpretation to determine costs and benefits within the financial foundations of educational institutions. The school business administrator employs accounting techniques to describe (1) the nature, sources, and amounts of revenue inputs; (2) the appropriation of revenues to various programs (or funds and accounts); and (3) the actual expenditures in these programs. These data are then related to program outputs or educational outcomes, so that citizens can understand the financial implications of program decisions and the program implications of financial decisions. In this way the schools are accountable to the public, and the public has information on which it can exercise its decision-making power in areas of financial policy.

Because of the recent and significant movement toward a program budgeting type of accountability to the public, the authors suggest that there is an additional level of the accounting, auditing, and reporting task: an internal accountability prerequisite to integrated and comprehensive planning. It has been established as a central focus of this book that the planning process must be a team effort. Planning inputs from individual specialists within the superintendency team are interactive. For example, programmatic and financial aspects of a staff personnel administrator's proposal can have an impact on the proposal lodged by the administrator in charge of instruction. There must be a free flow of adequate and valid information within the planning team. Each member is accountable to the team in order that individual plans and specific proposals can coalesce into an integrated educational program, which in turn can be proposed to and evaluated by the public.

School policy makers and administrators have responded to the public demand for accountability not only by implementing program-oriented accounting systems but also by decentralizing educational policy making and administration. The major vehicle used to accomplish decentralized administration is site-based management, described in previous chapters. This concept requires the implementation of an accounting system that provides budgeting, revenue, expenditure, and accounting data at the level of the building or administrative unit. These data are necessary for effective planning of the operation of the program as well as for holding the staff and administrators accountable for the decisions that are delegated to them.

Thus, school accounting is manifest in several ways and places throughout the school system. It is an important means of providing vital information for districtwide as well as site- or building-level financial decisions. It is crucial in providing a structure for holding the institution as well as specific policy makers and administrators accountable for their decisions and performance. Lastly, school accounting is an important vehicle for providing information to the public that they can use in formulating basic policy or responses to specific ballot issues pertaining to the operation of the schools.

School Accounting

A Definition

School accounting has been defined as . . . recording and reporting activities and events affecting personnel, facilities, materials, or money of an administrative unit and its programs. Specifically, it is concerned with determining what accounting records are to be maintained, how they will be maintained, and the procedures, methods, and forms to be used; recording, classifying, and summarizing activities or events; analyzing and interpreting recorded data; and preparing and issuing reports and statements which reflect conditions as of a given date, the results of operations for a specific period, and the evaluation of status and results of operations in terms of established objectives.[1]

Several ideas in this definition deserve to be highlighted. First, accounting deals with activities and events that affect both operational inputs (money, material) and the school's program. Secondly, the process of accounting incorporates acts of recording, classifying, analyzing, and interpreting data. A third idea expressed in the definition is that of recording conditions as of a given date and the evaluation of the status and results of operations in terms of established objectives. From this definition it is apparent that, as it constitutes important financial and programmatic inputs, the accounting function is an integral part of the planning process employed by the educational team.

Objectives of School Accounting

The definition implies that the accounting function serves several varied purposes in schools. Among the most important are:

- Maintaining an accurate record of significant details in the business transactions of the school system

- Providing a basis and medium for planning and decision making by both policy-making and administrative bodies at local, state, and federal levels
- Providing a control system to ensure the appropriate use of resources in the educational enterprise
- Expediting the process of setting priorities; establishing, analyzing, and selecting alternatives in the budgeting process; and establishing an operational blueprint for the school system
- Providing a medium for reporting the financial condition of the school system to the patrons of the school district, as well as to other groups and agencies at the local, state, and federal levels. This is done for purposes of planning and policy making, accountability, control, and comparative study.
- Providing basic input information to calculate and extend school district budgets, tax levies, and state and federal subventions or transfer payments

Emergence of School Accounting System

Since school accounting had its genesis in public accounting, which in turn sprang from business accounting, several basic principles of the latter can be appropriately used to design or evaluate accounting systems to be used in public schools. A primary difference between public school accounting and business accounting (other than the absence of a profit motive) is the presence of legal restrictions or controls on the sources and procedures for obtaining revenue for public education and on the purposes and processes for expending it. The fiscal controls placed on the school district by the state typically limit revenues to taxation, gifts, tuition, fines, fees, and transfer payments from state and federal governments. In many instances very specific controls are written into state laws. Strict control over expenditures tends to be the rule rather than the exception in most states. For example, in some states, teachers' salaries may not be paid unless a valid teaching certificate is on file in the appropriate office; or monies may not be expended for paying the moving expenses of the superintendent.

States exercise their plenary legal authority over the school districts as quasi corporations by specifying the accounting and other fiscal procedures to be used. Typically, the state requires a public school fund accounting system. Thus, all districts use a common system with common funds, accounts, definitions, and procedures. Usually a series of funds is set up including discrete sources of revenue to be used in each for specified purposes. Thus, each fund tends to be a unique entity. Within each fund the uniform accounting laws typically provide for a group of accounts that define, as legal restrictions, those transactions that may be made within the given fund. For example, in Ohio the expenditure for replacing a typewriter used for instruction must be charged to the 740 account—equipment, replacement—in the general fund. However, purchase of an additional typewriter to be used for instruction in a new school built with monies from a bond issue must be charged to the building fund—account 640, equipment.

School accounting systems, with their rather rigid state controls, serve another major purpose. The designation of funds and the construction of school budgets around the funds provide the baseline decisions and information needed to determine tax rates. Thus, in many states the officials or agencies so empowered use these financial data to designate the required tax rates, which in turn are extended by the tax department in the appropriate jurisdiction. For example, two basic property tax levies are calculated in Ohio, the current operating levy (required by the general fund budget) and the bond retirement levy (required to finance debt service).

Basic Concepts in School Accounting Systems

The science of accounting is made up of an organized body of knowledge and an orderly application of procedures. Three basic concepts are used in the accounting function in public school systems. School personnel with responsibility for general and fiscal policy decisions and those with responsibility for executing them must apply the concepts in order to utilize the information resources afforded by an accounting system. Frequently, specific terms used in an accounting context carry meanings quite different from those used (or misused) in lay jargon.

The Accounting Equation

The first concept is related to describing financial status at a given moment. What a school system or an individual is worth is equal to what is owned minus what is owed. Thus, the basic accounting equation is stated as:

Owned minus Owed = Net Worth

Accounting terminology translates the equation by substituting standardized terms.

- *Assets* are things owned.
- *Liabilities* are things owed.
- *Equity* is the difference between things owned and things owed and thus equates with net worth. When applied to school accounting, the term *fund balance* is used.

Thus, the equation becomes:

Assets minus Liabilities = Equity

If a school system has $500,000 in its bank account and owes $450,000 for teachers' salaries, its equity equals $50,000. The equation can be stated in several different forms with the above example:

Assets = Liabilities + Equity
$500,000 = $450,000 + $50,000 or $500,000 = $500,000

Liabilities = Assets – Equity
$450,000 = $500,000 – $50,000 or $450,000

Equity = Assets – Liabilities
$50,000 = $500,000 – $450,000 or $50,000 = $50,000

Since the accounting equation is an algebraic expression, it can be added to or subtracted from, provided the same amount is added to or subtracted from both sides of the equation.

In the following example, suppose that the school system increased its assets by $100,000. Using the equation Assets = Liabilities + Equity, assets would be increased by $100,000, so it would be necessary to add $100,000 to the other side of the equation. The actions and reactions of adding to or subtracting from any of the elements of the equation are governed by the following concepts:

1. One asset can be increased while another can be decreased by an equal amount. Invested funds, for example, can be converted to cash. Thus, the amount of assets remains the same although investment assets decrease and cash assets increase.
2. An asset can be increased while a liability is increased by an equal amount. Material that was ordered has been received but has not yet been paid for. The assets have been increased by the value of the material, but the liabilities have been likewise increased since the school system now owes the vendor for the material.
3. An asset can be increased while equity is increased by an equal amount. Fines, charges, and gifts received increase assets and at the same time increase the school system's equity.
4. A liability can be increased while another can be decreased by an equal amount. Money can be borrowed to pay a vendor's bill.

It must be recognized that changes in the equation may be made in combinations of the above actions and reactions since a single transaction may result in several simultaneous changes.

Since school accounting involves the reporting and recording of activities and events affecting the school system over a period of time, it is essential that the ongoing and changing financial condition be recorded. Thus, it is necessary to introduce a dynamic character or capability into the accounting system. This is accomplished by adding two elements to the basic accounting equation:

$$\text{Assets} = \text{Liabilities} + \text{Fund Balance} + \text{Revenues} - \text{Expenditures}$$

Revenues result from transactions that increase assets without increasing liabilities or from transactions that decrease liabilities. Revenue increases eventually increase fund balance. Typical revenue transactions are receipts of local property taxes, state subsidies, and grants or gifts. Monies obtained from a loan or a bond issue are not revenues, as they entail the creation of a liability in that they must be repaid.

Expenditures result from transactions that decrease assets and fund balance or that increase liability and fund balance. Typical expenditure transactions are the many expenses in carrying out the educational program: teachers' salaries, instructional supplies and equipment, support services and supplies, and the like. Payment of a loan is not considered an expense as it decreases liability and assets but fund balance remains the same.

The Accounting Process

The financial status of a school system changes as it transacts business that effects changes in its accounting equation. It is these transactions that are recorded, classified, and summarized in the accounting process. Transactions are originally recorded in a journal and from it are posted to accounts. Accounts are established for each asset and liability and for equity.

Because of the unique nature of school district accounting specified by individual states, which mandate discrete funds and accounts, public school system accounting procedures use the term *fund balance* rather than *equity*.

The accounts that reflect the action and reaction of the several transactions are commonly known as *T accounts*. The concept of debits and credits is built around the way data are recorded in each account. The left side of the T account is the debit side, while the right is the credit side (see Figure 7-1).

The derivation of the words *debit* and *credit* in the accounting context can provide an important insight into this concept. Sam Tidwell states:

> *The Latin word* debeo *means "owe." The history of the use of this word as it applies to accounting began when the only transactions necessary to be recorded were those with customers or suppliers. A charge against a person who owes appears on the left side of the account with that person. The left side of the account is the "debit" side.*
>
> *The Latin word* credo *means "trust" or "believe." The history of this word as it applies to accounting began at the same time as the word* debit. *The amount shown as owed to a person who trusts us appears on the right side of the account, which is referred to as the credit side.*[2]

To keep accounts in balance, or to maintain the accounting equation, there must be an equal use of debits and credits for each transaction. As indicated earlier, a single transaction might have two or more debits and two or more credits. However, the total amount of debits must still equal the total amount of credits. In a series of transactions the total debits must be equal to the total credits. The fact that the accounts are self-balancing through equal entry of both debits and credits identifies such a system as *double-entry bookkeeping*.

An application of the concepts of the accounting equation and double-entry bookkeeping with debits and credits can be illustrated in a rather simplistic example.

A school district has a balance of $100,000 when it opens its books at the beginning of the fiscal year. Over a period of time it completes a series of transactions, and they are to be recorded in the accounting system. In chronological order the opening balance and succeeding transactions are:

1. $100,000 in the opening balance is recorded.
2. $500,000 in local taxes is received.
3. $450,000 is paid for teachers' salaries.
4. $1,000,000 is borrowed from a local bank.
5. $100,000 in supplies is ordered and received from a vendor.
6. $150,000 is paid for salaries of noncertificated personnel.
7. $100,000 is paid to vendor for supplies.
8. $500,000 in state aid is received.
9. $1,000,500 in principal and interest on loan is repaid.

These transactions would be recorded as shown in Figure 7-2.

Opening balance (1): $100,000, so Assets are debited and Fund Balance is credited.

Transaction (2): The school system receives $500,000 in taxes, so Assets are increased by a debit and Revenue is increased by a credit.

FIGURE 7-1 T Accounts for the School Fund Accounting Equation

ASSETS		=	LIABILITIES		+	FUND BALANCE		+	REVENUES		−	EXPENDITURES	
Debit	Credit		Debit	Credit		Debit	Credit		Debit	Credit		Debit	Credit
Increase	Decrease		Decrease	Increase		Decrease	Increase		Decrease	Increase		Increase	Decrease

FIGURE 7-2 Illustration of the Application of the Accounting Equation and Double-Entry Bookkeeping

	ASSETS		=	LIABILITIES		+	FUND BALANCE		+	REVENUES		−	EXPENDITURES	
	Debit	Credit		Debit	Credit		Debit	Credit		Debit	Credit		Debit	Credit
	Increase	Decrease		Decrease	Increase		Decrease	Increase		Decrease	Increase		Increase	Decrease
(1)	100,000							100,000						
(2)	500,000										500,000			
(3)		450,000											450,000	
(4)	1,000,000				1,000,000									
(5)	100,000				100,000									
(6)		150,000											150,000	
(7)		100,000											100,000	
(8)	500,000										500,000			
(9)		1,000,500		1,000,500										
	2,200,000	1,700,500		1,000,500	1,100,000			100,000			1,000,000		700,000	

147

Transaction (3): The school system pays $450,000 in teachers' salaries, so Assets are decreased by a credit and expenditures are increased by a debit.

Transaction (4): The school system borrows $1,000,000 from a local bank, so Assets are increased by a debit and Liabilities are increased by a credit.

Transaction (5): The school system orders and receives a $100,000 purchase of supplies from a vendor, so Assets are increased by a debit and Liabilities are increased by a credit.

Transaction (6): The school system pays $150,000 in salaries for classified personnel, so Assets are decreased by a credit and Expenditures are increased by a debit.

Transaction (7): The school system pays $100,000 to the vendor for the supplies previously ordered and received, so Assets are decreased by a credit and Expenditures are increased by a debit.

Transaction (8): The school system received $500,000 in state aid, so Assets are increased by a debit and Revenues are increased by a credit.

Transaction (9): The school system pays $1,000,500 in principal and interest on the $1,000,000 borrowed previously, so Assets are decreased by a credit and Liabilities are increased by a debit.

In order to be certain that transactions have been properly analyzed and recorded, and that debits and credits have been equally applied, a *trial balance* is run.

School Fund Accounting and Operation

Accounting in public schools employs basic concepts in common with private sector accounting. However, given the public mission of the public schools and the statutory constraints and directives applied to them, the accounting procedures per se deviate somewhat from private sector practices. Sources and levels of revenue for the schools are relatively fixed by law and tax administration practices. Expenditures are likewise controlled. Thus, public schools use "fund accounting," which designates several funds, each having its own discrete purpose and appropriate expenditures and its own discrete source of revenues. Public school accounting is built around separate accounting systems for each fund. Most states have a fund for current operations—variously termed educational, general, or the like—for teachers' salaries, instructional materials, and so forth. Similarly, many states designate a building or capital outlay fund for fixed assets such as site, buildings, and equipment. Bond funds are established to pay principal and interest on school bonds that have been floated. Each of the separate funds is a separate accounting entity.

Given the several basic accounting concepts presented and the recognition that these are applied in the context of school fund accounting, the remainder of the discussion on accounting will be devoted to an examination of how the accounting process is applied. It will be built around the business administrator's responsibility for and in the accounting cycle.

Tidwell identifies ten basic steps in the cycle:

1. Journalize transactions.
2. Post transactions.
3. Prepare a trial balance.
4. Prepare a work sheet.
5. Prepare financial statements.
6. Journalize closing entries.
7. Post closing entries.
8. Balance, rule, and bring forward balances of balance sheet accounts.
9. Rule temporary accounts.
10. Prepare post-closing trial balance.[3]

As the school business administrator assesses his/her accounting responsibility, legal mandates and constraints must be recognized. States usually exercise their plenary authority by requiring an accounting for school district resources; by specifying the data, forms, and procedures to be used; and by assigning individuals fixed responsibilities in accounting and related functions. In many states these functions involve responsibilities shared among superintendents, boards of education (or their counterparts) or board secretaries, treasurers, clerks, school business administrators, and other local or state officials or agencies. Thus, it is extremely important that job expectations and working relationships be set up carefully and clearly to avoid confusion, role conflict, and muddled role expectation.

The recent movement toward site-based management (with budgeting, purchasing, and accounting responsibilities given to principals and directors of various discrete programs) highlights the problems of clarifying responsibilities and fixing accountability. Administrators in these kinds of centers have had decision-making authority delegated to them. It is necessary not only to clarify this authority and accountability but also to relate it to the rest of the system. Thus, the decentralized accounting mechanism for a given cost center must be an integral part of the accounting machinery of the whole school system. Program-oriented budgeting and accounting systems have been developed with this capability. Funds and accounts can be broken down where appropriations and expenditures can be identified by programs, courses, teachers, and objects in a given building or cost center. The major point is this: If management of educational programs is site-based, the accounting system likewise must be site-based.

The challenge is not met simply by a precise set of job descriptions and elaborate computer software. Ongoing working relationships must be developed and maintained if the organization so necessary for effective school fund accounting is to function. Accurate and reliable accounting data must be accompanied by an integrated decision-making system acting on the data. Site-based accounting data and decisions must be related to central administration and board of education accounting data and decisions. Thus, all levels must see the larger scene as well as that scene in which they play. Unfortunately, in the past many principals knew little of fund accounting and how accounting-based decisions impacted on their roles.

The Accounting Cycle

Several discrete and sequential steps characterize the accounting process. These are presented in the following subsections.

Initiating Transactions

The accounting cycle begins with the initiation of a financial transaction. This may occur in many different sectors of the school system. It may be the certification that taxes are to be collected, the consummation of a contract for construction of a building, or a teacher's requisition for art paper. In most systems the last type of transaction is the most prevalent.

The approval procedure for requisitions is usually a local administrative decision of which the business administrator must be knowledgeable. When the approved requisition data are committed to a purchase order, the school system becomes liable for its payment. Many state-mandated accounting systems require that funds be encumbered, or ''earmarked,'' to pay this obligation and thus subtracted from an asset account. When a school system recognizes revenues as soon as it gains a right to them and recognizes an expenditure as soon as liability occurs, the system may be said to use an *accrual basis* of accounting, rather than a cash basis, which records only those financial transactions involving cash receipts and disbursements.[4]

Thus, the encumbering process finalizes the contracting or purchasing act and initiates the accounting act by providing the document and data for the *journal,* a book of original entry in the accounting process. The contract or purchase order becomes a *voucher,* a business document that provides evidence of a business transaction.

Journalizing Transactions

The accounting office continuously gathers all the vouchers generated by the school system. These are analyzed in terms of debits and credits and recorded in the general journal. This book of original entry records all the transactions in chronological order (hence the term *journal*). Specific data on each page of the general journal include the date of the transaction, the specific accounts affected by the transaction, an explanation of the transaction, the posting reference—which indicates the specific location of the posting in the ledger(s)—and debits and credits to all accounts affected by the transaction. The concept of debits and credits discussed earlier is applicable to the general journal as well as to ledgers of the several different accounts.

After the opening entries have been recorded in the general journal, they are posted to the appropriate accounts in the general ledger. The general journal entries include the date, account identification, explanation, posting reference (the account number in the general ledger where the transaction will be posted), and whether the entry is a debit or a credit.

The General Ledger

A *ledger* is a group of accounts. All asset, liability, expenditure, revenue, and fund balance accounts make up the general ledger. In practice the simplistic examples of accounting concepts presented earlier have given way to more complex forms of recording and analyzing these data. The asset account in the accounting equation has been replaced by a whole series of asset accounts including cash; taxes receivable; revenue receivable from various local, state, and federal sources; and so forth. Liability accounts can run literally into the hundreds in some states. Equity, or fund balance, accounts are used in each individual fund of the accounting system and reflect the difference between current assets and current liabilities in these individual accounts.

Revenue and expenditure accounts were created to reflect a unique feature of governmental and school district accounting. Since revenues available to school systems are relatively fixed through local property tax levies, state aid appropriations, and rather predictable amounts of other income, and since there are rigorous state controls over expenditures, it is both possible and necessary to build in safeguards for raising and expending school system monies. Two related types of accounts, which assist in financial planning, are known as *revenue* and *expenditure summary accounts*. These summary accounts and their functions are:

- *Estimated Revenue Summary:* summarizes all revenue estimated to accrue during the given fiscal year
- *Revenue Summary:* summarizes all revenue actually received
- *Appropriations Summary:* summarizes the total amount appropriated by the board, including authorization of fixed amounts for specific purposes during the given fiscal year
- *Expenditure Summary:* summarizes all expenditures incurred, including those paid and unpaid, that result in benefits enjoyed during the given fiscal year
- *Encumbrances:* summarizes all encumbrances that are chargeable to and included in an appropriation for the given fiscal year

The revenue and expenditure summary accounts provide the school administrator with information on the nature and amount of expenditures set up in the appropriations, the nature and amount of expenditures to date, and the nature and amount of expenditures that are not yet encumbered. Revenue and expenditure summary accounts provide important planning tools for the school business administrator.

Posting the General Ledger

Transactions entered in the general journal are posted to the appropriate accounts in the general ledger. This process brings together or summarizes all similar accounts. The general ledger is made up of individual accounts. Each account incorporates data regarding its designation (cash, accounts receivable, and so forth), its account number (usually the state-mandated classification system), date of the transaction, explanation, the posting reference (designation of page or location of the transaction in the general journal), and the designation as to whether the transaction was a debit or credit to the particular account (same designation given the transaction in the general journal).

Recording Budgets and Appropriations

At or near the beginning of the fiscal year, school systems adopt budgets and appropriations for operations during the coming fiscal year. These basic financial decisions are transactions and must be recorded. The appropriation is used to establish estimated revenues and expenditures. These data are entered in the general journal and general ledger in a fashion similar to the entries that originally opened the books. The journal entry account title in the operating or current expense fund would be "Estimated Revenue" and would be a debit amount. The equal credit amount would carry the title "Fund Balance."

When the general journal entries for estimated revenue are posted to the general ledger, the same account titles and debit and credit assignments are entered as were entered in the general journal. Subsidiary ledger forms for the revenue ledger include account descriptions and numbers for each of the several revenue sources. Estimated expenditures or appropriations are entered in a similar fashion.

Recording Transactions

The preceding sections have discussed the principles of accounting, how the books are opened, and how budgets and appropriations are recorded. The latter two functions are performed only once each year, to prepare for the entry of the normal daily transactions.

Processing Accounting Data

Manual, machine, and electronic data processing have all been used in accounting systems in recent years. The basic principles of school accounting apply, however, in any of these. The latter two types of processing have advantages over manual accounting in terms of speed, multiple use of a given entry, and mechanical or electronic reliability.

Accounting machines are frequently used in small school systems. Through the use of carbons, multiple carriages, and the like, relatively complex accounting systems can be maintained by a few well-trained people. Larger school systems are moving toward online computer-based accounting systems with capabilities for numerous and complex accounting functions.

School Accounting in Contemporary Practice

Observers of contemporary school accounting readily note marked contrasts between concept and practice. These differences are due to the use of simplistic examples to convey an abstract concept—for example, use of T accounts to show relationships between and among debits and credits and among assets and liabilities. In contemporary practice, T accounts are not used in school fund accounting. Instead, state-mandated accounting systems have tended to be single-entry cash accounting systems with required encumbrance procedures. Often they were built around state-mandated line item budgeting systems. However, change is apparent in both state and school system procedures.

Many states have integrated mandated or permissive program-oriented budgeting systems into their required accounting systems for school districts. This not only reflects good management techniques but also attempts to improve fiscal and management accountability to school decision makers and administrators and the public they serve.

Contemporary budgeting practices include the movement from line item to program-oriented budgeting. Generally speaking, spending budgets are developed around the basic funds, and within each fund major program areas are identified. In the Ohio school accounting system, the general fund contains major functions (program areas) that include instruction, supporting services, community services, extracurricular services, non-programmed charges (payments to other governmental units), contingencies and interfund transfers, and other functions. Subsets of instruction are regular instruction (elementary, middle/junior high school, high school, other regular), special instruction (e.g., academically gifted, mentally retarded, physically handicapped), vocational, adult/continuing, and other instruction.[5] All funds and functions within each fund reflect similar breakdowns into smaller units of school system programs.

Within each function, objects of expenditures are classified. Major objects are employees' salaries and wages, employees' retirement and insurance benefits, purchased services, supplies and materials, capital outlay, capital outlay-replacement, and other objects. Each object is further detailed. For example, supplies and materials subsets include general supplies; textbooks; library books, periodicals, newspapers, films and filmstrips; food and related supplies and materials; supplies and materials for operation, maintenance, and repair; supplies and materials for operation and repair of motor vehicles; and other supplies and materials.

Contemporary program-oriented accounting systems often must accommodate site-based management, budgeting, and accounting. This is done through the inclusion of the operational unit or cost center in the accounting systems. Transactions are attributed to the appropriate administrative unit in the school system. Many transactions occur at the districtwide level—e.g., collection of taxes, salary contracts for the superintendent and others who serve districtwide concerns, and liability insurance. Some transactions may be attributed to a given division or department (e.g., pupil transportation, teacher personnel), while others may be attributed to a given school. Thus, the accounting system attributes each transaction to one (or more) cost center. Individual school systems assign code numbers to each cost center.

Special cost centers have been designated as special projects and are often supported by restricted monies that are earmarked and must be accounted for separately from the more general programs of the school system.

Beyond operational units and cost centers, even greater detail is provided when subject areas and subsets thereof are identified. Thus, an expenditure may be traced not only to a given school but to a given subject taught in a specific school and at a given instructional level.

For example, in contemporary practice, when Mr. Jones, a West Senior High School microbiology teacher, requisitions and receives a set of microscope slides for his class, the accounting system will ask:

1. What kind of transaction is this?
2. What fund is affected?
3. What function does it meet?
4. What kind of object is it?
5. Is it in a special cost center?
6. What is its subject?
7. To which operational unit should it be attributed?
8. To what instructional level should it be attributed?

Using the example of the Ohio accounting system and the purchase of the microscope slides, the transaction for budgeting, purchasing, and accounting purposes is illustrated in Figure 7-3.

A similar logic is applied to other school system transactions. In receipts, each transaction is identified (various revenue sources), the fund affected is designated, the function of the receipt is coded, and the designation is made if it is appropriate to special cost centers, subjects, or operational units.

Full implementation of this kind of accounting system provides a relatively detailed picture of how revenues flow into the several programs and how they are expended in each.

FIGURE 7-3 Coding an Expenditure Transaction

Transaction
Indicator

| 0 | 5 |

05 Expenditures-
Operational

Fund

| 0 | 0 | 1 |

001 General
Fund

Function

| 1 | 1 | 3 | 2 |

1000 — Instruction
1100 — Regular Instruction
1130 — High School
1132 — General Curriculum

Object

| 5 | 1 | 1 |

500 — Supplies and Materials
510 — General Supplies
511 — Instructional Supplies

Special
Cost Center

| 0 | 0 | 0 | 0 |

0000 — District Wide
(No Special Cost
Center)

Operational
Unit

| 1 | 0 | 5 |

105 — West Senior High School

Subject

| 1 | 3 | 0 | 2 | 2 | 0 |

130000 — Natural Sciences
130200 — Biological Science/General Science
130220 — Microbiology

Instructional
Level

| 5 | 4 |

54 — High School Grades 10–12

The specific processes of implementation are spelled out in the following description of the accounting procedures employed by a forward-looking school system of approximately 16,000 pupils.

A typical transaction is initiated by the principal, who requisitions materials for a given educational program under his/her direction. The teacher who originated the request determines the item and price per unit from a vendor's catalog, and the quantity needed. The principal approves the request, giving consideration to its educational merit and the building's program allocation for such materials for that year. The combination requisition-purchase order form is completed, and the principal fills in the code number that reflects the planning, programming, budgeting, evaluation system (PPBES) accounting classification (see Figure 7-4).

If approved, the business administrator signs the purchase order as purchasing agent, assigns a purchase order number, selects a vendor (if none was designated on the requisition), and submits the document to the chief fiscal officer.

At this point the data describing the transaction are fed into the computer for verification. The computer program classifies the transactions by codes and thus "compares" the unencumbered balances in the given account for the given building with the amount of the purchase order. If the computer picks up an error (e.g., wrong coding, insufficient unencumbered balances), an error is indicated and corrections must be made before the order is submitted to the chief fiscal officer for his/her approval.

The chief fiscal officer's function is to sign the purchase order. By law, this obligates the district, and the computer encumbers the funds necessary to satisfy the contract with the vendor.

In this particular district, cash balances are deposited in several banks according to transaction codes. Thus, bank balances and fund balances are automatically adjusted to reflect each transaction.

Up to this point in the accounting process, financial transactions have been reported (requisitions and purchase orders) and recorded (from the documents into the computer). A first step in the classification function has already taken place with the encoding of each transaction (date, purchase order number, fund, account, building, program object, and the like). The following steps illustrate how the computer will further classify, analyze, summarize, and report the financial condition of the school district. (See Figure 7-5.)

Journalizing

With the data from transactions (requisitions and purchase orders in our example) in the computer disk pack or memory unit, the accounting steps can be initiated. The way in which the data are processed is determined by the program. Since each program is discrete, no particular sequence of programs is necessary to complete the accounting process. However, in order to follow the logical sequence of steps described earlier, the initial step of journalizing will be described.

Several programs produce reports that equate with the general journal. A Daily Audit Report displays each transaction in sequence by date. The Cash Disbursement Journal displays all the cash disbursements in daily sequence. The Purchase Order Update Report is a journal that reflects the daily aggregations of descriptions and amounts of purchase orders. The computer program in our example district has the capability of combining

FIGURE 7-4 Purchase Order

FUND	SPECIAL COST CENTER	FUNCTION	OBJECT	SUBJECT	OPER. UNIT	INST. LEVEL	JOB ASSIGN.	AMOUNT
· ·	· · ·	· · ·	· ·	· · · · · · · ·	· ·	·	· ·	· · · · · · · · · ·
· ·	· · ·	· · ·	· ·	· · · · · · · ·	· ·	·	· ·	· · · · · · · · · ·
· ·	· · ·	· · ·	· ·	· · · · · · ·	· ·	·	· ·	· · · · · · · · · ·
· ·	· · ·	· · ·	· ·	· · · · · · ·	· ·	·	· ·	· · · · · · · · · ·
· ·	· · ·	· · ·	· ·	· · · · · · · ·	· ·	·	· ·	· · · · · · · · · ·

SEND ALL INVOICES TO:

SOUTH-WESTERN CITY SCHOOLS

2975 KINGSTON AVE.   GROVE CITY, OHIO 43123

TO:

DELIVER TO:

PURCHASE ORDER

SHIP PREPAID — VIA:

Material on this order is Exempted from the Ohio Sales Tax and Federal Excise Taxes.

Numbers listed BELOW are required on all invoices for payment.

PURCHASE ORDER NO.

VENDOR No.

FOR DISTRICT USE ONLY

DATE _____

REQUESTED BY _____

FUNC./SUBJ.

INSTR. LEVEL

QUANTITY	UNIT	DESCRIPTION	PRICE @	AMOUNT	OBJECT

TERMS OR CONDITIONS: Time of delivery is of the essence of this contract. Buyer reserves the right to refuse any goods and to cancel all or any part of this order if seller fails to deliver all or any part of the goods in accordance with the terms of this order. This contract may not be modified or terminated orally, and no modification or termination, nor any claimed waiver of any of the provisions hereof shall be binding unless in writing and signed by the party against whom such modification, termination or waiver is sought to be enforced, and by the treasurer of the School District who shall affix a new certificate to such contract by reason of such change. **PLEASE ACKNOWLEDGE RECEIPT AND ACCEPTANCE OF THIS ORDER.**

TREASURER'S CERTIFICATE

It is hereby certified that the amount required to meet the contract, agreement, obligation, payment or expenditure for the above has been lawfully appropriated or authorized or directed for such purpose and is in the treasury or in process of collection to the credit of the fund free from any obligation or certification now outstanding.

_____
Treasurer, Board of Education

THE BOARD OF EDUCATION
South-Western City Schools

By _____

Purchasing Agent

THE ORDER IS VOID UNLESS TREASURER'S CERTIFICATE IS SIGNED.

FIGURE 7-5 Purchase Order Flow Chart

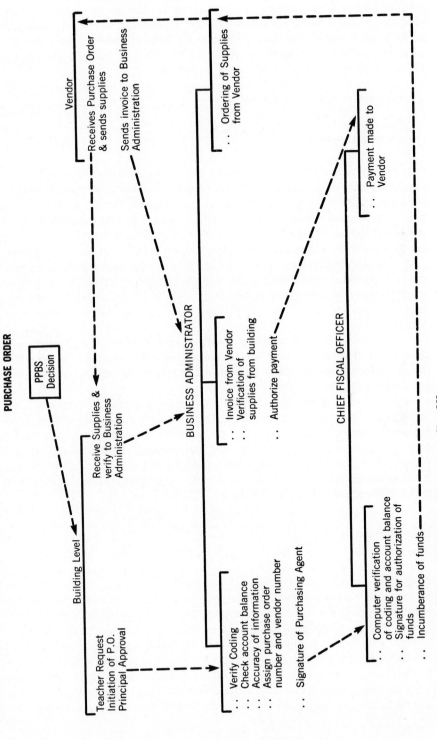

PURCHASE ORDER

PPBS
Decision

Vendor

Receives Purchase Order
& sends supplies

Sends invoice to Business
Administration

.. Ordering of Supplies
from Vendor

Building Level

Receive Supplies &
verify to Business
Administration

Teacher Request
Initiation of P.O.
Principal Approval

BUSINESS ADMINISTRATOR

.. Invoice from Vendor
.. Verification of
supplies from building

.. Authorize payment

CHIEF FISCAL OFFICER

.. Payment made to
Vendor

.. Verify Coding
.. Check account balance
.. Accuracy of information
.. Assign purchase order
number and vendor number

.. Signature of Purchasing Agent

.. Computer verification
of coding and account balance
.. Signature for authorization of
funds
.. Incumberance of funds

Source: Board of Education, South-Western City Schools, Grove City, OH.

157

payment for several purchase orders to a single vendor into one check, thereby reducing the overhead costs of multiple checks to one vendor. The journals serve the function of reporting the daily sequence of transactions and take the form of computer printouts that can be aggregated for weekly, monthly, or yearly reports. The data from the journals are used to create the several ledgers used by the school district.

The posting process (taking data from the journal and classifying and recording them in the ledger) is accomplished by the computer to produce the various ledgers.

The General Ledger

The format of the ledgers generated by this particular accounting system reflects both state mandates and the unique needs of the school district. A computer printout provides the status of each fund and each account maintained by the school district. Specific data for each include the original appropriation, adjusted appropriation, year-to-date expenditures, unexpended balances, outstanding encumbrances, and unencumbered balances. These same data are presented monthly to the board of education as part of the monthly financial report.

A second, but optional, general ledger classifies the same data by a program budget classification system developed by the district. This ledger shows the financial status by programs and cost centers (individual buildings). Modifications of this second general ledger can provide reports used by building principals and administrators of other cost centers.

Since the data fed into the computer include disbursements as well as purchase orders, checks to vendors are produced in a process parallel to the accounting process. Reports on checks issued include the check register (which reflects the vendor), the check number, accounting codes, and amount.

The Cash Position Report is used in our example district for purposes of cash-flow management. When checks are written and cash is received, the cash position of the district changes. The report reflects these changes and is thus considered a form of cash journal. Data on each fund include balances, cash disbursements, funds available, interim funds (which may be invested), and active funds (which may not be invested). Printouts of these data provide the bases for short-term investments. The report also reconciles cash-flow data with the amounts on deposit in each bank.

Balancing the Books

The function of balancing is accomplished in a continuous fashion as the accounting process progresses. By virtue of electronic verification and retrieval, a full range of balances can be programmed into the process. If imbalances or errors occur, the computer either rejects the transaction or records it on a special report. An example of the latter type is the Invoice Update Report, which provides a daily summary of all invoices. If negative balances emerge, adjustments in appropriations may be made. Another example is the Invoice Validation Report, which shows on a printout all instances in which vendors submit invoices in absence of, or at variance with, the original purchase order. This is particularly useful when partial payments are made on partial orders and the like. The faulty invoice is rejected, and the business office can then initiate the audit trail to resolve the problem.

Each of the reports derived from the journals and ledgers contains such balances as cash, fund, and account balances—encumbered and unencumbered, daily, month-to-date, and year-to-date balances.

Generally Accepted Accounting Procedures

One of the obvious weaknesses in the modified cash accounting system described here is that it deals only with current assets and liabilities. The cries for reform in education have included accountability, but are usually limited to educational results and spending decisions. Only recently have states concluded that school systems should incorporate accrual accounting into their programs. Thus, long-term assets and liabilities should be reflected in accounting systems. Modified cash accounting does not accommodate the liabilities of a multi-year teachers' salary agreement, depreciation of capital, or an early retirement incentive program. It does not accommodate investment interest earned beyond the current year, long-term debt, or the value of investments.

An alternative or supplementary accounting procedure has been put in place in some states and school districts to remedy this weakness. Generally accepted accounting procedures (GAAP) have had a long and rich evolution in terms of the application to school accounting. Its chronology has been summarized by Bernard F. Gatti.[6] He gave prominence to the report *Governmental Accounting, Auditing, and Financial Reporting* published by the National Council on Governmental Accounting in 1968, which spelled out generally accepted accounting procedures for state and local governments and ''. . . defined the modified accrual basis of accounting and included a model financial statement reporting format, the initial version of the *Comprehensive Annual Financial Report* (CAFR).''[7] Substantial impetus was provided by the Revenue Sharing Act of 1972 since recipients of these revenues were required to use a uniform accounting system mandated by the federal government. Since then many agencies have developed specific accounting standards that in turn have been reviewed for approval by various governmental and professional organizations. Generally accepted accounting procedures provide for the establishment of fixed asset records, maintaining accurate inventory records, selecting an auditing firm, and completing a series of specific tasks. An abbreviated description of the groups of tasks include:

- Cash and investment detail with budgetary and bank reconciliations
- Receivables such as taxes, accounts, and intergovernmental transfers
- Prepaid expenses such as insurance premiums
- Inventory and its valuation
- Fixed assets including general accrued wages, pension benefits, worker's compensation, and accounts payable
- Long-term liabilities including note indebtedness, bond indebtedness, bond and coupon account reconciliation, capital leases, claims and judgments, and compensated services
- Budgetary presentations including review of budgeted revenues and appropriations prior to year end, fund consolidations, working paper schedules for budget and actual data, statements, schedules, note reconciliation, and disclosures

- Reclassification of cash transactions including revenues, expenditures, capital outlay debt service, transfers, advances, and other financing sources and uses
- Trial balances, journal entries, and posting of cash[8]

Auditing

The concept of an audit is a logical part of the idea of the state's responsibility for public education and its accountability to the public. Auditing is the study of an accounting system in general, and specific accounts in particular, to verify their accuracy and completeness. Since states specify much of the accounting system used in most school districts, audits usually include checks on the legality of expenditures as well as the accuracy of the many entries and calculations.

Audits can be classified by at least two criteria. In terms of time sequences, audits can be described thusly:

- *Pre-audits* are conducted before a transaction is completed. In this type, accounts are checked to see if expenditures are proper and/or within the appropriation. Initiating the encumbrance procedure is a type of preaudit.
- *Post-audits* are conducted after a series of transactions has been completed. Usually the annual audit by a certified public accountant hired by the board at the end of a fiscal year or a periodic audit by a state auditor is considered a post-audit.
- *Continuous audits* are conducted by very large organizations to ascertain net worth or cash flow. School systems with computer capability might conduct their own continuous audits, especially if unique fiscal problems require monitoring the flow of revenues and expenditures.

The organizational affiliation of the auditor makes possible another classification of audits:

- *Internal audits* are conducted by individuals within the organization. In school systems this might be done (and sometimes mandated by the state) by a designated official reporting directly to the board of education, e.g., the secretary, clerk, treasurer, or comptroller. Usually someone on the superintendency team will verify the figures of the accounts in order to prepare various financial reports. Both of these constitute a form of internal audit.
- *External audits* are conducted by individuals from outside the school system. These may be private auditors employed by the board or state, regional, and federal auditors checking on legal conformity to the particular governmental requirements.

Auditors' reports are not designed exclusively to find crooks and embezzlers. Instead, they can be used by school officials to improve practices and build bridges of confidence with the community and professional staff. Educational needs can be evaluated with more confidence if this kind of assurance of validity is provided.

If computers are used in accounting and auditing, an audit trail must be established so that actual documents are available for each major step in the processing of the transaction.

Given the differentiation between internal and external auditing, the school business administrator's responsibility here is twofold. The administrator frequently has the responsibility of seeing that internal audits are conducted, in order to ensure the adequate functioning of the financial and business system and also to monitor the system to provide planning data to the administrative team. The status of the several funds and accounts and the cash flow will determine, for example, whether money should be borrowed to meet the October payroll, or whether a short-term investment in Treasury Bills is possible.

The responsibility of the business administrator and other fiscal officers is indirect and supportive in cases of external audits. Especially in state-mandated audits, the business administrator's activities are usually limited to providing the external auditor with ready access to information needed. Auditors need not only the accounts and previous financial reports, but also supportive information such as the vouchers, the minute book of the board of education (showing resolutions and authorizations for financial transactions), the school district policy manual and personnel records (showing certification and eligibility of personnel for various positions at given salary levels), the insurance register (showing policies covering only insurable risks), and the like.

In recent years state-mandated auditing has included student activity accounts because these have been judged to be "public monies," even if not generated from public taxes. External audits of student activity accounts are made in essentially the same way as external audits of conventional school district funds. However, because of the involvement of many teachers, and even students, in the accounting process, the school business administrator needs to provide much care and supervision in order to prevent teachers from using loose accounting procedures that might result in subsequent auditors' findings being lodged against the student activities accountant.

Reporting

The accounting and auditing processes have to do with generating and verifying information pertaining to the financial status of the school system. Reporting deals with disseminating the information to persons or offices that can use it to upgrade their understanding and concomitant decision making in school matters. The reporting aspect of accounting is extremely important, and without adequate reporting nearly all else that goes before has little impact on understanding, decision making, or planning. As a result, the accounting system should be considered as part of a total information system. Accounting reports are output from the accounting subsystem and input to other sub- and suprasystems.

Recent years have brought a sharply increased demand for information in all aspects of school affairs, particularly school business administration. The accountability movement demands answers to myriad questions. School administrators are thus faced with the general question: What is accountable to whom, for what, and in what way? This question suggests the necessity of developing a systematic overview of the entire school operation with responsibilities, roles, and relationships clearly allocated and delineated. In addition, it requires a management information system to disseminate appropriate information throughout the operation. Financial accounting and auditing data are important components of the lifeblood of the school organization.

Comprehensive Annual Financial Report

A relatively new format for reporting financial conditions of school systems has been developed in response to demands for greater detail and clarity of financial data. Parallel to these demands is the concern for financial reports that also enable reasonable comparability among school systems within and between states. These demands stimulated the publication of *Governmental Accounting, Auditing, and Financial Reporting* by the Governmental Finance Officers Association.[9] Of particular interest to school systems is the *comprehensive annual financial report* (CAFR). The format of CAFR utilizes GAAP to ensure interschool system comparability.

Because the report is not only comprehensive but also interpretative it is well suited to the general public and others who are not oriented to conventional accounting concepts and terminology. The major elements of the report include:

1. Introductory Section (developed by the school system)
    a. Letter of transmittal
    b. List of officials
    c. Organization chart
2. Financial Statements
    a. Combined—all government fund types
    b. Combining—all special revenue funds
    c. Individual fund schedules
3. Notes to the Financial Statements—explanatory materials
4. Single-Audit Section—schedule of federal financial assistance
5. Statistical Section—school system data presented in tabular form

The report is to be printed and distributed to appropriate officials and agencies.[10]

Supplementary information included in a CAFR provides a context for the reader that helps in the interpretation of the accounting data. This information includes:

- General governmental expenditures by function
- General revenues by source
- Property tax levies and collections
- Assessed and estimated actual value of taxable property
- Property tax rates of all overlapping governments
- Special assessment collections
- Ratio of net general bonded debt to assessed value and net bonded debt per capita
- Computation of legal debt margin
- Computation of overlapping debt
- Ratio of annual debt service for general bonded debt to total general expenditure
- Revenue bond coverage
- Demographic statistics
- Property value, construction, and bank deposits

- Principal taxpayers
- Miscellaneous statistics

The CAFR developed by the Southwestern City School District is characterized by its introductory statement:

> *The comprehensive annual financial report is presented in four sections: introductory, financial, single audit and statistical. The* introductory section *includes this transmittal letter, the school district's organizational chart and a list of principal officials. The* financial section *includes the general purpose financial statements and schedules, as well as the auditor's report on the financial statements and schedules. The government is required to undergo an annual single audit in conformity with the provisions of the Single Audit Act of 1984 and U.S. Office of Management and Budget Circular A-128, Audits of State and Local Governments. Information related to this single audit, including the schedule of federal financial assistance, is included in the* single audit section *of this report. The* statistical section *includes selected financial and demographic information, generally presented on a multi-year basis.*[11]

The increased intervention of, and hence accountability to, federal and state educational agencies has placed more pressure on school systems for accounting and auditing data. Developments within the local school system itself have also exacerbated the situation. Teacher organizations in their negotiation processes demand revenue and expenditure data. Citizens, clients, and taxpayer groups have taken advantage of long-standing public access and more recent sunshine law provisions.

School systems have acted to meet both legal and moral responsibilities to provide the data. As the superintendency team and site-based management concepts are adopted and flourish, the increased interdependency among these units demands full and free exchange of information in order to make the best decisions within the given circumstances.

Considering reporting from this posture, we can look at reporting to external agencies and internal units within the school system.

External Reporting

Federal and state law, along with policy, dictate what data, and in what format, must be reported to external agencies. Federally funded programs usually specify the accounting procedure to be used in describing the financial status and transactions made in connection with their grants. Probably the most important decision for the school business administrator (once involvement in the federally funded program is ensured) is how the specified accounting responsibility is to be executed. The total information system perspective is helpful as the school business administrator plans for a flow of school system information relevant to the data required in the federal specifications. In essence, this process requires the integration of local data and data channels with the required data and procedures.

Much the same is true for state-mandated financial reports. However, in most school districts the information system for the local district is structured around the state mandates. Thus, the monthly financial report for the board members usually uses the same data, format, and terminology as required in monthly or annual financial reports that the school system must file with the state education or finance department.

Financial reports to local agencies or groups are not usually limited to those mandated by the state. Thus, local boards and administrators have considerable freedom in providing data for their own design for these groups. Most school systems are required to publish or make available some kind of an annual financial statement or report. In addition, school boards frequently integrate this with an annual, or "state of the school system" report, to inform citizens of the status, problems, and accomplishments of the system. A considerable amount of interpretation of both program and finances is included.

Special reports of the fiscal status of the educational enterprise are frequently generated to illustrate the need to issue construction bonds, pass tax levies, and enact other public policy related to fiscal affairs. Unfortunately, the public often perceives such reports as attempts to inform only when the school has a predetermined solution and needs public ratification in the form of additional allocations. Out of this perception has grown the public demand for greater accountability on a continuous rather than a sporadic, crisis-oriented basis. With an understanding of school accounting, the school business administrator can satisfy the public demand for accountability by helping the administrative team design and develop meaningful kinds of reports that can relate the school system to the community in the most open and honest sense possible.

Public demand has had the effect of increasing the flow of mandated reports on programs in general, and financial information in particular. At the local school district level, administrators have become sensitized to the fact that citizens desire information above and beyond that which is typically provided by the board of education and the administration. School business administrators are called upon to make information available (and understandable) to individuals and citizens' groups. Under sunshine and open records laws, data are on the public record, available to all. This concept of responsible fiscal reporting is quite different from an earlier one limited only to meeting the letter of the law.

Other factors that call for the broadening of the reporting function are those related to increased involvement of the following processes in decision making: participative management, the establishment of common data bases in negotiation processes, the advent of new decision processes (such as PPBES) that call for different aggregations of data (costs by program rather than by object), and the necessity to make unusual and very difficult financial decisions (such as which schools should be closed because of declining enrollments and rapidly escalating costs). All the items of this incomplete list imply that much more financial and accounting data must be generated, ordered, and interpreted to ensure that needs and demands are met.

Internal Reporting

The internal reports that involve school accounting can also be perceived as one aspect of an information system. It is in this form that accounting can best be described as a planning tool for the superintendency team. If administrators in the office of the superintendent think of themselves as a team, and if they see their roles and behaviors in an interactive milieu, then it follows that each must have access to the data as well as the thinking of the others. Thus, the accounting system must provide data of a financial nature to each member of the team. These data are (1) indigenous to each member's responsibility and (2) relevant to all other operations of the school system and sufficient to provide a financial context for their programmatic character.

Furthermore, it is important that information regarding the nature of all available data and the channels that may be used to obtain it be made available to the whole team. In this way, accounting information is accessible to but does not inundate a whole staff, many of whom do not want or cannot use it at a given time.

Planning and decision making can be expedited through optimizing the quality and availability of relevant data. The school business administrator fulfills team responsibility not only by providing appropriate information, but also by integrating his/her data production process into the larger information systems at federal, state, and local levels. A significant move in this direction has been made by the U.S. Department of Education, with its development and publication of the State Educational Records and Reports Series. In addition to *Financial Accounting: Classifications and Standard Terminology for Local and State School Systems* (1973), other handbooks have been developed for property accounting, school activity accounting, and staff accounting. These handbooks establish uniform definitions and classification systems that provide a great deal of help to state and local administrators who seek to upgrade quality and uniformity of data among the several levels of government. Generally accepted accounting procedures and the comprehensive annual financial report described earlier are excellent tools to disseminate these kinds of data.

Summary

School accounting requirements and current practices have been drawn from the accounting arts and sciences developed in the business and public administration sectors. This chapter describes the function and objectives of school accounting. Principles of accounting are reviewed in order to afford an overview of the fundamental concepts and terminology and thus provide a school business administrator with sufficient knowledge to understand the data and reports generated by the school system accountant. The accounting equation is reviewed to provide an understanding of assets and liabilities. The process of accounting is reviewed in order to acquaint the reader with the concept of debits and credits and the interaction in the flow of transactions. The ten basic steps in the accounting cycle are applied to school business transactions in order to give a sense of sequence. Adaptation of the principles to contemporary manual, automatic, or machine accounting results in very complex and rapid processing. Few, if any, school business administrators have responsibility for actually operating such equipment. However, a knowledge of the accounting principles will enable him/her to read, analyze, and interpret the data and reports produced by such machines. In this way the school business administrator has the information needed to initiate, design, and implement plans in the school business sphere.

The accounting data generated provide the raw material for auditing and reporting. Audits are used internally (pre-audits) to monitor financial affairs. Post-audits are conducted after the fact to determine the accuracy of the system and the propriety of the transactions. Both audits and reports are important to maintain accountability and credibility in both the state and local communities.

Suggested Activities

1. Obtain a copy of your state system of classification of accounts and compare it with the accounting system being used by a local school system in your state. If there are variations between the two, try to account for them.

2. In many states the accounting responsibility is vested in an office other than that of the school district official. Find out how this responsibility is designated in your state. How does this affect the responsibility of the school business administrator?

3. Obtain a copy of a monthly financial report of a board of education. From it develop an interpretation that could be understood by a reasonably perceptive layperson.

4. With the cooperation of an accountant in a local school system business office, select a given transaction and trace an audit trail on it from its initiation to its final disposition.

Suggested Readings

Adams, Bert K., Quentin M. Hill, Allan R. Lichtenberger, Joseph A. Perkins, Jr., and Philip S. Shaw. *Principles of Public School Accounting.* State Educational Records and Reports Series: Handbook 11-B. Washington, DC: U.S. Government Printing Office, 1967.

American Institute of Certified Public Accountants. *Accounting and Financial Reporting by Governmental Units, Statements of Position 80-2.* New York: AICPA, 1980.

Drebin, Allan R. "Government versus Commercial Accounting: The Issues." *Government Finance,* 8 (Nov. 1979).

Hay, L. E. *Accounting for Governmental and Municipal Entities.* Homewood, IL: Irwin, 1980.

Lynn, E. S., and R. F. Freeman. *Fund Accounting: Theory and Practice.* Englewood Cliffs, NJ: Prentice-Hall, 1983.

Municipal Finance Officers Association. *Governmental Accounting, Auditing, and Finance Reporting Principles.* Chicago: MFOA, 1979.

Roberts, Charles T., and Allan R. Lichtenberger. *Financial Accounting: Classification and Standard Terminology for Local and State School Systems.* Washington, DC: Office of Education, U.S. Department of Health, Education, and Welfare, 1973.

Notes

1. Bert K. Adams, Quentin M. Hill, Allan R. Lichtenberger, Joseph A. Perkins, Jr., and Philip S. Shaw, *Principles of Public School Accounting,* State Educational Records and Reports Series: Handbook 11-B (Washington, DC: U.S. Government Printing Office, 1967), 260.

2. Sam B. Tidwell, *Financial and Managerial Accounting for Elementary and Secondary School Systems* (Chicago: Association of School Business Officials, 1974), 35.

3. Ibid., 76–77.

4. See Tidwell, *Financial and Managerial Accounting for Elementary and Secondary School Systems,* pp. 108–110, for more comprehensive discussion of cash, accrual, and modified accrual systems.

5. Thomas E. Fergusen, *Uniform School Accounting System—User Manual* (Columbus, OH: State of Ohio, Bureau of Inspection and Supervision of Public Offices, 1976).

6. Bernard F. Gatti, "ASBO's Certificate of Excellence Program: 15 Years of Professional Excellence," *School Business Affairs, 53,* 10 (Oct. 1987), 43.

7. Ibid.

8. Carroll L. McCammon (Ed.), *Ohio School Business Administration Manual* (Westerville, OH: Ohio School Boards Association, 1989), 77–79.

9. Municipal Finance Officers Association, *Governmental Accounting, Auditing and Financial Reporting* (Chicago: MFOA, 1968).

10. McCammon, *Ohio School Business Administration Manual,* 79.

11. South-Western City School District, *Comprehensive Annual Financial Report for the Fiscal Year Ended June 30, 1989* (Grove City, OH: South-Western City School District, 1989), 15.

_8_

Personnel and Payroll Administration

AN INTEGRAL PART of classified (noncertified) personnel and payroll administration is the establishment of and adoption by the board of a philosophy supporting its application within the school district. This philosophy must include such elements as: selection, training, retention, and promotion of classified staff based on ability; establishment of detailed job descriptions; implementation of the principles of human relations in dealing with staff members; provisions for an equitable salary and fringe benefit package; and the establishment of an appeals procedure for employees.

Planning plays a key role in the development of an effective and efficient way to administer classified personnel in any school district. Proper attention to classified personnel is often not provided due to lack of understanding of their role in an organization dominated by certified employees. Classified personnel ranging from custodians to accountants provide a major challenge to the school business administrator, who is often responsible for this phase of personnel administration in the district.

Challenges of Personnel Administration

The ability to administer any program in a period of unparalleled change is a major concern to the school business administrator. With resource reallocation and/or decline, reduction of personnel, aging buildings, penetrating questions of the value and outcomes of education, and decreased or at least questioning public support of education, to maximize the appropriate use of all personnel is a primary accomplishment. Equality of opportunity for all employees is the cornerstone of an effective personnel management program. The success of effective organizational productivity lies in creative, innovative staff development programs. These, of course, must be coupled with appropriate professional staff activities as the goals for the system are sought.

F. W. Taylor noted that human variability and performance can be used to discover better ways of doing work.[1] The school business administrator can testify to the truth of this assertion. It is in the administrator's office that technically oriented persons, clerically oriented persons, and supervisors of skilled and nonskilled employees must come together to discuss and work out common problems. Personnel reporting directly to the school business administrator are often of such different backgrounds and varying interests that personnel administration taxes the most ardent advocate of better human relations.

The school business administrator generally works with the classified personnel in the district, while certified personnel administration is carried out through the office of the assistant superintendent for personnel or by the superintendent in small systems. The school business administrator must manage his/her own office and may also be responsible for selection of custodial, service, and clerical personnel for individual schools, although the building principal generally is charged with direct supervision.

A plan for personnel classification is a logical outgrowth of the adoption of the philosophy of personnel administration by the district. The classification plan provides guidelines for recruitment, selection, orientation, in-service training, evaluation, promotion, and termination for all classified employees. The classification plan groups similar duties and responsibilities into common classes, hence the term *classified* personnel. This simplifies recruitment and examination processes by using common plans for performance tests and facilitates the formulation of common benefit packages and common evaluation procedures.

Labor-Management Relations

Today's management views on organized labor are considerably more sophisticated and far less emotion-laden than during the past few decades. Major changes have affected employment relationships and contributed to the lessening of overt anti-unionism. Findings from behavioral science research have led to an employee-centered management approach that was previously unknown. Far greater worker expectations have been fostered by a new social climate derived in part from a growing level of education and the spread of the world's most ambitious communications network. The old-time owner/manager holding a major exclusive proprietary interest in the business has now been substantially displaced, succeeded by the hired administrator oriented toward management as a profession. Finally, the right of workers to organize and bargain collectively free of employer restraint or coercion has been protected by statutes since the mid-1930s.[2]

While the preceding paragraph is not related directly to educational negotiations and management/labor relationships, its salient points indicate that there is more concern about overall employer/employee relations than had previously been accepted or encouraged by either side. Even though accommodation is the dominant attitude in many educational administrator-employee relationships, there are still at least six different types of philosophies that can be distinguished in the area of management-labor negotiations. These include:

1. *Conflict:* the intrinsic, uncompromising attitude that is now fading from the labor relations scene

2. *An armed truce attitude:* where employer representatives are motivated by what is in essence a workable advisory relationship

3. *Power bargaining:* where any relationships are focused on the balance of power, which is again generally considered in today's labor relations activity to be an untenable relationship

4. *Accommodation:* where the management view is still riveted on the traditional agenda of collective bargaining and there is a self-conscious employer unwillingness to discuss officially anything that cannot rather rigidly be construed as falling within these topics

5. *Cooperation:* involving full acceptance of the union as an active partner in formal plan, a decidedly rare occurrence

6. *Collusion:* behind-the-scenes negotiations leading to the success of more union-management harmony, in which employers have been known to bribe union officials to agree to bargaining table concessions and substandard contracts and sometimes to waive the formality of actually having a contract altogether[3]

Contemporary challenges to labor-management relations are numerous and varied. Unions are faced with declining numbers and changing characteristics of their membership. The interests of older and younger members differ, with older workers usually preferring increased benefits while younger workers often are most interested in wages. Minorities are not interested in seniority systems that hinder promotions and wage increases. Members of some professional groups value their status as individuals more than they do communal membership in a union. In general, most union membership has declined and public support is less strong than in previous periods. School business administrators need to note that the new inclusion of women in the labor market is likely to increase. For instance, in 1975, 40 percent of all U.S. women were in the labor market. By 1990, 61 percent of all U.S. women are expected to be in the labor market, and of the estimated 20 million employees expected to be added to the labor force, 11 million will be women. Substantial numbers of new applicants for jobs—even those not usually filled by women—will be female. Insurance concerns, flexible work schedules, and leave provisions are often substantially different for female employees than for males. Contract negotiations will need to reflect those differences.[4]

Additionally, the concept of site-based management often conflicts with general provisions that unions wish to include in contracts to cover services to the district as a whole. As will be seen in other sections, site-based labor-management conflicts often flow from contracted differences and from the attempt to use grievance procedures to extend (from a union perspective) or to loosen (from a management perspective) basic contract provisions.

Relationships of Subordinators and Subordinates

The general line-and-staff organizational chart of any school district shows the formal superior/subordinate relationships existing in the organization but often fails to show the actual organizational operating procedures, or the *informal* organizational structure for the system.[5] It is imperative that the proper superior/subordinate relationship be established in terms of the district's operational goals. Job competence and the ability to relate to other persons are important considerations when selecting staff applicants, but the weight of each factor often needs to be considered in specific instances within a district.

Concern for the individual is a basic part of any plan for better human relations with individual employees. Today's effective administrator recognizes the goals of the organization, the needs of people, and the effects of social and technological change in organizing a plan of operation that allows for variability among groups and yet shows concern for the individual.

When conflict develops, it is probably because groups (or individuals) have different and/or incompatible views. One often encounters these differences over such issues as wages, working conditions, and fringe benefit packages. Conflicts also often emerge as policy issues between board members and classified staff, between classified staff and community groups, and between classified staff and students. However, the school business administrator is most often engaged in managing conflict relative to the distribution of resources, including budget allocations, assignment of service staff, allocation of space, and/or issues of autonomy. Many of these conflicts emerge from professional negotiations and resulting contract disputes.

The expanded role of the school business administrator into conflict management often comes as a result of a team approach to the solution of problems by the district administration. The need to diagnose the degree of conflict and avoid serious results is a major factor in effective conflict management.[6] The old idea that if only one side wins, then neither side actually wins is a sound basis for conflict resolution. Collaboration, bargaining, and to some degree avoidance are all useful techniques in the appropriate setting.

In a time of difficult decision making, reduced budgets, and impasse situations among teachers and classified personnel at all levels, administrators are under tremendous stress from all sides. Parents demanding better education, school board members demanding accountability, and state boards of education mandating basic skills improvement have created a stressful situation where most school administrators are under significant pressures in the day-to-day environment in which they work. The standard stress management techniques of business and industry are certainly applicable and should be examined by the school business administrator and building principals responsible for the administration function.[7] These activities follow lines of good mental health. While a discussion of this material would be too broad for this text, it is important to note that administrative personnel maintain a proper perspective on their job, provide for themselves appropriate recreational and non–work-related activities, and provide a proper balance between job-related and non–job-related social and other functions.

Final contract determination does not mean that all issues are resolved until the contract expires. In reality the signing signals only the beginning of the usage and implementation of the document. Problems often emerge relative to the application and especially the interpretation of selected clauses of the agreement. The mechanism that allows for continuing the bargaining process during the life of the contract is the grievance procedure. The school business administrator is often a part of a grievance panel and may well be making interpretations for management in contract applications for such employees as custodians, food service personnel, and so forth. Contract administration is a joint responsibility of the union and of management.

Personnel Planning and Recruitment

Job Analysis

It is in the area of personnel planning and recruitment that the school business administrator can be of significant assistance to the total school district. Nothing needs detailed analysis more than the general question of what transpires in a school district, from the local school to the operations at the central office. It is imperative that district personnel constantly evaluate the requirements and responsibilities of each particular job.

Job Descriptions

A detailed job description is a must for each specific position within a school district, from data entry personnel to superintendent. Certain job descriptions are more routine, more easily established, and involve fewer nebulous statements than others. However, it must be realized that all job descriptions must be as detailed as possible and must be written clearly, so that the interviewer and the interviewee are able to evaluate the requirements of the position.

Job descriptions are developed from job analyses and detail the specific activities, responsibilities, and requirements of the position. These guidelines include skills necessary, types of responsibility, and limitations imposed by the job. Federal, state and local fair employment practices must always be considered in developing job descriptions. The more detailed the job description, the fewer the problems generally associated with the determination of whether a prospective employee fits. Following is a description of custodial duties for a large school system.

   I. Custodial Duties

      Custodial personnel of the public schools are responsible for:

        A. Cleaning, heating, minor maintenance and maintaining. . . .

        B. Providing services (cooperatively arrived at between the principal and head custodian) to the faculty and student body.

  II. Custodial Responsibility during the School Year

        A. During the school year the head custodian is directly under the supervision of the principal. In schools where there is more than one custodian, custodial helpers and maids are responsible to the principal through the head custodian. The head custodian is responsible to the principal for:

           1. Cleanliness and minor maintenance of the building.

           2. Heating the building.

        B. During the school year, custodians are responsible for providing certain services to teachers and the student body that are. . . .

 III. Custodial Responsibility during Summer Months

      All custodians who are on duty during the summer months are under the direction of the Director of Plant Operations and Maintenance, who will deploy them in. . . .

The final makeup of a job description can be influenced by the results of union agreements or civil service contracts in effect within the district. In areas of high unionization the slightest alteration in a job description requires union agreement or at least becomes a subject for negotiation at the time of the next bargaining session. Until that time the job description has to remain unchanged. Legislation has restricted such statements as ''male only'' or ''under 25 years of age'' in job listings and descriptions.

Personnel Selection

Supply and demand often influence personnel selection. The adage ''select the best person for the job'' is certainly not wrong, nor is it to be cast aside. It may be better to leave a position unfilled than to fill it with an improperly trained person or a person with a poor or unrealistic attitude toward the job or the world of work in general. No effort should be spared to select competent personnel and to compensate them adequately.

Personnel selection procedures should be detailed and available for review as part of general school board policy and procedures. Proper affirmative action practices must always be followed. In several states, laws have been adopted requiring that certain city school districts secure personnel classes from approved civil service lists. These lists are constructed from test results and personnel records for use by all governmental units. Where appropriate, some positions—nurse, engineering technician, and the like—require the applicant to hold a state license. Also, some positions may be covered under union agreements requiring the appropriate apprentice, journeyman, or craftsman designation. This brings about uniformity of pay scale across all agencies and is generally combined with a detailed employee classification structure.

Depending on the type and use of local board policy, building principal input into the selection of noncertified staff will vary. In those systems where major site-based expenditures are authorized by the principal, selection of personnel may be a major responsibility.

If personnel selection is a local function directed by the building principal, then the role of the school building administrator may be one of advertising, initial screening, contract interpreting, and so forth, as opposed to actual selection and placement of personnel. The varying responsibilities dictated by the two different roles certainly require different administrative application by the school business administrator.

The application of Title IX and affirmative action guidelines to the selection of employees for school districts clearly revolves around the need to avoid discrimination claims relative to sex and minority group hiring practices established by state, federal, and local authorities. The adherence to the published standards of affirmative action developed by the local school district and approved by the appropriate governmental bodies provides the basis for the school business administrator's selection process. The nondiscriminatory factors of Title IX relative to equal facilities, equal opportunities, equal access, and so forth for both male and female participants in any kind of selection process as well as the necessary affirmative action hiring practices relative to race, sex, handicapping conditions, and such must be strictly adhered to by the school business administrator. Care must be taken to ask only for appropriate information from a potential employee. Certain questions such as marital status and expected length of employment cannot be asked. However, questions related to job skills are appropriate. The Age Discrimination and Employment Act, which covers employers of twenty or more people in private organizations is designed to protect people who are at least forty years of age but under seventy from age discrimination in terms of replacement by younger workers or in terms of reduction of benefits or loss of tenure time and pension support through discriminatory firing practices. Presently there is no upper age limit for public employees. This act is only one of a recent group of such acts that have been concerned with producing equality among workers in terms of the general concerns of sex, race, marital status, and so forth.

Nothing is more damaging to a school district's reputation than a board of education that personally intervenes in personnel selection, recruitment, and/or retention of staff members, instead of setting policies for these activities. Once again, the school business administrator should exert whatever professional influence he/she can to be certain that proper personnel policies are established at the board of education level and that proper personnel selection is carried out within his/her own department.

Orientation, Training, Development, and Motivation

Job Orientation

Job orientation is a key element of success in any employment program. Proper instructions, job descriptions, and job analyses all give the newly hired staff member a way to orient himself/herself with what is expected and required to be successful in the position. An organization of any size should have a detailed orientation program. A specific plan should be implemented to introduce the new employee to the various functions of the organization. This gives the person ''a feel'' for who does what, why it is done, and how this fits into the overall operation of an effective school district. It is imperative that the orientation program be developed to such an extent that the person is made to feel important as a viable part of the organization, rather than ''just a certain person at a certain desk in a certain row.''

Material covered in an orientation session includes information on employee welfare, such as the district's fringe benefit package, insurance, sick leave and/or maternity policy, vacation schedules, and medical and hospital benefits. Additional points to be covered include job-related information on promotion policy, grievance procedures, and the manner in which jobs are classified and defined. A copy of the school board policy manual should be available to all employees. Detailed information as to the nature of the specific position being filled and its role in the system should be offered.

Job Training

The training of employees to be efficient in the school district is an important element of any successful program. The cost of training both old and new employees is extremely expensive and has been estimated nationwide for all types of employees to be approximately 140 billion dollars annually. The most basic and perhaps simplest training program is orientation for new employees. Usually, very little job-related material is presented; emphasis is on introductory information and housekeeping procedures, with the main purpose being to make employees feel comfortable in adjusting to their new work surroundings, particularly in the department or area in which they are assigned. The most important aspect of training, however, may be that which goes beyond the orientation phase and becomes a complicated process of technique and motivation as employees are persuaded to discard inefficient practices and learn new, more productive skills.

A logical beginning point to determine training requirements is the labor planning process. This is accomplished through job analysis, which defines appropriate knowledge in skill areas and performance appraisals that indicate how adequately these have been attained. Yet another approach in determining training needs is to review other organizational records, such as the results of accident reports; grievances; principal, student, teacher, and parent complaints; and employee attitude surveys, assessment center results, and skills test analyses.

Once the training needs analysis has been completed, the question of priority always arises. Since no school system has unlimited financial resources, the human resources department can cope with only a specific number of training programs. When the school board and/or superintendent's staff has set priorities, the next step is to choose the appropriate training methods.

Perhaps the most widely accepted training method is *on-the-job training,* usually conducted by the supervisor in the particular area in which the training is to occur. Pretraining steps include establishment of time tables to learn the skills, breaking the job into learning segments, having all materials available, and arranging a workplace as the employee would find it. The training steps include putting learners at ease and determining present skill levels, presenting the materials to be learned by questioning and repeating, having the employees perform the steps and explain them putting the employees on their own, and continuing to monitor their performance on a reduced basis as more comfort and success are evidenced within the program.[8]

Internships combining on-the-job training with classroom instruction ranging from local classes taught by in-house personnel to university and/or technical school faculty are another method of instructing and conducting training.

Apprenticeship training is similar to training occurring separate from the actual workplace but with similar equipment. It is often referred to as *vestibule training* in that it involves both on- and off-job site learning.

Probably the newest and most efficient, as well as one of the most promising, training techniques is computer-assisted instruction. The majority of such computer programs adjust the instruction to the level of the student, and material is selected to provide the student with the most beneficial format. The flexibility of computerized learning and computerized training is limited only to the complexity of the software that can be developed. In many instances computerized training can be developed for use with regular employees, learning-disabled employees, and employees with physical disabilities.

However, after the training program has been accomplished by whatever appropriate methods selected, the final step is to evaluate what has been accomplished. A training program should have taught the desired knowledge, and the new skills should result in the anticipated outcome at the workplace. Evaluation can be obtained very simply by taking a measurement before the training and then another afterward to determine difference. The cost benefits of new skills can be compared with the cost of the training program to determine a rough approximation of the benefits.[9]

Employee Development

As important as personnel planning and recruitment are to the overall development of an effective program within a school district, the development of employees once they are members of the organization is even more significant. The expenditures made on staff selection, orientation, and recruitment can be wasted if an effective developmental program is not established for the total school district and for those specific areas considered. These functions can be reinforced through the effective implementation of evaluation procedures and through proper overall personnel supervision.

Job obsolescence is a recent phenomenon for school districts and is directly related to the fact that more and more jobs have become technically oriented. Many of the operations responsibilities of the school district now are highly technical or involve at least a minimum amount of technical ability. The need for more general-purpose custodial staff and simply more people to do a job has vanished from public school settings as from other industrial and private sector situations. Many of the jobs performed by sweepers, cleaners, and painters, which required little or no technical capability, have now been replaced by positions of maintenance engineering personnel for which much technical expertise is required.

Economic necessity and better health care have combined to extend the work career of many school system employees. The desire of many employees to retire early has been tempered by the economic problem of retirement living. Furthermore, many people who wish to work at a second career are unable to find such employment and are keeping jobs for longer periods. While this reduces the cost of recruitment and training, it increases basic payroll costs and reduces the flow of new ideas (through personnel) into the organization.

In-service training, while as old as the concept of the professionally trained teacher, continually challenges the school district to select meaningful and rewarding experiences for its employees. Such programs are generally planned for the central office professional personnel and the teaching staffs of school districts but are often overlooked for classified and technical personnel. In-service training, or, more properly, staff renewal (given the proper philosophical and managerial foundations) can be quite useful in upgrading skills and developing knowledge that staff members lack when they come to an organization. Released-time may be provided for the attendance of these functions, and incremental pay schedules may be based on completion of certain predetermined courses or experiences. While specific prerequisites for every step of upgrading staff cannot always be identified as precisely as those for the CPS, rewarding and meaningful experiences can be provided when some thought and preparation are involved in their selection.

It is important that staff members be involved in determining these areas for staff in-service or staff renewal activities. Current employees may have the expertise to conduct certain classes or demonstrate the use of certain types of equipment. It is not an unusual practice to invite selected personnel from other divisions within the school system to give meaningful presentations in the staff renewal process. Cost and time considerations may make the use of in-house personnel desirable.

With continued pressure to maximize the use of scarce school system resources, the concept of shared resources for staff renewal activities is widely used. This can entail cooperation by educational cooperatives, boards of cooperative educational services, and independent districts or can simply be a shared experience between two adjacent districts.

Often experiences can be structured to use key personnel for larger groups at no additional cost or to use local personnel as team leaders for group discussions.

A feature of staff renewal programs that has gained national attention is the point system, or variable unit program. Under this plan, numerous opportunities—short courses, college credit work, travel, regular in-service days, and so forth—are assigned "points" based on a determination by a coordinating body of staff and administrators. Some experiences are mandatory, while others are chosen by each participant until a certain number of points is obtained. Individualization is a key consideration, and the flexibility of choices is generally welcomed by all participants.

Employee Motivation/Career Ladder

The area of employee motivation concerns all administrative personnel. A school business administrator is concerned not only with the day-to-day operations of his/her division but also with staff motivation to do the job. Motivation is directly tied to good personnel practices. For example, most employees work more efficiently if predetermined goals are set within each job description and if basic procedures for accomplishing the goals are established. If a list of available staff renewal opportunities is posted and policies on coffee breaks and lunch hours are spelled out, most employees function more effectively.

Motivation is also enhanced by the existence of salary increments based on predetermined and established criteria.[10] Established goals and responsibilities that are rewarded by promotions and pay raises are important to almost all employees. Small increments, awarded frequently, are generally more effectively used with clerical- and technical-level personnel than are yearly increments, which are more often awarded to professional-level personnel. Both spiraling wages and fringe benefits have not always accomplished the desired goal of motivation. Often these are viewed as a "right" rather than as a "reward."

Personnel Supervision

There is little question that supervision is necessary for all employees, whether it be specific, direct, and continuous, or a part of the general personnel policies of the organization. The supervision of any staff position is directly related to staff evaluation and, therefore, staff retention and/or termination. Insofar as possible, supervision should be a direct, responsive part of the organization in which the lines of supervision are open for two-way communication. Supervision is more effective when the supervisor and the boundaries of supervision are clearly identified. While supervision is distasteful to many classified personnel, it is essential to establishing an effective and well-ordered program. Supervision of any employee is always based on the job or position (as defined by the job description) for which the employee is hired. The basis of evaluation forms, questions, and so forth must be found in the job description as presented to the employee.

Veto powers of a building-level administrator are directly related to the amount of site-based control that board policy permits. With major site-based budgeting, principals traditionally have primary control over custodial, clerical, and to some degree operational staff at their site.

Staff Evaluation

All staff members are evaluated at periodic intervals. Much staff member evaluation occurs on a day-to-day basis, is informal, and is nonstructured. However, any well-structured organization has predetermined patterns for the evaluation of staff members. Whether evaluation takes the form of interviews, rating sheets, tests, or a combination of several of these, it must be done on a periodic and established basis. Figure 8-1 shows a Custodial Trainee Evaluation form for the Alexandria, Virginia, Public Schools.

Staff evaluations should be a cooperative venture. Under no circumstances should an evaluation become a "witch-hunt" procedure in which a supervisor is looking for faults in a staff member's performance. As with student evaluation, the goal is to determine areas of strength to be built upon and areas of weakness to be improved. One of the best ways to establish an evaluation policy is to provide within the policy for some degree of self-evaluation. Proper emphasis must be placed on the central activity within the staff member's job description. To give too much weight to an area that is not defined or understood by the employee to be a prime area of responsibility is unfair to the employee and is damaging to total employee-employer relations. The evaluation method must mirror the activities that are detailed in the job descriptions.

The total evaluation effort on the part of supervisors and staff members should be viewed as a constructive effort toward the improvement of the performance of the particular staff member and toward the betterment of the supervisory process under which that staff member operates. In keeping with this idea, it is well to consider that other resources beyond the local division, or even the department, may be called upon to facilitate the evaluation procedure.

In the last several years the development of job targets, work plans, and other organized schemes for planning what needs to be accomplished by individual staff members has become a major activity for many school districts. The development of each administrator's own job target or work plan for the year has become a major feature in the evaluation of most staff members within a system. The development of the work plan is a cooperative effort between the administration and the individual staff member. The supervisor and staff member determine what is expected from the staff member throughout the coming year. The year-end evaluation conference determines how successfully these goals have been met. First evaluation efforts may lead to overestimation or underestimation of employees on the part of certain staff members, but after one or two efforts, staff members come "on target."

Management by objectives (MBO) represents an umbrella approach for working with an entire organization. The key to effective use of MBO by the school business administrator and/or other members of the school administrative team is for all levels of the organization to have goals from which the objectives can emerge. Goals must be available from the very top (board) to the very bottom (employee) to be effective. The major feature of the MBO process of interest here is that the individual employee and his/her immediate supervisor agree on what the job responsibilities are and on written objectives to meet these responsibilities. A review of these objectives follows. Finally, the appraisal process occurs. The employee provides factual data on which performance can be judged. The degree of success in presenting these data then determines the reward (positive or negative) for the employee.[11]

FIGURE 8-1 Custodial Trainee Evaluation

ALEXANDRIA CITY PUBLIC SCHOOLS
Alexandria, Virginia
Department of Educational Facilities

CUSTODIAL TRAINEE EVALUATION

Employee's Name _____   Employment _____

SUBJECT	ABOVE AVG.	SATIS-FACTORY	NEEDS ADD.TRN.	COMMENTS
Personal Grooming				
Employee Relations				
Carpet Care				
Care of Equipment				
Use of Floor Buffers				
Use of Wet Mops				
Use of Dry Mops				
Use of Vacuums				
Use of Shampooers				
Floor Stripping, Sealing & Refinishing				
Spray-Buffing Techniques				
Toilet Room Cleaning and Sanitizing				
Classroom Cleaning				

Overall Evaluation: Above Avg. _____ Satisfactory _____

Needs Add. Training _____

_____

Additional Comments:

_____

Area Supervisor Signature   Date   Employee Signature

Distribution: Original to Personnel
                1 Copy to employee
                1 Copy to principal

Courtesy of Alexandria City Schools.

Promotion

Promotion policies in a school district should reward competence and experience on the part of employees and should spell out qualifications such as seniority and skill levels needed for promotion. The school business administrator and the planning team may work together to determine promotion policies for certified personnel, while the administrator alone is often directly responsible for promotion policies affecting a large number of noncertified personnel.

In many districts, union agreements determine most of the ground rules for promotion, both within a section and across division lines. Stipulations as to training, seniority, and pay schedules are covered in all union agreements insofar as these affect promotion policy. In districts where noncertified personnel are not covered by union agreements, a set of personnel policies should be established that guarantees rewards for those deserving them, yet protects the district against exploitation by certain staff members. Some employees can be covered under civil service, with the attendant rules and regulations associated with civil service appointments.

Employee Discipline

Employee discipline issues are a part of most negotiated contracts. Contract provisions discuss the types of conduct that are seen as inappropriate and spell out general codes of expected conduct including specific behavior and the results of specific behaviors (e.g., arrests, convictions). These provisions are part of the basic labor agreement, which also indicates the provisions for grievances. A portion of such a list, from the *Handbook for the Classified Personnel of the Metropolitan Public Schools, Nashville—Davidson County, Tennessee, 1988–1990,* provides examples of such agreements. Specific provisions of the agreement note:

> *An employee of the Board of Public Education shall not engage in any criminal, dishonest, infamous, immoral, or disgraceful conduct or behavior, activity or association which discredits the employee and/or the Board. Each employee is expected to conduct himself/herself both on and off the job in such a manner as to reflect credit on both himself/herself and the Board of Public Education.*
>
> *It shall be the duty of each employee to maintain high standards of cooperation, efficiency, and economy in his/her work for the Board of Public Education. Department heads or supervisors shall organize and direct the work of their units to achieve these objectives. When work habits, attitude, production, or personal conduct of an employee falls below a desirable standard, supervisors should point out the deficiency at the time it is observed. Warning in sufficient time for improvement should precede formal disciplinary action, but nothing in this section shall prevent immediate formal action whenever the interest of the Board of Public Education requires it.*
>
> *No regular employee in the classified service may be terminated, or suspended from the service, or demoted in pay grade, except for cause and after a hearing before the department head or other appointing authority.* [12]

Causes for Disciplinary Action
An employee in the Nashville Schools may be disciplined for just cause for the following actions, among others:

1. Neglect of duty.
2. Failure to perform his/her duties.
3. Inefficiency in the performance of his/her duties.
4. Any act of insubordination or disrespect toward a supervisor.
5. Excessive/habitual absenteeism.
6. Excessive/habitual tardiness.
7. Absence without notification or approval for leave. . . .[13]

Personnel Termination

Generally speaking, personnel terminations are not pleasant. However, some terminations are routine and should be viewed as such. Terminations that carry out board policies having to do with health, residency requirements, and so forth are viewed as routine policy actions and are carried out accordingly. There should be no ill will involved, nor should there be any reluctance to give the policy as the reason for termination of the employee.

As with many facets of promotion, termination procedures are often covered in union agreements. If this is the case, then most of the reasons for termination and the avenues open to both parties are outlined in detail. Alteration or abandonment of these procedures then becomes a point for litigation and/or union-management bargaining, and all situations remain static until negotiations can be conducted and completed.

In certain school districts, employment of noncertified personnel falls under civil service, and the rules and regulations associated with termination are specified. In some cases noncertified personnel may have tenure status in the school district.

In any situation involving employee termination, the school business administrator and the system's legal staff must ensure that due process is granted the staff members. As was stated in Chapter 2, an employee has every right to due process, and the school system is obligated to see that he/she is informed of rights and the avenues of appeal that may apply.

Terminations become unpleasant when a lack of productivity, a lack of ability, or an unwillingness on the part of the supervisor or the employee to work out a difference of opinion necessitates the employee's termination "with cause." The key word here is, of course, *cause.* To replace persons summarily in nonunion systems without justifiable cause is very damaging to the total morale of the school system. Though not issued formally, this kind of information will "get around." Proper review and appeal procedures should be built into board policies to cover any differences between professional and nonprofessional terminations within the system.

It should be made clear to the employee at the time of employment that there are avenues of appeal and that grievances can be pursued through legal channels. This action is a rare occurrence, but it can happen, and parties are under obligation to apprise each other of the situation. Termination within a fixed probationary period is a general feature of most employment contracts. The administration has an initial period to determine whether the employee has the necessary traits and skills to fill the job properly. Generally, the provisions for dismissal during the period are oriented toward management and are not as stringent as during a later term of employment. As always, however, dismissal should be based on concrete, documented reasons.

In the event of discharge, the following provisions regularly apply: (1) The employer will only discharge employees for just cause; (2) the employee being discharged has the right to meet with some union representative before leaving the employer's property; and

(3) if the employee or the union representative considers the discharge to be improper, a complaint normally shall be presented in writing through this representative within a specified number of working days. Generally, concerns have centered on procedural rights of persons terminated rather than the authority of schools to terminate or what is identified as substantive due process.

Contractual arrangements usually state that the employer has the right to discharge any employee for such actions as: (1) not returning from sick leave or leave of absences, (2) being under the influence of intoxicants or drugs, (3) falsifying records, (4) moral offenses, and (5) stealing board and/or other employee property. In general, the employer sends written notification to the employee at his/her last known address, stating that the employee has lost seniority and his/her employment has been terminated. In case of discharge for one of the reasons listed, a review may be possible in a special conference at a time agreed upon between the union and the employer.

Enrollment declines, fiscal and economic reductions, reorganization, reduction/elimination of positions, and other "just causes" have been ruled as appropriate reasons for a reduction in force. Generally, courts have held that a school board's good faith determination in these issues is sufficient ground for supporting the action. Strict adherence to affirmative action and Title IX guidelines are also important in termination activities.

In all situations the application of due process must be provided by the employer to the employee. Both persons have an obligation to participate in due process, and all efforts should be aimed at providing both sides with proper protection.

Retirements

An activity of business administrators that has peaks and valleys is the early retirement of staff members (certified and noncertified). Changes in state laws and/or economic conditions may result in early retirement opportunities offered by school districts. These permit employees to take either reduced benefits or full benefits based on service rather than age. In general, early retirement and the associated costs have to become a part of contracts or board policies.

Cash incentives for early retirement continue to be an option in some school districts. These are generally limited to personnel within a fixed number of years of retirement in terms of age and/or service. They provide a partial salary and continued insurance coverage. The success of these programs has been limited, with acceptance by staff (and faculty) "lukewarm." The impact of potential changes in social security retirement age limits is a concern for school business administrators but is not likely to affect most people currently employed. If changes occur, they will be phased in over time and be of limited concern for several years.

Retirement procedures among school personnel have undergone some changes. The impact of negotiated contracts countered with the loss of enrollments and revenues in many school systems has created a state of flux in the general area. One of the basic concerns of retirement is that the benefits of the retirement package are protected under the negotiated contract and that any school mergers or other alterations of the basic structure of the school system protect persons who have invested years of service in the organization. Many city or special school districts that have later merged with county or governmental units to create larger and broader-based school districts have faced this problem. An additional problem caused by budget reductions has been the need to carry an ever increasing portion of the resources allocated to the school district to provide for the retirement and, incidentally, medical and other fringe benefit packages of the large number of aging teaching and noncertified staff personnel in a district. The costs have become increasingly large as persons have held jobs for longer periods of time and as turnover in a job area has lessened. In order to deal with the problems of ''riffing'' faculty members, many school systems have elected to suggest to personnel within a given period of time prior to a normal retirement cycle that they take early retirement. This would both open a job for a younger employee and reduce the overall payroll, since younger employees generally make less money. The current federal government acceptable retirement age affects retirement plans in districts with negotiated contracts and in those districts without contracts that are covered by a general personnel policy for the next several years. The school business administrator must be attuned to these potential difficulties.

Professional Negotiations

The results of professional negotiations are felt throughout an entire school district. Negotiation activities on the part of one group of employees effect changes in the day-to-day activities as well as in the thinking of all groups within the district. The interaction of one group with another cannot be denied, nor can the direction the interaction takes be predicted. Success on the part of one group may not ensure success on the part of another group, nor does failure in one area by one group guarantee failure in that area by other groups.

Lieberman and Moskow define professional negotiations as:

> *A process whereby employees as a group and their employers make and counter offers in good faith on conditions of their employment relationship for the purpose of reaching a mutually acceptable agreement, and the execution of a written document incorporating any such agreement if requested by either party. Also, a process whereby a representative of the employees and their employer jointly determine their conditions of employment.*[14]

Negotiations have become regular features of personnel administration for the majority of school boards. School boards must be alert to the possibility of multiple kinds of negotiations, as well as the ramifications all have for the short- and long-range operation of the school district. Negotiations generally fall into the ''piecemeal'' or ''total'' approach. In the piecemeal approach, one issue at a time is considered, while in the total approach everything is settled or nothing is settled. The school business administrator may be a key member of the negotiation team of the local district. The majority of all negotiation activities have both short- and long-range fiscal results or ramifications. The administrator's fiscal expertise and knowledge will arm the board and/or other negotiation personnel with ample data on which to base decisions and/or make concrete offers, whatever type of negotiation pattern is established. However, negotiation plans and their implementation are the responsibility of the total team. The levels of negotiations most often follow a continuum from nonbinding to binding.

The data for the negotiating of contracts are specified in the master contract. On the date named the local educational agency or union and the board begin negotiations for a new agreement covering wages, hours, and terms and conditions of employment. The contracts often state that neither the local educational agency nor the union shall have any control over the selection of the negotiation or bargaining representatives of the other party and that each party may select its representatives from within or without the district. In some instances, state statute contains what can/cannot be negotiated. It is often recognized that no final agreement between the parties may be executed without ratification by a majority of either membership. However, the parties present have necessary power and authority to make proposals, consider proposals, and make concessions in the course of negotiations or bargaining, subject only to ultimate ratification. Normally the agreement may be modified only with the voluntary mutual consent of both parties in writing, signed as an amendment to the agreement. (For further information see *The Practice of Collective Bargaining* by Beal, Wickersham, and Kienart.[15])

It is hard to imagine a school district involved in complex negotiations without the assistance of the school business administrator. While the titles vary and responsibilities differ, he/she is an important player in the negotiations process.

Because so many union proposals have such a direct and often substantial impact on the local school budget, every school board must be sure it knows what the "price tag" is before agreeing to any proposal. Unions usually minimize the cost of proposals, hoping that a school board might not take the time to find out what it is being asked to pay out. Proposals for a comprehensive family dental plan, an improved longevity schedule, or payment for accumulated sick leave upon retirement can end up being quite expensive. The school business administrator is in an excellent position to tell the board about the real, not suggested, cost of these proposals. In many districts the administrator is the chief fiscal officer and can obtain the information for the board rapidly and in a manner using proper projection techniques that can show the long-term effect of such activities. Other data may be equally valuable, such as a distribution chart revealing likely future retirements. A length-of-service chart can be used to tell how much a longevity schedule pegged to service in the district would cost. One of the first steps in negotiations is to determine, for example, the current costs of persons employed and the relationship of indexing salaries or increasing health benefits to persons based on certain salary distributions and expected salary distributions based on longevity increases.[16]

The price tag of all negotiated union agreements must be known so that the total impact on a local budget, both short- and long-term, can be known. Proposals for a comprehensive family dental plan, an improved leave plan, provisions for accumulated sick leave payments or career ladder payments can have substantial costs for the next fiscal year and on into the future. These costs are generally fixed up to certain limits (e.g., cost of a system's share of family health insurance) but can be influenced by state legislative mandates. For example, state legislatures often pass enabling legislation dealing with payments for "climbing" career ladders and providing early retirement options. This legislation most often allows but does not fully fund the activity. These legislative mandates clearly affect the work of the local school business administrator. The issue seems to be magnified in those districts where large numbers of staff members are supported with local funds beyond the minimum foundation program.

The school business administrator is the key person to indicate the differences among "one-year," "real," "suggested," and "expected" costs of negotiation items. In dealing with all employee groups and in reacting to all employee questions, the ability to provide hard, clear data and to present them in an informative, understandable way is the key to dealing effectively with such issues. In addition to knowledge of the negotiation issues, one needs to know all that can be known about the negotiating terms from the union group.

Additionally, the school business administrator needs to be knowledgeable about trends in the area being negotiated. Good information properly presented strengthens the board's position. More importantly, this approach conveys the board's seriousness about covering union demands and stressing its own agenda.[17]

John Glaser, in the article "Alternative Labor Relations Practices: A Second Look" provides a list of elements of bargaining that may promote cooperation. A sampling of these is shown in Table 8-1.

Individual Negotiation

In total number of persons affected, the individual negotiation is one of the procedures least used by school districts. The vast majority of certified personnel and a similar-sized group of technical and supporting personnel in most systems are subject to some type of union, civil service, or local predetermined salary schedule. Whether the schedule is restrictive or flexible, a large percentage of persons in virtually all entry-level positions are covered by a set salary schedule. If such a schedule does not exist, it can be implied that the school board is in the business of administering the schools, rather than setting policy for its administrators to follow.

TABLE 8-1   Alternative Labor Relations Practices*

Elements of Bargaining That May Promote Conflict	Elements of Change That May Promote Cooperation
Attitudes	*Attitudes*
1. Managing is done "around the contract"	1. Managing is done "through the contract"
2. "Distributive" bargaining of separate interests with compromise only when necessary	2. "Integrative" bargaining of mutual interests
3. Mediation takes place only after impasse is formally declared	3. Informal mediation processes are built in so they happen continuously
Financial Structures	*Financial Structures*
4. Budgetary information is restricted by the district	4. Open budget processes and the introduction of financial formula
Bargaining Processes	*Bargaining Processes*
5. Bargaining is done from positions	5. Bargaining is done from problem statements
6. One person talks for each side	6. Everyone talks
7. Caucuses are frequent	7. Less frequent caucusing—groups communicate more openly
8. Frequent use of bargaining chips	8. Both sides strive for consensus/elimination of bargaining chips
9. Communications to the constituencies and general public are frequently conflicting and divisive	9. Communications with constituencies/public developed together

*Source: John Glaser, "Alternative Labor Relations Practices: A Second Look," *Thrust* (Feb./Mar.), 33–37.

Individual negotiations have a valid place in most school districts but usually pertain to key personnel such as the superintendent, selected other staff personnel, and possibly some technical employees. In elementary form, individual negotiations "boil down" to a decision between What am I offered? and What will I accept? In most districts there is a predetermined salary and fringe benefit range, and key exceptions provide override capabilities. The employee has in mind a basic salary figure set by the job market, geography, and salaries of peers. Other compensation in terms of activities, membership and other "perks" often is a major consideration in the final selection/negotiation process.

Final terms of the agreement should be subject to board approval and should be a matter of public record. Individual contracts are few, but they often cover the key employees within a district. It should also be remembered that individual negotiations often involve expenditures of funds in excess of selected fringe benefits paid directly to or for the employee, as well as extra or expanded auxiliary services such as clerical assistance, office space, or transportation.

Group Negotiations without Outside Consultation

The ability of groups of school employees, either certified or noncertified, to organize and act effectively without outside consultation is severely limited. Rarely can a single uniform goal or set of goals override personal differences to a degree that equals the cohesion and disengagement that outside consultation brings to personnel negotiations. It is unrealistic to assume that a board of education can enter into negotiation without readily available, expert consultation services. The group pursuing this avenue may soon find itself in the same position as the person who chooses to represent himself/herself in a court of law—virtually without representation.

Groups without outside consultation may prepare points for initial consideration, and key points for further consideration or confrontation may be identified, if not resolved. If time permits and the atmosphere allows, this avenue may be pursued. However, the group seeking to negotiate should not be shocked if this approach fails to bring expected results.

Group Negotiations with Outside Consultation

Outside consultation services provide expertise that is generally unavailable within most local employee groups. Professional negotiators usually have a balanced background that is useful in discussions with board representatives. Consultants can arm themselves with the pertinent information and then condense it to a set of goals and alternatives, including the extent of the demands a group is willing to seek.

The school business administrator is intimately involved in these negotiations since each result affects the funding of the school district for subsequent years. The results may be seen in salary figures, fringe benefits, and/or a multitude of other ways. Additionally, the business administrator is a prime information resource for the board throughout all negotiation considerations. The administrator's organization must be able to respond rapidly with accurate fiscal information and predictions.

The role of the school attorney in the negotiations process has taken on considerably more importance with the impact of reductions in enrollment and the need for attendant phasing out of staff. The major function served by the attorney in these areas is to interpret negotiated contracts and to certify that procedures followed are correct and appropriate. The chief negotiator for the board, often the school business administrator, must give attention to these rulings as well as have a view of the larger needs of the district. Just what can be negotiated from a budget and educational program position provides the information base for future contract work.

Administration of the Agreement

Any labor agreement establishes only the general framework for labor relations in the school system. At the time of contract signing, emphasis shifts to the actual application and administration of the contract and away from the rhetoric associated with its signing. As most negotiators agree, contract language is often broad and, to a degree, purposefully vague to allow agreement to be reached and to provide some flexibility for each side. Thus, the real success of a labor agreement rests with the day-to-day application and administration of what was signed. The climate of labor relations in any organization will, to a large degree, be determined by the extent to which the parties—the school district and whatever unions are involved—discharge their day-to-day understanding and application of the contract. The administration of the contract usually allows for some flexibility on both sides, but flexibility can create problems. Problems are then handled and settled through the grievance procedures of the labor contract which are discussed below. If, however, the bulk of bona fide labor problems cannot be solved at some level of the grievance procedure through the process of negotiation, the next step must occur—mediation or arbitration.[18]

Mediation

The techniques to resolve conflict range from relatively weak to very strong, starting with the fairly mild form—mediation—and ending with the strongest—arbitration.

Mediation has its success in settling disputes without duress. However, there are no generally accepted rules as to how to reach this resolution. Good mediators are persons who listen well. Selection of a mediator is agreed upon by both parties. Techniques of mediation are as varied as the characteristics of the mediator. The basic requirement of the mediator is that he/she be a good listener and work from a sound, basic approach to the task. Whether to meet with both sides together, how to discuss issues, what proposals to provide for consideration, and when to say an impasse exists are some of the questions with which mediators must deal. Mediators come from various sources, but all must be agreed upon by all parties. To assist both parties, the federal government provides—on a voluntary basis—the services of its Mediation and Conciliation Service.[19] Some states have added "fact finding" as a second step in the conflict-resolution process and yet removed from arbitration.

Arbitration

Arbitration is the reference of a dispute by voluntary agreement to some person judged impartial for determination of a final result.[20] The arbitration is based on information provided and arguments presented by both sides. In general, arbitration becomes an agreement by both parties that all other avenues including mediation, fact finding, and negotiation have failed. Either side may call for arbitration. Thus the arbitration is an agreement by both parties that they are willing to submit information to a disinterested third party who has no interest in the results, but whose decision will be considered to be acceptable to both parties. The costs of arbitration cover the preparation/presentation of the case, a report of the testimony, the arbitrator's fee, and administrative expenses. The major item of any arbitration is of course the cost of the arbitrator. These expenses generally are shared between the two parties. This is a negotiable fee depending on a variety of factors.

There are two kinds of arbitration—binding and nonbinding. Compliance with the award is compulsory in binding arbitration, whereas in nonbinding arbitration, compliance is optional. In nonbinding arbitration each party considers the award and makes the decision whether or not to accept it. Principally, nonbinding arbitration varies little from mediation if no final determination must be made. Since many employees fear reprisal from their employer, a no reprisal clause has become a common part of most grievance procedures. State law must be considered as the beginning point for the determination of any arbitration strategy.

Role of the School Business Administrator

The role of the business administrator on the professional negotiations team is a major concern for school districts. The role of the school business administrator in actual negotiations is determined, of course, by the board and the superintendent. He/she may be a part of the team, a consultant, or nonparticipant.

The school business administrator's responsibilities have become weightier in recent years with the advent of the new laws. The first prerequisite and responsibility for the school business administrator is the presentation of accurate data. Sunshine laws and other court decisions (e.g., *Oldbaur* v. *Drummond*, Bd. of Educ. 542 p. 2d 1309, 1310 [Okla, 1975]) indicate that all parties have the right to know and have access to certain kinds of data. What is supplied to one side must properly be supplied to the other. Information readily accessible to union negotiators must be equally accessible to the system negotiators.

The negotiated contract is designed to provide a "blueprint" for both parties. Major features of most contracts include district rights, staff and association rights, features of professional negotiations activities, and grievance procedures, as well as specifics such as vacations, transfers, leaves of absence, qualifications and assignments, conduct, disciplinary procedures, and seniority.

Contract provisions may limit management's prerogatives in personnel administration. Decisions on what can be done without union consultation and/or approval often are seriously limited by the agreement. The school board administrator must plan according to these limitations in all aspects of contract-personnel work.

Civil Service—Union Association

Any or all forms of negotiation noted previously can be used by employees working under union agreement, using their professional association as a bargaining agent, or by employees operating within civil service salary guidelines. The school business administrator is concerned with the activities of both groups because of the previously established or potential impact on the budget. The administrator must constantly keep the board apprised of future trends in the budget produced by contract items and/or the impact on the budget if requested items are granted.

Grievance Procedures

As noted earlier, grievance procedures are avenues that provide for the peaceful settlement of disputes that arise over the application or interpretation of the agreement or contract during the time it is in effect.[21]

Any grievance procedure should be handled through normal administrative channels. The general order of a grievance should be from employee to principal or immediate superior to superintendent, and finally to the board, with the principle of due process always observed. An employee should have the right to seek advice from any group he/she chooses and should always have the right of legal counsel.

More specifically, the nature of the negotiated contract will generally provide the key to all grievance procedures within the district. Whether these are procedures for contracted and noncontracted items or academic and nonacademic items, steps for grievance procedures will usually be spelled out in the contract.

A claim by the bargaining unit and/or individual is often sufficient to initiate a grievance procedure if there has been an alleged violation, misrepresentation, or misapplication of the provisions of a contract applicable to wages, hours, or conditions of employment. Grievance procedures provide for: due process for both representatives, the naming of a local representative for each side, the maintenance of grievance committees for the purposes stipulated, and the number of days indicated for each step of the procedure. Penalties are also set forth for failure of an aggrieved party to proceed from one step of the procedure to the next within the time limits. In general, grievance procedures specify a series of steps or activities that must be completed, in sequence, within a specified period of time. Both parties agree to be bound by the decision of an arbitrator, if one is called in, and agree that either party may enter judgment thereon in any court of competent jurisdiction. The use of an arbitrator is normally a last resort in the grievance procedure. Miscellaneous items occur in most grievance procedures, all of which are concerned with due process for the individual.

Each union negotiates its own grievance procedure. While there is variability in the language of contract clauses, there is much commonality in the fundamental features of a grievance procedure. Features generally specified include the following:

- What is the definition of a grievance?
- Who may initiate a grievance?
- How long does the grievant have to decide whether or not to file a grievance?
- What is the union's role in the process?
- Where should the grievance be filed?
- What are the procedural steps to follow?
- What are the timelines and deadlines?
- What is the final step?[22]

The grievance process benefits management, union members, and private citizens. Since any contract can become the focus of a dispute, ideally the grievance process provides a quick and inexpensive resolution of contractual disputes. Employees are given an opportunity to protest management decisions without fear of retribution and do so with the assistance of a union advocate. As has been noted, both parties to any labor contract have a vested interest in enforcing compliance of the terms and conditions of the agreement. While management has various discipline measures to ensure that employees honor the terms of the contract, the union must rely on the grievance procedure to enforce the contract. The union must enforce the contract or it will have little value and the union will have no power. Grievances also provide a vehicle for the union to react to management decisions and to protect the rights of employees.

The public also benefits from the grievance process because grievances are settled without disruption to the school schedule. Strikes, pickets, slowdowns, and other disruptive practices are not needed because employees accept the grievance procedure as a legitimate method of resolving differences. Consequently, disruption of the school calendar and the daily schedule of parents and students is greatly minimized.

While the benefits of grievance procedures are substantial, critics have identified several key problems. The process can be costly, time-consuming, and legalistic, and it often fails to met the needs of individual employees. This is especially true when binding arbitration is the final step. Because this quasi-legal process often involves lawyers and transcripts, a single arbitration may cost a union several thousand dollars, and a small union may not have the funds to arbitrate many legitimate grievances. When legitimate grievances are not taken to arbitration because of cost consideration, both the arbitration process and the union lose credibility.

If the best efforts of both sides fail and there is a strike, the system must be in a position to provide essential student, staff, and faculty support services necessary to maintain the health and safety of all parties. If a bus mechanics' strike makes the *safe* operation of buses questionable, then the buses should not operate. The inconvenience of no bus service does not override the safety of the child or an improperly serviced bus.

Strike contingency planning is but another role of the school board administrator. The availability of a detailed plan for dealing with the issues is the best way to ensure that the school will operate as successfully as can be expected during this emotion-charged time. Basic educational needs must be met, and every effort should be made to keep the instruction as close to normal as possible.

Personnel Budgeting

The establishment of detailed, written salary policies for all levels of employees within the school district greatly facilitates the solution of numerous personnel problems. A set salary policy for both certified and noncertified personnel is a must for effective and truly efficient operation of any school district.

Step-increment salary increase policy is the type of policy used by most school officials. Regardless of the system used, a detailed picture of the personnel budget plan is a must. Salary projections for general budgeting purposes are little better than guesses without an established framework within which to work. Staff turnover, court actions, annexation, and union agreements all have impact on salary policies within a school district. However, none of these can be allowed to set salary policy. Established policies for both certified and noncertified personnel have been identified as priority items. As previously discussed, salary policy and its implementation are important elements in staff motivation. An established and published board policy relative to salary and fringe benefits also helps a school business administrator to do his/her job more efficiently and effectively.

All states provide salary schedules for certified personnel that take training and years of experience into consideration. A bachelor's degree is the usual minimum training requirement. In lieu of a bachelor's degree, a journeyman union card or some other evidence of training/experience is often required of vocational/technical teachers. Doctorates must be from accredited colleges or universities. In general, the schedules indicate minimum salaries, which tend to be augmented in most districts. Augmenting of the state salary schedule normally occurs with increased training and experience, or increased responsibilities such as coaching, music direction, or yearbook coordination.

Fringe Benefits

Fringe benefits and their budget impact are of increasing concern to school business administrators and to the total administrative team of a district. As union agreements are negotiated, as civil service contracts are set, or as general employee contracts are established, the total dollar value of fringe benefit packages continues to grow. These benefits include vacations with pay, paid holidays, medical insurance costs for the employee and his/her family, group life and disability insurance, sick pay (leave), tax-deferred annuities, and many others. It is often possible for professional negotiators to use fringe benefits as a tradeoff against wages when a quantity discount would benefit both parties. For example, in an insurance plan where family coverage is offered but most persons choose single coverage, the value of the benefit for contract negotiation purposes may be calculated at the higher rate. In some systems a fringe benefit is available in terms of a sick leave incentive cash payment plan for persons who do not use accumulated sick leave. Extended medical care in such areas as dental services also has become a popular item. Continual attention to the direction and quantity of the growth in fringe benefit packages is an important job for the school business administrator.

Some of the fringe benefits for noncertified personnel include supplementary pay; license and dues allowance; maternity leave; personal leave; jury duty leave; military leave; health, life, accident, retirement, and disability insurance; and such miscellaneous items as meal allowances, uniform allowances, equipment usage, housing, credit union membership, automobile allowance, in-service training opportunities, and conference visitations.

In negotiations with groups of certified and noncertified personnel, the tradeoff of fringe benefits against wages is a major concern. In many instances the tax advantage of some fringes allows the employee to realize 10 or more cents on the dollar rather than the dollar value realized after taxes for each dollar negotiated in wages.

Employee Assistance Program

One of the recent innovations in employee-employer relationships has been the advent of the *employee assistance program (EAP)*. EAPs are programs that grow from a base of caring for persons as persons and also of concern for job performance and its relation to the individual employee. Under most conditions it is more desirable to rehabilitate a current employee than to recruit and train a new employee. While EAPs have greatest visibility in such areas as professional basketball drug and alcohol rehabilitation programs, they are a feature of many collective bargaining agreements.

Patterns for the EAP structure can be identified through the delivery models defined by Phillips and Older.[23] These models describe some of the more widely used program designs and are defined below.

> *Model 1:* Internal program providing one of the following:

> — Assessment and referral service
> — Assessment, referral, and counseling services
> — Internally based program services with an off-site location for assessment and referral service

> *Model 1A:* Internal program in which some or all counseling treatment and/or social services are provided within the organization

> *Model 2:* Service Center Program in which organization contracts with an independent EAP service provider

> *Model 2A:* Internal Program (with Service Center support) provides additional external Service Center resources as support, thus allowing options for assistance either on or off the work site

> *Model 3:* EAP Services located in Treatment or Social Service Agency (no internal services)

> *Model 4:* Union-based EAP in which EAP services are provided by union at the union office[24]

Summary

Planning for personnel administration is a multi-faceted feature of the school administrator's position. New developments in personnel policies and major changes in the role responsibilities of the school business administrator have created a new working environment. Changes in legislation, restructuring of collective bargaining units, and technological growth have had a significant impact. A lead role in personnel planning and recruitment as well as working in all areas of personnel development must be assumed. Participation in personnel budgeting and instructional support is visible but is seldom easily accomplished. The professional negotiation role has undergone major changes, and no end is in sight, as labor and management ideas must be blended with the ability and willingness of the public to pay. New ideas, new challenges, and new experiences are all part of the school business administrator's role in personnel and payroll administration.

Suggested Activities

1. What would be the role of the school business administrator in setting performance standards for classified positions within his/her district?

2. How does the school business administrator function as a part of the professional negotiations team? Should he/she serve in such a role?
3. What elements are needed in a plan for a reduction in force of maintenance/custodial personnel within your school district? The transportation system?
4. How is due process provided in personnel terminations in your district or school? Do social and/or gender factors have a place in such considerations?
5. How does the school business administrator plan for the institution of collective negotiations in his/her area of responsibility? For impasse situations?

Suggested Readings

Baer, Walter E. *Grievance Handling*. New York: American Management Association, 1970.
Bowin, Robert B. *Human Resource Problem Solving*. Englewood Cliffs, NJ: Prentice-Hall, 1987.
Drucker, Peter F. *The Frontiers of Management*. New York: Truman Talley Books, 1986.
Goodlad, John I. *A Place Called School*. New York: McGraw-Hill, 1984.
Greenhalgh, John. *School Site Budgeting: Decentralized School Management*. Lanham, MD: University Press of America, 1984.
Manese, Wilfredo R. *Fair and Effective Employment Testing*. New York: Quorum Books, 1986.
Rothwell, William J., and H. C. Kazanas. *Strategic Human Resources Planning and Management*. Englewood Cliffs, NJ: Prentice-Hall, 1988.
Stern, Joyce D., and Mary Frase Williams (Eds.). *The Condition of Education*. Washington, DC: U.S. Office of Educational Research and Improvement, 1986.

Notes

1. Rensis Likert, *New Patterns of Management* (New York: McGraw-Hill, 1961), 3.
2. Arthur A. Sloane and Fred Witney, *Labor Relations*. (Englewood Cliffs, NJ: Prentice-Hall, 1988), 2.
3. Ibid., 27–33.
4. Robert B. Bowin, *Human Resource Problem Solving* (Englewood Cliffs, NJ: Prentice-Hall, 1987), 234.
5. Warren Bennis, "Organizational Developments and the Facts of Bureaucracy," *Industrial Management Review*, Spring, 41–55.
6. Likert, *New Patterns of Management*, 9.
7. "Conflict Is the Acid Test for Superintendents and City Managers," *School Business Affairs*, Oct. 1981, 31.
8. Bowin, *Human Resource Problem Solving*, 259.
9. Ibid., 258.
10. Robert J. House and Terence R. Mitchell, "Path-Goal Theory of Leadership," *Journal of Contemporary Business*, Autumn, 81–97.
11. Douglas McGregor, *The Human Side of Enterprise* (New York: McGraw-Hill, 1960).
12. *Handbook for the Classified Personnel of the Metropolitan Public Schools, Nashville—Davidson County, Tennessee, 1988–1990*, 54–62.
13. Ibid., 55–57.
14. Myron Lieberman and Michael H. Moskow, *Collective Negotiations for Teachers: An Approach to School Administration* (Chicago: Rand McNally, 1966), 418.
15. Edwin F. Beal, Edward D. Wickersham, and Philip K. Kienart, *The Practice of Collective Bargaining*, 5th ed. (Homewood, IL: Irwin, 1976).

16. Marc Gaswirth, "The School Business Official Can Give the District an Edge at the Bargaining Table," *American School and University, 58,* 1 (1985), 36 & 40.

17. Marc Gaswirth, "Negotiated Employee Insurance Benefits Cost Money Too!" *American School and University, 58,* 12 (1986), 14.

18. Sloane and Witney, *Labor Relationships,* 226–27.

19. Beal, Wickersham, and Kienart, *The Practice of Collective Bargaining,* 412–13.

20. American Arbitration Association, *Labor Arbitration* (New York: AAA, 1976), 2–23.

21. T. M. Stinnett, "National Picture on Professional Negotiations," in M. Chester Nolte (Ed.), *Report on the School Administrators' Conference on Professional Negotiations* (Denver, CO: Bureau of Educational Research of Denver, 1964), 8–9.

22. Ned B. Lovell, *Grievance Arbitration in Education* (Bloomington, IN: Phi Delta Kappa Educational Foundation, 1985), 8.

23. D. A. Phillips and H. J. Older, "Models of Service Delivery," *EAP Digest, 2* (1981), 13–15.

24. Ibid., 12–15.

9

Purchasing, Warehousing, and Distribution

THE PRIMARY FUNCTION OF PLANNING for educational continuity is to undergird the educational process with logistical support at maximum efficiency. If the educator does not have the proper quantity and quality of educational supplies at the proper time, educational outcomes will be jeopardized. The educational continuity process should be administered as effectively and economically as possible so that the educational process can be maximally financed. This should be done within the policy structure of the board of education.

Purchasing. *subordinate to instruction*

Educators have the responsibility of determining the quantity and quality of educational supplies needed for the educational process. Different individuals within business administration handle different phases of the continuity process. Purchasing agents, accounting personnel, computer personnel, warehouse personnel, and delivery people all participate in the educational continuity process.

Purchasing is not an end in itself. Educational materials, supplies, and equipment are bought because they are needed in the educational process. Since purchasing has the primary purpose of implementing the work of other areas of the educational complex by procuring needed materials, it can be regarded as a service function. The implication of this view, however, is that purchasing considerations are subordinated to the aims, desires, and policies of those being served. This is to sacrifice, by default, the larger benefits and full potentialities of scientific purchasing policies and decisions.

The progressive view, which is gaining in acceptance, is that purchasing is coordinated with other phases of the school's activities, neither subordinate nor dominant, but working closely with other departments toward an optimal educational program. Purchasing involves the management of materials in flow, from the establishment of sources and shipping, through inventory and warehousing, to the ultimate delivery at educational stations. At every stage there are decisions to be made as to quality, quantity, timing, source, and cost. These decisions must be keyed to constantly changing educational business, and economic conditions that alter the immediate objectives and policies of purchasing from month to month.

Recent innovations in purchasing procedures include the just-in-time (JIT) purchasing practice being adopted by such industrial leaders as IBM, Motorola, and Harley Davidson, to name a few. JIT advocates suggest that it produces better quality while lowering inventories and cutting costs. It does require closer collaboration between the purchaser and the supplier and results in a smaller number of suppliers, who benefit from a more stable and predictable production schedule. Among the benefits noted by practitioners of JIT purchasing were "bare-bones inventory, reduced acquisition and handling costs, improved quality, and sometimes lower costs."[1]

Purchasing Powers and Responsibilities

Board of Ed. has authority to purchase

State Mandated

Whatever purchasing authority a school district possesses is granted by the state, purchasing power is not inherent but must be delegated to the local district through statutory law passed by the legislature or by rules and regulations of the state department of education. Thus, the state frequently mandates purchasing responsibility and authority, purchasing limits, procedures, forms, and so forth. For a more complete review of the place of the school system in the state legal structure, see Chapter 2 entitled "Legislative and Judicial Concepts Useful in School Business Administration." Before engaging in a purchasing activity, the business administrator must become familiar with statutory law governing purchasing in the public sector. In addition, he/she must peruse state department of education rules and regulations for educational purchasing. Many states have regulations requiring that all purchasing beyond a specified amount must be procured by sealed bids, meeting state bid-advertising and bid-allocating procedures. Other states require purchasing from state lists at stipulated prices. The various state requirements make it problematical, at best, for a local school district to pursue JIT practices.

Some states have specialized personnel to help with setting up purchasing procedures. Sample specifications for particular items are made available. Quality-testing procedures have been established by some states. Computer programs that will integrate purchasing, inventory, and delivery planning systems are available from some states. Before developing a system a business administrator should check to see what commercially prepared programs are presently available.

Federally Mandated

Restrictions imposed by regulations for particular grants must be read carefully and followed closely. Many will require that you purchase from organizations that employ fair labor practices. Others may require you to work with agencies that practice affirmative action in personnel policies. Other policies may suggest that you purchase from minority-owned business or service agencies. Some policies will necessitate renting rather than purchase of equipment. If the equipment will be utilized by the school system after the ending of a contract or grant, a rental-purchase agreement may be a wise consideration.

Centralized

When bidding is centralized at the district level, better purchasing criteria can be utilized. Purchasing personnel can be more specialized as to function. Central purchasing personnel should take care not to sacrifice educational qualities needed in order to have larger consolidation of orders.

Even when centralized purchasing is utilized, the determination of quality and quantity of educational supplies should be made at the site. This allows for adjustment of supplies to the individual programs being conducted at the site. Purchasing can be handled effectively at the site if the purchasing officials at the central office will serve in an advisory, consultative, and coordinating role.

Districts which have adopted site-based management as a functional tool for decentralization have found that purchasing is more productive when done in a highly centralized way. These districts have utilized site educators to develop minimum specifications for the many items used and to assist in evaluating the utility of particular items bid, but they have generally standardized the bid process as a central function. The sites actually prefer this, for it provides top quality while still maintaining the principle of site-based decision making.

Relationship of Purchasing to Educators

Ultimate responsibility for the type, quality, and quantity of materials to be bought must rest with those who use them and are responsible for results—the educators and support personnel. In this sense the using departments are the customers of the purchasing department, and they must be satisfied. This does not place the responsibility or authority for selection in the hands of the educators or the support personnel. Rather, their responsibility is to define accurately the product in terms of formula or analysis, accepted commercial standards, blueprints or dimensional tolerances, the intended purpose of the material or, in some cases, the identification of a product in the vendor's catalog. Most educational materials, supplies, and equipment are procurable in competitive markets from a variety of vendors, and it is the function of the purchasing department to select the particular materials and source most advantageous to the school system. Patronizing two or more alternative sources is desirable to stimulate competition or ensure continuity of supply, provided always that the essential requirements, as defined, are met. Some believe that purchases must be made from local vendors, as they are taxpayers. This should be discouraged unless local vendors meet competitive prices and other vendors are aware of this purchasing practice.

The request for materials states quantity needed and the date or time of delivery. The purchasing agent must check quantity ordered against need, particularly if an order deviates from past experience. It is part of the purchasing agent's duty to avoid duplication, excessive stock, and unnecessary rush orders that may disrupt the procurement program and cause unnecessary expense.

Once quantity and delivery requirements have been established, it is the responsibility of the purchasing department to decide whether the goods are to be bought in a single lot, in a series of smaller transactions over a time span, or in a single long-term contract with delivery schedules specified according to needs.

Commercial aspects of the transaction negotiations such as price, delivery, guarantees, terms and conditions of contract, and adjustments for over- and undershipments or deficiencies in quality are the responsibilities of purchasing. For most school systems the purchasing function includes following up on delivery, reconciling receipts and vendors' invoices with purchase orders, and passing invoices for payment. Inspection and quality testing of purchases should also be handled by the person or persons responsible for purchasing, although this function can be contracted to an outside firm. The purchasing department is also responsible for storekeeping, warehousing, and complete accountability for materials until they are issued to the using department. With most purchases under federal titles, this is not an easy task.

Large Systems

In large systems a purchasing department will include buyers in the different areas—e.g., supplies, equipment, and capital equipment. The total operation may be computerized with reorder points, purchase orders, and normal order follow-up handled through a computerized system. The process may be highly formalized and regimented, sometimes to the detriment of the educational programs. Purchasing must remain a support role and not become the primary role in material selection. In large systems the process may become greatly isolated from the educator.

Small Systems

One of the myriad of duties of the business administrator in a small system may be the purchasing agent function. The process may not be as formalized and regimented as in a large system. With the advent of microcomputers the process can be computerized. On the other hand, material specifications, advertising for bids, bidding, placing orders, order follow-up, invoice approval, delivery, and warehousing may be handled clerically. The educator may be more highly involved in the selection process.

Site-Based

Purchasing at the site level allows greater adjustment for program differences. Faculty and staff may feel much more accountable for selecting items as well as for prioritizing purchasing when funds are scarce. The central staff still would assist in a consulting and coordinating role. Without proper coordination, purchases may be made in inefficient quantities. Follow-up on purchase orders should still be done by the central staff. If too much of the purchasing procedure is handled at the site, the district may have to consider staff duplication or have generalists handle specialized functions.

Legal Aspects of Purchasing

In an industrial setting the purchasing agent, as indicated by the title, is an agent authorized to make valid contracts of purchase for his/her company. Many vendors are aware of the role of the industrial purchasing agent and assume that the same relationship exists within the educational setting. Because this is not so, school administrators should develop comprehensive job descriptions for their purchasing personnel, with definitive statements as to authority and responsibility.

A primary rule for purchasing personnel is to consult the school's legal counsel on any doubtful or controversial points in the analysis of unusual or obscure legal terms in the vendor's forms and in the phrasing of clauses and conditions that are to be incorporated into purchase agreements. Because purchase orders issued or contracts signed are legal docu-

Purchase order is a contract
Purchaser + vendor have to both sign.

Board has the authority to purchase

ments, it is not enough that a purchase be economically sound; it must be legally sound as well—both the agreement itself and the way it is carried out. Many governmental requirements regarding labor conditions, employment practices, fair competition, and the price and distribution of goods have legal implications.

Unless a purchase order is issued in acceptance of a specific bid or offer by a vendor, it is not a contract; it is an offer and will become a contract only when it is accepted by the vendor. This is the reason that ''acknowledgment copies'' of purchase orders are sent with the original order to be signed and returned by the vendor. It has been held in various courts that a signed order given to a traveling salesperson is not valid until accepted by his/her employer. Salespeople are not agents of the company and are generally legally allowed a degree of ''puff'' about their product. A contract, to be valid, must impose an obligation upon both parties. The obligation is on the buyer's part if the demand is hypothetical or the quantity to be delivered is conditioned solely by the will of one of the contracting parties. Date and time of delivery and price should be integral parts of the contract.

Warranties are of two types: express and implied. In the absence of express warranties for quality, fitness, or performance of a product by a seller, an implied warranty is in effect if the buyer relies on the seller's judgment and skill to determine that the goods shall be reasonably fit for the purposes described. In invoking the warranty clauses of a contract, the purchaser is under obligation to take action as soon as deficiency of goods or breach of warranty is observed.

Making a purchase involves a transfer of title to the merchandise from vendor to buyer. If goods are sold and shipped f.o.b. (free on board) the vendor's location, the purchaser automatically takes legal title. By doing so, he/she assumes full responsibility for accidents, contingencies, damage, loss, or delay by the carrier. The purchaser must determine the best route of shipment, suitable insurance, and installation or handling of materials upon arrival at destination. If goods are shipped f.o.b. buyer's location, title passes to the buyer when goods are delivered by the carrier.

Legal fraud has been defined as any act, deed, or statement made by either a purchaser or vendor, before the purchase contract is formalized, that is likely to deceive the other party. A vendor is not liable for fraud if the evidence proves (1) that the vendor or the salesperson made a false statement after the contract was signed, (2) that the vendor or salesperson did not know that the quality of the merchandise was not as claimed in the contract, or (3) that the buyer did not rely on the vendor's statements concerning the product. If a buyer inspects merchandise before entering into the contract, he/she, if experienced with the merchandise, is expected to practice good judgment in decision making.

If a contract agreement is made on the basis of fraudulent acts or statements, the contract is not valid. A delay in claiming fraud or a payment made after fraud is discovered may destroy the basis for rescission and damages.

There are many more aspects of law that affect purchasing. In planning the purchasing routine, the person responsible should work very closely with the school board's attorney in preparing procedures, purchase forms, and contracts.

Schools deal with a much broader spectrum of materials and services than does the average industrial firm. Challenging specifications are especially important and fruitful. A researcher's or teacher's knowledge of his/her field does not necessarily entail knowledge of economics and the market availability of equipment and supplies needed to conduct teaching and research. The purchasing manager, by working with the academician well ''upstream,'' can save time and needless worry and save the institution money.

Standard components cheaper to use.

Relationship of the Purchasing Role in Educational Budgeting to Roles of Other Administrative Divisions

The purchasing function is an integral part of the administrative milieu. In the area of budget planning, whether short- or long-term, the purchasing group can be instrumental in costing out educational programs. Purchasing personnel, because of training, experience, and current understanding of costs, can be extremely beneficial in the development of program budgets. The purchasing agent can assist educational personnel in exploring possible new instructional materials and media. In maintenance and capital outlay programs, purchasing personnel can perform the costing function. As cost-benefit analysis and cost-effectiveness analysis become common evaluative planning procedures in the educational world, purchasing personnel can give valuable operational inputs. In buying for a hospital, a university, a school system, or some governmental unit, where the profit motive and competitive factors are absent, the goal should be to obtain maximum value for the expenditure of a fixed budget appropriation. Purchasing efficiency in institutional and governmental administration helps to make the materials dollar go farther, thereby either reducing the necessity of raising additional funds by taxation and appropriations or releasing available funds for an extension of services.

Purchasing—the Act

The fundamental objectives for a purchasing department can be summarized as follows:

- To plan a program of educational materials and equipment procurement that will optimize the educational output of the system
- To maintain continuity of supply to support the educational program, with the minimum in inventory consistent with educational need, safety, and economic advantage
- To avoid duplication, waste, and obsolescence of materials and equipment
- To maintain standards of quality in relation to suitability of use
- To acquire materials and equipment at the lowest cost consistent with quality and service required
- To help the educational system maintain maximum instruction efficiency at all times

Purchasing personnel must remember that they are serving a support function for the educational system. They must not become so involved with the purchasing act itself that the product becomes cumbersome.

Requisition

In a purchasing procedure the first step is to determine the need and authority necessary for the purchase. Essentially, the individual, school, or department initiates a standard requisition that implies a need. An administrator is delegated the authority to determine the validity of the expressed needs. One copy of the requisition will remain with the initiator. Multiple copies will go to the approving authority. (The number of copies is determined by the steps involved in the particular system.) A copy will be returned to the initiator indicating whether the requisition was approved. If approved, a copy will go to the warehouse to see if the item is already on hand. If the item is not on hand, a signed copy of the requisition will go to the purchasing department. The purchasing department should standardize purchases whenever this does not negatively influence the educational process.

Specifications

There are many reasons to control the quality of purchased items. Correct quality improves the morale and efficiency of those in the system utilizing the purchased items. Without a clear statement of why or how the purchased items are to be utilized, legal responsibility falls to the buyer if the vendor ships under an honest misunderstanding. The buyer may then be responsible for all or part of the defective goods if quality requirements on the purchase order were incomplete or unclear. The purchasing department must:

- Know what is wanted and pass the information on to the vendor.
- See that the vendor performs according to the purchase quality specifications.
- Take necessary steps to protect the school system against financial loss from materials or parts that do not meet the purchase specifications.
- Utilize suggestions from the vendor where they promote desirable quality and reliability.

Vendor notification of rejected items should be handled by the purchasing department because: (1) The buyer is instrumental in the negotiation of a mutually acceptable agreement—i.e., the purchase order has been placed by the buyer, and the buyer is more familiar with the entire picture; and (2) vendors are more likely to resolve quality problems and negotiate quick turnaround or replacement if they are dealing with the person responsible for additional business.

Quality must be defined. It is, specifically, the sum or composite of the properties inherent in a material or product. Every definition of quality is predicated on some unity of measurement understood by purchaser and vendor.

Chemical analysis is one method of measurement. The formula of a cleaning compound measures its usefulness and safety on various types of materials and its efficacy in removing various types of dirt or foreign matter. The sulfur, ash, and BTU contents of coal indicate the suitability of a fuel for use in a particular power equipment installation and its measure of heat efficiency. The school system may need to employ outside testing agents for this type of quality control. Another possibility is to buy products meeting federal purchasing specifications, e.g., motor oil, floor waxes, ink, cleaning solutions, and lunchroom detergents.

Physical tests provide a measurement of quality in respect to properties such as the tensile and shearing strength of metals and fibers; the bursting, folding, and tearing strength of paper; and the elasticity, ductility, opacity, resistance to abrasion or shock, and resistance to sunlight or moisture of other materials. Performance or guaranteed output may be a basic measure of quality, and the purchaser's proper description of intended use makes this the responsibility of the vendor.

If the purchasing is done by brand name, the phrase ''or equal'' should be added to the statement, or there occurs the serious disadvantage of limiting procurement to a single vendor and thus eliminating the competitive element, except insofar as competition may exist in distribution.

The actual description or definition of quality is sometimes avoided by inviting prospective vendors to match a sample submitted by the purchaser. This practice is justified under certain conditions—in the case of special, nonrepetitive items when absolute quality requirements are not a significant factor, or when the size and importance of the purchase do not warrant the effort and expense of formulating a more definitive buying description.

In many commodity fields there are well-established grades or quality designations that are known to vendor and purchaser. Where this is the case, the commercial description of desired qualities is simplified by reference to the appropriate grade.

There are some items, usually of a technical nature, the quality of which cannot be sufficiently defined by any of the preceding methods, so that formal bid specifications must be prepared. The specifications should state the means or basis for testing purchases. Nonessential quality restrictions should be avoided because they can add to cost and difficulty of procurement without adding to utility or value. Definitions that unnecessarily restrict competition should be avoided. Conformation to established commercial and industrial standards should be encouraged. Analysis of function to be performed should receive primary consideration in preparing specifications. Minimum standards should be stressed so that anything meeting the standards can be considered.

In summary, it cannot be stressed too strongly that the quality requirements of purchased goods are properly determined and defined by those who are responsible for their utilization.

Before an order is placed or a quotation is requested, the purchasing official must specify what is desired so that prospective vendors can intelligently quote prices and fill orders. Specifications may be very simple or considerably detailed, as shown in the following examples:

8d common wire nail is a generally understood term and requires little explanation.

Smooth-on no. 4 plane or equal is also generally understood.

Ink, writing, blue-black to meet federal specifications #TT-1-563b of October 1, 1968 is more detailed.

Items of office equipment may require a lengthy description of type, style, material, and sometimes method of construction. In addition to the description, specifications should state ''or equivalent.''

Quantities

The second decision a purchaser must make, after determining the right quality to buy, is how much to buy. Purchase quantities must maintain a balance between current educational needs and the advantages of volume buying and must be supplemented by an inventory reservoir of materials, to which current purchases are added and from which currently needed quantities are withdrawn.

The determination of optimum ordering quantity is a mathematical computation. Besides the basic purchase, there are many factors to be taken into consideration: the unit cost of items in various lot sizes, the average inventory resulting from purchasing in different quantities, the number and cost of negotiations and issuing a purchase order, and the cost of carrying materials and equipment in inventory. The utilization of computers in purchasing has expedited the determination of optimal orders. A school system with definitive cost accounting can use the following formula for determining optimum quantity:

$$E = \frac{2UP}{I}$$

where: E = economic order quantity (in dollars)
      U = annual usage (in dollars)
      P = cost of issuing purchase order (in dollars)
      I = cost of carrying inventory (as a decimal percentage of value)

A computer can implement an entire purchasing system for standard stock items. The key to its value and effectiveness is its ability to determine optimum ordering and stock quantities and to control reorder points and quantities once proper inventory standards and policies have been established.

Automation of the mechanical features of the purchasing procedure is valuable in itself. Increased use of the computer has developed with experience. Among the operations that are now performed electronically are:

- Automatic reordering for stock: replenishment, including the writing of the purchase order
- Follow-up of all open purchase orders; not only the "machine" orders for stock items, but also the manually written orders for nonstock, nonrepetitive, custom-made items
- Checking of invoices and payment of invoices by automatic writing of the check
- Distributing charges to the proper account code
- Providing statistical data for quality control, vendor rating, and similar purposes, including the direct interpretation of such data by machines

Factors influencing quantity are the time required for delivery from the time the order is issued and manufacturing costs per item if special items are ordered. Quantity economics are involved when considering the costs of transportation and storage facilities. Market trends can also influence optimum purchasing quantities. See Figure 9-1.

Quotations

Price is meaningless unless it is predicated on adequate quality and quantity, assured delivery, reliability and continuity of supply, maximum efficiency in educational utilization, and minimum downtime because of service needs. To establish a right and realistic price, buyers properly insist upon firm bids. Competitive bids are almost mandatory in government purchasing because of possible charges of favoritism and patronage and the need to conserve taxpayers' money. Negotiated prices are not necessarily incompatible with competition. In almost all cases negotiation starts with a firm bid, but many further modifications may be made before the optimum balance is achieved among quality, service, and cost.

There are three types of discounts that concern the buyer in the consideration of price. Trade discounts are set up on a graduated scale that is applicable according to the vendor's

FIGURE 9-1   Three Phases of Planning for Educational Continuity

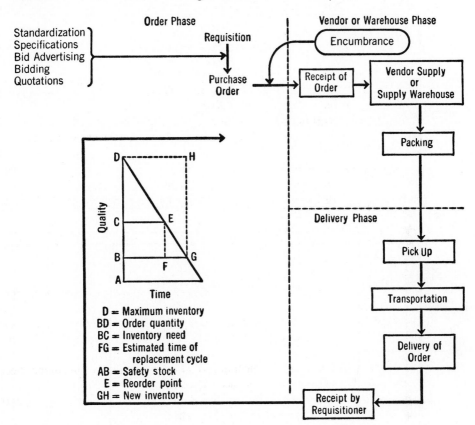

D = Maximum inventory
BD = Order quantity
BC = Inventory need
FG = Estimated time of
        replacement cycle
AB = Safety stock
E = Reorder point
GH = New inventory

classification of customers. The purchaser's responsibility is to see that the school system is in the most favorable customer classification possible. This is a proper subject for negotiation with the prime supplier, distributor, or both.

Quantity discounts offer lower unity prices on large quantity orders. The buyer's responsibility is to adjust his/her ordering practices to the most advantageous quantity price break. (See Figure 9-2 for a sample price quotation request form.)

Cash discounts are an inducement to prompt payment of invoice charges and are earned only when payment is made in accordance with stipulated terms. The purchaser's responsibility for this potential saving includes (1) seeing that proper cash discount terms are incorporated in the order, (2) securing invoices promptly from vendors, (3) processing invoices promptly and getting them to the proper paying agent, and (4) securing extended discount privileges when unavoidable delays are encountered.

The objective evaluation and rating of vendor performance have lagged behind the measurement of other factors in purchasing. The buyer is aware in a general way that some vendors require an excessive amount of expediting effort and are consistently late in deliveries and that rejections for inadequate quality are more numerous for some than with other vendors. Many times these same vendors are slow to assemble or service equipment

FIGURE 9-2   Sample Price Quotation

```
                        BOARD OF EDUCATION
                        MEMPHIS CITY SCHOOLS
                        2597 Avery Avenue
                        Memphis, Tennessee 38112

                                          Date  May 1, 1973

TO  John Smith Publishing Co.        QUOTATION DUE:  May 9, 1973

    1111 First Avenue

    New York, New York  10021
                        PRICE QUOTATION
THIS IS NOT AN ORDER--PLEASE QUOTE PRICE ON THIS FORM ONLY


QUANTITY|      ARTICLE AND DESCRIPTION      |UNIT|PRICE|TOTAL|

  1 ea.|   MIDNIGHT SHADOW by Danny Charles |    |     |     |




REMARKS:


TERMS:_____      SIGNED_____

DELIVERY FOB:_____      TITLE _____
                             FROM   E. P. Williams
FOR:  Tech High School       TITLE  Buyer
         School or Department
```

Source: Courtesy Memphis City School System.

or may do so incorrectly. A computer for which downtime due to lack of service is measured in days rather than hours can make the initial purchase price a rather insignificant portion of the total cost. Purchasers should establish a system of vendor evaluation and consider the results in determining the lowest responsible bidder.

Bidding

Two common classifications of bids in educational purchasing are formal and informal. *Formal bids* have the following requirements: public advertising, public opening, and award to the lowest responsible bidder. Award is culminated by the issuance of a contract document. *Informal bids* are the telephone quotation and the (preferred) written quotation when the dollar value is less than the required statutory limit.

Formal bid procedures should be followed unless exceptions are defined by regulation or are bona fide emergencies. Complete openness and impartiality are essential to protect the bidder and the school system.

Advertising   Public advertising for bids is an open invitation to all qualified potential bidders to participate. All common advertising media should be utilized. Newspaper advertising is a must and is usually required by law. Since advertising has its limits, invitations to bid should be sent directly to all interested potential bidders. School systems can cooperate with each other and other governmental agencies to develop potential bidder bids.

Bidders should be evaluated. A performance record should be compiled for each vendor, listing late deliveries, noncompliance, rejection, and other problems.

Bid and Contract Documents   The important characteristics of bid and contract documents are that they be clear, logical, and as standardized as possible in order to produce the greatest number of low qualified bids. The document set should include:

1. A copy of the legal advertisement
2. Instructions to bidders
3. General bid conditions
4. Special bid conditions
5. Item specifications
6. Bid proposal forms

Each bidder should be furnished two complete sets of documents, one set to be returned with proper documentation execution and signatures, the other to be retained by the bidder for reference.

Bid Processing   Formal bids should be submitted in sealed envelopes, color coded or otherwise easily identifiable. Bids should be placed in a locked receptacle until official bid opening.

Bid Opening   Both the opening and the tabulation of bids should be under the control of the person responsible for the purchasing function. Bidders, reporters, and interested citizens should be invited to attend bid openings. Bids should be opened and read aloud for the benefit of those attending.

Late Bids   Reasonable time should be set for the submission of bids. Bids received beyond the time limit should be returned unopened.

Bid Errors   Bidders making genuine errors should be allowed to withdraw bids without prejudice. However, the withdrawals should be noted on the vendor's evaluation records. Repeated withdrawals may indicate some shoddy practices. Courts generally allow withdrawal of bids on the following conditions:

1. That a mistake of a clerical or mechanical nature was made
2. That the bidder was not guilty of culpable negligence

Award   Most statutes on purchasing require that the award be made to the lowest responsible bidder. Making correct value judgments when considering awards is a primary purchasing management responsibility. Impartial professional judgment is necessary, and thorough documentation of reasons for awarding to any other than the lowest dollar bidder is prudent, because the notion persists that governmental agencies should take the lowest bid regardless of related factors.

Award is usually confirmed for a contract or purchase order. The basic elements of legally enforceable contracts are:

- Offer and acceptance
- Parties competent to contract
- Legality of subject matter
- Sufficient consideration

Security Requirements   Bid deposits in the form of certified or cashier's checks, money orders, or currency are more common than bid bonds. Performance bonds do not necessarily guarantee the faithful performance of contracts; they simply provide for responsibility by a third party. If the vendor defaults, the bonding company becomes responsible and may be sued for relief by the school system.

Aggressive action by the school's legal representative can serve to improve a vendor's fulfillment of a contract. This kind of action has not been utilized as much as it should be.

Vendor Evaluation   Each competing supplier is evaluated on quality, price, and service. Quality evaluation is simply the supplier's record with respect to meeting required specifications; it is measured as the percent of its material that is rejected. Quality evaluation can be secured from quality control if this group is performing its proper function. Price evaluation in its simplest form is the figure quoted in each bid. Service evaluation includes prompt submission of data, response to inquiries, delivery performance, special services rendered, and other intangibles. Under ordinary purchasing situations these factors, properly weighed, should be sufficient to evaluate vendors.

Ethics   Ethics are probably more critical in educational than industrial purchasing. This is especially true because of increasing interrelations among business, government, and institutions. Control of attempts at "backdoor selling" is frequently more difficult in institutions than it is in industry. In theory, collusion should be easier to control in schools and hospitals than it is in industry; in practice, this is often not the case. Trustees, donors, board members, and alumni on occasion bring great pressure on institutions to purchase their companies' products. Normally, such purchases (if made on any basis other than quality, service, and price) should be resisted.

Purchasing Cooperatives or Consortia   Many states with a multitude of small districts may want to form purchasing cooperatives or consortia. The consolidation of orders into larger units may bring about more competitive bidding. Orders can be consolidated into more efficient order quantities. Truckload or carload lots can be more economical with present high freight rates. Deliveries can be routed to individual districts or buildings. In some purchasing cooperatives, warehousing may also become a joint venture.

Site-Based Purchasing   This is very useful if the district maintains many unique programs at the building level. Particularly with larger units, optimum order quantities may be generated at the site. The central purchasing personnel should still serve in a consultative role. The central office will serve a coordinating role for smaller site orders.

Purchasing—the Follow-Up

The establishment of centralized purchasing is a reflection of overall school board philosophy and policy. It immediately entails a series of interdepartmental policies related to lines of authority, channels of procedure, and departmental relationships. These interdepartmental policies should be carefully defined and made a matter of record, for they determine the scope and responsibility of the purchaser. Policies might include such matters as authorization to make requisitions, permission for vendor representatives to contact school personnel, final responsibility for specifications, and value analysis.

The Requisitioner
The first step for the requisitioner is to advise the purchasing department of a need, defining it in sufficient detail for ordering purposes and supporting the request with the necessary approvals to authorize a purchase. Definition of the need includes a description or code identification of the material wanted (this may be as simple as giving an item number in a specific vendor's catalog), the quantity requested, and the date by which it will be needed. School policy should explain carefully the procedure for approving requisitions initiated at any place in the educational system. Some larger school systems develop a system catalog that includes all standard items used in the educational systems. The teacher then simply lists the catalog and item number on the requisition. See Figure 9-3 for a sample requisition.

The Purchase Order
See Figure 9-4 for a sample purchase order. This is the instrument by which goods are procured to fill a requirement. Essential information on every purchase order includes: name and address of school system, identifying order number, date, name and address of vendor, general instructions (marking of shipment, special shipping information, number of invoices required, and so forth), delivery date required, shipping instructions (destination, type of carrier, traffic routing, packaging requirements, receiving hours), terms and conditions of the transaction, description of materials, quantity, price, appropriate discount information, and signature.

FIGURE 9-3 Sample Requisition

Form 14634

BOARD OF EDUCATION OF THE MEMPHIS CITY SCHOOLS
Requisition For Supplies Materials or Service

Original (Retained by Purchasing Dept.)

_____ 19 _____

№ **12404**

School or Department _____

Delivery Address _____

Whse. No.	Fund	Location	For Use By Requisitioning Agency	Approx. Cost of Item	Purchasing Dept. Only					Purchase Order No.
Func.	Obj.	Quantity	Whse.Stock No.	Exact Description, Specifications and Nomenclature of Articles							

Justification Of Need _____

Approved _____ Title _____

Signed _____ Title _____
Requisitioner

Source: Courtesy Memphis City School System.

208

FIGURE 9-4 Sample Purchase Order

```
1 VENDOR COPY                                          PURCHASE ORDER
Subject to Conditions    BOARD OF EDUCATION             No.
  on Reverse Side              OF THE
                         MEMPHIS CITY SCHOOLS
                          PURCHASING DIVISION           DATE
                           2597 AVERY AVENUE
                          MEMPHIS, TENNESSEE 38112
                                                        REQ NO. 87311C
                                                        DATE
```

			DELIVER GOODS F.O.B. OR PREPAID TO:
TO	Moore Office Sales	SHIP TO	Memphis High School
	2200 So. Courtney		100 Elm St.
	Memphis, Tenn. 38114		
			MEMPHIS, TENNESSEE 38112

VENDOR CODE	LOC CODE	T.I	TERMS	F F O
2260	300	pa-ew	2%	Prin.

QUAN. RECEIVED	QUANTITY	ITEM NO.	DESCRIPTION OF ITEM	UNIT	PRICE	TOTAL
			F1 9410-730			
	1 ea.		13" Typewriter	ea.		115.00
	1 ea.		Ten key adding machine,	ea.		125.00
			seven list - eight total			*240.00
			with credit balance			
			F1 2210-400			
	1 ea.		Bates List Finder	ea.		* 4.95
				Grand Total		244.95

WILLIAM P. WILLS, Director of Purchases

Source: Courtesy Memphis City School System.

The purchase order should be prepared in multiple copies. The original is the vendor's copy. A second copy should also be sent to the vendor, to be signed and returned as acknowledgment and acceptance of the order. Additional copies are useful for the following purposes:

1. Copy to the receiving department as notice that a shipment is expected and to facilitate identification
2. Copy to the accounting department as notice of the commitment, to be reconciled later with the invoice and receiving reports as authorization for payment and also to encumber the account for the amount of purchase order—this will be adjusted when an invoice is received
3. Copy to the requisitioning department as confirmation
4. Copy for follow-up or expediting purposes (see Figure 9-5 for sample purchase expediter)

Color coding will facilitate routing and processing.

FIGURE 9-5 Sample Purchase Expediter

BOARD OF EDUCATION
MEMPHIS CITY SCHOOLS
PURCHASING DIVISION
2597 AVERY AVE.
MEMPHIS, TENN. 38112

Purchase Expediter

PLEASE REPLY IMMEDIATELY

☐ BY PHONE

☐ BY WIRE

☐ ON THIS FORM

PLEASE SAVE YOUR TIME AND OURS, BY COMPLETING THIS FORM RATHER THAN WRITING A LETTER. FORM MAY BE RETURNED IN A #10 WINDOW ENVELOPE. FOLD AS INDICATED AT UPPER LEFT.

To
John Smith Publishing Co.
1111 First Avenue
New York, New York

DATE

OUR PURCHASE ORDER NO.	YOUR INVOICE NO.	YOUR ORDER NO.	INVOICE DATE	INVOICE AMOUNT	REFERENCE
120120	B7702	W2871		$159.50	

ORDER INFORMATION

1. ( ) Please rush PRICES.
2. ( ) Acknowledge our order and give SHIPPING DATE.
3. ( ) Please mail us ACCEPTANCE COPY of our Purchase Order.
4. ( ) Is this order considered COMPLETE?
5. ( ) Please inform us about items BACK ORDERED.
6. ( ) CHANGE made on above order. Please acknowledge.

SHIPPING INFORMATION

7. ( ) RUSH shipment. ADVISE earliest shipping date.
8. ( ) Will you SHIP on date requested?
9. ( ) WHY did you not ship as promised? WHEN will you ship?
10. ( ) IF SHIPPED advise method.
11. ( ) What PARTIAL shipment can you make and WHEN?
12. ( ) When can BALANCE of order be shipped?
13. ( ) Please make certain order is SHIPPED VIA_____
14. ( ) Please make SHIPMENT RELEASES as shown under Remarks.

ACCOUNTING INFORMATION

15. ( ) We require_____INVOICE COPIES.
16. ( ) INVOICE enclosed RECEIVED IN ERROR.
17. ( ) We are RETURNING attached invoice.
18. ( ) PURCHASE ORDER NO. incorrect or missing.
19. ( ) PRICE ☐ TERMS ☐ DISCOUNT ☐ do not agree with quotation.
20. ( ) Please forward CORRECTED INVOICE or CREDIT MEMO for following reason.
   ( ) Quantity incorrect.   ( ) Extension incorrect.
   ( ) Should be F. O. B. destination. ( ) Unit price incorrect.
   ( ) Material wrong or defective.
21. ( ) SALES TAX not applicable. Exemption No. is_____
22. ( ) We have no record of RECEIVING INVOICE NO._____ shown on your statement. Please send duplicate invoice.

SERVICE AND OTHER INFORMATION

23. ( ) If order has been shipped, MAIL INVOICE today.
24. ( ) Please forward CERTIFIED WEIGHT slip.
25. ( ) Please forward SHIPPING NOTICE.
26. ( ) Please show PURCHASE ORDER NUMBER on papers referred to or attached.
27. ( ) Material not received. TRACE AND ADVISE.
28. ( ) Please forward receipted FREIGHT BILL.
29. ( ) We have NO RECORD of transaction covered by your invoice. Advise date of shipment, name of person placing order and furnish signed delivery receipt.
30. ( ) Please complete and return our REQUEST FOR QUOTATION dated_____

REMARKS

SIGNED

Reply

Balance will be shipped from our warehouse May 15.

DATE   SIGNED

PLEASE RETURN THIS COPY TO SENDER WITH REPLY
PINK COPY IS FOR YOUR RECORDS

Source: Courtesy Memphis City School System.

The Warehouse

The warehouse department is responsible for receiving incoming goods; signing and checking the carrier's delivery notice; identifying and recording incoming goods; reporting receipt to purchasing, inventory control, and quality control personnel; and making prompt disposition to the appropriate department.

Institutions have the same two reasons for storing items as do industries—economy and service. However, institutions also have a third reason—campus congestion. Overcrowding of supply facilities can be alleviated by using vendors' storage. Using the vendor as an extension of the institution's storage system can free funds for other purposes and contribute to procurement efficiency.

Accounting

The purchasing department's copy of the invoice is checked against the purchase order number to identify shipment and avoid duplication. Prices and terms, f.o.b. point and transportation charges, and quantity and quality are verified, and prices are extended. When all this is done, the invoice is passed along from the purchasing to the accounting department and serves as a voucher for payment through the disbursing office. An earlier copy would have been sent to accounting for encumbrance of funds in the proper account.

Inventory Control and Warehousing

There has been for some time a growing awareness of the importance of inventory control as a planning and policy function of the school administrator. The school administrator must strive for maximum utilization of school equipment and supplies and prevent the breakdown of the educational process from lack of school supplies. The size of the school system's inventory depends on the delivery service of vendors. When vendors carry complete inventories, school systems need not do so.

Flow of Materials

Having a current and long-range storage plan is one key to consistent and efficient warehouse operation. Some questions that must be asked in planning proper warehousing and flow of materials are as follows:

- How much space is required to store items properly?
- How many units are normally withdrawn as an order?
- What is the maximum number of items to be stored at any one time?
- What type of storage is best (considering weight, shape, and handling)?
- What handling equipment is necessary to transport the item?
- How often is the item withdrawn from stores?
- Where is the item most frequently used in the education process?

Storeroom Layout

Good storeroom layout attempts to achieve eight objectives:

1. A straight-line flow of activity through the warehouse
2. Minimum handling and transportation of materials
3. Minimum travel and waste motion of personnel
4. Efficient use of space
5. Provision for flexibility and expansion of layout
6. Security against pilferage
7. Ease of physical counting
8. Minimum material deterioration

Control

Efficiency and economy in inventory control can greatly enhance the educational program. As individual learning processes require greater and more complex planning, the acquisition, storage, and delivery of educational materials and equipment become more important. Some advantages of efficient inventory control are that it:

- Expedites educational planning throughout the system
- Promotes buying economies by determining needs scientifically
- Prevents duplication in ordering because it offers a clear picture of present materials available throughout the system
- Facilitates the exchange of materials and equipment throughout the system
- Minimizes losses from damage due to transit
- Reduces losses from mishandling and theft
- Aids cost accounting and the development of a program budgeting system
- Aids in cost comparison between and among programs and departments
- Provides data for perpetual inventories and therefore can lead to reduced insurance costs
- Minimizes the investment in inventory

Inventory control can be expedited through the utilization of a computer. All material receipts and issues for each stock item are fed to the computer daily from keypunched records. There is no hand posting of stock records. The computer performs all the additions and subtractions so as to show the current inventory status of each item at all times and automatically compares this figure with a previously established reorder point. The computer signals when an item reaches reorder status so that purchasing action can be taken to replenish stock in accordance with predetermined inventory and ordering quantities.

The evolution of technology, particularly the microcomputer with its tremendous information storage capacity and its ability to generate status reports and to signal inventory status, gives purchasing and warehousing personnel a powerful tool to use as plans are adopted for the equipment and supply needs of a school district.

The ordering quantity in the system is fixed in the machine memory. It is possible to program a system for (1) fixed ordering quantity with variable ordering frequency; (2) fixed ordering frequency with variable ordering quantity; or (3) at the expense of some additional computations and running time, variable quantity and variable ordering frequency. The first system is deemed advisable, since the fixed ordering quantity achieves the advantages of ordering in full package lots rather than broken package quantities, ordering in the most favorable quantity discount brackets, and ordering in lots conforming to full pallet loads.

If the reorder point and quantity are set with accurate consideration of lead time and safety stock requirements, and if all vendors keep their delivery promises, the system is completely automatic. If an emergency arises because of failure in delivery or abnormally heavy use of an item, the machine signals the emergency and the buyer handles it manually, either by expediting an open order or by placing an emergency order to supplement the normal flow of material.

Provision is also made for automatic consideration of stock status within "families" of items—related items procured from one source. Thus, stock items frequently go on order without manual assistance of any kind.

Salvage

Efficient purchase and inventory control limits the generation of surplus and scrap items. Requisitions must be screened carefully to avoid overbuying. If surplus occurs, a centralized purchasing system can often meet the needs of one particular school through the salvage from another school.

Selling

To dispose of surplus or salvage, one should first contact the original vendor. Many times he/she may have an outlet for extra materials or equipment. Second, there is the established trade of surplus and used equipment dealers. If the surplus items have any general utility and marketable value, such dealers constitute a logical outlet. Another possibility is direct sale to other possible users. Many business publications and association bulletins have sections devoted to the listing of surplus materials and equipment.

Leasing

An alternative method of procuring equipment, which circumvents the salvage problem, is leasing instead of outright purchasing. Leasing of equipment that reflects continuous innovations due to technological advancement (e.g. computer hardware) is especially advantageous. Additional advantages of leasing are as follows:

- It postpones large capital outlay but permits the use of modern equipment at low initial cost.
- Equipment can be tested in actual use, bypassing the risk of buying the wrong machine or equipment.
- Maintenance costs are minimized or can be included as a part of the leasing arrangement, thus reducing the need for highly specialized personnel within the system.

Destroying

Almost every school system has had, at some time, the sad experience of destroying obsolete texts, library books, equipment, or educational materials. Before considering destruction as a solution, all salvage alternatives should be considered. If these alternatives have been considered and costs are prohibitive, then destruction may be a possible answer. However, even though economically sound, destruction may be a poor alternative from a public relations standpoint.

Educational Materials en Route—Distribution

Distribution is the way teaching materials and equipment move from one place of need to another. A steady, constant flow of materials between learning stations is very important. Time spent in transit is time wasted as far as optimal use in the learning process is concerned. Use of teachers or school administrators to deliver materials to the next point of use is very inefficient utilization of high-cost professional personnel. Clerical or hourly employees can perform this function efficiently and economically.

Scheduling

By Request

In smaller school systems, materials and equipment may need to be moved throughout the system upon request. Some of this movement can be done during the hours when schools are in session. Directions to the messenger must be explicit to ensure pickup of materials at the correct location and delivery to the proper place for optimal utilization the next day.

Routing

Larger school systems may have regular delivery routing between schools within the system. Studies should be made to determine delivery priorities. General supply deliveries can be scheduled to avoid peak periods of educational materials movement. Flow charts and linear programming techniques can be used to plan optimal distribution of educational supplies and materials.

Central versus Decentralized Storage

Many authorities advocate the decentralization of supply storage. Decentralized storage is complementary with site-based management. If a system has chosen the site-based model, it would probably enhance its operation with decentralized purchasing, receiving, storage, and so forth. With the increased cost of transportation, it is cheaper to decentralize storage. Supplies can be made available much more quickly, particularly if deliveries are not made on a routine, short internal basis. Alternative supplies may be more readily recognized by the requisitioner. Conscientious employees may exercise more care in seeing that supplies do not become obsolete.

Authorities favoring the centralization of storage argue that decentralization adds to the supply management problem. They argue that under decentralization it is much more difficult to keep accurate inventory records and cost supplies to various departments, and

FIGURE 9-6   Vehicle Log for Mail and Distribution and Warehousing

VEHICLE LOG FOR MAIL AND DISTRIBUTION AND WAREHOUSING				
		DATE: _____		
DRIVER'S NAME	TRUCK NO.	DESTINATION	TIME OUT	TIME IN

Source: Courtesy Memphis City School System.

also to keep supplies current and fresh. Supplies may tend to become the sole property of the particular building where they are housed and not be moved to meet needs throughout the system. It may be more difficult to protect against pilferage under the decentralized system.

Most systems of fairly large size try to balance the centralized-decentralized storage issue by providing storage space for a limited amount of supplies at the building level while still achieving economies of purchasing scale by storing greater quantities centrally. In this manner, buildings are charged for consumables as they order and use them, control is much more effective, and the economies resulting from mass purchasing can be achieved.

Evaluation of Purchasing, Inventory, and Distribution Systems

Members of the purchasing groups must remember that their function is to support the teachers and other educational personnel. Educational usage of supplies, materials, and equipment must first meet the educational criteria for best utilization. Decisions of the purchasing group must not impede the efficiency of the educational team. The purchasing function must have as its primary objective the provision of quality materials, supplies, and equipment of the right quantity, on time. If this objective is not accomplished, economies and technical efficiencies become worthless. Bearing this objective in mind, however, does not mean that one carries out the purchasing function without consideration of economical methods of purchasing and distribution. It should be recognized that through effective and economical procurement, more and better equipment and supplies can be provided. This efficiency is important, as very few school systems have all they need of instructional supplies, materials, and equipment of the proper quality.

The inventory group is responsible for seeing that educational items are stored at the lowest possible cost that does not detract from the quality of items. Item obsolescence, pilferage, and deterioration must be a charge against the inventory personnel. Cost of handling items should be compared with similar school systems with comparable costs.

Evaluation of the distribution system focuses on the time between requisition arrival and delivery as well as the cost of daily deliveries throughout the system. Cost must be prorated to the total delivery system. If supplies do not arrive in time for an educational activity to take place, the system has failed. The educational process is the primary function of an educational system as well as the support system.

Summary

Every principle of good procurement applies to purchasing, inventory control, warehousing, and salvage in all types of institutions. Good purchasing follows the same guidelines for industry, government, and institutions. However, nonprofit institutions often lack the motivation for cost-control efficiencies that may exist in competitive industries and institutions.

The purchasing, warehousing, inventory and distribution functions in schools involve more than the acquisition of materials to keep them running. Instead they are perceived as determining how schools are operated and this implies a function that is directly tied to the purposes of schools. Thus, purchasing should not be viewed as a peripheral service but instead an integral part of the educational program. The difficulty arises when considerations of economy, efficiency, and cost effectiveness are introduced. The function of school business administrators as introduced in Chapter One characterizes this dilemma. In short, both instructional and business considerations (and personnel) must be involved in these decisions.

In decisions related to purchasing, teachers and instructional personnel must be involved in determining the nature of instructional materials necessary to carry out the teaching strategies most appropriate to reaching instructional objectives. This is operationalized by involving teachers and instructional personnel (especially site-based administrators) in the development of educational specifications for the materials and the estimated or requested quantities. Considerations of economy, efficiency, and cost effectiveness involve school business administrators who use their expertise to locate materials to meet the established specifications, submit requests for bids, evaluate the bids, and submit recommendations for purchase.

Many of these decisions are formulated in conjunction with the budget development and implementation processes. A prime example is that of evaluating the purchase in terms of its effectiveness—was this a good buy? Cost effectiveness relates cost to the degree which objectives were met as a result of the particular purchase. These data are then considered in the budget for next year.

Warehousing in the school business administration context is more than merely storing materials until they are needed. A major cost component of any material is related to providing accessibility—having what one needs when one needs it. School business administrators must balance optimum accessibility with cost. What is the cost of warehousing a whole year of supplies as opposed to warehousing only a week's supply through the year? To what extent does the discount of large volume buying offset the costs of warehousing a year's supply? Concepts of just-in-time purchasing and economic order quantity described in this chapter speak to management techniques useful to the school business administrator.

Distribution is closely tied to warehousing and inventory. These concepts also relate to having materials available to the user at the appropriate time and at the least cost to the organization. Because the flow of needed materials in classrooms and other school departments is often uneven and unpredictable, the problem for the school business administrator is planning a distribution system having considerations of both flexibility and cost effectiveness. Instructional personnel involvement can again be useful in designing the system. Teachers, for example, can understand if they plan and adhere to weekly warehouse requisitions, they can reduce these overhead costs and subsequently have an argument for a larger budget for instructional materials the next year.

Salvage of obsolete, damaged, or surplus material is an important topic for school business administrators as it revolves around the concept of optimum use of resources. By definition these kinds of material are not contributing to reaching educational objectives. Thus, these assets should be liquidated and then, as liquid (cash) assets, be used in a productive manner.

Suggested Activities

1. Explain why collusion can take on a different form in institutions than in industry.
2. Explain in some detail why purchasing goods and services for large institutions requires special abilities.
3. Diagram an automated purchasing and inventory system.
4. The uninformed person sometimes envisions an automated purchasing system as one in which most purchasing personnel are simply replaced by a huge computer. This is not true. What jobs do people perform in operating an automated purchasing system? Discuss the importance of these jobs.

5. Explain how a computer can calculate the economic order quantity (EOQ) for a particular material. From a buyer's point of view, what problems might you anticipate regarding the computer's ability to calculate accurate and valid EOQ values? Explain.
6. When a purchase (or sales) contract is created, what specific actions constitute the offer and the acceptance?
7. List and discuss the essential elements of a contract.
8. Discuss the warranty protection a purchaser has when he/she makes a purchase.

Suggested Readings

Alijian, George W. (Ed.). *Purchasing Handbook,* 4th ed. New York: McGraw-Hill, 1982.

Ammer, Dean S. *Materials Management and Purchasing,* 4th ed. Homewood, IL: Irwin, 1980.

Barlow, C. Wayne. *Purchasing for the Newly Appointed Buyer.* New York: American Management Association, 1970.

Corey, E. Raymond. *Procurement Management: Strategy, Organization, and Decision Making.* Boston: CBI Publishing, 1978.

Dudick, Thomas S., and Ross Cornell. *Inventory Control for the Financial Executive.* New York: Wiley, 1979.

Heinritz, Stuart F., and Raul Farrell. *Purchasing: Principles and Applications,* 5th ed. Englewood Cliffs, NJ: Prentice-Hall, 1971.

Kudrna, Dennis A. *Purchasing Manager's Decision Handbook.* Boston: Cahners Publishing, 1975.

Lee, Lamar, and Donald W. Dobler. *Purchasing and Materials Procurement,* 3rd ed. New York: McGraw-Hill, 1977.

Leenders, Michael R., Harold E. Fearin, and Wilbur B. England. *Purchasing and Materials Management,* 7th ed. Homewood, IL: Irwin, 1980.

Page, Harry Robert. *Public Purchasing and Materials Management.* Lexington, MA: Heath, 1980.

Zenz, Gary J. *Purchasing and Management of Materials,* 5th ed. New York: Wiley, 1981.

Notes

1. S. Dorst, ''MRO & JIT: How the Pros Pull Them Together'', *Purchasing* (May 1986), 62–68.

_10_
Maintenance and Operation

ONE OF THE KEY PLANNING ROLES of the school business administrator is in the maintenance and operation of the plant, equipment, and service facilities. Billions of dollars have been spent for constructing and equipping currently operating school plants in the United States. Additional amounts have been spent on rehabilitating older facilities to make them more energy-efficient and environmentally safe; adding much needed equipment to meet current demands of instructional programs such as education of the handicapped, vocational-technical education, and science; and providing more comfortable, usable, and safe facilities in terms of thermal and physical environment, lighting, and noise control. These facilities and expensive, complex equipment must be maintained and kept operational.

The school business administrator's maintenance role is to oversee the functions associated with repair, replacement, and upkeep of all school facilities. His/her role in operations is to oversee the housekeeping functions, the performance of scheduled upkeep procedures, and plant security for the entire system. Maintenance is concerned with those activities required to keep the facilities and equipment of a system in condition. (See Glossary for definitions.) Operations is concerned with keeping such facilities and equipment open and/or ready to be used. As a part of the administrative team, the school business administrator should join with other staff members to determine a philosophy of maintenance and operations and push for its adoption by the board. The philosophy should allow for the development of policies for maintenance and operations and provide the framework for developing procedures to execute these policies.[1]

Many contemporary educational problems demand that maintenance and operations policies be well conceived and effectively administered. The utilization of educational facilities in a period of restricted budgets presents new and unique problems. Declining budgets for school districts are often first reflected in decreased levels of funding for maintenance and operations. The inflationary spiral has affected maintenance and operations as it has all other areas of costs. Increased costs in such products as paper, training materials, and fuel, coupled with increased wage and fringe benefit costs, have produced a major strain on budgets. Improved construction practices and more energy-efficient heating/cooling systems have helped to reduce costs, but these have not overcome the massive increases in other areas.

Decisions to delay capital improvements such as new roofs or new boilers and to reduce general maintenance by painting less often or making fewer service calls for word processors and audio/video equipment are initial results of reduced budgets. Since most educational institutions are as much as 85 percent salary-intensive, the tendency to apply the budget ax to maintenance and operations is quickly seen. While a ''fair share'' cut is reasonable, short-term savings can be easily transferred to long-term major costs for replacement of poorly maintained facilities and/or equipment. The concept of using a *cost stream*—the cost flow of a project—is a major management tool for the school business administrator. Figure 10-1 presents a cost stream showing such cost factors as research, investment, operations and maintenance, and phaseout. A plan like this presents a quick, graphic look at the idea of cost concepts as related to maintenance and operations.[2] It also represents the interrelationships among the several factors (e.g., irresponsible purchasing decisions could result in extraordinarily high maintenance and operations costs).

With the emphasis on energy-efficient construction nationwide and on the continued importance of maintaining successful energy conservation activities, the maintenance and operations function of a school district, university, or community college becomes even

FIGURE 10-1   Sample Cost Stream

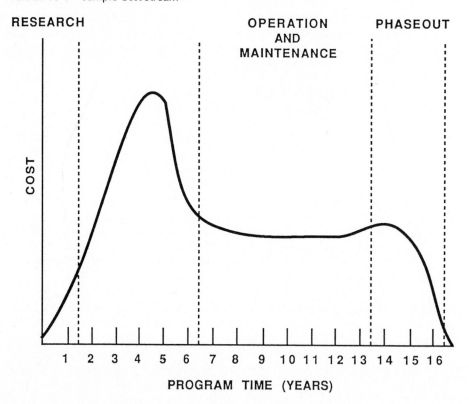

more important. One major way for the school business administrator to deal with the emphasis on energy conservation in maintenance and operations is through an efficient energy audit system for all facilities in the district. Principals, as site managers, need specific assistance in working with energy-related problems and all other problems of maintenance and operations.

It is important for the school business administrator, especially in urban centers, to be aware of which areas are considered maintenance and which areas are considered operations under local union agreements. The union agreement spells out in great detail what can be done by the maintenance staff and what can be done by operations personnel. The importance of this role differentiation should not be overlooked when planning for both the selection of personnel and for budget items to be considered by the total school system. Day-to-day operations of schools can be affected by the school business administrator's success or failure in dealing with maintenance and operations union demands. Many school districts do not have union representation for maintenance and operations personnel, but the difficulties of selection, evaluation, and retention still face the local district. Whether professional negotiations are a part of the school business administrator's role or not, he/she is often directly responsible for the use of major portions of the budget as it relates to maintenance and operation of school facilities. The necessity to plan with other key members of the administrative team therefore assumes major importance.

Maintenance

Maintenance is the function of the school system associated with upkeep, repair, and replacement that ensures continuous usability of the physical plant, equipment, and service facilities. Ensuring availability for continuous use is the key priority in any maintenance program and is the essential point illustrating the need for planning on the part of the school business administrator. The development of the system's maintenance philosophy and the establishment of policies necessary to implement this philosophy in daily operations are vital to a successful maintenance program.

Besides the maintenance philosophy developed by the district, the school business administrator must adhere to the legal responsibilities of state and local building codes. In many instances certain worker accident laws do not apply solely to schools but are a part of the overall operational policies of a district.

With a stronger emphasis on site-based budgeting, local building administrators have major responsibilities for maintenance and operations. These responsibilities extend to making broader decisions in funds usage, scheduling activities, and personnel administration. The extent to which site-based budgeting for maintenance and operations is implemented is a function of local policy and philosophy. In many instances the school business administrator is charged with responsibility for systemwide and local building projects. These shared responsibilities are a major feature of decentralization in many school districts and provide an opportunity for collegial efforts.

The effective organization of the maintenance program is essential to the success of the day-to-day operation of the local schools. It is through maintenance, for example, that school buses run on schedule and that heat is available in a building when needed. The overall philosophy of maintenance should begin with maintenance functions in initial facility planning. Other major considerations include the concept of educational obsolescence versus physical obsolescence, the practice of preventive maintenance, contingency planning in the event of budget reductions, the role of the maintenance staff in capital projects, contract versus local staff, priority of maintenance functions, and cost analysis. It is a recognized fact that in most situations the success and cost of maintenance of buildings and equipment are tied to the initial planning and construction of the facility. This is an illustration of where a cost stream analysis is an invaluable tool for the school business administrator. Low-cost, high-success maintenance can often be ensured with proper advance planning, which can affect the choice of materials used in the construction of buildings; selection of equipment for heating/cooling, student workstations, laboratories, shops, and cafeterias; and purchase of consumable supplies for the operation of equipment, plant, or grounds.

Low cost of initial construction is not always the best solution if it is recognized that many school buildings have an expected life span in excess of fifty years. The actual construction cost of a building is generally considered inversely proportional to the cost of maintenance of that facility. For example, it can be expected that a poorly or improperly constructed building will cost much more than the average 1.5 to 2 percent maintenance figure generally accepted for overall school building maintenance. Maintenance costs are often in excess of 7 percent for poorly constructed buildings. Maintenance costs can be significantly influenced by decisions made at the time of construction.

The school business administrator, as a team planner, must seriously consider the problem of educational obsolescence versus physical obsolescence of school plants. This question addresses the point at which, regardless of the effectiveness of continued maintenance programs, the building ceases to be viable for use in the instructional program of the school district. The function rather than the maintenance of the facility becomes the issue. Structural alterations, program changes, and so forth are an integral part of such considerations but the ultimate decision to dispose of a property will probably be made on both a programmatic basis and a maintenance/operations basis. It is here that the role of the school business administrator again meshes with those of other members of the administrative team in planning relative to the overall school program. Decisions to abandon well-maintained buildings are hard, but an objective look by all members of the team allows for the proper interchange of data that can facilitate a consensus decision.

It is generally false economy on the part of a school board to reduce outlays for maintenance programs when a budget squeeze comes, since deterioration of a building improperly maintained is potentially more costly than the current expenditure necessary to maintain it at an acceptable and usable level. Occasionally budget considerations do require that maintenance programs be curtailed or even halted in certain areas. The key to doing this without major implications centers in the time lapse and the selection of items to be curtailed.

Most maintenance persons would agree that a cut in a program such as roof replacement is to be desired rather than a general across-the-board reduction of, say, 15 percent in the total maintenance budget. The rationale supporting this is simple. It is far easier to convince a school board to reinstate a total program, such as roof replacement, than to replace a 15 percent cut in the total maintenance budget.

One overall consideration should be paramount in the maintenance program: It is difficult to convince the general public that a quality educational program can be or is being carried out in poorly maintained buildings.

School people agree that the success of academic programs is hard to "see," unlike the physical appearance of school facilities. The basic approach to good public relations through good maintenance is really common sense. Keep paper and other litter removed; keep entrances and exits free of clutter; clean and keep interiors painted, water fountains cleaned, and all areas well lighted. Inside public areas should be clean, neat, and safe. The equipment used in maintenance and operations activities should be in good repair. Uniforms should be clean, and workers should be clean and as neat in appearance as possible considering the job situation. Since many visitors see ball fields and other sports facilities on their initial arrival, outside ground appearance is especially critical. All restrooms, but especially those used by visitors, should be checked regularly with strict attention to the provision of adequate supplies and proper security.

Public relations makes sense for schools, and physical appearance is where public relations is easiest to showcase.

Organization of Maintenance

All maintenance programs are concerned with the basic elements of safety, serviceability, energy conservation, and general economy. There are basically three plans of maintenance for school district consideration: (1) the local system maintenance program, (2) the contracted maintenance program, or (3) a combination of these. For example, some districts service their own office machines (both for staff use and instructional purposes), while others contract with outside vendors for the service. The economics of each plan must be examined in all maintenance and operations programs. Scheduling of maintenance activities on the second or third shift should also be considered for improving building security. Management concepts such as cost-utility are a major asset in determining the "best" program.

As noted previously, energy conservation is a major concern in maintenance work throughout the district. While extensive illustrations are not possible, key areas of energy conservation are in transportation, thermal conditions of buildings, and initial selection of equipment and materials. General energy conservation practices include proper training of personnel. For example, the availability of school buildings for use by community groups should be studied not only for the cost of custodial care but for energy usage.

Similarly, decisions to reopen schools after brief, weather-related closings need to be examined in terms of the energy needed to restore the building to an acceptable thermal level. A check of publications of the Council of Educational Facility Planners may be useful.

There are a number of factors to be considered in examining a district-operated maintenance system. If a school district operates its own maintenance program, it can avoid delays and costs associated with taking bids, opening them, and perhaps negotiating for services or materials of equal quality. Overhead costs charged by companies performing maintenance functions can be eliminated. An additional factor that might influence the decision on contractual versus noncontractual service is that there need be no time delay with a local (i.e., in-house) maintenance system, although time delays do occur locally and must be a part of local contingency planning. Other advantages of local maintenance systems are that it may be possible to make more efficient use of personnel in terms of scheduling peak-load or peak-time operations and that local district employees can often be required to provide higher standards of workmanship than can the contractor working for a profit.

However, there are some problems associated with implementing an in-house maintenance operation. Many maintenance functions require very specialized types of procedures that may not be needed more than two or three times a year, and the skilled employees necessary to accomplish this work may be too expensive to include in the local staff. Specialized equipment or tools that require a physical structure or materials not generally associated with a local school district maintenance program may cause problems. Another factor is maintenance scheduling. For example, some types of school repairs cannot be made under certain weather conditions. An additional factor in favor of contracted services is that while time and money may be saved at the bid phase of work by having local personnel perform the job, the costs related to equipment, depreciation of maintenance buildings, special insurance, sick leave pay, and so forth add to the budget. The scheduling of needed seasonal work may also require that a district consider contracted services for periods such as summer vacations. The use of these services is dictated by workload and local vacation schedules.

Capital outlay projects are another cause for policy decisions regarding contracted versus noncontracted services. To use maintenance crews to build bookcases or lay sidewalks may cause the routine maintenance program to be neglected. Again, if the school business administrator uses the planning function in a proper manner, he/she can determine the approximate amounts of time when crews can be used on capital projects, scheduled projects, or emergency requests. Whatever type of maintenance program is used, some tradeoffs are made. Relations with unions, establishment of a plan for dispatching personnel, and organization of work units are some of the features of maintenance programs that vary with the type of program used.

Regardless of the organization of the maintenance program in the district, an individual plan for each structure and/or item of equipment must be established. A replacement schedule for bus engines, a plan for roof upkeep on each building (including a replacement cycle), and a painting plan for each building are musts for effective planning and allocation of scarce resources. Table 10-1 shows a replacement schedule for the bus fleet of a large school district.

Cost Analysis

A competent school business administrator should be able to predict, within an acceptable range, the year-end balance for maintenance projects. Cost data for each job for which funds are encumbered should be compiled for the current year and used in making budget projections. Records for several years should be maintained for use in long-range planning. Accounting problems often occur in unfinished jobs when, for example, materials on hand are used without appropriate requisition records or materials to be purchased cost more than estimated. Funds for maintenance should be allocated on a systemwide basis rather than on a building basis. This provides for flexibility in the use of funds and does not allow needed services to be omitted at one site while ''make-work'' projects are being accomplished at another.

TABLE 10-1   Transportation Vehicle Replacement Summary

Vehicle Type	Year	Date Placed in Service	Quantity	Last FY Usable
66 Passenger	1984	October 84	9	FY 93
66 Passenger	1984	January 84	2	FY 93
66 Passenger	1984	February 84	3	FY 93
66 Passenger	1984	August 84	11	FY 93
66 Passenger	1984	September 84	5	FY 93
66 Passenger	1984	October 84	23	FY 93
66 Passenger	1985	March 85	5	FY 93
66 Passenger	1985	September 85	2	FY 93
66 Passenger	1986	September 86	3	FY 93
66 Passenger	1986	October 86	4	FY 93
66 Passenger	1986	September 87	1	FY 93
66 Passenger	1987	September 87	7	FY 93
66 Passenger	1987	October 87	1	FY 93
66 Passenger	1988	September 88	9	FY 93
66 Passenger	1989	November 89	9	FY 93
			94	
87 Passenger	1980	September 80	4	FY 95
			4	
48 Passenger	1986	December 86	1	FY 96
			1	
12 Passenger	1985	September 85	2	FY 95
12 Passenger	1986	September 86	2	FY 96
12 Passenger	1987	February 88	1	FY 98
			5	
27 & 28 Passenger	1978	November 88	1	FY 89
27 & 28 Passenger	1985	January 86	1	FY 93
			2	
		Total	106	

A 1988 study by the *American School and University* magazine showed school districts budgeted $446 per student for maintenance and operations expenditures during the 1987–88 school year. This study revealed that these costs represent approximately 13 percent of the median net current expenditure of $3,500 per pupil. Included in these figures was an average cost for fuel of $47 per student, $65 for electricity, and $32 for equipment and maintenance costs.[3]

Types of Maintenance

The key element in any maintenance program is not its complexity, its cost, or its organizational scheme, but simply its effectiveness. This effectiveness is measured each day in many ways in numerous locations, from central office to athletic dressing rooms to laboratories. The major types of maintenance fall into four classifications: (1) preventive,

(2) periodic, (3) recurring, and (4) emergency. The divisions overlap to a degree, but each has a separate function. Often a combination of two or more operations must be made to ensure adequate service.

The use of private maintenance contractors when services are obtainable at a fixed price through competitive bidding often can be more cost-effective than employing special workers within the district. Several factors can influence the decision to purchase maintenance. These include:

1. The difficult task of keeping the optional number of employees with specific skills under contract
2. Reduction in collective bargaining problems
3. Fixing of contractor's fees for supplies and materials for a specified time

Additionally, the provision of this support service is guaranteed for the life of the contract. The expertise of the contractor also can be determined and successful work guaranteed with performance bonds. Since every agency has an obligation to provide the best possible service at the lowest possible cost, contracting for maintenance could be the way to go. However, each situation has unique variables involved, and decisions should be based on individual circumstances.

Preventive Maintenance

Preventive maintenance is the program for servicing machines, systems, and structures devised to prevent a breakdown of the total system or any one of its component parts. For example, a preventive maintenance plan is set up for all parts of a lathe or band saw in a shop to inspect specific points for stress or wear that indicates possible failure in the future. Checking for proper tension of belts and springs on various machines is another example of preventive maintenance. The purpose of preventive maintenance schedules is to maximize the useful life of a piece of equipment, a structure, or an operating system and therefore preclude or at least delay a breakdown that could render it unusable. In terms of cost return, one of the most worthwhile items in a school budget is the cost of a properly planned preventive maintenance program.

Preventive maintenance has not been practiced in many schools because manpower needs are so acute in other areas that there is no time for this function. Secondly, preventive maintenance is often not practical due to lack of an easily administered inspection service. The planning function that provides for accurate control records and schedules is a necessary part of a successful preventive maintenance program. Recordkeeping is discussed later in this section.

Preventive maintenance—performing the tasks that keep the "place" operational— has become a greater concern, in part, due to increased federal safety regulations, rising insurance costs, and the increased cost of equipment. Implementing a preventive maintenance system as a part of a system's long-range management program is of major importance. In general, a good preventive maintenance system should have effects such as:

- Producing a complete and accurate inventory of building components and equipment
- Reducing the frequency and number of emergency repair responses

- Providing cost collection and analysis tools to assist in budget preparation
- Increasing the effectiveness of facility maintenance
- Implementing a flexible and easily operated system

As exemplified in a Seattle, Washington system, the main goal of a preventive maintenance system is to fix something before it requires emergency repairs, which are often costly and time-consuming. Preparation to implement a district preventive maintenance program means an examination of existing criteria for selection, construction of the automated system, analyses of the pilot program, refinement of elements and criteria selected, and implementation of the manual and automated procedures needed to operate the program on a full-scale basis.[4]

The preventive maintenance schedule (PMS) is planned to provide for condition monitoring and inspection to take place in a programmed way through an automatic checklist. This allows for good management techniques and an improved overall environment for risk managers to present well-documented information to insurance underwriters. It is important to note the relationship between risk management and this particular area of management and operations. Again, coupled with an emergency management system, utility expenses and overall energy costs will be monitorable and possibly reduced. Such a system allows for review of what was done, how it was done, and what it cost to be done.

In the final analysis this management tool provides a strong element of accountability and a basis for budgetary decisions. The PMS system takes care of the routine decisions and allows maintenance staff to focus on more creative activities, thus increasing effectiveness and productivity.

Periodic Maintenance

Periodic maintenance is scheduled on a reoccurring or a contractual basis for equipment and facilities at predetermined times. Generally speaking, periodic maintenance schedules are set up to be accomplished on specific days or at specific times. Performance of periodic maintenance is often associated with equipment in school office and in teaching areas such as business education, home economics, and/or trade and industrial programs. However, building maintenance functions such as painting can also be scheduled on a periodic basis.

Recurring Maintenance

Recurring maintenance is more closely related to the day-to-day operation of facilities and use of equipment. Where periodic maintenance schedules are not in force, or where the need to have repairs made in a short period of time is important, a recurring maintenance plan is needed. This plan provides that equipment be maintained at full operational status regardless of the number of service calls needed.

Emergency Maintenance

Emergency maintenance means, of course, to fix or repair equipment or systems that have ceased to function. The basic differences between recurring and emergency maintenance are the time frames in which they occur and the cost factors. For example, an emergency maintenance plan for a computer system that is in operation twenty-four hours a day is always in effect. With recurring maintenance, several hours might lapse between the breakdown of the item and the arrival of maintenance personnel.

Figure 10-2 provides a sample building maintenance survey. Many useful references are available which detail school building maintenance procedures. These sources provide reference lists and explanations beyond the scope of this chapter and should be examined carefully by the school business administrator.

Selection and Training of Personnel

As is true with any other function of the school operation, the selection and training of maintenance personnel have a significant impact on the success of the maintenance program.

FIGURE 10-2   Building Maintenance Survey Sample

```
                    BUILDING MAINTENANCE SURVEY


    School _____

    Date of Construction _____ Number of Teachers _____

    Enrollment _____ Type of School:  Grades: _____

    Number of Classrooms _____ Size of Site _____

    Pupil Capacity _____ Type of Construction:

                                        Exterior _____

                                        Interior _____

    Additions:  Date _____ Type (size and type wall

    construction) and/or Renovations _____


    Number and Size of Regular Classrooms

    _____ Classrooms @ _____ sq. ft. with _____ floor covering

    _____ Classrooms @ _____ sq. ft. with _____ floor covering

    _____ Classrooms @ _____ sq. ft. with _____ floor covering


    Special Areas (in square feet) such as Science, Commercial, Home
    Making, Health, Art, Music, Shop, others

    _____ _____ sq. ft. _____ sq. ft.

    _____ _____ sq. ft. _____ sq. ft.

    _____ _____ sq. ft. _____ sq. ft.
```

Different patterns of selection and training emerge in school districts of different sizes and geographic locations. As noted in a previous section, larger school systems often have union agreements covering both maintenance and operations personnel. Under these circumstances some of the elements of training and selection may be covered by union assignment stipulations based on union membership, journeyman worker status, and so forth. Stipulations in most, if not all, union agreements detail specific competencies to be expected from each employee; at the same time, the scope of each position is defined. Actual selection is generally left to local systems, but qualifications are spelled out.

Where the size of the school district warrants, a supervisor should be employed to direct the maintenance program. The supervisor should report directly to the school business administrator and/or the assistant superintendent for buildings and grounds. The supervisor's responsibilities include recommendations concerning personnel selection, evaluation and retention, and training for all maintenance personnel. The supervisor also has major responsibilities in scheduling staff and providing data for effective recordkeeping in areas of materials and supplies.

In a small district the school business administrator may be charged with planning the maintenance function and also may act as the direct supervisor. In small districts the problems of personnel selection may be compounded by the scarcity of competent persons available locally. If this is the case, extensive training programs may be needed to gain the level of competence necessary to handle maintenance of the expensive and highly technical equipment often found in school laboratories, electronic shops, and so forth. However, factors such as cost, time, and staff turnover might make extensive individual training impractical.

Extreme care should be exercised in a district's decisions about using student employees in both the operations and maintenance programs. Insurance regulations, union agreements, and federal and state laws are three areas of concern to all maintenance and operations employers. The type of maintenance service (local versus contracted) established by the local district also affects the role of the school business administrator and the nature of the maintenance staff.

Maintenance Records

One of the most important parts of any maintenance program is keeping adequate and complete records. It is imperative that an exact record of all maintenance functions within a school district be kept and that this information be available to the appropriate personnel within the district. Only through the proper selection of maintenance forms and the proper completion of these forms can the cost-effectiveness of a maintenance program be determined with any accuracy. These data provide the day-to-day record of the maintenance of each building and of each item of material used. Work schedules also provide useful data for planning staff usage and reflect what is to be accomplished over a specific period of time. These facts are important for the determination of cost-effectiveness factors, for the determination of current maintenance fund balances, and for advanced planning within the school district.

The accuracy and completeness of maintenance records have become a major concern of school business administrators. With declining funds for physical maintenance, materials, and supplies and the accompanying loss of flexibility in hiring staff and/or contracting for services, accurate and complete records are the key to effective and efficient use of available funds. Accurate custodial equipment inventory records will allow for cost-effective purchases, while eliminating inefficient warehousing of surplus materials. Bulk purchasing of custodial supplies, for example, is only efficient if the use cycle warrants such purchases. Accurate inventories also allow for effective use of tools and equipment at multiple sites, thus avoiding costly duplication in purchasing. Only through accurate maintenance records can an effective plan for use of both personnel and scarce resources be made.

The availability of all maintenance records may be enhanced through the use of an effective management information system, a concept described in an earlier chapter. The use of computer facilities for collection, reduction, and processing of data provides concise, dependable records in various formats with a high degree of reliability. Figure 10-3 shows a custodial equipment inventory that includes a maintenance record and remarks section.

Plant Operation

Plant operation consists of day-to-day activities such as cleaning, heating, and grounds care. Generally, the term *plant operation* is limited to a specific building (or set of buildings) located on one site. The basic element of any quality plan for plant operation is the establishment of cost estimates for item implementation and completion.

As discussed in the section on maintenance, a school district's philosophy of operations is a determining factor in the success of any program. Establishing an acceptable level of cleanliness, delineating staff responsibilities, developing personnel policies, and describing the role of the custodians and other operations staff members must also be understood and supported by the board.

Boards of education are responsible for providing the necessary funds for the operation of buildings. Since school buildings often represent a million dollars or more in construction costs, plus a comparable amount in furnishings and equipment, funds expended on the day-to-day operations should provide for high-quality plant care. Funds allocated for custodial services for each school building should be sufficient to provide a level of building care appropriate to its operation, thus increasing the useful life of each building.

The roles of the principal and systemwide personnel in plant operations are determined by board policy. The degree to which the concept of site-based management is implemented determines the scope of each participant. Some responsibilities of local building administrators and system personnel are similar. Supervision of personnel and responsibilities for implementation of negotiated agreements are critical elements for both levels of administration. Procedures must be known and responsibilities understood for effective plant operation.

Under a site-based management concept the role of the principal in effective operations practices is greatly expanded. While hiring and training usually will remain centralized functions, the majority of the daily responsibilities for custodial use and supervision rests with the principal. These responsibilities include the distribution of time (within district guidelines) and conflict resolution. The principal is also responsible for cooperative use of time, prioritization of jobs, and maintaining appropriate standards.

FIGURE 10-3 Custodial Equipment Inventory

ALEXANDRIA CITY PUBLIC SCHOOLS
Alexandria, Virginia
Department of Educational Facilities

Custodial Equipment Inventory

School _____   Date _____

Equipment	No. on Hand	Make	Model No.	Size	Serial No.	Accessories Part	Part No.	Maint. Record & Remarks

Courtesy of Alexandria City Schools, VA.

Energy and Resource Conservation

As all school business administration personnel now know, energy costs are a major factor in operating any school system, community college, or university. These costs have skyrocketed in the recent past and are likely to continue on an upward spiral for some time. Thus, the school business administrator, other central office staff, and local school staff have to assess energy and resource conservation opportunities within the district. Opportunities for conservation are widespread and should be examined in terms of total system and individual building application.

Energy/Supplies

A recycling program for consumable supplies should be considered. In general, the school business administrator, who has knowledge of the expenditures of the district for consumable supplies, energy, transportation and other factors, is the logical person to spearhead a serious examination of all areas of possible conservation. This should not be a one-time-only operation but an ongoing, regular process that is implemented at all times by all employees and users. For example, it is possible to facilitate a 25-percent reduction in energy consumption in a particular school building and systemwide. School systems should explore the area of alternate energy resources where appropriate. For example, use of passive solar heating in areas of the South and West should be considered when new construction occurs. Savings in heating costs, air-conditioning costs, and consumable supplies are feasible and should be examined in terms of their impact on programs throughout the district.

An *energy audit* is a major item in determining energy usage and needs and in projecting potential savings. A survey of all physical facilities should be made to determine the current usage, conditions, and estimated costs of any upgrading to bring facilities into the most energy-efficient state. A plan can then be developed for usage, capital improvement, and the identification of specific needs requiring further evaluation. While not a "cure," this plan will give direction to determining trouble areas warranting further investigation. Of course, some facilities will require more work than initially indicated, but generally speaking, these estimates will prove a reasonable guide. It is realistic to expect implementation of only a portion of this plan in a short period of time.

The audit should be conducted by a representative team competent in areas of specialization. A detailed project schedule should be developed that allows for multiple checkpoints and provides for setting target dates. The school business administrator is probably the logical team leader and should assist in outlining objective standards for each component. Current cost records should be readily available as well as other pertinent data so that an early overview of project needs can be made and appropriate administrative bodies notified.

Energy Management

While administrators are properly concerned with many important day-to-day issues of program implementation, data manipulation, word processing, and budgetary applications, the nonglamorous responsibilities and concerns of energy management often pass through offices and by boards without a real understanding of their impact on budgeting resources and facilities use. One of the best ways to conserve is to use a microcomputer-based unit designed to provide control and energy management functions for heating, ventilating, and air conditioning (HVAC) systems.

The "bottom line" of energy management is that when computer technology and energy demands are merged, the potential for real dollar savings is tremendous. Basic management systems, for which there are several major vendors,[5,6] work from an energy control unit, a microcomputer, visual display terminals, a printer, and a power line communication system for controlling all energy-consuming equipment. In general, energy management systems utilize a set of control points for which parameter bands are established. These parameters are monitored by the computer to determine if the system is working within the predetermined limits of each of these parameters. When a parameter is not satisfied (i.e., when a reading indicates an "out of range" response), an "alarm" appears with some type of action message giving vital, diagnostic instructions to management systems personnel.

Operating Scheme

Any of the accessible areas or items in a management system which can be accessed have parameter levels which can be altered. For example, starting time for building cooling or heating is a flexible feature of any system and is controllable based on decisions about when school activities start or stop, the level of cooling/heating desired, and time pattern variability for weekdays and weekends/holidays. Decisions also may be influenced by the number and type of activities that take place in a particular area (e.g., computer laboratory versus general instruction).

Cost Reduction

Cost factors of energy management systems are always major considerations. Some vendors offer "paid-from-savings programs" in which building owners may pay for purchase, maintenance, and financing of energy management and building automation systems with funds to be realized from savings after the system installation. Length of payback depends on how well (or if) the user was maintaining thermostats and time clocks prior to system installation. Two major decisions must be made when installing an energy management system either as a retrofitting of an existing structure, as the addition of facilities to an ongoing operation, or as a "ground-up," basic installation. The first decision concerns the type of energy management system that is to be installed, and the second concerns the installation of the appropriate devices, sensors, monitors, and the like through which the program can function.

An appropriately designed and utilized energy management system is a cost-effective investment.

Organization of the Custodial Department

Individual school building operations may be part of a systemwide program or may operate independently under a supervisor appointed by the central office. The difference basically depends on district size and maintenance philosophy. When a systemwide plan for providing custodial services is used, the director of operations (and/or maintenance) is charged with the responsibility of providing services for all schools in the district. The use of head custodians or supervisors is a necessary part of this program and any other plan where several employees work in the same building. Proponents of systemwide plans say better use of staff can be accomplished, while opponents say it violates the basic management theory that the principal is responsible for his/her building. Both plans have merit, and consideration should be given to each. Figure 10-4 shows custodial standards including assignment, production rate, and normal frequency of occurrence.

Maintenance and operations are closely associated. Because of this factor and the related factors of cost, storage, and training, a single director of maintenance and operations may best serve a school district. District size will determine the best organizational scheme, but policies related to control are key elements in whatever organizational plan is followed. The person(s) responsible for maintenance and operations may report to the assistant superintendent for business or (in a small district) to the superintendent. Whatever the maintenance and operations plan, the centralization of services, materials, procurement, and personnel selection is essential to the effective operation of a school district.

No single group of activities is as important to the success of the overall operations program as the selection, training, assignment, and supervision of staff. As was discussed in the introductory section of this chapter, union agreements regarding operational and custodial personnel often determine the qualifications of persons to be selected, job definitions, and the scope of assignments. Thus, responsibilities for operations functions or maintenance functions are fixed. Again, the size and the geographic location of the system play significant roles in determining requirements for staffing.

FIGURE 10-4   Custodial Standards

Custodial Standards		
Assignment	*Production Rate (Avg)*	*Normal Frequency*
Locker Days Includes policing floor areas, benches, etc., of loose paper and trash; sweeping, wet/dry mopping floors; dusting exterior surfaces of lockers, wall tile, ledges, shelves, cabinets; spot mopping, scrubbing, stripping, refinishing floors; washing/polishing lockers inside and outside.	Sweeping: 70 sq.ft./min. Dusting: 140 sq.ft./min. Locker dusting–72 sq.ft./min. Locker washing–2 min. ea. Ext. Locker washing–3 min. ea. Int.	Daily Daily Daily Three (3) times/year Annually
Shower and Dressing Rooms Includes policing all areas, hosing down showers and disinfecting area; wiping, washing, polishing mirrors, fixtures.	Hosing and disinfect– 25 sq.ft./min.	Daily when in use
Gyms, Multi-Purpose Areas Includes policing area of loose paper and trash; spot mopping as needed; dry/damp mopping as needed; dusting bleachers, chairs; spotting walls; clean offices, game rooms, toilet rooms as needed.	Sweeping gym floors– 200 sq.ft./min. Dusting gym floors– 400 sq.ft./min.	Daily when in use

Courtesy of Alexandria City Schools, VA.

Selection

All staff members in the operations areas should be selected according to criteria established by the board of education and administered through the superintendent's office. The selection process should be inclusive enough to ensure that the school district "gets its money's worth." Factors such as health, skills, character, and attitude should serve as bases for establishing selection criteria. Figure 10-5 illustrates the duties, job features, examples of work, required knowledge, skills and abilities, and acceptable experience and training for a custodian.

FIGURE 10-5   Duties of the Custodian

```
                        DUTIES OF THE CUSTODIAN


    GENERAL STATEMENT OF DUTIES:

    Performs routine building cleaning and semi-skilled maintenance
    tasks and related work as required.

    EXAMPLES OF WORK:  (Illustrative only)

    Sweeps and mops floors and stairs;
    Dust desks, woodwork, furniture, and other equipment,
    Washes windows, walls, blackboards, sinks, and other fixtures;
    Polishes furniture and metal furnishings;
    Empties waste baskets, collects and disposes of rubbish;
    Clears snow and ice from walks and driveways;
    Mows lawns, trims shrubs, rakes leaves, and performs a variety of
        other grounds-keeping tasks;
    Operates a coal or oil low-pressure heating system, including fir-
        ing and removing ashes;
    Delivers packages and messages;
    Checks operation of clocks and bells;
    Puts out and takes in traffice safety signs;
    Arrange chairs and tables and other equipment for special use of
        school buildings;
    Repairs window shades, replace light bulbs, soap and towels;
    Paints rooms and equipment, repairs furniture and makes minor
        plumbing, electrical, and carpentry repairs;
    Prepares and maintains a variety of records and reports.

    REQUIREMENTS:  (Illustrative only)

    Knowledge of building cleaning practices, supplies, and equip-
    ment; working knowledge of the operation and maintenance of heat-
    ing equipment and ability to make minor plumbing, electrical,
    carparentry, and mechanical repairs.  Ability to follow oral and
    written directions; willingness to do custodial and other manual
    tasks, good physical condition.

    DESIRABLE EXPERIENCE AND TRAINING:

    One year of maintenance experience, or equivalent training.
```

The implementation of Title IX guidelines relating to sex discrimination in hiring practices and the Privacy Act relative to collecting data on such factors as sex and marital status have had a significant impact on hiring practices for custodial and maintenance personnel. Factors of health, skills or competencies, and so forth are still of major importance, but the application of stereotypical sex roles has been affected by the implementation of the Title IX guidelines.

In school systems with a decentralized operations model, school building custodians are selected by the principals. However, the principals should work within guidelines established by the system and with awareness of the previously identified factors of sex discrimination, privacy, and so forth. In general, the building principal relies on the school business administrator as a key resource person; thus, the school business administrator may become involved in hiring practices even in a decentralized model. It is often the school business administrator's responsibility to coordinate any policy revisions or policy changes that might affect hiring practices throughout the district. He/she must also review union agreements and, in addition, may need to ensure that union agreements are properly explained to a potential employee and are properly honored.

Under no circumstances should the awarding of custodial positions be viewed as a reward or established as a patronage system. However, criteria for selection of custodial staff should not be viewed by the board as a mandate to interview all potential employees at any level. The actual selection should be recommended to the board by the member of the superintendent's staff with this assigned responsibility. In many districts a supervisor is charged with the responsibility of administering the total program of maintenance and operations.

Since buildings need to be maintained twelve months a year, building custodians and maintenance personnel need to be employed year-round. Some reassignment to other operations areas is a possibility, but twelve-month employment is necessary to attract and keep quality personnel. A reasonable package of fringe benefits also serves as a plus factor in attracting competent personnel. A high turnover rate among personnel at this level is as costly as high turnover in teaching staff. The cost may be even more pronounced if key skills are involved.

Training

Even though staff members are hired with certain skill levels, in-service training affords the opportunity to sharpen general skills in building operations as well as to introduce new techniques and products to a large group. Group training and demonstration is a most effective method of providing necessary and useful information. Preschool workshops at which a wide range of activities are discussed fill a valuable role in a school district. At these sessions the entire operations plan for the year can be reviewed, questions answered, and new techniques or refinements of old plans introduced. Care should be taken to secure input from present custodial and maintenance personnel for use in planning future training programs as well as for improved efforts in decision making, procedures, and work practices.

Assignment

The assignment of custodial staff to individual schools should be made in accordance with established board policies. Criteria for assignment should be determined by members of the superintendent's staff and recommended to the board. These professional staff members are better able to provide specialized inputs and to apply general personnel criteria useful in avoiding charges of patronage or favoritism at certain schools or with certain persons.

An appropriate number of custodial persons should be assigned to each building to maintain each building at an acceptable level in accord with board policy. Figure 10-6

FIGURE 10-6   Sample Custodial Analysis

```
                           CUSTODIAL ANALYSIS


    Name of school . . . . . . . . . . . .   Jones Elementary School

    Number of custodians . . . . . . . . .         3 1/2

    Total square feet of floor space . . . .       49,295

    Square feet per custodian. . . . . . . .       14,084

    Type(s) of floor:

                 Vinyl asbestos tile   AREA:  Classrooms and halls

                 Ceramic tile            "    Restrooms

                 Quarry tile             "    Kitchen

                 Concrete                "    Basement halls, stairways
                                              Classrooms, halls, cafe-
                 Asbestos tile           "    teria, and gymnasium

    Salary per custodian (monthly):

                 Full-time custodian          $230 (10 months)

                 Part-time custodian          $115 (10 months)

    Number of students enrolled. . . . . . .       1035

    Equipment:

                 floor brushes                wet mops

                 corn brooms                  deck or stock mops
                                              wringer buckets with
                 dust pans                    rollers and casters

                 dust mops, hall mops         force cup
                                              electric scrubbing and
                 waste paper baskets          polishing machine

                 step ladders                 toilet bowl brushes

    Remarks:
```

provides a custodial analysis for an elementary school, and Figure 10-7 shows a custodial assignment formula. As noted earlier, it is inappropriate to construct a building and not maintain it at an acceptable level. That acceptable level of maintenance also will indicate what central office services need to be allocated. Through these activities the proper cost factor can be projected for long-term budget work in areas of personnel, purchase of supplies, and maintenance scheduling.

Assignments are determined in a number of ways; one of the more common is by some type of square footage measure. It is important for the school business administrator to give some consideration to a factor-weighing scheme based on the type and use of the facility rather than on size. Laboratories, auditoriums, gymnasiums, science laboratories, and athletic dressing rooms all have unique cleaning problems, and size may not be an effective common denominator in assigning work to a group of custodians. Figure 10-8 shows suggested custodial work time for selected activities.

Supervision

Day-to-day supervision of a custodial staff occurs at the system or at the building level, depending on the operating plan adopted by the board. As previously discussed, if the principal has direct responsibility for the condition and maintenance of the facility, it is necessary that the custodial staff be responsible to him/her. If maintenance responsibility is assumed at the system level, an operations manager is responsible. If more than one custodian is working at a single facility, one should be designated as head custodian.

The head custodian, the principal, the general maintenance operations supervisor, and other appropriate staff should plan work schedules on a short- and long-range basis. Whenever possible, each staff member should be involved in evaluation of his/her own competence. This facilitates explanation of work expectations and assists in producing a

FIGURE 10-7   Custodial Assignment Formula

```
Enrollment ÷ 250 = Number of full time positions (N₁)

N₁ x 16,000 sq. ft. = Sq. Ft. covered in N₁

Total Sq. Ft. - Allowance above = Remaining Sq. Ft.

Remaining Sq. Ft. ÷ 25,000 = Number of part-time positions (N₂)

                      or

         E ÷ 250 = N₁ (12 month positions)

         N₁ ÷ 16,000 = X₁

         Sq. Ft. - X₁ = X₂

         X₂ ÷ 25,000 = N₂ (10 month positions)
```

Courtesy of Chattanooga Public Schools, TN.

FIGURE 10-8 Custodial Work Time

OPERATION OR TASK	AMOUNT OF WORK	TIME NEEDED
Clean classroom	1 Room	20 minutes
Spray-buff classroom	1000 sq. ft.	40 minutes
Clean Adm. Area	1000 sq. ft.	20 minutes
Clean & Sanitize Gang Toilet Room	1 Room	27 minutes
Clean & Sanitize Small Toilet Room	1 Room	7 minutes
Sweep & Wet Mop Dining Area	1000 sq. ft.	45 minutes
Clean & Sanitize Drinking Fountain	1 Fountain	2 minutes
Sweep or Dust Mop Corridors	1000 sq. ft.	5 minutes
Spray Buff Corridors	1000 sq. ft.	30 minutes
Sweep Sidewalks	1000 sq. ft.	8 minutes
Spot Clean Walls, Doors	1 Room	5 minutes
Police Grounds	Per day	30 minutes

sense of accomplishment in the daily work assignment. Plans should be made for exceptions in custodial requirements since special cases do arise for additional services.

Continuous evaluation should be made of all maintenance and operations personnel in the district. Annual efficiency reports should be prepared on each person by his/her immediate supervisor. General supervisory evaluations should be made where appropriate, and the sum of all ratings should serve as the basis for retention, transfer, and/or merit salary adjustments.

When a school system changes from systemwide to site-based management at the building level, the principal's role and responsibility change in both maintenance and operations of the physical plant. The principal becomes more accountable for the day-to-day applications and for the operations plans and has more input into the overall operation of a school facility than under total central administrative organizational plans.

Reduction in Force

As discussed in Chapter 8, declining enrollment and limited teacher turnover have forced school systems to reduce personnel at all levels. This condition, coupled with general budget woes, has created a need to reduce staff by greater numbers than natural attrition provides.

Any reduction in force of maintenance and operations personnel has a serious impact on the general care and usability of all facilities and equipment. As such major items as painting and roofing are delayed, the question of how much delay is possible becomes a real issue. At what point does delay cause significant structural damage? More efficient scheduling of personnel and better care by staff and students will help, but a certain level of care and maintenance is required for general usage of all facilities and equipment.

Union Agreements

Union agreements cannot be overemphasized with regard to setting up maintenance and operations programs within the school district. The role of the union is crucial in many districts and is becoming an increasingly important aspect of all school business administration functions. In general, union agreements provide for such features as recognition rights, seniority, job shifting, vacancies, regular and overtime pay, and fringe benefits including hospitalization, vacations, leaves of absence, and military leaves. Other elements of the union agreement include the rights of negotiation and specific considerations for grievance procedures.

Inspections

Safety inspections should be planned as a regular part of the maintenance and operations schedule of a school district. A detailed plan for this procedure should be established for each building in the district. Implementation of this plan should be coordinated with manufacturer recommendations for items of equipment so as to comply with local fire, disaster, and civil defense regulations. Inspection teams should be established, trained, and granted adequate fiscal resources and time to function. The use of manufacturer representatives, local governmental personnel, and/or community members should be encouraged, but the supervision of these persons should be handled by the responsible representative of the local school district.

Inspections should be made promptly of potential safety hazards noted by parents, school personnel, students, or others. Necessary corrections should follow or adequate warning procedures be initiated until such time as proper repair or removal of the potential hazard can be made. General health inspection procedures may fall in the area of maintenance and operations, but adequately trained personnel must augment the general staff if these inspections are to be made effectively.

Unlike the asbestos threat (which is discussed at length in a following section), the hazard posed by naturally occurring radioactive gas, more commonly referred to as *radon,* is not yet well identified. The main question, of course, is how much of a problem is it in the schools and what can be done to rectify the situation.

Radon is a colorless, odorless, tasteless gas that occurs as a result of the natural breakdown of uranium found in almost all soils. Radon seeps into buildings through holes and cracks in foundations and is generally a threat only in an enclosed space where concentrations can soar to unacceptably high levels. The concern is that some studies have shown that extended exposure to high concentrations of radon can lead to lung cancer. Many persons are yet unaware of the issues of school exposure and how much of a threat it really poses.

Unlike asbestos, however, the money and time needed to detect radon are minimal. Short-term tests can be performed in less than a week and generally cost less than $20. The cost of making a school nearly radon-free can be as little as a few thousand dollars. The key to radon elimination, or at least control, is to prevent its entering a building or to dilute it. Since many school systems are well ventilated, their air exchanging systems have managed to dilute any potential threat. The major areas of concern include basements and first floors, especially when these areas are used for the placement of younger children (i.e., kindergarten, nursery school, preschool programs).

Environmental Hazards

The location of a school site should be determined on the basis of educational needs of children and the broad needs of the host community. Careful planning of the learning environment during this phase of development includes the identification of present and future needs. Health or environmental educators note that chemical, biological, and physical environmental health hazards at school sites are concerns of the school business administrator and the school district. Basic environmental health considerations used in selecting a school site include proximity to sources of air, noise, and water pollution and potential for earthquakes, tornadoes, severe wind storms, and floods.

Environmental factors may not determine a school location, but awareness of their influence will play a major role in the comfort, health, and safety of personnel who spend time there. Evaluation of potential redevelopment of existing sites to improve energy use, grounds utilization, and safety are also a part of the school business administrator's overall concern.

The maintenance and operation of laboratories is one example of a major concern in terms of providing appropriate health safety systems in which faculty and students work and study. Indoor air pollution is another factor facing schools. The inhalation, ingestion, inoculation, and absorption through the skin or mucous membranes of chemical contaminants can be a major factor in health concerns. The contamination of building air with asbestos also is a significant environmental health factor.[7]

An often overlooked aspect of the electronic office found in many school locations is the vulnerability to electrostatic discharge (ESD). Computers are particularly vulnerable since, while controlled by electrical current pulses, machines are unable to differentiate between command pulses and the random pulse of ESD. Environmental area treatment seems to be the most likely (and the most cost efficient) since floor covering specifications can be included in bids requested by the school.[8]

While PCB exposure is a minor problem, it can be of concern in some schools. Leakage from PCB-containing ballast in florescent light fixtures is a possibility. Generally, only light fixtures manufactured before 1978 are of concern. It is expected that natural replacement plans and energy-saving procedures will negate any problems with PCBs.

Asbestos Management

The removal of asbestos-containing materials, which have been identified as present in many schools across the country, has proven to be a costly and, in many cases, disruptive process. The intent of asbestos removal is to make the environment safe in the contained area of school buildings and to provide an asbestos-free environment.

The Asbestos Hazards Emergency Response Act (AHERA), which regulates primary and secondary public and private schools, went into effect December 14, 1987. This act set up stringent requirements for operations and maintenance programs in schools and required all local educational agencies to have their facilities inspected for friable asbestos by a certified inspector. The law also required that a plan for training custodial and maintenance personnel in the handling and removal of asbestos be submitted to the state agency by October, 1988.

It is now evident that another wave of asbestos litigation will impact public and private schools. It will probably strike from a wide range of new defendants including persons presently unaware of their own personal liability. A further discussion of this appears in Chapter 13, which covers risk management.

Pest Control

An area often overlooked in custodial services is pest control. In urban locations this is usually a contracted service, while in more rural settings local personnel deal with the problem. Under the terms of most contracts with outside sources, each building would be serviced in its entirety once each year during the summer months. Monthly treatment is provided to designated areas within each building—food service areas, restrooms, and so forth. Other areas are treated on an "as needed" basis. Thus, it is important that on-site staff include preventive pest control measures in the regular building maintenance program.

Pesticides

School districts are faced with an increasingly difficult issue relative to the uses of chemical pesticides, including even those that can be bought locally "off the shelf." In general, chemical pesticides are a fact of life in most school districts and in most school buildings, but in the last several years, more and more concerns have been raised relative to the widespread and generally uncontrolled use of chemical pesticides. As a result, many school systems have adopted policies that require officials to monitor and record each pest population, to determine the level of pests that can be tolerated before any action is taken, and to identify all nonchemical alternatives to pesticides that can be used to control a particular pest. This would include such things as the use of traps or, in some instances, the introduction of the pest's natural enemies.

Clearly, one of the major factors of pest control is pest prevention. By placing emphasis on preventive education and good housekeeping measures at all levels, the numbers and varying types of pests can certainly be reduced. The centerpiece of all policies relative to integrated pest management programs is clearly the close monitoring of pest population and the use of nontoxic pest control methods. In instances where the situation is a major problem, many techniques that can be used have been around for a long time but have not been used because of a reliance on pesticides. In addition, other procedures that can be performed routinely and as part of a regular maintenance program can save a school system several thousand dollars by reducing the need for pesticides, which are a large expenditure in many districts. However, in some instances, chemicals are necessary, and their use is determined by weather, climate, and humidity levels in a particular area rather than by practices under the control of the business administration or the board.

Plant Security

The security of the physical plant and equipment is a major concern of local boards of education and directors of maintenance and operations, as well as of local law enforcement agencies and the general public. Damage to school buildings is increasing each year. Incidents of window breakage, paint smearing, destruction of toilet facilities, forced door locks, and so on are reported daily in local papers and are discussion points at all gatherings of school administrators and business managers. Since few school systems are able to provide security guards for their facilities, it is more important than ever that proper security measures be exercised from the board of education down to the local school custodian. Detailed descriptions of what areas are to be secured and how they are to be secured must be determined for each building in the district. Proper locking devices, alarm systems, and surveillance systems must be decided upon by the local boards and installed at appropriate locations.

Electronic systems with automatic dialers have become a major feature of security work. Most fire and intrusion systems are linked to the 911 emergency system. In a 1988 survey by *American School and University* magazine, approximately 26 percent of the respondents indicated a major concern with security; yet only 8 percent had a director of safety. Perhaps of more concern for the future, in the same survey 58 percent of the respondents indicated their district had a drug problem.[9]

School security needs today are substantially more complex compared even to recent years. The possibility of physical threats to faculty, staff, and students has been added to the recurring concerns of threats to property from theft and vandalism. These threats come from both inside the building (e.g., students attacking faculty or other students) and from outside the building (e.g., nonschool persons entering the school grounds to sell drugs or to abduct children). School locker and hall monitors are one method of security but, as time-tested as these are, they may not be sufficient for today's problems.

Clearly, school size, location, and demography affect issues of security. In areas of high crime, schools are no less vulnerable than convenience markets, gasoline stations, liquor stores, or houses. The decision to fence school grounds or to add locking devices and lights is based on identified problem frequency. Determining what security services are needed and how these will be provided has a major impact for the school business administrator. The basic reason, as is often the case, is that effective security costs money— but a lack of adequate security can cost substantially more.

Contracting for certain types of security services may make good financial sense for some school systems, especially smaller ones, rural systems, or those without major security difficulties. It is often cost-effective for large school systems, especially urban ones, to establish their own security forces. A possible cost-efficient alternative is to employ a private security firm to provide the support needed. The type of services and the degree of expertise sought are functions of what must be protected in terms of property and personnel.

The improvement of school security is a complex task that often requires physical security measures and the involvement of trained personnel. The goal of any security system plan is to both deter crime and provide additional safety measures. The service may be directed at ensuring surveillance and crime reporting, not necessarily the capturing of persons caught in the act. Other security systems may provide physical protection from bodily injury or harm. Electronic monitoring systems (e.g., television cameras, listening devices), expanded lighting, new locking devices, and securing background checks on appropriate personnel, especially those who have access to the buildings at times other than normal security hours, may well be reasonable expenditures of funds.

Involved with security of programs, buildings, and personnel is the issue of risk management (insurance) in terms of protection, personnel, and protection of buildings, grounds, and equipment. Costs associated with risk management are addressed in a later chapter, but often security needs and security involvement influence the risk management program of a particular school system.[10]

A continuing problem facing local school districts is lost or stolen keys. The cost of replacing locks and keys in a building can amount to several thousand dollars. One successful approach has been to charge these costs to the loser of the keys. Once this policy is established, loss rates tend to go down.

A goal of each system should be an antivandalism program. Whether this is an educational program, a community assistance program, or a combination of a number of approaches, the entire administrative team should assume shared responsibility. Input from various sources should be welcomed, and no avenues should be closed that can lead to a reduction in vandalism in the school district. With relatively high energy costs likely to continue, energy conservation and its relation to plant security and operations become important.

Vandalism prevention measures considered to be major contributions to plant security include extra outside lighting, extra inside lighting, night custodians, use of plastic glazing material, school citizenship programs, and security patrols. Another major factor in plant security is proper planning for security measures while the building is still on the drawing board. School plant planners must work with architects to identify features that will lessen vandalism in future buildings. An alarm system, whether local, central station, or direct connect, is still seen as a first line of defense in any plant security program. A review of educational facility planners' designs can be important to business administrators as they plan the renovation of current facilities and the construction of new ones.

Some specific approaches to security for school facilities include the implementation of programs using students and/or community members as patrol groups. The use of an "internal" or an "external" security force has helped many school systems. Both systems may alienate students if personnel are not carefully screened. Both of these methods are rather costly. Another method of curbing vandalism is working with the staff and students. Development of an *esprit de corps* can help very much to reduce vandalism. This is a rather inexpensive system that works with varying results.

Other physical security measures include audio alarm systems, magnetic door contacts, window foils, and vibration detectors. Closed circuit TV is a possibility in the plan calling for scheduled maintenance during the second and third shift. The presence of personnel is always a major deterrent to crime.

The training of systems-level personnel in security procedures is often overlooked in many school districts. A key feature of a security program can be the training of central staff, who in turn train building-level staff. Through this procedure systemwide policies can be transmitted and understood at all levels, which facilitates the flow of personnel across all levels and provides a consistent operations policy.

Scheduling of Custodial and Maintenance Services

Routine custodial services and certain types of maintenance are performed during the school year. Housekeeping chores, small repair projects, and selective replacement work can take

FIGURE 10-9   Sample Custodial Schedule

```
                    CUSTODIAL SCHEDULE


  7:00-7:15    Put up flag, unlock doors, turn on lights in all
               areas.

  7:15-8:00    Check on rest rooms.  Clean administrative and
               guidance offices.

  8:00-8:30    Clear student activity center and corridor
               around this area.

  8:30-9:00    Clean dressing room areas.

  9:00-11:30   Clean foyer and lobby and take care of preventive
               maintenance as noted on repair list.

  11:30-12:30  Assist in the feeding operation.

  12:30-1:00   Lunch.

  1:00-1:30    Clean walk-off mats after children have come in from
               recess.

  1:30-2:30    Clean the following rooms now vacated due to dismi-
               sal:  kindergarten, EMR* #1, EMR #2, SMR, + rest
               rooms in student activity center.

  2:30-3:00    Clean the gym and state area.

               *Educable Mentally Retarded
               +Severely Mentally Retarded
```

place without disrupting the instructional program. Figure 10-9 shows the schedule for one custodian for one day. Some major capital projects may be undertaken or finished during the school year if proper safety standards can be met and if construction can be combined effectively with noise control to allow for the normal continuation of classes. Of course, emergency repairs may need to be made at any time during the school year, with a certain amount of inconvenience resulting.

In isolated instances a one-day interruption or rescheduling of classes is not beyond question to accomplish an inside task such as ceiling repairs or lighting corrections. These activities cannot be accomplished by the staff available to the system if all such tasks are left to periods when school is not in session. Even if additional personnel were available, the cost could prove prohibitive. Another factor to be considered is that staff members under full-time contract must be continuously utilized.

Planned maintenance activities not accomplished during the school year must be accomplished during periods when schools are closed. Activities that must be carried out during closed periods are those that create major disruptions or require that utilities be suspended or that no persons be allowed to use facilities for an extended period of time.

Work such as sanitary facility replacement, replacement of water systems, major painting, or paving access roads must be scheduled when school is not in session.

Summary

Advanced planning and scheduling by the system's administrative team are the keys to an effective maintenance and operations program, as with all system activities.

A philosophy of maintenance and operations must be established by the board, and policies to implement the philosophy in the day-to-day school setting must be established. Decisions concerning contracted services versus system-provided services; procedures for selecting, training, and retention of staff; and budget priorities are all related to a successful maintenance and operations program. Clearly, concerns relative to energy usage and conservation are paramount for the school business administrator. Costs continue to rise and supplies are "iffy" in some areas. The need to monitor energy programs is of continuing importance. Additionally, environmental concerns ranging from noise pollution to asbestos removal are increasing. Costs for building modifications or improvements and possible litigation is of more than passing interest. Safety and security issues are more than ever under review by the board and the school business administrator.

The school business administrator should supply the cost analysis data representing many facets of maintenance and operations needed for effective decision making. Planning is the key for the successful merger of these needs with other needs throughout the district.

Suggested Activities

1. How can the school business administrator ensure that he/she is operating a cost-effective custodial program under a site-based management plan?
2. How should decisions be reached regarding use of contract versus system-supplied maintenance services?
3. What is the value of in-service training for school custodial personnel? How should this training be organized and evaluated?
4. Develop a plan for the maintenance of the school buildings in your district. What records are necessary? How does the MIS facilitate this plan?
5. How should a maintenance program be organized in a time of reduced funding and reduction in staff?
6. Design a plan for removal of asbestos and/or related materials at your site or in your system.
7. Develop a plan for community and other group use of your site.

Suggested Readings

Brooks, Kenneth W., Marion C. Conrad, and William G. Griffin. *From Program to Educational Facilities*. Lexington, KY: Center for Professional Development, College of Education, University of Kentucky, 1980.

Educational Facilities Laboratories. *The Economy of Energy Conservation in Educational Facilities: A Report from the Educational Facilities Laboratories—Revised.* New York: Educational Facilities Laboratories, 1978.

Guide for Planning Educational Facilities. Columbus, OH: Council of Educational Facility Planners, International, 1985.

Hawkins, Harold L. *Appraisal Guide for School Facilities.* Midland, MI: Pendell, 1977.

Hawkins, Harold L., and H. Edward Lilley, *Guide for School Facility Appraisal.* Columbus, OH: Council of Educational Facility Planners, International, 1986.

Sleeman, Phillip, and D. M. Rockwell, (Eds.). *Designing Learning Environments.* New York: Longman, 1981.

Notes

1. Guilbert C. Hentschke, *Management Operations in Education* (Berkeley, CA: McCutchan, 1974), 205–28.

2. Ibid., 211

3. Dorothy Wright, "17th Annual Maintenance and Operations Cost Study, *American School & University, 60,* 8 (1988), 32.

4. Richard C. Locke, "Automated System Programs Preventive Maintenance," *School Business Affairs,* Jan., 1987, 24–27.

5. Automated Logic Corporation, *System 20/20* Specifications (Marietta, GA, 1989).

6. Honeywell, *Delta 21 System* Specifications (Minneapolis, MN, 1989).

7. Daryl E. Rowe, "Healthful School Living: Environmental Health in the School," *Journal of School Health, 57,* 10 (1987), 426–31.

8. Thomas L. Rennie, "Shock Treatment," *American School & University, 60,* 9 (1988), 13.

9. Kenneth Lindbloom and Joel J. Summerhays, "School Security: An AS&U Survey Part I," *American School & University, 60,* 12 (1988), 17.

10. "Quick Tell Me How to Buy . . . Security/Fire Equipment," *American School Board Journal, 161,* 8 (Aug. 1974), 12.

_11_

Capital Asset Planning and Management

planning process [handwritten]

THE SOCIETY OF THE NINETIES is changing in many ways, some of which we have not seen before. These changes are not necessarily bad. As planners we will be facing new challenges and opportunities. Traditional planning methods are diverging in order to meet the need for more extensive involvement in the planning process.

In order to provide a suitable learning environment to meet current and emerging educational needs, a planning process must include participation of educators, planners, governing boards, students, and community representatives and agencies. This participation has both an educational and a planning function. The planning process follows a sequential pattern from getting organized to gathering information and developing priorities, to making statements of program and facility needs, to exploring options and refining them, and, finally, to follow-through and implementation. Planning is very important in the construction of educational facilities and in the conduct of the total capital outlay program of a school system. The business administrator plays a major role in planning.

who - nature of the
what student [handwritten]

Comprehensive Strategic Planning

Comprehensive strategic planning can be visualized as a continuous process involving the following:

1. Development of procedure
2. Formulation of goals
3. Collection of data
4. Development and evaluation of alternative means of goal assessment
5. Building of a master plan
6. Assessment of goal achievement
7. Evaluation and adjustment of master plan
8. Reassessment of goals

Comprehensive strategic planning should be future-oriented, with consideration given to both short- and long-range alternatives.

Involvement of Key Participants

The need for greater participation is more apparent today than it ever has been in the past. With all the pressures being exerted on the schools, the need for involvement is becoming more urgent. Facility planning in particular needs the input of parents, citizens, students, faculty, staff, and the governing board. When all of the following groups are involved, the planning is improved.

1. *Chief Administrator:* This person will have primary responsibility for the overall planning. He/she will control or delegate responsibility for establishing parameters of decision making for the different groups. All groups must be reminded that the governing board will make the ultimate decision because of legal responsibility.

2. *Facility Planner:* This person may be a member of the central office staff or may be employed as a consultant from the private sector, university, or state department of education. Since the planner's role is so important, careful screening of applicants as to expertise and time commitment to the project is most important. This person will work closely with the business administrator.

3. *Faculty and Staff:* If the facility is to be accepted fully, the faculty and staff must be involved, particularly the ones who will move into the new facility. Participation in planning will not only create a better plant but will also cause better acceptance of the planning process and support for the finished facility. Educational specifications, particularly as they relate to educational goals and programs, are the forte of the staff and faculty.

4. *Community:* A committee made up of representatives of the total community should reflect the demographic, social, economic, religious, and racial makeup of the community. It should include citizens, parents, and leaders in the community. This kind of committee can be particularly useful in assisting the staff in translating goals into desired programs and curricula. Often such a committee can assist in determining the political viability of each alternative.

5. *Governing Boards:* This group will make the final decision as to the facility to be built. For many boards this should be the limit of their involvement. If some board members want greater involvement, they can serve on community committees as members of the community, not as board members. They should be encouraged not to dominate the committee.

6. *Students:* Students are usually considered as part of the community group. Special care must be taken to see that students have proper input. If this is a problem, students may need to be grouped separately so they can be heard. The age and experience of the students must be considered in soliciting their input.

7. *Others (Multiple Agency Personnel):* If other agencies are going to share the facilities regularly or on a part-time basis, they should be included in the planning. With declining and shifting enrollments, alternative ways of using facilities must be considered. In addition, such specialists as state department of education staff and other state agency staff, e.g., state fire marshal, architects, engineers, city and regional planners, real estate brokers, and attorneys (including special bond attorneys) will be an integral part of the planning process.

Program Analysis

The primary goal of facility planning is to develop the best environment possible for the desired educational program. In this context, program includes not only the things to be learned but the full complement of services to be provided. Program analysis should give adequate attention to the overriding goals, purposes, and philosophy of the school organization as well as to the specifics of the program. A needs assessment should be an integral part of the analysis. All the planning must be future-oriented; the program to be housed must be the program of the future rather than the program of the past. All phases of the program must be analyzed, including curriculum offerings, the instructional plan, supporting services, and operating policies.

Context Analysis

The objective of context analysis is to gain some perspective that will provide a foundation for understanding the nature of a program. Context analysis can be directed through the following series of questions which are designed to suggest items for inclusion without being restrictive or exhaustive.

Demographic Analysis   What are the demographic characteristics of the community?

1. What is the distribution of ages within the community?
2. What is the racial makeup of the population?
3. How is this racial makeup changing?
4. Do identifiable ethnic subgroups exist within the population?
5. What percent of the total population currently can be identified with each ethnic orientation?
6. How is the ethnic pattern changing?
7. What are the basic patterns of migration in and out of the community?
8. What is the educational level of the community?

Economics and Employment   What are the economic and employment characteristics of the community?

1. Would the community best be described as urban, suburban, or some combination of these?
2. Is the community growing, stable, or declining in an economic sense?
3. Who are the major employers?
4. Are there industries or occupations that dominate the community?
5. What is the current rate of unemployment?
6. What percentage of mothers work outside the home?
7. What is the mean family income?

State of Texas puts no money into School Housing.

Housing   What is the nature of housing in the community?

1. What portion of the community lives in single-family dwellings?
2. What is the average value of a dwelling unit?
3. What portion of the population lives in federally- or state-subsidized housing?
4. Is housing generally oriented to ethnic neighborhoods, economic stratification, or some other identifiable pattern?

Recreation   What recreational opportunities are available?

1. Is public recreation available?
2. What are the kinds of offerings?
3. What private recreation opportunities exist?
4. What, if any, recreation needs are not currently being met?

Coordinate Education   What educational opportunities exist outside of the organization focused on in this study?

1. What preschool opportunities exist?
2. To what extent do students attend preschool?
3. What religiously oriented schooling is available for students in elementary through high school?
4. What other private schooling is available for students in elementary through high school?
5. What public offerings are available for students in elementary through high school?
6. What is the nature of any post–high school vocational training available in, or nearby, the community?
7. What college or university experiences are available?
8. Are any adult enrichment activities offered in the community?
9. Are there any major unmet educational needs?
10. Are any major changes in these educational opportunities likely?[1]

The objective of the context analysis is to provide a foundation from which the program can be reviewed.

Educational Goals

Broad-based participation in the process of goal determination is desirable. A common approach is to utilize a representative sample of the total community, including faculty and students. Support from the community will be needed to develop crucial, future-oriented goals. In educational organizations the primary goals must be related to learning. Since goal development for an organization is very time-consuming, it may be advantageous to utilize some previous goal statements, particularly if time is limited. The following list of goals was developed as part of a research project by Phi Delta Kappa. These goals are an excellent starting point for the development of goals by a particular school. The process outlined by Phi Delta Kappa seeks widespread community involvement.

1. *Attainment of a General Education*
2. *Development of Skills in Reading, Writing, Speaking, and Listening*
3. *Development of Skills for Examining and Using Information*
4. *Development of Desire for Learning Now and In the Future*
5. *Knowledge and Understanding of Changes That Take Place in the World*
6. *Development of Pride in their Work and of a Feeling of Self-Worth*
7. *Development of Good Character and Self-Respect*
8. *Appreciation of Culture and Beauty*
9. *Use of Leisure Time*
10. *Development of Ability to Make Job Selections*
11. *Acquisition of Respect for and Ability to Live and Work Well with People*
12. *Development of Qualifications for Good Citizenship*
13. *Understanding and Practice of Democratic Ideas and Ideals*
14. *Acquisition of Respect for and Ability to Get Along with People who Think, Dress, and Act Differently*
15. *Practice and Understanding of the Ideas of Health and Safety*
16. *Preparation for Entering the World of Work*
17. *Understanding and Practice of the Skills of Family Living*
18. *Development of Skills for Good Management of Time, Money, and Property*[2]

Regardless of the approach taken, the end product must be a list of the organization's goals, with group consensus that the list includes the system's basic goals. Since goals are usually not of equal importance, a system of prioritization must be developed. Participants can prioritize the goals and help achieve consensus by ranking each goal on a scale of 1–5 (5 being the most important). This method can be used by members of groups with each group reaching consensus before moving on to the next level in the organization.

The resource inputs include students, curriculum, faculty, staff, services, time, and materials. The nature of each of these resource inputs is first analyzed, and then a description of how each will be organized and utilized becomes the program to be implemented. This analysis and description is primarily a professional task and should therefore be the primary responsibility of the professional staff; however, other school personnel, pupils, and citizens can provide helpful insight.

How the resource inputs are organized and utilized will define the various types of instructional and service spaces required to house the desired program. The program will also define the scheduling of activities, time allotments, group sizes, and other programmatic aspects that determine quantitative aspects for the projected enrollment to be housed. The space determination index is a straightforward tool to determine either the operating capacity of a building or the number of rooms or teaching stations that will house a projected enrollment. Indexes can be used to evaluate the adequacy and capacity of existing facilities or to establish the kinds and numbers of spaces needed in new construction or remodeling.

Quantitative Aspects of Need

The multiplicity of factors affecting future enrollments makes enrollment forecasting precarious. The implications of error in estimates can be drastic. If enrollment projections are too low, it may take three to five years of additional time to get adequate facilities. If projections are too high, valuable resources will be wasted on unneeded facilities.

Future Enrollments

Births, deaths, and migration are the three primary factors affecting population change. With the energy crunch the Sun Belt is experiencing the greatest in-migration. Out-migration is occurring particularly in the inner cities of major metropolitan areas. Efforts are being made to upgrade the inner cities to reverse the tide of out-migration. Technological development and societal change have been major factors in birth rate decline. Improved birth control techniques and changes in attitude toward size of families have been most consequential. Large families are no longer an economic asset but a liability. Educational factors such as entrance age, retention/promotion policy, geographic boundary changes, and nonpublic schools also affect future enrollment.

Methods of Forecasting Enrollments

Some of the records needed by each educational planner are:

- Summary and analysis of school census, including migration data
- Annual resident births
- New residential dwelling construction
- Studies of private and parochial enrollment
- Enrollment density by residential sectors of pupils attending public schools
- Analysis by both ages and grade of annual changes in public school enrollment and holding power
- Index of school plant utilization
- U.S. Census

If demographic data are relatively stable, enrollment histories can be used as a basis for forecasting enrollments for the near future. In this section only a few of the forecasting techniques will be discussed. The methods may be applied at the district or site level. (Two models are presented in Chapter 3.) Refer to works in the Suggested Readings at the end of this chapter for a more detailed review of forecasting techniques.

Evaluation of Existing Facilities

Plant evaluation for the purpose of planning is basically a data-collection process for decision making and not a process of discussion. Planners should refrain from decision making until all basic data have been gathered. The evaluation should seek building and site data concerning five basic aspects of the total plant: location, health and safety, environment, program adequacy, and numerical adequacy. Plant evaluation is especially needed in a period of declining enrollment, tight finances, and high interest rates.

A listing of every space should be prepared for each building. This should include location, dimensions, present use, and number. Special rooms will need modifications in data requirements to reflect their particular utilization. A program needs assessment must be prepared prior to the on-site visitation.

For most facilities a single line drawing, blueprint, or sketch is satisfactory. As long as it is fairly accurate in scale, it is better than construction blueprints. Basic data must be collected for each facility—e.g., date of construction, site, square footage, and a listing of rooms built or added. The site size will be expressed in acreage and should be checked with the state's minimum standards. Faculty, custodians, and maintenance staff can help you identify major maintenance needs (e.g., leaky roof, ineffective heating, and deteriorated plumbing).

Health and Safety

The evaluation of a facility for health and safety should be fairly detached. If recent inspections have not been made, Occupational Safety and Health Act (OSHA) inspectors, Title IX, and Public Law 94-142 inspectors should be a part of the evaluation team. Points to be considered for fire safety include fire alarm systems with provisions for the hearing-handicapped, adequacy of exits with the physically handicapped in mind; type of construction with respect to combustion; safeguards in dangerous areas such as kitchens, boiler rooms, shops, and labs; condition of fire extinguishers; adequacy of combustibles storage; and condition of electrical services. The structural soundness should be checked by a structural engineer. The planners can check for obvious signs of deterioration such as cracking, leaning, or bulging of walls, rotting or damage to wood, or weakening of masonry.

In determining sanitation adequacy, the quality of the water supply, adequacy of drinking fountains, and the location, condition, and number of restrooms must be checked. The general cleanliness of a building should be noted along with freedom from unsightly storage and control of vermin and rodents. The facilities must not present undue barriers to the handicapped. The overriding concern must be people rather than property. The facility must be adequate for the health and safety of all occupants, including students, faculty, staff, and visitors.

Environment

Environment is most often defined as the surrounding conditions and influences that modify the actions of human beings, their mental and physical comfort, and their ability to see and hear properly. The essential reason for building schoolhouses is to produce a working climate where the physical factors in the classroom are controlled. A controlled environment of heat and cold, moisture and dryness, air motion, and the like must be maintained so learning can progress effectively. The preponderance of data on safety, absenteeism, and efficiency in offices, industry, and schools leads to the conclusion that human performance deteriorates rapidly at a temperature above or below a relatively narrow comfort zone. Students experience a small reduction in learning ability whenever room temperature deviates from the optimum. On the other hand, educational leaders believe that the amount of learning by average students in a proper thermal environment increases approximately 40 percent. Another benefit of temperature control is lower building operating costs, which usually offset operating costs for air conditioning. Temperature control is easier to control when carpet covers the floor. The thermal environment must be carefully evaluated.

Guiding principles of proper classroom lighting have been established that contribute to a more comfortable, efficient, and pleasing environment. Approximately 80 percent of all learning is acquired through vision. Therefore, proper lighting and balanced lighting are necessary for correct optical hygiene. Proper lighting should be directly on the task and should eliminate glare. There should never be more light on the eye than on the task. Nothing in the central field of vision should have less than one-third or more than three times the task brightness. In the peripheral field, brightness should not be less than one-tenth or greater than ten times the task brightness. If the planners find that lighting problems exist, evaluation by a lighting engineer is advisable.

In the design of school buildings or remodeling of older buildings, architects and administrators need to be reminded of the psychological effects of color and the use of correct lighting. Carefully planned experiments by psychologists have proven that modern principles of color applied to schools will greatly improve the scholastic performance of students, especially in the earlier years. A well-designed environment not only facilitates learning new subject matter but also reduces behavioral problems. In evaluating old buildings as well as planning new buildings, planners should utilize the most recent research on the use of color.

Program Adequacy

The real problem is to obtain a good functional measure of either capacity or utilization that is related to the operating program rather than to abstract standards. Certain ideas about a capacity measurement technique have been crystallized into the following criteria:

- Program-related functional use of the building should be studied.
- Capacity problems should be related to programmatic utilization rather than through status studies.
- All significant capacity-related factors should be included.
- Factors utilized should lend themselves to objective measurement.
- The application should be universal.
- Arbitrary standards should not be involved.
- Application should be relatively easy.
- Results should be easily interpreted.

Numerical Adequacy

Criteria of numerical adequacy are based on the assumption that capacity is integrally related to the educational program and policies of the school system being studied. An analysis of capacity is related to the following factors:

- Number and types of teaching stations
- Quality of rooms
- Size of rooms and number of pupil stations
- Desirable average class size
- Room assignment policies
- Nature of educational program
- Number and length of class periods
- Alternative schedules
- Multiple sessions
- Specialization of rooms
- Diversity of subject selection

A multiple factor formula for determining capacity is:

$$FC = \frac{TS \times OS \times I \times E}{PI}$$

where FC = facility capacity for given subject area
TS = teaching stations in subject area
OS = optimum class size in subject area
I   = total effective periods of instruction per week
E   = average total school enrollment per periods of time
PI   = the total pupil periods of instruction per week

While evaluating a facility, it is desirable not only to identify any existing problems or shortcomings but also to begin thinking about potential solutions.

Analysis of Financial Resources

The capital budget includes all expenditures related to creation or improvement and maintenance of major facilities. Capital expenditures are usually regarded as long-term, while operating expenditures—even though recurring—are short-term. The history of local responsibility for financing school construction is neither sound nor realistic: Well-funded districts have ample funding for elaborate facilities, average districts with major effort can fund moderate facilities; and poor districts cannot afford improved facilities. Some states are beginning to provide partial funds for capital outlay. Federal funding for capital outlay appears rather bleak. Federal Impact Law 815 was for school construction and is no longer operative. Lingering effects of ''Reaganomics'' suggest that federal funds for school construction will not be available for some time.

State Responsibility for Capital Funding

Some of the major responsibilities of the state education agency, in addition to establishing needed policies and guidelines for capital funding, should include:

- Helping local school systems to plan and provide for effective use of funds to bring about improvements in their educational programs, instructional environment, and facilities
- Assisting in or arranging for periodic studies to determine advantages and disadvantages—including inequities in various aspects of the program—and to recognize areas in which improvements are needed
- Collaborating with other agencies in dealing with aspects with which they are concerned, such as site determination and location, transportation, safety standards, energy conservation techniques, joint use of facilities, and so on

A few states have established a special agency to develop regulations and to coordinate and oversee provisions for financing school plant construction. These agencies, although presumed to be primarily concerned with finance, usually influence bond issues and support policies that affect the educational program. This should not be. All state responsibilities relating to school construction should be vested in the state education agency. Determination of need; development of program; educational specifications; funding sources; architect selection; construction; health, safety, and energy principles; and project follow-up should be under the direction of the state education agency.

Although the courts consider education a function of the state, most states have given little attention to financing capital outlay. Some states have given temporary or emergency assistance for school construction. Others have encouraged a long-range view of such funding by providing grants for the purpose of assisting local school systems in the construction of facilities. Only Hawaii provides full funding for facilities, but then Hawaii has only one school system to serve the entire state. Other states contribute at a low of 3 percent for Arizona to a high of 96 percent for Maryland. For a more detailed discussion of patterns of state support for capital outlay, see the American Institute of Architects' *State Requirements for School Construction*.[3] Table 11-1 shows the pattern of state support for 1987. With the possible declining local tax base, taxpayer revolt, and high interest rates, business administrators must use ingenuity in working with state department personnel and legislators to develop more effective methods of financing capital outlay.

It is becoming clear that equity concerns will ultimately dictate that states become more involved in the funding of capital outlay at the district level. Indeed, the marked increase in the number of states that participate in providing at least partial funding for capital outlay between 1976 and 1987 reveals a trend that suggests a continued recognition of the need to become more involved at the state level.

Local Capital Funding through Bonds
Bonding is the most prevalent local method of funding capital outlay. Other less utilized approaches include pay-as-you-go, reverse funding, building authorities, and lease purchase. Planning the bond marketing procedure very carefully can lead to substantial savings.

Voter Approval   Methods of approval of bond issues vary among the states. In fact, many school districts have been having tremendous problems with securing voter approval. Desegregation, inflation decreasing enrollments, overutilization of the property tax, citizen dissatisfaction with the public schools, expansion of programs without commensurate funding by the state and federal government, and government regulations, e g., OSHA, Title IX, and Education of the Handicapped, have all led to questioning of school facility funding.

Planning Bond Issue   Several basic decisions must be made concerning the specific bonds. The denominations may have a very important impact on the ease of marketing an issue. Generally, large banks, trust funds, and other large-lot purchasers desire large denominations. Conversely, individuals and buyers for small institutions desire small denominations. A wide range of denomination size can enhance the bond sale.

Interest rates on municipal bonds are determined largely by the character and the financial capacity of the issuer, length of term of issue, and the relative availability of investment funds at the time of the sale. Many school districts, through past experience, issue bonds with the maximum maturities allowed by the state. This is very expensive for the district that has a relatively constant school facility need. Bond maturities should be kept as short as feasible. If longer maturities are utilized, call features may allow earlier retirement if economic conditions permit.

TABLE 11-1 Sources of Support for School Capital Outlay

State	School Funding				Planning Requirements		
	% Local	% State	% Federal	% Other	State Pre-Planning Agencies	Community Involvement	State Plan Review
Alabama	67%	30%	3%	0%	No	No	Yes
Alaska	50%	49%	1%	0%	Yes	No	Yes
Arizona	94%	3%	3%	0%	No	No	No
Arkansas	100%	0%	0%	0%	No	No	No
California	15%	80%	3%	2%	Yes	No	Yes
Colorado	100%	0%	0%	0%	No	No	Yes
Connecticut	20%–60%	40%–80%	0%	0%	Yes	No	Yes
Delaware	40%	60%	0%	0%	Yes	No	Yes
Florida	66%	28%	1%	5%	Yes	Yes	Yes
Georgia		74%			Yes	No	Yes
Hawaii	0%	100%	0%	0%	Yes	Yes	Yes
Idaho	100%	0%	0%	0%	No	No	Yes
Illinois	30%–80%	20%–70%	0%	0%	Yes	Yes	Yes
Indiana	100%	0%	0%	0%	No	No	Yes
Iowa	100%	0%	0%	0%	No	No	Yes
Kansas	90%	0%	0%	10%	No	No	Yes
Kentucky	36%	64%	0%	0%	Yes	Yes	Yes
Louisiana	100%	0%	0%	0%	No	No	No
Maine	32%	68%	0%	0%	Yes	Yes	Yes
Maryland	4%–22%	78%–96%	0%	0%	Yes	No	Yes
Massachusetts		50%–75%			Yes	Yes	Yes
Michigan	100%	0%	0%	0%	Yes	No	Yes
Minnesota	45%	3%	2%	50%	Yes	Yes	Yes
Mississippi	50%	50%	0%	0%	Yes	No	Yes
Missouri	100%	0%	0%	0%	No	No	No
Montana	95%	0%	5%	0%	No	No	Yes

TABLE 11-1 *Continued*

State	School Funding				Planning Requirements		
	% Local	% State	% Federal	% Other	State Pre-Planning Agencies	Community Involvement	State Plan Review
Nebraska	100%	0%	0%	0%	No	No	Yes
Nevada	100%	0%	0%	0%	No	No	No
New Hampshire	40%–70%	30%–55%	0%	0%	No	No	Yes
New Jersey	68%	32%	0%	0%	Yes	Yes	Yes
New Mexico					Yes	No	Yes
New York	40%	40%	0%	20%	Yes	Yes	Yes
North Carolina	100%	0%	0%	0%	Yes	Yes	Yes
North Dakota	80%	20%	0%	0%	No	No	Yes
Ohio	90%	10%	0%	0%	Yes	Yes	Yes
Oklahoma	95%	0%	0%	5%	Yes	No	Yes
Oregon	100%	0%	0%	0%	No	No	No
Pennsylvania	60%–80%	20%–40%	0%	0%	Yes	No	Yes
Rhode Island	70%	30%	0%	0%	Yes	Yes	Yes
South Carolina	78%	21%	1%	0%	No	No	Yes
South Dakota	100%	0%	0%	0%	No	Yes	Yes
Tennessee	100%	0%	0%	0%	No	No	Yes
Texas	99%	0%	1%	0%	No	Yes	Yes
Utah	87%	12%	1%	0%	Yes	No	Yes
Vermont	70%	30%	0%	0%	Yes	No	Yes
Virginia	100%	0%	0%	0%	No	No	Yes
Washington	20%–90%	20%–90%	10%	0%	Yes		Yes
West Virginia	50%	28%	12%	10%	Yes	Yes	Yes
Wisconsin					No	No	Yes
Wyoming	90%	10%	0%	0%	No	No	Yes

Note–blank entries indicate information was not available.

Source: State Requirements for School Construction (Washington, DC: The American Institute of Architects, 1987).

Serial bonds (bonds maturing annually or semiannually from year of issue to termination date) are self-administering and require little management by the local fiscal agent. Because of their popularity these bonds may not command the low interest rate that may be available for term bonds (bonds paid at the end of the bonding period with only interest paid during the intervening period). If state statutes permit the utilization of term bonds and the district has the fiscal acumen to handle such a bond, the term bond may be an alternative that deserves careful consideration.

Retaining a Bond Attorney   In order to consummate a bond sale, a bond attorney whose decision is recognized by the ultimate buyer must be retained and must give favorable legal opinion. His/her service can be invaluable in planning and administering a bonding program. The bond attorney should draft the original bond resolution or ordinance, as well as the notice of bond election and the form of the ballot if an election is required under local law. Once voters have approved the issue, the bond attorney reviews preparation of the prospectus, notice of sale, other financial advertisements, and all materials presented to underwriters for bidding purposes. After the bonds have been sold, printed, paid for, and delivered, he/she renders a final legal opinion.

Advertising Sale   Recent widespread rejection of bond issues by school patrons has emphasized the importance of good public relations for the entire bond issue procedure.[4] Assuming passage of the bond issue by the electorate, a notice of sale will be required by state statute. Legal requirements can usually be met by advertising in a newspaper of general circulation throughout the district. Bids on school bonds can be encouraged by advertising in the *Daily Bond Buyer* or the *Wall Street Journal*. Pertinent data regarding the issue and community should be forwarded to underwriters and potential investors. See Dewey H. Stollar's *Managing School Indebtedness* for a detailed account of steps to follow in marketing municipal bonds.[5]

Bond Rating   A borrower who obtains an AAA rating has the most coveted but most carefully granted financial rating it is possible to acquire. Since secondary market bond buyers accept these ratings religiously, a borrower with a high rating can attract more investors, pay lower interest rates, and profit generally from the esteem bestowed upon such a rating in the business world. Dun and Bradstreet, Moody's, and Standard & Poor's are the major raters of school bonds. Once a favorable rating is obtained, the local district must meet an annual financial records requirement for continuation of the rating. Failure to complete forms will automatically discontinue rated status, which can be detrimental to the future sale of bonds.

Post-Sale Planning   Almost all school districts face the necessity of future capital outlay expenditure. Therefore, it is obviously important to earn and retain the good will of the financial community by properly performing all required services after a sale is accomplished. Prompt payment of principal and interest is essential, and it is highly desirable to keep bond owners, rating agencies, and underwriters informed of the financial status and progress of the school system and the community.[6]

Attorney General approves the bond sale.

State Capital Funding

Although under the Constitution education is a function of the states, states have been reluctant to support capital outlay projects. Voter resistance to the passage of operating levies and bond issues is forcing many states into making arrangements for financing school facilities. Many states have passed large bond issues that, based on proper planning and voter approval at the local level, are shared with the local school system based on need and matching local funding. Multiple agency utilization of facilities virtually necessitates state involvement in financing of the jointly utilized facilities. States are generating capital funds through current operating funds, general obligation bonds, state building authorities, loans, rental agreements, and grants.

Federal Capital Funding

Federal support for public school construction has been quite limited. Some funds have been available since World War II to finance facilities in locales heavily affected by defense need. This aid may disappear under the present administration. Although federal aid has been inconsequential, there have been many recommendations to increase it. Two reasons are often cited for increased federal support: (1) It could be used to equalize interstate resource disparity, and (2) it would shift the tax burden away from the regressive property tax to the progressive income tax.

Alternative Capital Funding

Several creative, innovative mechanisms for providing capital outlay resources to school systems have become available. Among the more creative is the use of public building authorities to plan and build school facilities to lease to the school system. Typically, the lease provides the option for the school system to retain ownership upon completion of the leasing period.

In the typical building authority mode (Chicago, for example), the building authority is established by state statute and empowered to sell municipal bonds for the purpose of planning and building school facilities. The building authority leases the school facilities to the school system at a cost that covers the principal and interest on the bonds and the cost of the building authority operation. Provision is usually made for the facilities to become the property of the school system upon the retirement of the bonds and attendant costs. An increasing number of cities and states have used this process to plan and build facilities, particularly those facilities that generate funds that can be used to retire the bonded indebtedness. Many states have used a state building authority to build college and university facilities, especially dormitory and union facilities that have potential for generating funds to be used in retiring the bonds.

Among the many other options being utilized by creative business officials in their quest for options to traditional methods of financing capital outlay expenditures for the school system are the following:

1. *Rental of facilities.* This is particularly effective in areas that show great immediate need for school housing and where population projections show that the need is temporary and will subside after a few years. A number of school systems including Lansing and Flint, Michigan and Fort Worth, Texas have utilized this strategy to solve space needs for early childhood and early elementary facilities.

Contractor - you pay him 90% of whats on the building site.

2. *Sharing of facilities with other agencies.* Many housing authorities provide space for education, health, social services, and other tenant needs in the complex of the authority. Often space needed for early childhood programs is located in the facility and provides a convenient and close environment for the children of the project.

3. *Private sector provision of facilities.* Increasingly, the private sector will provide facilities to the public school system in return for the school system operating a school on the premises to serve either the employees (retraining and development) or the children of the employees (daycare and early childhood education).

Planning the Sequence of Steps in Construction

Planning capital outlay involves several discrete and sequential steps. The business administrator will either supervise these steps or will be heavily involved in their coordination. Steps to be implemented are:

1. Develop educational specifications.
2. Develop architectural plans and specifications.
3. Review architectural plans and specifications.
4. Solicit competitive bids.
5. Award contract.
6. Complete construction.
7. Select and procure furniture and equipment.
8. Orient and train faculty, staff, and students.
9. Occupy facility.
10. Conduct postoccupancy evaluation.

The degree of business administrator involvement will depend on the size of the system. If the business office is large, specialists under the business administrator's supervision will handle many of these details. In smaller systems the business administrator may be solely responsible for supervision of most of these steps.

Educational Specifications

Educational specifications should be developed into a written report that summarizes the operational planning discussions and becomes a communication device from the educational planners to the architectural planning team. Educational specifications are a statement of the design problem to be solved by the architectural planning team. Specifications should be provided for new construction projects, major additions, and extensive renovation projects. Ideally, the educational planning group should include the administrative staff, paid consultants, and personnel who will occupy the facility on completion of the construction. If the staffing has not yet been established, then personnel who are working with the same, or similar, program should be chosen. Within this planning group it is important to involve staff familiar with all the functions to be housed, whether instructional or service. Those involved should be knowledgeable and active in their field since they will be participating in the detailed planning of a facility likely to be in use long after all involved have retired. Developing educational specifications precedes architectural planning, and direct involvement of the architectural staff is not necessary.

Planning participants will need time to discuss, analyze, reflect, and investigate findings as details of the spaces are established. It would not be unusual for a major project to require six to eighteen months of lead time for completion.

Failure to design a particular project in relation to the overall plan involves substantial risks and can prove costly in terms of both money and functional effectiveness. Analysis should encompass the total program most broadly defined, including both the major programs involved plus all supporting activities; it covers both indoor and outdoor activities, ''off hour'' and regular hour events, and activities of casual users as well as those regularly served by the facility. Good educational specifications promote economy and make it possible for the architect to do a better job without unnecessary delay. Interpretation and clarification will require continuous communication between the facility planner and the architect. Major steps in the development of educational specifications include the following:

1. Review of tactical facility planning
2. Development of the basic program outline
3. Determination of quantitative requirements
4. Determination of specific qualitative requirements
5. Preparation of the written document

Multiple Agency Utilization   If several agencies are going to utilize the building, representatives of all the agencies should be involved in the planning. Extra time will be needed for this process because personnel from the other agencies will not be experienced in developing functional specifications.

Quantitative Aspects   The first product of quantitative determination should be a listing of (1) every room and space needed for instruction and service functions, (2) the number of each type of space, and (3) the capacity of each. The list should include all learning spaces, support facilities for students, administrative and staff facilities, service facilities, facilities for public use, maintenance facilities, and outdoor spaces.

Qualitative Aspects   Once the list of needed rooms and spaces has been computed, attention must be shifted to the qualitative side. Attention must be directed to questions dealing with location, activities anticipated, furniture and equipment, and special considerations associated with the space. In planning these spaces, personnel associated with them are the best source of expertise. It is imperative that building area planning committees understand prior planning efforts and decisions so they can meet the constraints already established. Consideration should be given to the relationship between spaces and concerns for proximity or separation of spaces. For each space the furniture and equipment to be used should be listed. Space footage estimates or dimensions should not be included unless exact dimensions are necessary for proper functioning of a room or space. Educational specifications can serve as background for in-service training of both faculty and staff.

Architectural Planning
During tactical planning and the development of educational specifications, the educational facility planning group has had the primary role, with the architect serving as a consultant.

Upon completion of educational specifications, the architect assumes the primary role and retains it for the duration of construction.

Role of Architect   Whether a school building project is large or small, the architect's normal services are similar. It should be noted, however, that special services are often contracted by special arrangement. The following are normal services of architects.

1. The architect assumes responsibility for the implementation for the project in all phases.

2. The architect prepares all contractual arrangements between the architect and the owner and between the owner and the contractor. The legal complications of any construction project can only be appreciated by one who has been involved in producing a school plant from start to finish. The problems involve code requirements; controls by public agencies; real estate legalities; bonding; inspection reports; progress payments; preparation, administration and enforcement of contract documents; lien laws; recording of all project amounts; certification of construction personnel; and determination of the degree of acceptability of all work performed.

3. The architect aids the client in programming and analyzing school needs. This consultation phase involves administrators, curriculum personnel, teachers, consultants, planners, and engineers. In the interest of expediting the project, site surveys and soil testing may be completed during this phase. These surveys and tests are not normally covered by the architect's fee.

4. The architect, after thorough study of the program, the site, the financial limitations, and the predilections of owners and boards, prepares tentative design studies for review. Generally these are revised several times as review teams make their evaluations. Preliminary drawings usually require detailed illustration of conceptual ideas.

5. The architect develops his/her schematic work by refining all drawings and preparing in detail illustrations of the plan, site development, features of construction, and equipment. Usually he/she prepares outline specifications for materials, determines the type of construction, and prepares a statement of probable construction costs. Work completed at this point constitutes the preliminary phase. Normally, one-fourth of the architect's fee is paid at this time.

6. The architect develops the construction documents (including working drawings, specifications, general conditions, bidding information, and contract forms), covering in detail general construction, site development, structure, mechanical systems, materials, workmanship, and responsibilities of all parties. The technical knowledge and experience required to coordinate the architectural details with electrical, mechanical, and structural engineers is today one of the most complex skills of any profession. Professional competency in these areas not only has direct influence on costs, but determines to a great extent the level of performance of the completed buildings.

7. The architect obtains approvals for proposed construction from all agencies, including the bureau of school planning, the division of architecture, the state fire marshal, local and regional planning boards, and other controlling agencies such as the highway department, flood control agencies, the health department, and so forth.

8. The architect guides the client in the selection of contractors and in the crafting of their contracts and administers and supervises the work of the contractor. The architect must keep project accounts, issue certificates of payment due to contractors, and expedite all change-orders in the contracts as needed. He/she verifies acceptability of shop drawings submitted by various subcontractors and manufacturers and maintains standards for workmanship, materials, and appliances. He/she makes periodic inspections at the site and reviews progress and workmanship with the inspector and the construction superintendent. He/she must pass on and certify the satisfactory completion of all work.

Architects furnish many special services. Most school building projects require some type of special architectural service such as civil engineering services beyond site surveys and soil testing, acoustical engineering, and services of landscape consultants and color consultants. If theaters or kitchens are included in a building project, services should include specialists for stage design, rigging, or kitchen layout.

Architectural services are also required in many instances when communitywide population projections and land utilization studies are made for the master plan of a total district's site needs. All applications made by school districts for funds under a state school building aid law usually require architectural services.

Other special services involve extra work on the architect's part that was not anticipated at the time his/her contract with a school district was signed. Such services might include:

- Revising previously approved drawings and specifications at the written request of the owner
- Preparing documents for alternative bids or change-orders at the written request of the owner
- Consultation and professional services concerning replacement of any work damaged by fire or other cause during construction
- Arranging for work to proceed in case of default or insolvency of a contractor
- Administration of a prolonged contract in excess of 25 percent of the stipulated time

Fees for Architectural Services   Historically, the architectural fee schedule for school work in several states has been 8 percent of the construction price. Some districts today use a sliding scale based on the size and complications of the project. Architects sometimes ask for an additional fee beyond the normal 8 percent when they are required to provide special services.

Construction of a typical secondary school from initial work with the client to completion requires about three years. Typical elementary school projects can be completed in approximately eighteen months from beginning to occupancy. Smaller projects take less time. During this period the architect attempts to conduct his/her business so that it will show a profit. This requires a high degree of managerial skill. The architect must not only maintain his/her office and all the accompanying overhead of normal business expenses, but must pay for a wide variety of skilled personnel. The architect as a businessperson will attempt to maintain a profit for services rendered even when fees are reduced. This can be done only by gearing the whole operation to a particular fee and setting time schedules and services accordingly. Cutting time means cutting services, with lamentable architectural results virtually guaranteed.

part of the med is the time line.

Selection   Selecting an architect must be done objectively and impersonally. Since architects tend to specialize, it is advisable (1) to limit choice of an architect from among those who have given special attention to school building planning, and (2) to select an architect whose services and school buildings have given satisfaction. The architect should have the following qualifications:

1. It is important to secure an architect with training and experience that will be useful in the planning of an educationally sound school building. An architect specializing in school building construction projects should profit from his/her experiences in building other school structures and can assist the school in determining educationally useful features in the new building.
2. He/she should be able to design school buildings in terms of a specified program of education.
3. He/she should plan buildings that are economical in terms of usable space, construction costs, and maintenance costs, and at the same time not sacrifice utility, appearance, or durability.
4. He/she should be able to prepare plans and specifications that are clear and complete.
5. He/she should be a competent executive in drawing contracts, investigating bidders, and coordinating the work of contractors.
6. He/she should provide or secure all engineering services. His staff should be able to provide supervision during construction.
7. He/she should have a good reputation in all personal and professional dealings.

Construction Plans and Specifications   The first step in construction planning is the development of a potential schematic solution to the educational specifications. The architect develops diagrams indicating various possibilities for organizing spaces in the facility and on the site. During this phase the needs stated in the educational specifications take shape, the architect's creative talent is expressed, and highly visible decisions related to the project are made. These should be approved by the governing board before moving on the next step, design development.

The design development stage includes determination of the basic materials and finishes, as well as the structural, mechanical, and electrical systems; furniture and equipment layouts are also prepared during this stage. This stage should not be started unless the project is fully funded because the architect's costs will be quite substantial for this phase.

The construction document stage includes the preparation of complete working drawings and construction specifications based on the approved design development documents. Working drawings establish physical detail: location, shape, relationship, and size; construction specifications establish quality, standards, requirements, and criteria. Site sheets show location of all facilities on site, any shrubbery, and final elevations and contours desired. When working drawings and construction specifications are finished, the project is ready for bidding and construction.

Review of Plans and Specifications   The educator should feel no hesitancy in criticizing the plans. The architect is skilled in design but the educator is in a position to evaluate whether a proposed plan is likely to meet teaching/learning needs. The assistance of an educational planner can be extremely important in the review of plans.

Construction Contracts   The contractors accept responsibility for this phase of the project planning. The architect maintains a supervisory role and must approve all alterations and payments. The educational planner should generally follow the construction and be fully informed to see that everything progresses according to plan. However, the planner will not be directly involved in any project supervision. It is important that the architect serve as a communications link between each contractor, the planning staff, and board. In fact, it is good practice to have the architect prepare written progress reports on a regular basis.

A change-order is a plan or specification alteration occurring after the contract is in effect. Some change-orders are unavoidable; an oversight in planning or unexpected developments may force a change. A sequence of change-orders indicates poor review of plans or inadequate architectural supervision or both.

Bidding of Contracts   Competitive bidding is generally required by law and is usually detailed in state statutes. Bid specifications must be precise enough that all bidders are bidding on an equal basis. When utilizing manufacturer names and model numbers to indicate quality wanted, the phrase ''or equivalent'' must be added, or bidding will be highly restricted. Bid notices generally must be advertised in a local newspaper that will go to clipping services. The architect will contact some bidders, particularly those with whom the architect has had good experiences in the past. F. W. Dodge or a similar group will advertise your construction project for a fee. Although timing of bids is a major factor in both number of bidders and amount of bids, the architect and owner influence bidding. If the architect is well organized and precise in the specifications, lower bids will be forthcoming. Any bids not conforming to all requirements must be rejected. All bid documents should contain the provision for bid rejection. The lowest bid does not have to be accepted; most states require that you pick the lowest responsible bidder.

Awarding of Contract   Contracts must be awarded for every construction project and should be drafted by the architect or attorney and reviewed by legal counsel. The contract must contain the following:

1. Legal name of contracting parties
2. Contract sums and stipulations
3. Responsibility for supervision of work
4. Completion date
5. Procedure for payment
6. Procedure for
   a. Acceptance of project
   b. Final payment

Architects may use the standard American Institute of Architects (AIA) contract or the architect's standard contract form.

Clerk-of-the-Works   This person is employed by the governing board and is responsible for inspecting the project to ascertain that the project is developing according to plans and specifications. This person should be jointly selected by the architect and the governing boards. Any concerns are relayed to the architect for action. If the architect is daily supervising the project, the role of the clerk is less important.

Progressive Construction Techniques

This textbook is written primarily for educational staff, particularly the educational planner and the business administrator. Therefore, some of the latest building construction techniques—modular construction, fast tracking, and construction management—will be described. These techniques have been used for some time in other construction. All have their advocates and disbelievers. All save money under particular construction needs. Educators must understand these techniques, where each is appropriate, and the advantages and disadvantages of each.

Modular Construction
The modular construction technique has been widely used in building apartments and motels. Many are built in a factory setting and assembled at the site. Only the foundation and basic utility services are built on site. In school construction small modules are combined. These modules are combined to form a basic classroom. The lighting system, doors, demountable walls, and chalkboard are planned to fit the module. This system was pioneered in California and Florida. It requires standardization to the point that programmatic differences may be ignored. The main advantages are that it saves expense and time.

Fast Tracking
Through critical path method (CPM) or program evaluation and review technique (PERT), overlapping of planning and construction steps can occur to the point that a facility can be completed in a much shorter period of time. (For a more detailed discussion see Chapter 3.) Many times, in order to get the construction completed quickly, proper planning is sacrificed. The fast tracking method allows planning to occur while other phases of the construction are underway. This is extremely costly if changes are made after the project is underway. The problem of costly errors can be diminished if fast tracking is only applied to construction rather than to both planning and construction.

Construction Management
Construction management is the newest of the three techniques discussed here. This method is usually combined with fast tracking. The construction manager is employed at the same time as the architect and starts working with the planners at that time. He/she is the one familiar with construction costs, techniques, and practices. He/she serves the role of general contractor and is paid the same fee as the architect. All contractors serve as subcontractors. Under proper conditions this method will save both time and expense. A major disadvantages is that it is difficult to find well-trained construction management personnel. Second, since this method is relatively new, contractors are not familiar with it and therefore are reluctant to accept it.

Procurement of Furniture and Equipment

Furniture and equipment influence educational outcomes and therefore should receive attention at the earliest stages of operational facility planning. The selection process should involve a variety of individuals including the general staff, facility planner, architect, equipment consultant, and equipment supplier. Coordination can be handled by the architect, system administrator, or equipment consultant. If the architect has the proper experience, he/she can perform most adequately as coordinator because (1) the entire project will be coordinated and (2) the responsibility will be clearly established. Using an equipment consultant or system administrator creates a coordination problem. Conflicts often arise over issues such as the union status of workers, access to areas of the facility, and storage space as equipment arrives. If the architect does not have proper training, then the school administrator or equipment consultant should be chosen, depending on who can give the best service without interfering with the total workload. All built-in equipment must be a part of the regular construction contract. The coordination of a simple project such as a built-in sink involves coordination among the following: the general contractor who has responsibility for the basic construction, the floor covering supplier who carpets or tiles around the cabinet, the plumber who connects the sink, the electrician who provides electrical service, and the cabinetmaker who fabricates the built-in unit.

Selection

The first task, selection, involves compiling a list of all the furniture and equipment desired. It is important to try to consolidate and minimize the number and types of items. Every effort should be made to standardize furniture and equipment as long as such standardization does not seriously affect the basic function of requested items. This should be a collaborative effort involving input from faculty, staff, and other members of the planning team. Flexibility will be required should the need arise to adapt to emerging programmatic needs.

Procurement

The preparation of bidding specifications is a technical task and should be delegated to a person knowledgeable in equipment specifications. Specifications should be written as simply as possible but with sufficient preciseness to avoid ambiguity. In using brand names as a generic term, ''or equivalent'' should be added to encourage other bidders. The instructions to bidders should contain such information as where and when bids are to be received and opened, bonding requirements, affidavits needed, where delivery is to be made, whether bids are to include installation, and treatment of alternative bids. State legal requirements must be met as to places and length of time to advertise. Ample time between advertising and bid opening will ensure that bidders have sufficient time to prepare bids. Most state statutes require a public opening and reading of all bids. No attempt should be made at the bid opening to evaluate and award bids. The evaluation is a tedious and time-consuming activity: Bids must be checked for compliance with specifications; alternative bids must be checked; and delivery schedule, guarantees, and quality levels must be checked to see if they meet or exceed specifications.

Once the order has been settled, items received must be inspected to make sure that (1) they are the items that were ordered, (2) the right quantity has been received, and (3) they are in satisfactory condition. Coordination of deliveries and installation with the construction schedule must not be overlooked or left to chance.

Orientation and Training Programs

Once the construction of the facility is completed, the school business administrator and members of the team involved in planning and construction turn the facility over to the instructional personnel. These personnel, with advice from the school business administrator and construction team, have the responsibility to see that the facility is fully used for the purposes intended.

The community should be encouraged to tour the new facilities. Students can be trained to make excellent tour guides. Public relations should be addressed very early in the construction process.

The media should be encouraged to cover the following activities:

1. The board's decision to construct a building
2. Site tour
3. Architect's selection
4. Overview of schematic plans
5. Bidding
6. Groundbreaking
7. Open house and/or dedication
8. Opening day

Both the faculty and student body must be oriented to a new facility. With both groups a lecture and slide presentation of the new building is a good initial step. This should be followed by a general tour of the entire facility. Time should be allowed for a later in-depth visit to facilities of major importance to the individual. Student groups should be broken down into manageable divisions.

In addition to in-service education concerning operation of the educational program and selection of learning experiences, the staff needs to be oriented to a multitude of operating procedures. The following list is suggestive, not exhaustive.

- Specific opening day plans and schedules
- Student registration
- Scheduling for students
- Orientation of new students
- Procedures for ordering supplies
- Equipment repair and service procedures
- Use of intercom and public address system
- Communication with parents
- Preparation of instructional aids
- Use of specialized equipment

- Relationships with service and support staff concerning heating controls, cleaning, dining procedures, and other matters

The need to train the entire staff before the building is completed cannot be overstressed.

Additional Planning Considerations

The school business administrator's role in planning construction will involve consideration of physical factors peripheral to educational specifications but conducive to an atmosphere in which education can proceed. These peripheral factors include vandalism control and conservation in the face of decline. Security and energy management were both discussed in Chapter 10's section on plant operations; they will be addressed here in a construction planning context.

Planning for Vandalism Control

Vandalism is an unfortunate but very real fact of life. It is not confined to the inner city, rural, suburban, or other type of educational setting. It is a widespread phenomenon that educational facility planners must consider in planning buildings if those structures are to remain functional and attractive. Planning is a major deterrent to vandalism. For the safety of persons and property, the following ideas merit consideration.

- Provide a system of emergency telephones at strategic locations.
- Channel building exit paths onto well-lighted and traveled paths where nighttime use is heavy.
- Avoid alcoves and recesses, both in and outside of buildings.
- Create a system of emergency lighting in facilities where evening use is common.
- Light the premises (in spite of energy problems). Light is a deterrent to criminals and vandals.
- Avoid staff offices in isolated portions of buildings.
- Avoid large shrubbery masses.
- Locate bicycle racks near well-traveled pathways.
- Provide automatic locking of interior doors.
- Provide well-lighted pedestrian paths between major activity centers and parking lots. Unintentional footholds such as decorative wall structures, hardware, and roof drains should be avoided.

Proper design of facilities can help control vandalism. If vandals cannot gain access to the roof, they cannot damage the roofing or equipment on the roof or enter the building through skylights and entry hatches.

Entrances must be safe and inviting but secure. Glass that cannot be easily broken must be used. Hardware must be of high quality and resistant to vandalism. If the public has access to portions of the building, these should be grouped and barriers to the the rest of the building installed.

Play areas should be highly visible from major streets. Plantings and facilities must be strong and able to withstand damage from stray balls and players. If the school furnishes meeting places, they should be highly visible and easily secured.

Many walls are easily vandalized. Names, letters, and signs should be placed out of reach. Walls should be nonabsorbent and easily cleaned. If graffiti is not removed it seems to invite more.

All interior hardware should be recessed and protected. Tamper-proof screws can be useful in fastening hardware throughout the building. Durable plastic, vinyl, and fiberglass should be used in furnishings.

There are many types of security alarm systems on the market today. The selection of an appropriate system merits careful consideration by the planning staff. Systems vary in style: They may sound a loud alarm on the outside of the building, signal an intrusion to the system's security office or signal the local police headquarters. Changes are occurring so rapidly that only careful planning will indicate what is best for your particular site and facility.

Energy Decline

Despite warnings over the years from many scientists, the energy crisis shocked us. Typically, we reacted by clamoring for more, bigger, and different sources of energy. For the first time we started seriously to explore the heat of the sun, the power of winds and waters, the warmth of the Earth, the fission of the atom—energy we hoped would be available, renewable, and infinite.

About one-third of the total energy used in the United States is used in buildings. Most of the 74 million residential buildings and 1.5 million commercial buildings in the country were constructed when energy was not a major consideration. Their designers incorporated few, if any, energy-conserving features into their plans. Owners undertaking new projects were more concerned with initial construction and labor costs and did not require projections of a building's energy consumption or costs of operation over the life of the building. The result is a tremendous waste by most of the existing inventory of U.S. buildings.

In all facility planning the business administrator must remember that: (1) buildings today waste energy; (2) through proper design the wasted energy can be saved; (3) energy shapes buildings; (4) buildings shape how people live, work, and play, and (5) energy can be saved without sacrificing aesthetics and human values.

On a more positive note, superior planning can save a tremendous quantity of energy in erecting new structures, as well as in retrofitting older structures. Specifically:

1. *Select the right direction for the building to face.* Twenty percent of a building's energy consumption can be saved through proper orientation.
2. *Reduce the building's volume.* Often a building's volume can be reduced by as much as one-third by trimming the fat through efficient design without sacrificing the needed spaces.
3. *Use outdoor spaces to save energy.* Courts, covered walkways, porches, patios, breezeways, and the like—protected from the hot summer sun and the cold winter wind—can save energy.
4. *Provide daylight.* If the building is divided with a sunlit atrium corridor, people may turn off the lights.
5. *Use the wind to cool.* Planning outdoor areas to take advantage of breezes can help influence the total climate (and energy consumption) of a building.

6. *Keep the sun out of buildings*. Deeply inset windows and windows with large overhangs can bring a reduction of as much as 25 percent in heating load.
7. *Stop heat transfer*. Well-insulated buildings use 50 percent less energy that uninsulated ones.
8. *Bury the building*. Earth is a good insulator.
9. *Design efficient mechanical systems*. New mechanical systems are much more efficient than old ones.
10. *Use the right kind of glass*. Quarter-inch glass allows 80 percent of the solar energy to penetrate.
11. *Design lighting for specific tasks*. Proper fixture orientation and reflective colors can increase illumination by 30 footcandles without increasing energy consumption.
12. *Respect the region*. Respect and respond to climate.
13. *Use computer-assisted management*. Both individual room lighting and heating can be controlled by computer.
14. *Use solar-assisted heating*. All water can be heated by solar energy.

Saving energy is complex. Only through careful planning can the hundreds of variables be given simultaneous consideration. Many of these complex variables will need the attention of architects and engineers. For the on-site planners and business administrator, understanding of the following guidelines will promote energy control related to building design.

- Use the climate. Put the elements to work.
- Make the envelope—the outside structure of the building—lean and clean. The more walls and roof area, the more energy it takes.
- Design on the edge of comfort zones. People can wear more or less clothing to suit individual comfort needs.
- Use energy-efficient systems for cooling/heating, lighting, wall/roof components, and fenestration, the design of wall openings that let in air, light, and view.
- Provide controls—automatic or on-off switches—so energy can be saved when spaces are not in use or when systems need modification.

Through proper planning we can do many things to reduce consumption of resources. We know how to bounce light off the ground into deep, interior spaces; how to cut building costs by decreasing the perimeter and lowering ceilings, yet have quality natural lighting; how to funnel the cooling wind around the people who use our buildings; and how to design pressure walls to ventilate leeward spaces, even reversing the direction of the wind and increasing the velocity. We have also learned how to modify the outdoors with windbreaks and sun packets, using the outside for functional activities. The key is control. Through proper planning, control of environment and resources is possible.

Planning for Decline

Comprehensive planning is an integral part of any new construction project for a growing school district. Many school systems are not growing but rather are suffering from a decline in students, with concurrent surplus facilities. Comprehensive planning is just as important when planning for decline. Most school administrators' training and experience have been focused on growth and expansion. For many school systems this is not the trend of the future. Administrators must plan to cope with scarcity, inflation, and decline. Facilities that are well planned from the outset in terms of flexibility of use, energy conservation, and security may contain features that mitigate some downturns and expedite rehabilitation or multiple agency use.

Enrollment Decline

Over the next fifteen years American schools will experience a series of fluctuations in their enrollments because of demographic changes. Even as high school enrollments were slowly reaching their (probable) twentieth century zenith in the 1970s, the overall enrollment began to decline. In the 1990s elementary enrollments are expected to increase, while secondary school enrollments continue to decline. These changes in enrollments are the result of past changes in the birth rate—the baby boom and bust—and expected changes. Demographers expect a rise in births shortly as the aging ''baby boom'' babies plus those who have delayed childbearing begin to settle down and have children of their own. This will affect elementary school enrollments in the 1990s.

Enrollment fluctuations will vary among school districts depending on past and current migration patterns (and, to a lesser extent, on local differences in fertility and school attendance). For example, secondary school enrollments were expected to decline nationally about 25 percent between 1976 and 1990. However, areas now experiencing in-migration may well show an increase while other places have an even more precipitous decline.

Both long-range plans and more immediate preparations depend on reasonably accurate estimations of probable enrollment changes. Although the national trends in enrollment are fairly well known, it is the local districts that will have to deal with the changes. The development of state and local capabilities in enrollment estimation and forecasting is therefore strongly recommended.

Financial Base Decline

Because finance and organizational policies in American education are in a tumultuous state, the financial base for education is shifting. The lack of planning and of full recognition of implications has caused school districts to be ridiculed for not meeting the contradictory standards imposed on them. The changing economy, the shifting job market, the conservative shift by the populace, the rise in teacher militancy, changes in social conscience as to redistribution of resources, an increasing antagonism toward taxes, and ballooning inflation have all contributed to the declining financial base. The trend toward ever larger units of school population continues in the absence of persuasive analyses that the movement has achieved the objectives held either by its past or present advocates. Indeed, the trend persists despite evidence to the contrary that it has produced any cost saving or educational gains, and it may have damaged citizen allegiance to public schools and lay control over them. This illogical planning approach has accelerated the financial decline.

Consequences of Decline

The evaluation of education in America has been based on the psychology that"bigger is better.'' We are having difficulty in coping with the fact that growth is declining. Some of the adjustments that are being made are rehabilitation, mothballing, and multiple agency utilization.

Rehabilitation

Our lifestyle has been characterized as disposable as long as natural resources and energy were inexpensive. Because of the current limited resources and energy, this trend is being reexamined. Declining enrollment has refocused the space concern. Educational quality of space is becoming a primary priority. The upgrading of facilities is being accomplished under a variety of terms: renovation, revitalization, restoration, recycling, rehabilitation, retrofitting, and modernization.

In determining the practicality of rehabilitation, some basic questions must be asked. They are:

- Will an educational facility be needed in the general location for an extended period of time?
- Will the rehabilitated facility meet the requirements of the anticipated educational program reasonably?
- Will the plant improvement be economically feasible? If the facility cannot be redesigned to meet programmatic needs, then renovation is moot. In addition, the site must be adequate in size.

Through renovation, most older facilities can be made energy-efficient through installation of new windows, doors, and mechanical systems. Cost of custodial services must also be accounted for. Renovation is generally considered feasible if (1) the project cost is below the 50 percent level (of new construction), (2) retrofitting will add another twenty-five years of use to the plant, and (3) program adequacy can be achieved.

In recent years several formulas have been proposed for determining the appropriateness of a proposed rehabilitation project. The Boles formula compares the pupil cost per year of operation for both proposed retrofitted and new facilities. The formula is as follows[7]:

$$\text{Pupil Cost per Year} = \frac{\text{Estimated Cost of Facility}}{\text{No. of Yrs. Estimated Life} \times \text{No. of Pupils}}$$

The computation must be done for both the proposed rehabilitated facility and a new facility. There are some serious weaknesses to this formula: (1) It is assumed that both facilities are of equal educational quality; (2) older facilities may have features (e.g., auditorium) that may not exist in new buildings; (3) older facilities may have undesirable features that cannot be corrected; and (4) no allowance is made for variations in operation and maintenance costs.

The Castaldi formula is more complex and deals with the educational adequacies that the Boles formula ignores.[8] The Castaldi formula demonstrates that modernization is justifiable if

$$\frac{(C_e + C_h + C_s)}{(L_m)(I_a)} = \frac{C_r}{L_r}(Ce + Ch + Cs) = Cr$$

where

C_e = total cost for educational improvements
C_h = total cost for improvements in healthfulness
C_s = total cost for improvement in safety
I_a = estimated index of educational adequacy
L_m = estimated useful life of modernized building
C_r = replacement cost of the facility considered for renovation
L_r = estimated life of replacement building

The three factors added together $(C_e + C_h + C_s)$ equal the cost of modernization. One problem with dividing the retrofitting cost is that many costs have multiple effects. The reader should be cautioned that neither the Castaldi formula nor the Boles formula allow for increasing operating and maintenance costs. The business administrator must take these costs into consideration.

Site-level planning for renovation projects is no different than for new facilities. In fact, both should originate at the site and should be a part of the master plan for facilities.

Mothballing

Some communities have decided simply to board up unused schools and hold on to them until the space is needed again (and current birth rate projections indicate that many schools may be needed again). Vandalism and the effects of decay make this the least desirable solution to the problem of excess space. Curriculum innovations and program changes make it even less likely that a reopened building will suit future educational needs.

In ever increasing numbers, school boards are brushing up on public relations techniques to convince angry citizens of the necessity for school closings. Too often an administrator will recommend the closing of a school without consulting the community it serves. This is unfortunate because school closings, emotional as they are, offer a real opportunity for increasing communication between differing sectors of the community.

Multiple Agency Utilization

Educators should be anxious to involve the lay public in school closings. The total citizenry has endowed the school system with the responsibility for educating the young and has supplied it with funds to build and run school facilities. School boards and administrators are trustees of community property. They cannot, in all fairness, dispose of a building without considering the wishes of the building's real owners.

Summary

Of all the activities American people engage in while living and working together, perhaps none expresses in material form so many aspects of our culture as school construction. The growing national concern for the improvement of education is undoubtedly one of the most pronounced phenomena of our time. Dimensions of education—purposes and content, methods and materials, as well as financial support and status—have been dramatically influenced during the past decade by forces inherent in rapid cultural change. Educators in every corner of the nation have examined the educational process with the full realization that the future of this nation and of the free world depends in large measure on the excellence of education.

One cannot help feeling a change in the tempo of our educational programming. Perhaps the most distinguishing characteristic of any living thing is that it is forever changing. A school facility that never changes gives a good indication that the program within is dead or was never alive. Therefore, in order to provide for a living, dynamic, and effective educational program, a flexible plant containing the kinds of teaching areas needed to implement the program must be arranged. The educational program must change; therefore, the facility housing the program must be flexible in order to implement this change. The ferment of ideas in education affects every feature of the school plant—namely, flexibility, furniture, equipment, thermal control, acoustical control, and visual and color control. Since buildings are of such a permanent nature and have such a direct and definite influence on the educational process, educational leaders are very much concerned with planning buildings to meet educational needs.

Suggested Activities

1. Prepare a PERT network for the planning of a capital outlay project of your choosing. In doing this, proceed through the following steps:
   a. Identify the activities involved in the project.
   b. Draw the PERT network, showing the sequence of the activities.
   c. Estimate the time required to complete each activity.
   d. Compute the time required to complete the entire project and the times at which each activity must be completed in order for the entire project to be completed on time.
2. Outline steps to follow in preparing educational specifications for a particular phase of a building program with which you are familiar.
3. Develop an overview of what should be included in a prospectus for both the primary and secondary bond market.
4. Prepare a plan for staff, students, and community involvement in planning educational facilities.

Suggested Readings

Abend, Allen C., Michael J. Bednar, Vera J. Froelinger, and Yale Stenzler. *Facilities for Special Education Services*. Reston, VA: The Council for Exceptional Children, 1979.

Castaldi, Basil. "Personalized Instruction and Programs," *Council of Educational Facility Planners Journal, 19,* 1, (Jan.–Feb. 1981), 8–10.

Council of Educational Facility Planners. *Energy Sourcebook for Educational Facilities*. Columbus, OH: CEFP, Int. 1977

Daniels, Farrington. *Direct Use of the Sun's Energy*. New York: Ballantine Books, 1977.

Hawkins, Harold L. *Appraisal Guide for School Facilities*. Midland, MI: Pendell Publishing, 1976.

Naisbitt, John. *Megatrends*. New York: Warner Books, 1982.

Peters, Thomas, and Robert Waterman, Jr. *In Search of Excellence*. New York: Warner Books, 1982.

Waterman, Robert, Jr. *The Renewal Factor*. New York: Bantam Books, 1988.

Notes

1. Kenneth W. Brooks, Marion Conrad, and William Griffith, *From Program to Educational Facilities* (Lexington, KY: Center for Professional Development, College of Education, University of Kentucky, 1980), 30–31.

2. Phi Delta Kappa, *Educational Goals and Objectives* (Bloomington, IN: Phi Delta Kappa, 1972), 32–33.

3. The American Institute of Architects, *State Requirements for School Construction* (Washington, DC: AIA, 1987).

4. For additional information on public relations and community involvement aspects of capital outlay programs, see Philip K. Piele and John S. Hall, *Budgets, Bonds, and Ballots: Voting Behavior in School Finance* (Lexington, MA: Heath, 1973).

5. Dewey H. Stollar, *Managing School Indebtedness* (Danville, IL: The Interstate Printers and Publishers, 1967), 22.

6. Ibid.

7. Harold Boles, *Step by Step to Better School Facilities* (New York: Holt, Rinehart, and Winston, 1963), 90–92.

8. Basil Castaldi, *Educational Facilities Planning, Modernization, and Management* (Boston: Allyn and Bacon, 1982), 358.

12

Cash Management

PART OF THE ROLE that school administrators assume is the responsibility for the use of financial resources. This responsibility includes not only expending resources to best achieve programmatic and related goals but also acting in a fiduciary or stewardship role with the school system's liquid assets. The latter role includes the wise and prudent investment of these resources. Local taxes, state and federal aids or grants, and miscellaneous revenues pour into school system treasuries at a rate that does not on a day-to-day basis match expenditures. Thus, "surplus" monies are frequently available for investment. For example, real property taxes usually are collected every six months, so early in each six-month period there is often a large balance in various funds. These are usually drawn down to small balances by the end of the period, and the cycle is repeated.

Responsibilities of public finance officers include not only the provision of security, but the wise and prudent investment of these monies. The rationale for investing "inactive" monies is to optimize the amount of revenue available for eventual expenditure. Thus, investment of available revenue will retain or increase the purchasing power of public monies dedicated to providing an educational program. In this function, school administrators play the role of good stewards of public monies.

The Nature of Cash for Investment

In its simplest form, cash for investment is stated as:

Revenues – Expenditures = Cash for Investment

School systems receive revenues from federal, state, and local sources. Federal revenue is largely tied to specific programs with discrete dispersement schedules. Typically, state revenue is transferred to school systems on a fixed and regular schedule that is reasonably predictable. Local revenue payments in the form of property and other taxes dedicated to school systems are made on a relatively fixed schedule also. Local taxes are less predictable due to the nature of changing tax rates, assessment procedures, tax delinquencies, and the like. Miscellaneous local charges, fees, and other sources are also subject to change. On the whole, the largest sources of revenue are relatively predictable, but only if underlying variables are taken into consideration.

The expenditure component of the cash for investment equation is governed by both policy mandates and school system discretion. Certain obligations of the school system must be met on a fixed schedule, e.g., tuition payments from one system to another, fees due to state agencies such as the auditor's office or the teachers' retirement system, and debt service payments to retire bond issues. The larger part of total expenditure is, at least in part, governed by school board and administration discretion. Salaries and payroll procedures are usually negotiable items, although there are certain specific mandates such as minimum salary provisions, pay periods, deductibles, and the like. The purchase of supplies, equipment, services, and capital assets is a permissive power granted to the school system within general parameters of state policy. However, the timing of such expenditures is largely determined by the board and the administrative staff. Many expenditures can be timed to coincide with the flow of revenue and thus even the cash flow.

Cash Flow

The concept of cash flow is derived from the analogy that revenue flows into a pot and that expenditures flow out of it. At a given moment the pot may hold a relatively large amount of cash if revenue exceeds expenditure. If at the next moment expenditure exceeds revenue, the amount of cash in the pot would be reduced. All organizations with fiscal systems experience the dynamics of cash flow. An important consideration then is how cash flow should be managed to maximize its benefit (or, perhaps, minimize its liabilities).

The initial step for such consideration in a school system is describing and analyzing the cash flow. This is prerequisite to the development of both a management strategy and a set of management tactics to reach investment goals. Given the unpredictables and the systematic changes from year to year, multi-year analysis is necessary to obtain useful trend data. It is desirable to review several past years of revenue and expenditure data and then forecast a year or two of anticipated revenue and expenditures. Cash-flow forecasting should be based on explicit assumptions of enrollments, staffing, salary levels, program costs, and other expected expenditures. Revenue forecasting likewise should be based on explicit assumptions of local property valuation, tax rates, tax delinquency and abatements, and other local sources of revenue such as tuition, fees, and investment income. State and federal sources should also be forecast—again these based on explicit assumptions related to the criteria or formula components used by the funding agency.

Table 12-1 is an illustration of an annual fiscal forecast for a general fund on a month-to-month basis. The forecast was developed by an analysis of the actual cash flow for each month of previous fiscal years. The same format is used to record actual receipts, expenditures, and ending cash balances.

The ending cash balances for each month give insights as to cash that is available for investment. A more precise—but still not absolute—figure can be obtained by using the same format but calculating the balance on a daily basis. Most school systems with aggressive investment policies have provisions for monitoring the daily cash flow.

A careful analysis of cash flow can reveal several ways to increase or optimize cash available for investment. Prompt payment of bills from vendors who offer discounts is

TABLE 12-1 South-Western City Annual Spending Plan SM-1

		(00) ANNUAL EST.	(01) JANUARY	(02) FEBRUARY	(03) MARCH	(04) APRIL	(05) MAY	(06) JUNE
	BEGINNING CASH BALANCE	$2,519,490	$3,057,122	$4,793,894	$6,312,666	$3,851,444	$2,698,344	$6,077,154
1.	REAL ESTATE TAX	$22,277,154	$4,000,000	$4,000,000	$0	$0	$0	$0
2.	TANGIBLE PERSONAL PROPERTY TAX	$6,353,128				$1,253,128		
3.	INVESTMENT EARNINGS	$600,000	$40,000	$55,000	$55,000	$50,000	$50,000	$50,000
4.	PROCEEDS FROM BORROWING	$0						
5.	OTHER	$736,000	$61,000	$61,000	$62,000	$61,000	$61,000	$62,000
6.	FOUNDATION PROGRAM	$26,621,826	$2,241,000	$2,241,000	$2,241,000	$2,241,000	$2,241,000	$2,240,826
7.	ROLLBACK AND HOMESTEAD EXEMPTION	$1,914,016			$257,000		$957,016	
8.	OTHER	$575,000	$32,000	$32,000	$32,000	$32,000	$32,000	$27,000
9.	PUBLIC LAW 874	$0						
10.	OTHER	$70,000	$6,000	$5,000	$6,000	$6,000	$5,000	$0
11.	TRANSFERS AND ADVANCES IN	$225,000						$90,000
12.	TOTAL RECEIPTS (LINES 1-11)	$59,372,124	$6,380,000	$6,394,000	$2,621,000	$3,643,128	$3,346,016	$8,552,980
13.	TOTAL RECEIPTS PLUS CASH BALANCE	$61,891,614	$9,437,122	$11,187,894	$8,933,666	$7,494,572	$6,044,360	$9,798,112
14.	SALARIES AND WAGES	$40,314,456	$3,120,000	$3,430,000	$3,620,000	$3,464,000	$3,465,000	$3,520,456
15.	FRINGE BENEFITS	$9,943,116	$736,000	$872,000	$737,000	$736,000	$737,000	$1,504,116
16.	PURCHASED SERVICES	$3,956,045	$339,000	$330,000	$329,000	$330,000	$329,000	$332,045
17.	MATERIALS, SUPPLIES & TEXTBOOKS	$2,321,535	$195,000	$150,000	$150,000	$199,000	$329,000	$198,535
18.	CAPITAL OUTLAY (INCL. REPLACEMENT)	$457,595	$30,000	$60,000	$38,000	$34,000	$36,000	$34,595
19.	REPAYMENT OF BORROWING (PRIN + INT)	$197,000						$197,000
20.	TRANSFERS AND ADVANCES OUT	$723,730	$33,228	$33,228	$208,222	$33,228	$33,228	$33,228
21.	OTHER	$0						
22.	TOTAL EXPENDITURES (LINES 14-21)	$57,913,477	$4,643,228	$4,875,228	$5,082,222	$4,796,228	$4,799,228	$5,819,975
	ENDING CASH BALANCE (LINES 13 MINUS 22)	$3,978,137	$4,793,894	$6,312,666	$3,851,444	$2,698,344	$1,245,132	$3,978,137

		(07) JULY	(08) AUGUST	(09) SEPTEMBER	(10) OCTOBER	(11) NOVEMBER	(12) DECEMBER
	BEGINNING CASH BALANCE	$2,519,490	$855,262	$4,745,034	$2,551,806	$5,765,578	$3,331,350
1.	REAL ESTATE TAX	$0	$6,000,000	$200,000	$5,100,000	$0	$2,000,000
2.	TANGIBLE PERSONAL PROPERTY TAX	$0	$0	$0		$0	$0
3.	INVESTMENT EARNINGS	$40,000	$45,000	$60,000	$65,000	$50,000	$40,000
4.	PROCEEDS FROM BORROWING	$0					
5.	OTHER	$61,000	$61,000	$62,000	$61,000	$61,000	$62,000
6.	FOUNDATION PROGRAM	$2,196,000	$2,196,000	$2,196,000	$2,196,000	$2,196,000	$2,196,000
7.	ROLLBACK AND HOMESTEAD EXEMPTION	$0	$0	$0	$957,000	$0	$0
8.	OTHER	$5,000	$32,000	$32,000	$32,000	$31,000	$31,000
9.	PUBLIC LAW 874	$7,000	$0	$0	$0	$0	$0
10.	OTHER	$0	$5,000	$6,000	$6,000	$6,000	$6,000
11.	TRANSFERS AND ADVANCES IN	$135,000	$0	$0	$0	$0	$0
12.	TOTAL RECEIPTS (LINES 1-11)	$2,444,000	$8,339,000	$2,556,000	$8,417,000	$2,344,000	$4,335,000
13.	TOTAL RECEIPTS PLUS CASH BALANCE	$4,963,490	$9,194,262	$7,301,034	$10,968,806	$8,109,578	$7,666,350
14.	SALARIES AND WAGES	$2,800,000	$3,000,000	$3,350,000	$3,620,000	$3,425,000	$3,300,000
15.	FRINGE BENEFITS	$736,000	$736,000	$737,000	$940,000	$736,000	$736,000
16.	PURCHASED SERVICES	$329,000	$330,000	$329,000	$330,000	$329,000	$330,000
17.	MATERIALS, SUPPLIES & TEXTBOOKS	$140,000	$180,000	$275,000	$240,000	$205,000	$190,000
18.	CAPITAL OUTLAY (INCL. REPLACEMENT)	$70,000	$20,000	$25,000	$40,000	$50,000	$20,000
19.	REPAYMENT OF BORROWING (PRIN + INT)	$0					
20.	TRANSFERS AND ADVANCES OUT	$33,228	$183,228	$33,228	$33,228	$33,228	$33,228
21.	OTHER	$0					
22.	TOTAL EXPENDITURES (LINES 14-21)	$4,108,228	$4,449,228	$4,749,228	$5,203,228	$4,778,228	$4,609,228

281

advised in order to minimize expenditures. Daily monitoring of the cashing of payroll checks reveals the "float" that is available for two, three, or four days of additional investment time. School systems can earn additional interest dollars if payment of large sums is made at the last possible moment. Examples of this practice include making payments to retirement funds, insurance programs, and the like by courier rather than by mail. The same concept applies in receiving large amounts of revenue. School system agents frequently will pick up checks for state reimbursement or warrants from the local taxation administrator for the system's property tax allocation. Even more sophisticated methods have been introduced to expedite the obtaining of these revenues. Wire transfer service may be available where local or state government treasurers can wire transfer the monies from the local or state agency account to the account of the school system. These transactions are nearly instantaneous. Such techniques are examples of cash concentration—providing for the prompt acquisition of revenue for investment purposes.

Investment Considerations

A successful school system investment program requires careful planning and a deliberate strategy. Although private sector investment programs have some similarities to those found in school systems, there are marked differences. Private sector investment is similar to school system investment programs in that both are sensitive to the market. The yield rates of both are related to supply and demand of investment money. The rates of return on U.S. Treasury notes and bills are reflective of the amount that investors are willing to commit to them, which in turn is related to the relative rate of return compared to other investment options.

All investments carry some risk, and the degree of risk is related to the amount of yield as demanded by the market. Both private sector and school system investments have an inherent risk-yield relationship, although the nature of it in each is somewhat different. This will be discussed in more detail in a following section.

Nearly all legitimate investments carry some restrictions. In the private sector these may be characterized by the regulations of the Securities and Exchange Commission. School system investment programs are severely constricted by state policy since school systems are agents of the state. Additionally, local restrictions may be enforced by boards of education through their permissive powers.

Differences between private sector investment programs and those of school systems are observable when the basic premise of each is considered. In the private sector, investments are made on the expectation of future earnings. A private sector investment cliché states that one should invest only what one can afford to lose—suggesting a speculative orientation. In school system investment programs the premise is more related to retaining and protecting assets. It must be acknowledged, however, that private investors also seek the latter goal and that school system investment programs are designed to enhance the liquid assets of the system.

A second major difference is the range of investment instruments that may be used. Most states have relatively severe restrictions. These usually allow purchase of government issues backed by the full faith and credit of the federal or the state government. Some states permit school systems to purchase collateralized commercial paper. At the same time they may prohibit speculative investments such as junk bonds or ventures into the futures markets. Investment strategies vary also in that school systems are not permitted to buy securities through leveraging or on margin.

The major considerations that guide a school system's investment program (listed below) are essentially the same as used in private sector programs, but they vary somewhat in specific applications.

1. *Does it conform to legal restrictions?* The fundamental restrictions are spelled out in state permissive legislation. Major provisions include permissive powers of school boards, the sources of revenue from which investments may be made, and the term of the investment period, e.g., within the fiscal year or beyond the fiscal year. State policy usually spells out the nature of the investment instruments, as previously described, and how the investment authority is exercised. Accounting and reporting procedures for investments are frequently incorporated in state policy.

Local policy is an extension of state policy and tends to be procedural in nature. For example, the school board may authorize the business administrator to invest all balances of specific funds in repurchase agreements in a given bank over weekends or holidays.

2. *What is the nature and amount of risk to be assumed?* It is axiomatic that all investments carry risks. However, it also is generally accepted that school system investment programs are not speculative in nature. Thus, the risks are restricted by statute or policy. Bank deposits are backed by collateral, but the value of the collateral may fluctuate given changing market conditions. Treasury notes and bills are guaranteed by the federal government, but only at par. So there may be some risk if a note or bill was purchased at a price over par since at maturity the principal repaid will be at par. However, if interest earnings are considered, the return of principal plus earnings might far exceed the purchase price. Thus, the nature of risk is relative. It is incumbent on the school business administrator to be aware of the risks of doing nothing, as well as the risks of developing an investment program to obtain maximum return on a minimized risk.

3. *What is the yield?* The yield on investments derives from either or both interest earned or appreciation (or depreciation) of principal. The most secure instruments (e.g., Treasury notes or bills) repay the principal at par, so the yield is derived from the interest. However, if the buying price was over $100.00 at par, the net yield at maturity would be reduced. If the buying price was under $100.00 at par, the net yield at maturity would be increased. If a security is sold prior to maturity, the appreciation or depreciation (difference in purchase price and selling price) would be calculated as a part of yield.

4. *What is the degree of liquidity?* Liquidity is an important consideration in developing a school system investment portfolio for several reasons. Because cash flow is irregular, invested cash may be needed before scheduled maturities or at the last possible moment before bills are paid and checks are cashed. Because market conditions change, the prices of investments may change. Interest rates and therefore yields may change since new issues reflect the current rates, which may be higher or lower than earlier ones. Consequently, it may be advantageous to "swap" issues. This tactic will be discussed in a later section.

A volatile cash flow suggests the desirability of highly liquid investments. These might have disadvantages of lower interest yield but the advantage of less costly transactions. For example, certificates of deposit (CDs) may offer an interest rate higher than that of a repurchase agreement, but withdrawing a CD before maturity incurs a substantial penalty.

Investment Instruments

A wide variety of instruments is available for school system investment programs. Each has its own unique characteristics as to risk, yield, and liquidity. Naturally, the school system official with investment authority must limit his/her choices to those investments which meet state and school system statutory standards. In most systems, investment opportunities for large amounts over long periods of time are relatively few. Thus, shorter-term investment instruments suited to unique cash flows are the most popular. However, as the following sections dealing with investment strategies and tactics suggest, it is possible to sell, swap, or spread long-term securities and derive the advantages of relatively high interest, possible appreciation, and reasonable liquidity. Some of the major groups of investment instruments are described in the following subsections.

U.S. Treasury Bills, Bonds, and Notes

Treasury issues are backed by the U.S. government and are considered the lowest-risk investment. They are sold at government auctions and thus reflect the interest rates in effect at the time of sale. School systems usually buy and sell these instruments on the open market through brokers. Since the bond interest rate is fixed, changes in interest rates in the financial markets are reflected in the price on the face of the instrument. For example, a 7-3/8 percent 30-year $1000 bond to mature in May 1996 may be discounted to 93-27/32.

Treasury bills have maturities of thirteen, twenty-six, and fifty-two weeks and are issued in $10,000 denominations. Treasury notes of $5,000 denominations mature in two or three years, while $1000 notes mature in four to ten years. U.S. bonds are issued for thirty years in $1000 denominations.

U.S. Government Agency Bonds

A host of government corporations issue bonds to specific government-sponsored activities. Most familiar are the Federal National Mortgage Association (Fannie Mae), Government National Mortgage Association (Ginnie Mae), and Federal Home Loan Mortgage Corporation (Freddie Mac). These are largely secured by mortgages but are not wholly insured by the full faith and credit of the government. They may be purchased through banks or brokers.

Certificates of Deposit

School systems use CDs in the same ways that other investors use them. However, the banks that issue CDs may make special provisions for large amounts with shorter maturities to serve the unique interests of the school system. A major criterion for selecting a bank to deal with is whether the CD is collateralized—i.e., fully secured by U.S. treasuries or other insured securities. School systems have encountered problems when CDs were secured by bad loans and the bank or savings and loan association went into receivership. Penalties are charged for early withdrawal (before scheduled maturation).

Repurchase Agreements

Repurchase agreements (REPOs) are used for relatively short-term investments (even overnight or over a weekend). A school system agrees to invest its funds for a given number of days and takes title to bank securities as collateral. At maturity the bank repurchases the securities, and the school system receives the original investment plus interest. These investments tend to be highly liquid, and the risk is governed by the quality of the collateral. The yield is relatively low, but certainly greater than that obtained from a checking account.

Money Market Certificates, Money Market Funds and Passbook Savings

These conventional instruments are designed for the general public but are sometimes used in school system investment programs. Yields reflect the going interest rate. Ordinarily relatively small amounts can be invested, since there is reasonably high liquidity. Risk is related to the collateral provided by the bank, so this becomes a major concern.

Commercial Paper

Several states permit school systems to purchase commercial paper (corporate bonds and the like). These instruments usually carry a relatively high rate of interest and thus reflect a relatively high risk since they are not backed by government securities but instead by the financial resources of the issuing corporation. An example of the worst selection is that of ''junk bonds'' used in leveraged buy-outs in the corporate takeovers of the late 1980s. On the positive side, high-quality commercial paper is available with relatively little risk in AA-rated utility bonds and other similar issues.

Selecting among Alternative Instruments

School officials with responsibility for investment programs have many alternatives suited to the unique cash flow and investment objectives of their school systems (see Figure 12-1). Investments may be made for the long or short term, for relatively high or low yield, and with varying degrees of liquidity. The investment program may be simple with only REPOs and CDs or with complex and changing packages of investment instruments to fit the ebb and flow of available cash.

Investment Strategies

Any investment strategy must be predicated on a policy dealing with investment and depository activities. State statutes usually cover the latter regarding both security for cash and other assets as well as the school system personnel who are responsible for investment decisions. Legislation spells out conditions under which cash may be invested. Consequently, it is crucial that local policy be developed to detail the ways in which school system investment officers may choose to exercise these powers.

Policy and procedural guidelines should include the following considerations:

- The objectives of the investment program
- The designation of in-house and/or contracted investment counsel or services
- The authority and responsibility of the investment officer or agency
- The procedures to determine cash flow and other basic data necessary to make investment decisions
- The procedures to determine the sources and amounts of investable cash
- The designation of the minimum and maximum investment maturities
- The investment instruments to be used

FIGURE 12-1 Selected Investment Instruments

Instrument	Minimum Amount	Issuer	Liquidity	Risk
U.S. Treasury Bill	$10,000	U.S. Government	Immediate	Least
U.S. Treasury Bond	1,000	U.S. Government	Immediate	Least
U.S. Treasury Note	5,000 1,000	U.S. Government	Immediate	Least
U.S. Government Agency Bonds	5,000	U.S. Government Corporations	Immediate	Little
Certificates of Deposit	Varied	Banks, Thrifts	Fixed Maturities	Limited Insurance
Repurchase Agreements	Varied	Banks, Brokers	Immediate	Little
Money Market Certificates	Varied	Banks, Thrifts	Fixed Maturities	Limited Insurance
Money Market Funds	1,000	Brokers, Mutual Funds	Immediate	Varies with Collateral
Passbook Savings	Minimal	Banks, Thrifts	Immediate	Limited Insurance
Commercial Paper	Varied	Brokers	Immediate	Varies with the financial status of the corporation

These policies and procedures should communicate clearly the intentions of the school board regarding the investment program. This is difficult since an essential element in investment is the free market system, which is in constant motion. Policies need to give considerable latitude to the investment officer, but within explicit parameters set by the board. As the national and international economies change, interest rates shift on all forms of securities. When risk increases, rates increase; when available capital increases, rates decrease. As a result of these interactive changes, investment portfolios may need frequent alterations given the school board's objectives for yield and parameters of risk.

A key step in developing strategies for investment is using cash-flow analysis to determine the nature of investment potential. This topic was discussed earlier and speaks to the question of when and how much one should invest.

A second step deals with the nature of yield on investments. As just mentioned, yields change as economic conditions change. A strategy must speak to the question of how to optimize the yield of a given or alternative investment instrument. The concept of the *yield curve* is central to this strategy. Investments with shorter maturities usually yield less than investments with longer maturities. A *normal yield curve* ascends as maturity is extended. Even within a fixed period of time, yields of related investments respond in different ways.

An *inverted yield curve,* the converse of the normal yield curve, is characterized by instruments with shorter maturities having higher yield and those with longer maturities having lower yields. For example, if the economy has the prospect of stagnation (and thus lowering corporate dividends and needing less capital), investors may flee the stock market and move into Treasury notes, bills, and bonds. This "oversupply" of capital may reduce the interest rate the government must pay to sell these securities.

A *flat yield curve* is no curve at all. Although an infrequent phenomenon in the absolute, yields on securities may tend toward a flat yield when there is little difference in yield between short-term and long-term securities. This situation is like a resting period within fixed income markets. Factors that have contributed to a flat yield curve include actions by the Federal Reserve Board to increase short-term interest rates to decrease the money supply and in turn dampen the threat of inflation. In recent years these increased interest rates were also a part of the strategy to stabilize the value of the dollar against the currencies of other nations.

Figure 12-2 illustrates the three types of yield curves.

Investment strategies can be built around yield curves and the periodic changes of yield for various investment instruments. Not all instruments respond in precisely the same way to changing economic and fiscal conditions. Thus, an analysis of yield curves may suggest several alternative reactions or tactics. One might shift investments from short to long maturities, or vice versa. One might "swap" treasuries for CDs or vice versa. One might roll over short-term maturities. The nature of investment tactics will be described later.

A third premise for building an investment strategy is related to the determination of the goal for investment yield. *Benchmark* is the conventional term for this concept. School system investment officers and boards of education should base their investment strategy on the nature of cash flow and an explicit policy reference to risk-yield relationships. The concept of the benchmark and its implementation are described by Jeffery B. Flynn:

> *Chances are, your school board members or others in your district probably have many different ideas about what constitutes successful investing. To those who are adverse to risk, a six or seven percent return may seem quite reasonable. These folks likely are among the millions of people who invest their personal funds in passbook savings accounts.*
>
> *Others who dabble in options or futures markets with personal funds may see anything less than double-digit returns as complete investing failure.*
>
> *One group or the other may perceive your investment performance as a failure whatever your level of investment return. In order to be judged fairly, you will need to establish some sort of guideline as an investment benchmark. In doing so, you will be setting forth a measure to which your performance can be compared.*
>
> *The benchmark you select should be in keeping with your own individual investment philosophy. For example, if you employ a frequent short-term rolling approach to investing, chances are that your average maturity is also relatively short. However, if you prepare accurate cash flow forecasts, you may be able to invest in longer term maturities. This approach generally rewards the investor with higher returns associated with upward sloping yield curves. Therefore, it is important to select a benchmark commensurate with the average maturity of the portfolio. This would represent a fair target for return comparison. If your investments have an average maturity of 176 days, for example, an appropriate benchmark might be a six-month Treasury Bill.*
>
> *Let's examine in general terms, how the benchmark can be used to evaluate relative performance. [See Table 12-2. Yields shown in the chart are actual as of October 4, 1988.]*
>
> *As you can see from the statistics, the weighted average maturity of the portfolio is 129 days and the weighted yield is 8.048 percent. If you select a benchmark with approximately the same maturity you may choose either the 120-day or 150-day Treasury Note. As of the same date, these yields were 7.65 percent and 7.76 percent respectively. Therefore, the portfolio is roughly outperforming its benchmark by 10 to 30 basis points, depending on which benchmark you selected.*[1]

FIGURE 12-2 Yield Curves

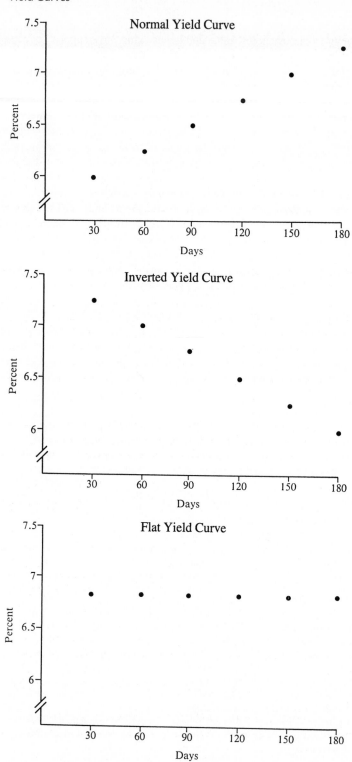

TABLE 12-2 Example Investment Returns

Investment Type	Amount	Percent of Portfolio	Weighted Average Buy Yield	Weighted Average Maturity
Total Repurchase Agreements	$1,000,000.00	8.33%	7.900%	42 days
Total Bankers Acceptances	$984,100.00	8.20%	8.078%	72 days
Total CDs and Bank Investments	$3,000,000.00	24.99%	7.540%	31 days
Total Treasury Securities	$2,547,428.67	21.22%	7.980%	211 days
Total Agency Securities	$4,471,170.83	37.25%	8.453%	180 days
Total Investment Portfolio	$12,002,699.50	100.00%	8.048%	129 days

Portfolio Average Weekly Earnings at Buy Yield—$18,575.68.

Enclosed within the benchmark concept is the strategy of diversification to spread risk. *Diversification,* or "putting one's eggs in more than one basket," is appropriate for the short term as well as the long term. The former is important with recent disclosures that banks and savings and loan associations with insured accounts have gone into receivership and federal insurance may not cover all the CDs held by school systems. In the long term, global economic systems are developing that will affect on the financial market in the United States. As more investment options appear, there will be both greater competition and opportunities for investment. Money managers in school systems will need to monitor these trends carefully to select those instruments that provide suitable diversification.

The *investment pool* is an investment strategy used in many small school systems where investments are small and short term, and where cash managers have neither the time nor experience to maintain an investment portfolio. Several states have developed such pools for state and local governmental units. Specific provisions vary, but most states by aggregating the monies of large numbers of units invest in Treasury bills or Treasury notes. The pool establishes its own cash flow and invests in high-liquidity instruments. Because the maturations are short, the returns are relatively low. The major benefit to school systems, however, is relatively easy access. The yield is determined on the basis of the amount of a school system's investments and the yield of the pool each day. (If a school system has invested 1 percent of the pool, it will have earned 1 percent of the interest for that day.) Cash managers can monitor the performance of the pool against that of alternative instruments. Liquidity, safety, and convenience appear to be the major strengths of these programs.

A similar but almost universal strategy is that of a board of education contracting with a bank or other agent for *cash management services*. Not only does the bank assume responsibility for making the investments, but it also aggregates all school system fund balances into one investment pool, usually called a *concentration account*. This has the advantages of the bank determining and monitoring cash flow on a daily basis and thus investing larger sums, which usually command higher interest rates. A bank can theoretically invest every dollar every day since it has ready access to a whole range of investment instruments.

Zero balance accounting (ZBA) is an implementing concept for developing the concentration account. All other accounts in the school system are established for given purposes. As accounts payable, they carry a zero balance, and all monies are aggregated in the concentration account from which investments are made. School officials write checks on the various accounts payable. When these checks clear with the bank, the exact amounts are drawn from the concentration account on a daily basis to cover each of them. Thus, cash balances are fully invested each day.

Investment Tactics

Because the financial and investment markets hold so many uncertainties, it is necessary or at least opportunistic to make adjustments in the way an investment plan or strategy is actually carried out. Investment tactics are the specific actions taken to implement an overall plan or strategy. It is not practical to describe here the full range of investment tactics available to the school system investment officer. The following are described as examples of some of the generally recognized types.

Riding the Yield Curve

A conventional strategy might call for investments in given instruments—Treasury bills or notes for example—to be held to maturity. However, under some conditions it may be advantageous to sell these securities before maturity. A study of yield curves is the means by which such decisions may be made. The tactic, known as "riding the yield curve," is exemplified by the decision as to whether it is more advantageous to buy a 90-day Treasury bill and hold it to maturity or buy a 180-day bill and sell it after 90 days. Investment agents can calculate the net return on these two options by considering the discounted purchase price of both and the discounted purchase price at maturity for the 180-day bill at the end of 90 days. If there were no interest rate changes, it would be concluded that the purchase of the 180-day bill would be advantageous since the normal yield curve for longer term bills is higher than that of short term. One must remember that Treasury bills are bought and sold at discounts that determine their relative interest rates. In the case of the 90-day matured bill, there is no discount, while the remainder of the 180-day bill would have the same discount as the 90-day bill. Thus, the school system would have the interest earnings on its 90-day investment at a substantially higher rate than the 90-day bill. However, for this tactic to be successful, the yield curve must be a stable, normal curve. If the discounts change, there is an interest risk.

The following example illustrates the concept of riding the curve.

Let's assume the purchase of a six-month T-Bill generates a 7 percent return if held to maturity. Assuming that rates stay about even, in three months, the original six-month T-Bill will actually become a three-month T-Bill which . . . is yielding 6-1/2 percent. If that T-bill were sold after being held for three months, the actual return on that T-Bill for the time it was held would be 7.52 percent. (If the original amount invested was $96.63, the amount received when sold at 6-1/2 percent was $98.44.) [sic] When the difference is annualized and multiplied by the days held divided by 365, it equals a 7.52 percent return. This return is 52 basis points better than the original purchase yield. As a matter of fact, if interest rates are unchanged and the yield curve has a positive slope to it, selling T-Bills prior to their maturity will always offer a better holding period yield than the original purchase yield. Often, in the short amount of time left for investment of the funds, a Repurchase Agreement would be a good choice. Repos usually pay more than very short maturity T-Bills.[2]

Spreads

A tactic related to changing yields rather than stable yields is that of "spreads." During periods of economic instability there are variations in interest rates between closely related instruments such as Treasury bills and Treasury notes. Generally speaking, in periods of uncertainty, risks are perceived to be greater and interest rates increase. When concerns of inflation are reduced, interest rates tend to go down. Treasury notes with shorter maturities in the latter situation need to be reinvested more frequently. If these economic conditions persist, they will be reinvested at rates lower than the longer-term Treasury bills. Thus, yield curves for these two treasuries will show a spread. Treasury notes, because of the interest risk, will be discounted more deeply and thus be purchased with higher interest rates.

Swaps

A somewhat more speculative tactic is the swap. In essence, a security is sold in order to buy another. The objective is to enhance the value of the overall investment portfolio by increasing the yield to maturity of these securities. The swap should not be consummated unless the yield to maturity is definitively increased. Factors such as different maturities and the direction of the yield slopes over the periods of both maturities must be considered. The relationship of spreads over the two maturities must also be put into the analysis. A third factor that must be included is the direct and indirect costs associated with swaps. Direct costs are those related to brokers' fees while indirect costs are those related to time, information acquisition and analysis, and the like.

Short-Term Rollovers and Matching

Tactics appropriate to school systems with uncertain or uneven cash flows tend to center on a series of short-term investments. In many instances these instruments, such as REPOs or CDs, are frequently rolled over when it appears that there will be sufficient cash for investment. The interest rate on these short-term instruments is relatively low, and the time expended for withdrawal and reinvestment is considerable.

A tactic providing greater yield is that of matching. Investment maturities are matched with anticipated expenditures by means of a well-designed cash-flow analysis. Such an analysis can reduce uncertainty and thus enable the investment officer to buy longer-term securities and avoid the short-term rollover. If necessary, the longer-term security can be sold before maturity and, given a normal yield curve, will produce a greater net interest than that achieved by the alternative of short-term rollovers.

Odd Lots and Round Lots

A related tactic that is applicable on a much larger scale is buying odd lots or round lots. The former, in Treasury bills or notes, is an amount of less than one million dollars; the latter is one million dollars or more. Brokers' fees for odd lots are greater than for round lots, and thus a matching tactic is useful when purchasing these securities.

Arbitrage

The practice of arbitrage—for example, taking the proceeds from a sale of a school system bond issue and reinvesting them in securities that pay an interest rate higher than that of the bond issue—has long been an investment tactic in public school systems. School bond issues are usually exempt from federal and state income taxes; thus they carry lower interest rates. The spread between interest on bonds and interest paid by Treasury bills or notes can be nearly two percentage points. In most cases the proceeds of a bond issue are drawn down as construction is completed, so it is appropriate to calculate the cash flow for this revenue. Presently the future of this "golden goose" is in jeopardy as the Tax Reform Act of 1986 contains limitations on arbitrage. It is unclear as to what extent school systems may continue the practice.[3]

Summary

The investment of idle cash in school systems is a legitimate exercise in the stewardship of public monies dedicated to providing public education. Investment protects or enhances the purchasing power of these dollars, which will eventually be expended for educational services.

A cash-flow analysis is a prerequisite to determining the amount for and timing of investments. Such an analysis provides the data necessary to make decisions as to the optimum kinds of investments to make. In most situations a variety of instruments will provide the portfolio best fitted to the cash-flow analysis. Typically, long-term securities carry higher interest rates, so these are well suited to the proportion of cash available for a relatively long term. Those parts of the cash flow over the given period of time that constitute small amounts and/or shorter terms of investment potential can be invested in instruments suited to maturity and amounts indicated.

Factors that must be considered in developing an investment program for a school system include legal constraints, risk, yield, and liquidity. The public nature of the gathering, use, and investment of school system monies is the most important concern since it guides all other considerations. Risk, yield, and liquidity are interrelated, and thus policies must be developed to guide investment decisions. High yields carry with them high risk—principal risk and interest risk. Liquidity comes as a tradeoff with risk and yield, also.

Investment policy also suggests alternative strategies that can be employed. Yield curve analysis, market analysis, and the establishment of an investment benchmark are useful in determining a general investment plan. In carrying out a plan, an investment officer has a host of tactics available. Tactics are employed to optimize investment in a changing market economy. Techniques of rolling or matching, riding the yield curve, and buying and selling on the basis of spreads are used in day-by-day investment decisions.

Every school system has some opportunity for investment. However, to achieve satisfactory results it is necessary at the minimum to develop a cogent and complete policy, a comprehensive cash-flow analysis, and an overall strategy. Investment tactics can be rather simple or very complex, depending on its components, risk, yield, and liquidity. Return on investment is an important bottom line. However, an even more important line is that the investment program is a means to the end of providing increased support for the educational program.

Suggested Activities

1. From your school system's fiscal and/or accounting reports, develop a cash-flow history over the past four or five years. Develop some general conclusions as to possibilities for the investment program.
2. Based on Activity 1, develop a specific proposal for an investment program (compatible with school system policy) involving long-term (longer than one fiscal year) and short-term (shorter than one year) planning.
3. Survey several local banks and brokers to ascertain current interest rates, minimum amounts to be invested, maturity periods, and other data relevant to investment options.
4. Interview the investment officer of your school system about the investment program. Focus on the nature of cash flow, the investment policy and its interpretation, the strategy and tactics employed, and the annual investment return.

Suggested Readings

Dembrowski, F. L. "Alternative Methods in Evaluation of School District Cash Management Programs," *Journal of Education Finance, 6* (Summer 1980).
———. *A Handbook for School District Financial Management.* Park Ridge, IL: Research Corporation of the Association of School Business Officials, 1982.
Dembrowski, F. L., and J. Biros. *Handbook of School/Banking Relations.* New York: State Association for School Business Officials, 1981.
Everett, R. E., and Dale S. Fausch. "Arbitrage: IRS Attempts to Further Limit School District Borrowing Power," *School Business Affairs, 49,* 9 (Aug. 1983).
MacPhail-Wilcox, Bettye. "Doing More with Less: A Preliminary Study of School District Investment," *Journal of Education Finance, 8,* 3 (Winter 1983).
Pogue, G. A., and R. N. Bussard. "A Linear Programming Model for Short-Term Financial Planning under Uncertainty," *Sloan Management Review, 13,* 3 (Spring 1972).

Notes

1. Jeffery B. Flynn, "Ensuring Investment Success," *School Business Affairs, 54,* 12 (Dec. 1988), 56.
2. Jeffery B. Flynn, "Investments—A 'Rolling' Philosophy or 'Matching' Philosophy?" *School Business Affairs, 54,* 7 (July 1988), 57.
3. Ward Weldon, "Arbitrage Interest Rubs and School District Borrowing," *School Business Affairs, 55,* 1 (Jan. 1989), 10–13.

_13_

Risk Management and Insurance

RISK DEALS WITH THE VARIABILITY in a series of outcomes that occur in a specific situation over a defined period of time. Risk exists whenever the future (or absolute outcome) is not known. The management or control of that risk must then become the responsibility of some decision maker.[1] Since the risk factor in school systems generally includes the loss of property, the school business administrator becomes one of the key decision makers for the district in managing the risk. In this chapter the idea of a comprehensive risk management program for school districts is presented so that the proper balance between cost of protection and the degree of risk a district is willing to assume can be generated. Due to inflation, negotiated contracts, and a wide range of other concerns, achieving a proper balance involves more than the decision to simply "buy insurance."

Risks are a day-to-day concern but take on greater meaning when related to choices in planning and purchasing specialized insurance coverage for a wide variety of responsibilities for the district or other educational unit. Several factors affect the implementation of an effective risk management program. In general, risk management includes the identification and measurement of risk, as well as the processes for dealing with losses in all areas—from property to people. One should be concerned with identification of potential risks in all areas for which the school district has responsibility, the potential for loss (in hard dollars), possibilities and costs for reduction or elimination of these risks, and a plan for regular review of potential and actual losses. Public schools often overlook major areas of liability risk, neglect to take advantage of cost savings with certain deductibles, purchase insurance containing major flaws in scope of coverage, and/or fail to regularly review plans of coverage.

Specifically, public school liability coverage should provide protection for school administrators, teachers, and other employees. Concern should be given to personal injury/liability suits, malpractice claims by parents pertaining to student treatment or negligence, personal injury claims against teachers based on disciplinary acts, inadequate workers' compensation coverage for all independent contractors working at school sites, and inadequate bodily injury liability coverage for buses and/or outside transportation services. To help reduce losses, systems need to develop and manage a comprehensive risk management program. The need to identify, evaluate, and eliminate risks is the purpose of such a plan.

Historically schools have not dealt with the concept of risk management very well. However, rapid and significant changes in the way schools are viewed by the public and the courts have caused a major rethinking in this area. Many public school officials are devoting more effort and time to identifying and reducing potential risk and to educating all faculty and staff on the need to be alert to possible areas of concern. From a practical standpoint, systems are now seeking help from experts in risk management and sound advice from lawyers in contract negotiations and in determining loss potential.

Risk management includes both financial management and the use of physical and human engineering techniques. Therefore, the risk manager must be able both to isolate areas of risk in program and facility and to appraise the cost of reducing risks by installation of safety equipment, appropriate modification of facilities, and other actions.[2] When a decision is made to take a risk, either because it is unavoidable or because it is essential to system objectives, the risk manager will normally attempt to maximize security by reducing the chances of loss by taking countermeasures or by transferring the financial effects of the risk to others through the use of insurance or some other hedging device.[3]

As the risk manager of a school system, the school business administrator, or the designated risk manager, should determine which incidents should be reported to the insurance carriers. Failure to report occurrences/events to a carrier can often cause problems when one attempts to make a claim under an existing policy.

The concept of risk management is a key element for the school business administrator to consider in the area of insurance planning. Of course, the concept requires the system to analyze its needs and requirements and assign the level of risk it is willing to assume. Beyond this level of risk, based on an actuarially acceptable standard, the system must be prepared to pay for insurance protection.

The degree or amount of risk a system is willing to assume is determined by a number of factors. In property insurance, factors include the age and condition of buildings, equipment, and motor vehicles; possible natural disasters; and history of loss. The business administrator must weigh the costs of protection against the costs of replacement and recommend a plan for insurance procurement. In some instances the school business administrator must consider ''insurability at all'' with regard to property. For example, many school districts must face the fact that some structures are not insurable at an affordable cost. This often occurs in urban districts where many buildings are of such construction and age that the cost of bringing them into compliance with fire codes and thus making them insurable at a reasonable cost is impossible. Age of building and general maintenance results (condition of structure) prevent some facilities from being insured. Self-insurance (discussed later) is often not the best but the only option available.

In assuming the responsibilities of risk management, the school business administrator must accept the job of educating members of the board in the area of risk management as well as many other areas. The purpose of insurance is to prevent loss of life, injury to personnel, and loss or damage to property. The board must understand the available options and the potential results of all insurance options as well as noninsurance.

Finally, with risk management the establishment of a loss control program is a major concern. The purpose of prevention of loss is a relatively new concept, with the goal of saving the system more than the program costs. Basically, a loss control program is designed to uncover *potential* areas of loss and suggest ways to fix them or reduce the possibility of loss as a result of this activity or situation. Issues as diverse as playground checks to asbestos control are covered in a loss control program. The cost of claims is, of course, what makes insurance costs escalate; thus, the reduction of claims (or even the elimination of claims) will affect the cost for a district. The plan must, however, save more than it costs to be salable to boards or to make financial sense to the school business administrator.

An aggressive risk management program is characterized by these activities:

- Identification of risk
- Measurement of risk
- Risk-handling techniques
- Risk control
- Risk funding

As with maintenance and operations, the availability of data for establishing a good risk management program can best be supplied through the development of an effective management information system. With accurate, regular data collection and a means of processing, school business administrators can review, plan, and predict an effective program. Elaboration of the MIS concept appears in Chapter 5.

The Role of Insurance

The most popular method of managing risk is that of purchasing insurance. For practical purposes, *insurance* is defined as a promise by an insurer to an insured of protection and/or service. *Protection* means making good a financial loss, and *service* means rendering aid of various sorts in connection with the promise of protection. The promise is made only to the extent that the loss may be caused by fortuitous events and, with certain exceptions, promised protection is legally enforceable only to the extent of actual loss. Large fiscal loss potential such as protection of bank deposits or workers' compensation are usually uninsurable risks by agencies other than the federal government. The *insurer* is the person or organization making the promise; the *insured* is the person or organization subject to loss to whom the promise is made.

To clarify further the concept of insurance, a discussion of insurable risks is appropriate. There are many risks of economic loss that no insurance company would be willing to accept. Conversely, there are a number of conditions that make a risk insurable. While some kinds of insurance are written where one or more of these conditions is not present, their absence acts as a danger signal to the insurance company, which then must take extra precautions to protect itself.

The conditions that make a risk insurable are:

1. The peril insured against must produce a definite loss not under the control of the insured.
2. There must be a large number of homogeneous exposures subject to the same peril.
3. The loss must be calculable and the cost of insuring it must be economically feasible.

4. The peril must be unlikely to affect all the insured simultaneously.
5. The loss, when it occurs, must be financially serious.

The major techniques for eliminating risk exposure include:

- Avoidance
- Reduction
- Assumption
- Transfer

In the years following the mid-1980s, the insurance industry as a whole experienced substantial difficulties, that translated into problems for the school business administrator and school districts in general. These problems have manifested themselves in three major areas—premium increases, coverage restriction/availability, and lower capacity. The increased costs and unavailability of insurance are easily understood items, but it is notable that the actual supply of insurance is shrinking. Since the demand for the product is stable, the "loss of capacity" in prices has caused prices to escalate, with school districts paying more for the same or, in many instances, less protection.[4]

One of the key factors in the complex area of risk management for schools and school districts is criminal noninsurability. Since insurance against criminal acts is not possible, by a school or anyone else, if an employee were to engage in such activities as theft or child molestation, for example, insurance against these acts by the district also is not possible. No criminal claims could reasonably be made against the district, but civil claims could be initiated. If civil claims are made, then the school or district would react as with any other lawsuit.

Because most persons respect professionals, the members of any profession are expected to meet high standards. As a result of this, what the professional owes the community or what the professional is viewed as owing the community often constitutes high stakes. Basically, the issue centers on what people expect from professionals. When they do not get what is expected, they sue! One caution is noted in the concern that liability claims have gone too far in many instances. Awards are seen as too high, and in some states legislation has been introduced to limit the amount of such awards. The application of this concept to education and/or educational activities is spotty, and an insufficient number of instances have been recorded to determine a trend or pattern of results.[5]

In many instances, the school district employee purchases a personal/professional liability policy to cover themselves against such instances. The National Education Association and Council for Exceptional Children both provide such coverage, often as part of the dues package, to members or other persons willing to join. Another method of individual coverage is through riders for homeowners' policies. These, however, are often weakened by substantial exclusions to the coverage.

A second contributing factor to the complexity of risk management has been the increase in the tort liability regarding negligence in the proper maintenance of school buildings, property, and equipment. As with litigation in general, school litigation in areas associated with proper maintenance is on the increase.

In typical negligence suits various courts have described the hypothetical prudent person as one capable of average knowledge and ordinary skills. However, because of the special relationship between the school and students and the professional status of educators, courts have held schools to a higher standard of care than is expected of average persons.

Negligence is any action falling below a certain standard that results in an injury to another person. If nonpreventable, the accident is not the result of negligence. Usually four elements must be present to constitute actionable negligence: (1) a duty must be owed; (2) there must be a failure to perform this duty; (3) a close connection between this failure and the injury must exist; and (4) actual loss or damage must result.

To avoid this problem, school business administrators must be responsible for the proper maintenance of equipment and facilities under their control. Courts have long been concerned with issues covered by areas such as:

- Knowingly having or providing a dangerous environment likely to be frequented by children who, due to age or inexperience, do not realize the danger
- Providing an attractive nuisance situation (i.e., playgrounds) that attract children but are not properly maintained
- Maintaining grounds, buildings, and equipment in an improper manner
- Failing to provide proper inspections for all school-related items

The best alternative to litigation is, of course, the avoidance of injuries through the use of precautions. To reduce the risk of litigation and to protect the health and safety of students and others, policies and procedures should be developed that demonstrate reasonable care and include the following precautionary plans:

- A regularly scheduled inspection program including all areas of buildings and grounds. The inspection program should be documented by areas and items inspected, dates, and personnel involved.
- The notification of all personnel (potential users) of any possible dangerous conditions if the district administrators know, or have reason to know, of such conditions.
- Conscientious efforts to ensure that all personnel understand that the school district has the affirmative duty to exercise reasonable care not to provide or to hold equipment or property that they know, or have reason to know, is dangerous for its intended use. In this light, ongoing in-service concerning proper maintenance should be scheduled.[6]

Planning Insurance Acquisition

The insurance buyer for a school system has direct contact with the insurance field and its limitations. In selecting an agent to handle insurance for the schools, the administrator must investigate abilities of the possible agents to determine which can best meet the school's needs. Familiarity with the market and ability to cover unusual risks are evidence that the agent or broker is well informed and is keeping abreast of developments in the field.

Many school districts have made it a practice to award school insurance business to local agents regardless of the cost. The explanation for this practice has been that the local board should do business with local taxpayers. Since substantial amounts of local district revenue come from state and/or federal sources, the board has no obligation to subsidize local businesses. However, the board does have an obligation to make the best use of local tax dollars. Indeed, the board must maximize risk reduction at minimum cost. The board should examine the possibility of using the competitive bidding process for insurance acquisition as it does to secure supplies and materials. Several bids should be received, since the same coverage is not provided at the same rate by all companies. Care should be taken if the sealed bid approach is used because this procedure may obligate the district to award a contract to the lowest responsible bidder. Informal bids can allow for more flexibility in the determination of the quality and extent of insurance services needed. There is not a "pat" answer for reconciling these differences, since local situations often provide the best guidelines for selection of services.

The practice of placing insurance contracts with certain agents or companies used in the past is still a regular practice in some districts. Because some of the major pressures on a local board are in the area of insurance placement, a sound board policy should be established. The board should set guidelines for who can bid, the amount that can be placed, specifications of the insurance program, and so on. These guidelines, along with a decision to seek professional assistance from insurance boards, state department staff, and others, will place the process on the necessary professional level.

Many district risk managers often prefer to view insurance as a service rather than a product. By viewing insurance as a service, they argue that the relationship between an agent or a broker is substantially more important than a few dollars saved when all insurance is purchased on a low-bid basis. As in purchasing procedures, service is an important consideration. Many risk managers are viewing contracts of three years or more as a minimum to have with one company. This time frame allows for development of long-term relationships and may avoid unnecessary delays and long-term litigation of some claims. Risk managers generally believe long-term relationships are especially important in the areas of transportation and bus fleet insurance.

The possibility of "locking in" coverages for specific rates for a specific period of several years is also an increasingly popular option. The ability to hold costs by dealing with longer-term fixed cost packages or perhaps with a smaller year-to-year adjustment also is gaining interest.

Coverage of "what you should have" compared with "what you might have" and "why" is presented in Table 13-1. This illustrates only a few of the many risk management issues facing school districts and school business administrators.[7] In this table, the first column shows a desirable type of coverage, while the second suggests what should be a goal. The righthand column explains why the "should have" is a good idea.

Agents and Brokers

An *agent* is an individual, or sometimes a partnership or corporation, licensed to represent a particular insurance company in a certain area. He/she may be a general agent, allowed to hire and supervise other agents, or a soliciting agent, responsible only for his/her own production. An agent may represent more than one company, particularly in the property insurance field, while holding a specific agent's contract with each company. As the company's representative he/she frequently has the authority to "find" risks for the company (except in life insurance), to collect premiums, and sometimes to investigate and

TABLE 13-1   Insurance Coverage

What You Should Have	What You Might Have	Why
Property		
Blanket limit for real and personal property	Scheduled limit for building	One limit applies (administrative ease)
	Scheduled limit for contents	
Blank limit for all locations	Scheduled limit for individual locations	One limit applies (administrative ease)
General Liability		
Combined single limit for bodily injury/property damage	Separate limits	One limit applies to bodily injury and property damage
Broad Form CGL endorsement provides 13 ext: i.e., contractual liability, personal injury, etc.	Not provided	Fills many gaps in the general liability policy

settle small claims. When a school system places business with several agents throughout the district, coordination of the insurance program can become rather cumbersome. Under these circumstances the district may appoint an agent of record who will then assume the coordinating role with all other agents involved. This arrangement can be a tremendous time-saver for the district.

When buying property insurance particularly, it is sometimes better to deal with a broker. A *broker* is the representative of the insured, whose job it is to place the insurance on the most advantageous terms for the client. Brokers can do business with any company licensed in the state and try to obtain the maximum protection of the client's property for the lowest premium.

Although a broker represents the insured rather than the insurer, he/she is compensated, on a commission basis, by the insurer. Despite the possible conflict of interest that this entails, brokers are very useful to buyers of large amounts of insurance, since they are expert in fitting the various types of available insurance policies to the needs of the buyer, and they know which company's policy is most appropriate in a given situation. In nearly all states the law does not recognize the existence of life insurance or health insurance brokers, though many property insurance brokers also hold life insurance agents' licenses.

Insurance Contracts

Legal Requirements

The same basic set of laws that govern all types of contracts also govern insurance contracts. Specific legal requirements vary from state to state, and care should be exercised to secure correct advice in the wording and stipulation of insurance contracts. There is actually a special body of law to handle legal problems associated with insurance. One key point is that insured parties (such as the school district) rarely participate in the drafting of the actual contract. In some instances the state, not the insurer, drafts the contract. A final point of concern is that many insurance options are valid in only one state. A major concern is tort liability.

A *tort* is a civil wrong (other than a breach of contract) for which an award of damages is appropriate. School boards generally become involved in tort liability as the result of an injury or accident. Through the years, courts have held school boards as corporate entities to be immune from liability as long as they were operating within the scope of legislative authority. Individual board members are not protected when they exceed their authority and act in a nonresponsible manner.

Legislation is such a variable and school system situations are so change-oriented that school business administrators and other responsible school officials need to be alert to current legal changes. One specific area of concern is the issue of ''educational malpractice.'' Since disenchantment with education is very real, a rash of suits charging ''John graduated but can't read'' can be expected. Changes in legislation are occurring rapidly, and these laws and court decisions will have a major impact on schools in the next several years. Again, fees for a top-flight risk management consultant and/or attorney are generally money well spent.

Fortunately for the consumer, insurance contracts are highly standardized as a result of statutory or administrative directives, voluntary agreements, or customary practice. Otherwise, choosing among the policies issued by thousands of insurers would be extremely difficult.

For example, in most states the standard fire policy is prescribed word for word by statute. All insurers, domestic or foreign, writing fire insurance in those states must use the prescribed policy. Consequently, (1) the insured need not consider differences in policy language when selecting an insurer, (2) all the insured are subject to the same treatment, (3) policy conflicts do not arise when two or more insurers are required to provide the necessary protection or become involved in the same loss, (4) court interpretations of the contract become more meaningful, (5) the insured and insurance agents save time and energy in contract analysis, and (6) loss experience can be pooled for rate-making purposes.

Structure of the Insurance Contract

All insurance contracts, whether consisting of policies plus forms or policies only, contain provisions that can be classified as (1) declarations, (2) insuring agreements, (3) exclusions, (4) conditions, and (5) endorsements. In many property or liability insurance contracts, the provisions are grouped into these five categories and labeled accordingly, but in other lines the provisions must be rearranged to achieve this grouping.

1. *Declarations:* Declarations are statements by the insured, on the basis of which the insurer issues the contract.

2. *Insuring Agreements:* These are the provisions that distinguish one contract from another.

3. *Exclusions:* Many exclusions may be nullified by endorsement, though some are absolute. Exclusions are perils, persons, property, or situations not covered by the insurance contracts.

4. *Conditions:* A condition is a provision in the contract with the insured must comply in order to enforce his/her rights under the contract.

5. *Endorsements:* If endorsements are added to the basic contract, they supersede any provisions in the contract with which they are in conflict.

Types of Insurance Options

Property Insurance

The term *property insurance* encompasses coverage for buildings and their content. It also covers physical damage to any kind of real property such as buses and equipment. Coinsurance clauses in most property policies state the insurer must pay only the part of the loss the amount of insurance bears to the amount required to escape any penalty. For example:

$$\frac{\text{Amount of Insurance}}{[\text{Coinsurance \%}]\,[(\text{Value at Time/Loss})\,(\text{Loss})]} = \text{Amount Paid by Insurer}$$

Until 1949 there were two distinct types of property insurers: Fire and marine companies owned casualty subsidiaries, and vice versa. State insurance laws required that the two classes of property insurance be written by separate corporations. Since that year the same company has been able to write all lines of insurance, but vestiges of the artificial pre-1949 schism between casualty and fire companies are still evidenced by the differences in clients served.

General methods of valuing property—real estate or personal—vary from area to area. However, certain basic patterns of this valuing are used most often by the risk manager individually or in combination with others. These methods include original cost, market value, tax value, and replacement value. Each of these methods include variations based on local situations.

The value for which any structure should be insured is the *sound replacement cost* after such items as depreciation, site acquisition, and architects' fees are removed. Since costs of construction and general replacement costs for furnishings and equipment change frequently, district personnel must make every effort to keep records up to date. Accurate and frequent appraisals are the surest method of having the proper information available for determining the appropriate insurance program. The selection of a commercial appraisal firm, a broker, or the employment of a staff member with proper appraisal credentials is money well spent. Insurance companies often take local appraisal at purchase but reserve the right to have commercial appraisal when a claim is filed. For the same reason, frequent appraisals help prevent a needless expenditure of district funds for excessive insurance on uninsurable interests.

Replacement cost insurance for buildings should be considered where appropriate, especially in the case of relatively old buildings. To fail to adequately cover the replacement costs of equipment and furnishings and/or to purchase amounts of insurance far in excess of what will be an acceptable replacement cost is not economically sound practice. A "rule of thumb" is that full replacement cost of insurance increases the cost by 25 to 40 percent, with these increases influenced mostly by type of structure (e.g., a technical school building) and age of structure. Adherence to fire safety codes and inflation are two other key considerations.

All school districts are faced with many insurance needs other than those previously noted. Burglary, robbery, theft, glass, and boiler and machinery insurance are some of them. Limited coverage and broad coverage are available for boilers. Specifics are determined by state and local regulations. Glass insurance is generally restricted to the plate type and/or other special types. Coverage for burglary, robbery, and theft is determined by the legal definitions of each of these items. The all-risk type of insurance may be used rather than certain specific coverages.

Property insurance contracts often have specific modifications made to reflect special situations. One of the more common could be the addition of an endorsement covering vandalism—from glass breakage to total building destruction. School systems may elect to add this endorsement or to have insurance cover a percentage of the replacement costs because full coverage is too expensive.

Fire and Casualty Insurers

In the United States, school property insurance is written by these types of insurers: stock companies, mutual companies, and reciprocals. Stock companies have a major share of the business, with approximately three-fourths of all property insurance and with 5 percent of the total capital and surplus available for protection of policyholders.

Stock Companies

A stock life insurance company is, like any other corporation, owned by its stockholders, who are desirous of profit. It is managed by a board of directors elected by the stockholders and by officers chosen by the board. If the company realizes a profit, the stockholders receive dividends; if business is unprofitable, reserves are depleted. Many stock insurance companies issue nonparticipating policies; these companies charge a fixed, definite premium, and the policyholders share through dividends in the profits of the company.[8]

Mutual Companies

There are four types of mutual companies: assessment mutuals, advance-premium mutuals, factory mutuals, and "specialty" and "class" mutuals. Many write only fire insurance and allied lines. In some companies all members participate in the management of the company. Many advance-premium mutuals charge a lower initial premium than do stock companies, while others pay out the profits from their lower operating expenses in the form of policyholder dividends.[9] Though one receives dividends in profitable years, the policyholder cannot be asked to pay anything additional in years when operating results are poor. Since by definition, mutual companies operate on the ability to assess policyholders if economic conditions warrant, many states will not allow insurance purchases from mutual companies, as these assessments are considered a noninsurable risk. State law for schools often specifies that only nonassessable purchases are possible.

Reciprocals

A reciprocal, or interinsurance exchange, is an insurance carrier without any corporate existence. The members pay an advance premium and are also liable for assessments of a stipulated amount. Theoretically, a reciprocal should be able to provide low-cost insurance for its members, since its cost of acquiring business, a major expense of most insurers, is so low. This may be an excellent form of insurance coverage for school districts.

State Insurance

Some states operate school insurance programs. North Carolina covers elementary and secondary schools. Some of the state programs are handled through the state department of education, while others are handled through the state insurance department. Many programs parallel self-insurance (discussed in the following section) in that the local districts do not pay premiums. If administered correctly, these programs are much more economical than insuring through private agencies because they lack the high overhead common to many insurance firms. This practice has not spread, primarily because of the strong insurance lobbies in most states.

Self-Insurance

Many administrators in large school systems recognize that because of district size, risk has already been spread, and thus money might be saved by adopting a program of self-insurance rather than buying insurance from commercial companies. Normally, a self-insurance fund is established, small annual appropriations are made into the fund, the accumulated reserve is invested, and the earned interest is added to the reserve. As the accumulated reserve increases through adding the annual appropriation and interest, the system gradually phases out policies held in commercial companies. Ordinarily, the first buildings phased out of the commercial policies are the relatively low-risk units; conversely, high-risk buildings are the last to have commercial policies dropped. Only when the business administrator and the school board are convinced they have adequate reserve to cover the reasonable probability of loss should the school system become completely self-insured. Self-insurance may also operate on a deductible basis, where the first $100,000 of loss is paid by the district and any additional amount is covered. This allows for lower rates, yet provides coverage for the major loss.

Since there is never complete assurance that the point of adequate reserve to cover probable risk has been reached, boards and business administrators must exercise considerable judgement. Considerations that must be entertained in making this decision are:

1. The magnitude of the spread of risk
2. The general comparability of value of the several buildings in the system so as to prevent distortion in the spread of risk
3. The general comparability of risk of the several buildings of the system so as to prevent distortion in the amount of risk
4. The geographic separation of buildings to avoid multiple loss from a single fire
5. Transition of coverage from commercial companies to self-insurance in the low- to high-risk sequence

6. The probabilities and magnitude of future expected losses, based on current risk exposure rather than on past loss records
7. The fiscal alternatives available to the school system to replace a loss exceeding the revenue available in the self-insurance fund
8. The ability of the school system to maintain the self-insurance fund at the level necessary to provide adequate protection[10]

Self-insurance as *pooling* is a means that numerous school boards are using to become self-insured. Some insurance industry personnel see public agencies devoting approximately 50 percent of all property and casualty insurance premiums to self-insurance by the mid-1990s as compared with the current 7 to 10 percent. Major reasons for this growth include such areas as:

- Premium dollar savings/access to markets
- Improved coverage/limits
- Claims and cash management
- Market stability

The structure of the pool is very important. Most pools are structured with the loss fund followed by an aggregate loss fund protection policy. An illustration of a pool structure appears as Figure 13-1. Pooling is clearly not for all school districts. It is important that the issues are clearly understood by all participants and that all participants are willing to "go the distance."[11]

Most school systems do not use self-insurance for all their needs. For example, commercial insurance could still be purchased on such items as boilers or computers if extensive/expensive inspections are part of the coverage. Administrators in some school districts have been able to expand their self-insurance programs into such areas as general liability and motor vehicle.

No Insurance

One possibility in a very large district or state that has a good reserve of bonding power is to carry no insurance. This is used for state buildings spread throughout the state, including higher education facilities that are a part of the state system. If no insurance becomes the option, the major area of concern is the substantial loss from a natural or man-made disaster such as fire, flood, earthquake, tornado, or riot. As noted earlier, the age and condition of some buildings make this a necessary option in some instances.

Group Purchase/Cooperative Insurance

It may be to the economic advantage of school districts to utilize groups in which they participate on a regular basis for the purchase of insurance at group rates. For many years various school business administration groups have attempted to develop meaningful property insurance programs. Some of these are now beginning to be implemented. Coverage provided under such plans generally includes fire and extended coverage, van-

FIGURE 13-1   Loss Fund

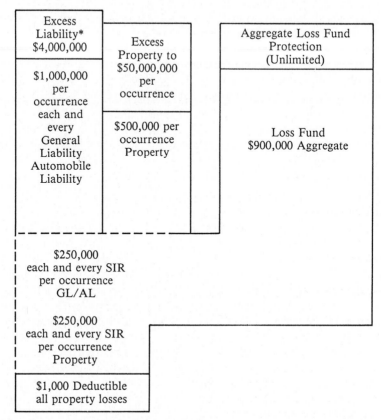

Excess Liability* $4,000,000	Excess Property to $50,000,000 per occurrence	Aggregate Loss Fund Protection (Unlimited)
$1,000,000 per occurrence each and every General Liability Automobile Liability	$500,000 per occurrence Property	Loss Fund $900,000 Aggregate

$250,000 each and every SIR per occurrence GL/AL

$250,000 each and every SIR per occurrence Property

$1,000 Deductible all property losses

Please note: The Loss Fund is set at $900,000 Aggregate which indicates the members cannot be liable for any amount above $900,000.

*Optional by District.

dalism, "all risk," theft, employee dishonesty, musical instrument floater, and boiler machinery. In general, a group purchase plan calls for a sliding scale of minimum loss deductibles related to the value of insured property. Obviously, the various loss deductibles may be increased if a particular school district wishes. There are some advantages to group purchase, including (1) overall rate reduction; (2) establishment of true insurable values of property; (3) establishment of an operating loss prevention and fire safety program; (4) more speedy processing of claims; (5) adjustment of amounts of insurance; and (6) review of the program by an external agency, which might provide additional input not previously available.

An interesting recent innovation in insurance coverage is the emergence of insurance boards. Under this plan local agencies and/or agents work together to service school accounts. If one of the members gets the contract, one-half of the premium goes to the insurance board for use in civic activities that assist the school system. The other portion of the premium goes to the agent. This service generally results in reduced premiums as well as providing funds for civic programs. Thus, the school district benefits two ways.

Cooperative insurers are organized for the benefit of the policyholders who elect the management and bear the insurance risks. The three types of cooperative insurers generally found are: (1) advance-premium mutual corporations, (2) pure assessment mutual corporations, and (3) reciprocal exchanges. Medical and dental expense associations such as Blue Cross/Blue Shield closely resemble the advance-premium mutual corporation. A detailed discussion of the technical differences among the groups would be too lengthy for inclusion here. The interested reader can secure information from the insurance board representative, broker agent, and/or insurance publications.

Liability Insurance

Liability insurance is written to cover any insured party's responsibility for damages due to bodily injury, death, and so forth. Two areas of liability—general liability and vehicle liability—are covered in most school district policies. (Vehicle liability is discussed in another section of this chapter.)

Liability insurance is a complex area for any school district and should be closely studied by the administrative team. An overall comprehensive insurance plan to cover the district is to be preferred over scheduled plans. Workers' compensation (see next section) is designed to cover injuries to school employees, and such injuries are generally not covered in liability programs. Liability insurance is not an accident policy, and payment of a claim need not be made until damages are awarded in a court. State statutes and the determination of what constitutes neglect affect decisions to such a degree that a board must insure for self-protection. In most states, school districts may not be held liable for injuries to pupils or other persons. This legal position has led to the establishment of nominally priced pupil accident insurance plans where coverage is purchased by parents. Group rates apply, and coverage is usually restricted to the school day and time spent traveling to and from school. Competition in interscholastic athletic events is usually excluded in these policies. Insurance covering these athletic events is purchased by athletic departments and/or parents for the specific sport in which the pupil participates. Teachers, administrators, and other school personnel are turning to personal liability insurance at a rapid rate.

All school districts must maintain an effective security program for staff, faculty, and students. The school site and district as a whole have an obligation to provide as "risk free" an environment as possible, but it is not possible to "guarantee" safety of all people at all times. The risk must be reduced, but it cannot be removed.

One of the more important developments in the area of commercial general liability (CGL) policies are the changes required by a shift to the "claims made" form of coverage from the traditional "occurrence" basis of coverage.

Occurrence policies cover all losses that happen during the time the policy is in force, even though a claim is not presented until a later time. Under the claims-made type of policy, the coverage would be provided by the policy that was in effect when the claim was made or the lawsuit was filed.

The Insurance Service Office (ISO) prepared revisions to the CGL policy, which included the change to the claims-made format. Although not in widespread use, the claims-made policy raises four basic issues. These are the:

1. Inclusion of an annual aggregate policy limit
2. "Retroactive date" feature
3. Notice of claims and occurrences from the insured to the carrier
4. Primary policy's tenure with terms of excess or umbrella policies[12]

Items related to these concerns will become a larger problem as more districts switch to this type of policy. Perhaps the key difference—and most interesting feature—is the fact that under a claims-made policy, the carrier of record at the time of claim filing is the responsible company. With such questions as long-term effects of asbestos exposure, for example, a company has a very difficult time projecting losses or potential claims. Additional problems facing schools include the so-called "long tail." Since most students are minors, they are not required to file lawsuits or make claims for injuries suffered at school or school-related types until they reach the age of majority. Thus, the potential number of claims is unknown for long periods of time. Additionally, the newer forms exclude pollution coverage altogether. Again, possible pollution caused by asbestos removal is the most likely source of problems. Finally, injuries sustained by large numbers of persons at a school event must be reported. However, notification of injury does not substitute for a claim and would not trigger coverage. If notification is not made, the carrier could cancel coverage or require some type of exclusion.[13]

One of the more recent concerns is that architects and engineers generally are excluding services related to asbestos removal from their contract and are requiring owners (i.e., school boards) to hold them harmless from any claims. While not usually a problem with K–12 systems, hazardous waste is also routinely excluded. Issues related to excluding pollution-related claims are not as clear but also are generally excluded.

The ISO, the insurance organization that prepares recommended policy forms for use in the United States, has made substantial revisions to its commercial general liability policy. Three major issues are covered in these sweeping changes. These are:

1. The change from *occurrence* basis of coverage to claims-made basis of coverage
2. Exclusion of coverage for all forms of pollution
3. Including the costs of defense within the coverage limits of the policy

As with all insurance policies, care must be taken to read and understand policy provisions. One illustration, Figure 13-2, of the differences between policies addressing the issues noted in the previous paragraphs is illustrated by material provided by the Insurance Service Office, Incorporated—"Commercial General Liability Coverage" and the same form providing "claims made coverage."[14]

Employee Insurance

Employee insurance programs constitute one of the major insurance items for a school district. Workers' compensation and medical insurance are the two major items of employee-related expense and will prove to be major items for consideration in the planning role of the school business administrator.

FIGURE 13-2   Commercial General Liability Coverage

Section I—Coverages
Coverage A. Bodily Injury and Property Damage Liability

1.   Insuring Agreement
    a.   We will pay those sums that the insured becomes legally obligated to pay as damages
          because of "bodily injury" or "property damage" to which this insurance applies. No
          other obligation or liability to pay sums or perform acts or services is covered unless
          explicitly provided for under SUPPLEMENTARY PAYMENTS—COVERAGES A
          AND B. This insurance applies only to "bodily injury" and "property damage" which
          occurs during the policy period. The "bodily injury" or "property damage" must be
          caused by an "occurrence." The "occurrence" must take place in the "coverage
          territory." We will have the right and duty to defend any "suit" seeking those damages.
          But:
          (1)   The amount we will pay for damages is limited as described in SECTION
                 III—LIMITS OF INSURANCE;
          (2)   We may investigate and settle any claim or "suit" at our discretion; and
          (3)   Our right and duty to defend end when we have used up the applicable limit of
                 insurance in the payment of judgments or settlements under Coverages A or B or
                 medical expenses under Coverage C.

Workers' Compensation

In most situations, district employees, both certified and noncertified, are covered under
provisions of the state workers' compensation law. Any particular exclusion to this law
should be noted in negotiated contracts between the individual and his/her particular
bargaining unit. Generally, in cases where physical disability resulted from compensable
accidental injuries sustained while on the job, employers augment payment employees
receive from workers' compensation. Many contracts state that beyond a specific day, in
this case the seventh, the employer pays the employee the difference between the workers'
compensation payment prescribed by law and his/her regular weekly income to the extent
and until such time as the employee has used his/her accumulated sick leave. In many
instances, payments are provided beyond this period and can be charged against compensable leave on a prorata basis computed on the relationship of differential pay to the regular
weekly pay, until compensable leave is exhausted. Any further payments would have to be
negotiated as a part of the individual contract.

   Rates for insurance coverage are, of course, determined by the dollar value of past
claims. As claims increase, rates for coverage increase. Thus the school business administrator, site personnel, and other central administrators can play a key role in avoiding
increased rates through a vigorous accident prevention and risk management plan. A regular
plan of inspections, preventive maintenance, and risk avoidance through education can help
hold the line against rate increases across several insurable areas. A team effort to identify
risks and reduce them is necessary for an effective program. In some school districts,
especially in larger urban areas, self-insurance for workers' compensation coverage is often
provided.

   No benefits are payable in the case of injury resulting from willful intent. Specific
injuries, medical expenses, disability, and death are covered in workers' compensation
programs. In several states workers' compensation is required for all public employees,
while in others the school district is held to be liable for the risk. Rates for workers'

compensation are based on employee compensation and the risk value associated with specific jobs within the district. Special cases or situations may be covered by adjusted rates for the specific district. A good accident prevention program, coupled with regular physical examinations and strict adherence to safety rules, is an effective method of reducing workers' compensation claims for any school district.

Medical Insurance

Group medical insurance programs with options to cover both the employee and his/her family (spouse and/or children) are features of virtually all plans. This coverage is often an integral part of union agreements or other negotiated packages. Coverage has increased in recent years to include major medical and disability or income-protection programs as well as death benefits. More recent program additions have included dental coverage and psychological services. Expanded programs that allow for the purchase of additional life coverage at low group rates are often available. Additionally, the option to convert term coverage to ordinary coverage now exists for many employees.

Prepaid health plans that offer comprehensive medical care for a fixed fee have become a feature of a large number of school-based medical plans. These are most commonly characterized by the term *health maintenance organization (HMO)*.

HMOs are established to provide medical coverage for a single fee and cover a wide variety of services, outpatient to major surgery. HMOs are of two major types:

1. Group practice plans provide medical services at centers staffed by salaried physicians. Laboratories, X-ray facilities, and pharmacies are on the premises so members can obtain outpatient services at one central location.
2. Individual practice plans offer medical care in the private offices of doctors under contract to them. One advantage is a wider choice of physicians. These doctors sometimes receive a monthly payment for every member who has enrolled with them.

HMO packages have come under fire in recent years since many are cutting services because of a loss of revenues. If the goal of providing good coverage for reasonable costs cannot be maintained in this way, school districts must seek other alternatives, which may well mean more expense

One key feature often overlooked by risk managers is a possibility of organizing a wellness program for employees, both faculty and staff. The general effects of *wellness programs* nationwide have been good, with these results felt in lowering of some health insurance premiums, reduction in absenteeism, increased productivity, and enhanced faculty/staff morale. Since many adults are in poorer health than they believe, most wellness programs are started by showing personnel they have a problem or a potential problem. Problems are a necessary part of the overall plan provided by the district since early identification of a problem is vital for the effectiveness of the wellness program. Early identification and treatment of a problem are substantially in the interest of the school district since they may eliminate long-term recovery or loss of job performance capability by faculty or staff members. Many other benefits accrue to a school district having an established wellness program, but one of the most important is that the tangible costs of health care may be reduced.[15]

Unemployment Insurance

The implications of recent court decisions have made school employees eligible for unemployment insurance in cases that were not previously covered. For example, in some states, teachers who were considered to be eligible for unemployment insurance during periods of unemployment or layoff become eligible for unemployment fringe benefits of a magnitude not previously experienced by local districts. State plans for unemployment insurance coverage are at best heterogeneous. Some are liberal and others are very restrictive. Problems abound with regard to covered groups, especially part-time employees. The risk manager must keep abreast of current legislation at both the state and federal level. The school business administrator and planning personnel have to consider the burden these payments place on the annual budget and plan to meet them. Since expenditures occur after the fact, the school business administrator has a major problem with allocation of the funds for this expense. The watchword here is adequate planning, so that the proper compensation units can be built into the budget.

Alternate Financing for Risk Management

If, as many risk managers believe, the insurance crisis of the mid-1980s is not the last such upheaval in the area, alternative forms of risk financing may be needed. One such form is the *capital assets market*. This approach is characterized by a district's administrator analyzing its exposure to loss, conventionally insuring some loss potentials, retaining (self-insuring) some loss potential, and creating a quasi-insurance entity—by borrowing in the capital assets market to replace some types of coverage. In short, the district has established its own insurance company.

The goal of the capital markets approach to risk financing has four subunits:

1. To stabilize the cost of risk financing
2. To stabilize the availability of coverage
3. To stabilize the availability of limits of liability
4. To provide control over the district's destiny

Basic emphasis of this plan is on stability and control, not cost saving. However, substantial cost savings can accrue with proper management techniques. Problems remain to be addressed for any district, including areas of legal and internal revenue regulations, but these are manageable. State legislative edicts and local legal concerns are other areas that must be examined by the school district administration, the board, and the necessary legal staff members for districts. This approach, however, is an important development and is worthy of consideration under appropriate circumstances. It can assist school districts in being released from a portion of the cyclical concern noted with the insurance industry.[16]

Insurance Records, Maintenance, and Protection

It is imperative that all school district records are maintained in a safe and yet accessible manner. Insurance records and all other records within the school district must be protected to the degree that the value of the documents warrant. For example, there are crucial, important, useful, and nonessential insurance records. It is imperative that each type of record is classified by category and that appropriate procedures are established to ensure that vital records are protected. Proper security measures must also be maintained when transporting data to and from vaults so that they can be used. As is true with most other records in today's society, insurance records can be maintained on microfilm or microfiche at relatively little expense and stored at a distant location, so that there is always a retrievable copy in the event of a natural disaster or a civil disorder.

The use of the MIS will be a major feature of a records system. It is also important—again, with the use of the MIS—that insurance records are designed to feed back into the fiscal accounting procedures so that the school business administrator can direct these materials into the day-to-day flow. This will allow for the use of particular items of information for projections relative to system costs or bid and contract lettings. The discussion of a disaster recovery plan in Chapter 6 also is of interest to the risk manager.

Personnel and Contractor Concerns of Risk Management

Negotiated Contracts

Expanded insurance benefits—dental, psychological, and so forth—have become a major issue for negotiations in recent years. While the need for increasing wages is still of paramount importance, many employee groups (and employees) see the "fringe benefits" of insurance, vacations, and such as fruitful areas to use for bargaining. The actual benefit to the employee may be several times the equivalent percentage increase in wages. Improved plans in all areas and extension of services have been prominent in recent teacher bargaining positions.

Riffing of Staff

Riffing is the reduction in force (RIF) that occurs when staff are discharged. The determination of insurance coverage when staff riffing occurs is a matter of serious concern to both school system and employees. A general position has been that the language of the contract set by collective bargaining will determine any insurance provisions for persons affected by a RIF. Thus, the issue is one of policy and contract. In those systems without contracts, school board policy should be in place to avoid suits and other legal problems.

Retirement Changes

Legislation at the federal level allowing for early retirement is now being reviewed. However, many school districts include early retirement incentives to reduce the effect of riffing. Under many plans, persons within a specified number of years of retirement are given a "bonus" to retire early. This prevents the dismissal of a new faculty/staff person and also lowers the general employee total for the system. The extent or full impact of this practice is not fully known.

Surety Bonds

A *surety* is a person, group of persons, or company guaranteeing that other persons will fulfill a valid obligation to the school district. There are several kinds of surety bonds available to public school districts and to the school business administrator. These include contract, court, license, and permit bonds. Each of these bonds guarantees that under a particular situation, such as a performance contract, failure to perform a certain activity or produce a certain acceptable level of work will be covered for the completion of that contract in accordance with its terms. Contract bonds help to eliminate incompetent and/or dishonest contractors from bidding, since a contractor without a good reputation is unlikely to be able to secure a bond. The advantages of bonding in general include: the district's assurance that its contract will be completed or that the surety company will have the contract completed; that incompetent or dishonest contractors will have difficulty in obtaining contract bonds; and that construction progress will be aided, since payment of bills is guaranteed in a performance bond or in a separate payment bond. Bonds affecting individuals are aimed at ensuring the performance or faithfulness of another party under an ''honesty of the employee'' bond. Under such a bond, if a public employee is careless or dishonest, any losses incurred by this activity will be covered. These are generally referred to as *fidelity bonds,* although they are technically a type of surety bond.

Vehicle Insurance

Insurance coverage associated with school transportation is a multi-faceted aspect of a school district's total insurance program. Planning on the part of the school business administrator in order to recommend coverage requires input from many school district sources, including the district's legal counsel, the personnel supervisor, union representatives, the purchasing agent, and the transportation director. Policies in a vehicle insurance program might include, among others, comprehensive, collision, fire, theft, liability, medical, and extended coverage.

Additionally, the school business administrator, as part of the administrative team, has the responsibility of providing information to all involved in the use of private automobiles for school-related functions. It may logically fall to the school business administrator to keep abreast of the latest judicial decisions in this area and to advise appropriate administrators, parent groups, coaches, and teachers of current laws. He/she may also be expected to give suggestions as to types of insurance coverage needed, or recommend additions to existing private coverage necessary to provide adequate protection.

Drivers of school buses are, of course, liable for negligence that causes personal injury or property damage. Negligence may also apply to the school board. The school business administrator must know the extent of coverage permitted or required by the state. Questions must be answered about the extent of coverage provided for drivers, passengers, and property. Safety training programs for drivers as they relate to a reduction of insurance premiums, efforts to regulate pupil conduct for the protection of equipment, and other safety considerations may well be a partial responsibility of the school business administrator.

Occupational Safety and Health Act

A major concern of all business administration personnel is the implementation of and the reaction to federal and state laws. One of the major pieces of legislation now affecting school systems and likely to continue to do so over the next several years is the 1970 Occupational Safety and Health Act, which mandates certain operating standards for various kinds of activities, structures, and job situations. For example, activities in the areas of transportation, maintenance, school plant management, and so forth all contain features covered under the Occupational Safety and Health Act. Thus, the necessity of providing adequate documentation and attention to detail in accident prevention, while it has always been present, is of paramount importance now. The application of the Occupational Safety and Health Act to the environment of workers as regards noise pollution and air pollution, as well as accident prevention, is a key feature of any safety program within the district. The application of the act is subject to the prevailing attitude of the current federal administration.

The implementation of this legislation, while probably causing an extra outlay of funds, may provide a "break" in terms of insurance premiums. The establishment of a rate structure that supports these particular innovations may well provide significant rate reductions. Many boards do not avail themselves of the opportunity to negotiate insurance rates. Thus, the opportunity to examine insurance programs in detail and to negotiate rate structures is an advantage that the introduction of OSHA may bring into sharper focus.

General decisions related to OSHA work have varied over the last several years on how the degree of enforcement would be made relative to school systems. Current government policies to reduce regulations could have a major impact on the rigor with which enforcement of OSHA standards takes place.

The OSHA acts of the early 1980s included a right-to-know law designed to help employees reduce and prevent adverse health effects from exposure to workplace chemicals and other hazardous substances. School districts are responsible for identifying such materials and substances, for providing information concerning employees' rights, and for providing necessary training and retraining of all employees in these areas. While often considered "another law, another form," school districts must consider the risk factor of such issues and take appropriate steps to educate and inform their employees of possible problems. The laws are designed for the protection of all employees and are thus a concern of the total district and especially the school business administrator with responsibilities of risk management and loss control. Investment in the safety, health, and welfare of employees and also students makes the implementation of such laws a must.[17]

Summary

This chapter discussed the major planning responsibilities of the school business administrator in the insurance program of a school district. Insurance contracting, including such facets as declarations, exclusions, conditions, and endorsements, was presented. Aspects of insurance acquisition, property insurance, fire and casualty insurance, state insurance, self-insurance, and their interrelationships were discussed. Information on insurance record-keeping and valuation, and discussions of employee insurance, surety bonds, vehicle insurance, and other kinds of insurance was provided.

It is clear that since a major part of the school business administrator's role is to maximize returns on educational dollars spent, protection of school funds, persons, and property is an integral part of this function. Protection involves expenditures; wise protection, however, is a vital part of effective planning.

Suggested Activities

1. Design and conduct a risk management survey for your school district.
2. Under what circumstances could competitive bidding for insurance not be desirable?
3. What are the major functions of insurance for a school system?
4. What are the conditions in your school that could make a risk insurable? Uninsurable?
5. How is insurable value determined?
6. Would self-insurance, coinsurance, or no insurance be suited to the district in which you work or last worked? If so, how? If not, why not?
7. What are the key issues in insurance acquisition, and how would you weight the various options to determine the necessary coverage for your site or system?

Suggested Readings

Adams, John F. *Risk Management and Insurance: Guidelines for Higher Education.* Washington, DC: National Association of College and University Business Officers, 1972.

Castle, Gray, and Robert F. Cushman. *The Business Insurance Handbook.* Homewood, IL: Dow Jones-Irwin, 1981.

Duncan, K. A., and D. I. Harris (Eds.). *Computers in Education.* Amsterdam: North-Holland, 1985. (A collection of journal and magazine articles.)

Hadden, Susan G. *Risk Analysis, Institutions, and Public Policy.* Port Washington, NY: Associated Faculty Press, 1984.

Rejda, George E. *Principles of Insurance.* Glenview, IL: Scott, Foresman, 1986.

Williams, C. Arthur, Jr., and Richard M. Heins. *Risk Management and Insurance,* 5th ed. New York: McGraw-Hill, 1985.

Notes

1. C. Arthur Williams, Jr., and Richard M. Heins, *Risk Management and Insurance,* 4th ed. (New York: McGraw-Hill, 1981), 3–22.

2. John R. Adams, *Risk Management and Insurance: Guidelines for Higher Education.* (Washington, DC: National Association of College and University Business Officers, 1972), 3.

3. Ibid., 2.

4. Joan M. Sherman "Do you understand your insurance program?" *American School & University,* 57, 8 (1985), 61–63.

5. D. R. Dunklee and R. J. Shoop, "School Facilities' Negligence: A Minefield Fraught with Litigation," *School Business Affairs,* 52, 6 (1986), 36–39.

6. Ibid.

7. Sherman, "Do you understand your insurance program?" 62.

8. For additional information regarding rate structures, see David L. Bickelhaupt and John H. Magee, *General Insurance,* 8th ed. (Homewood, IL: Irwin, 1970).

9. Additional information on the use of insurance dividends can be found in Albert H. Mowbray, Ralph H. Blanchard, and C. Arthur Williams, Jr., *Insurance,* 6th ed. (New York: McGraw-Hill, 1969).

10. S. L. Rosenthal, "Self-Insurance Pools: Fantasy or Reality?" *School Business Affairs, 53,* 6 (1987), 28.

11. T. F. Maedke, "Cooperative Purchasing of Insurance and Risk Management Services," *School Business Affairs, 54,* 6 (1988), 35–39.

12. J. G. McConnell, "The 'Claims Made' Policy," *American School & University,* 58, 12, 19–25.

13. Ibid.

14. Ibid.

15. D. Robinson, "How Well Do You Know Your HMO?" *Parade Magazine,* February 12–13, 1989.

16. R. G. Rudolph, "Risk Financing For Schools: The Capital Markets Approach," *School Business Affairs, 54,* 6 (1988), 27.

17. Michalene H. Roll, "The OSHA Communication Standard and State Right-to-Know Laws," *School Business Affairs, 56,* 7 (1990), 26–30.

_14_

Auxiliary Services

AUXILIARY SERVICES generally provide the school business administrator with most of the severe day-to-day problems encountered in the typical school system. While these services are not directly related to the teaching-learning situation, their absence makes it impossible for the primary function of the school to continue. Because auxiliary services are so important to the normal operation of a school system and because the efficient operation of these services enables the educational process to proceed with a minimum of distraction and disruption, considerable planning effort must be devoted to their appropriate injection into the total operations of the school system.

In planning auxiliary services, the school business administrator must first adopt the premise that these services are support services to the teaching-learning situation and not ends in themselves. Additionally, the function of auxiliary services is to enhance the educational environment and to make possible the most efficient learning situation. Therefore, auxiliary services personnel must see themselves as support personnel and must be able to make adjustments as needed to accommodate the learning process.

Since auxiliary services often involve the provision of a specific service at a specific time, e.g., food services and/or transportation, careful planning of the logistical details is crucial to success. Optimum use of expensive equipment also requires careful attention to logistics.

With the rapid increase in collective bargaining across the country, the business administrator must develop expertise in contract management as it pertains to those departments over which he/she has direct line responsibility, such as food services, transportation, and operations. Because of the crucial nature of the business role in the negotiations process, the business administrator is an important member of the management bargaining team. The dual realities of collective bargaining and contract administration add importance to the strategic planning function of the business official.

There are a number of school systems across the country that are developing alternatives to the traditional manner of providing for auxiliary services. Increasingly, school systems are going to the private sector for the provision of auxiliary services. The rationale is that auxiliary services are not the main function of the educational system, that those services are most efficiently and effectively provided by the private sector, that by getting competitive bids for these services they are provided at minimal cost to the taxpayer, and that the educational system has enough to worry about without becoming involved with auxiliary services. Of course, the down side of the argument is that the local system loses control when these services are privatized and that the quality of the service may be compromised as a result. For the business administrator, privatization reduces the burden of being responsible for several employee groups, each with unique needs and demands. In addition, the school system gets out of the fringe benefit business, the cost of which is dramatically increasing with no sign of letting up.

While auxiliary services include such items as attendance services, health services, student activities, and community services, the services that most often become a part of the school business administrator's direct responsibility are food service and transportation. These are services over which the business administrator is apt to have direct line responsibility, as opposed to a staff relationship in the instructional support activities. It is therefore appropriate for a school business administration text to deal in some depth with the planning of food services and transportation programs. The authors examine these functions with awareness that nuances of region and geography and variables of local and state policies make generalizations hazardous.

The move from a traditional pattern of organization to a site-based management emphasis further complicates the provision of auxiliary services. Rather than develop a standard, inflexible set of auxiliary activities, the business office must now consider local unit needs in the development of transportation schedules and food services.

Consideration of local preferences and needs may cause some deviation from traditional unilateral decisions, but once physical and financial constraints are identified, the process does simplify. Strategic planning requires that the clients, in this case the building principals, be involved and be participants. While more time-consuming, it ultimately leads to better understanding of the limitations, more unity in the final decision, and a better service for the students.

Transportation Services

What was once a rural phenomenon has become an accepted service provided to over half of the public school children in the United States. In addition, a sizable proportion of parochial school pupils are provided transportation services. The transportation of school children began at a time when the country entered the automotive age and was a real stimulus to the development of consolidated school systems. The breakthrough in transportation led to the elimination of small, inefficient school systems and greatly assisted in the establishment of the comprehensive school systems of modern America. As paved highways and improved vehicles were developed, the service area of a school system could be expanded, until today it is not unusual for children to be transported many miles to schools suited to their educational needs. Indeed, in some of the more sparsely populated sections of the country, it is quite common for children to be transported over fifty miles to school. The sight of fifty, one hundred, even two hundred school buses parked on a school transportation site is no longer unusual. The big yellow vehicle going down the road has become a common sight to most American drivers.

As the nation's highways became more highly developed and as the variety and size of vehicles increased, many other important uses of the transportation services were introduced. With the advent of smaller vehicles (six- to fifteen-passenger) and more specialized vehicles, moving particular children to special schools (e.g., handicapped, gifted) became economically feasible. The use of buses as mobile classrooms and as learning laboratories was also introduced. More recently cities and newly emerged suburbs have come to depend on transportation services for a number of tasks besides basic transport between home and school.

Even more recently the use of transportation services for desegregation purposes, including transportation to alternative schools, magnet schools, and for court-ordered student transfers among regular schools, has expanded the use and scope of the typical transportation department. Emerging "schools of choice" legislation in many states will add to the complexity of strategic planning for the transportation system.

Among the more demanding state mandates requiring school business administrator action and concern are the following:

- Seat belt requirements
- Bus safety requirements
- Changing eligibility for transporting students
- Bus driver requirements

Actions to be taken by the business administrator must be predicated upon federal law and statutes for the particular state and should reflect an ongoing concern for the safety of children. For example, Public Law 94-142 requires that vehicles used to transport students suffering from certain handicaps meet certain requirements and capacities. These requirements, e.g., hoists, wheelchair capacity, ramps, and so forth, require special specifications and attention from the business administrator.

Thus, the school business administrator's task of planning to meet the transportation needs of a school system becomes a complex, often frustrating endeavor. Not only must the primary function of moving children to and from school be attended to, but the important tasks of moving children for purposes of educational quality and educational equality must also be addressed. Recent decisions mandating the "mainstreaming" of students previously assigned to special schools further complicate the logistical difficulties involved in planning transportation services.

Since the planning and implementation of transportation programs are neither exotic nor desirable chores compared to the spectrum of duties normally assigned the business office, the service dimensions must be emphasized and rewarded. There are many considerations that must be resolved in order to implement a transportation program.

Planning Considerations

Crucial decisions as to what kinds of transportation are important to the educational programs of a school district must be handled at the policy planning stage. Questions to be addressed include:

1. Is the transportation system to be used only for moving children to and from school?
2. What are other legitimate uses of the transportation system?
3. What are the constraints (legal and otherwise) on the transportation system?

4. What benefits can accrue to the students through expanded use of the transportation system?
5. What federal, state, and/or local regulations affect the transportation system?
6. How do children qualify for transportation services? Is distance the only criterion, or are physical traffic concerns also important?
7. What portion of the educational resource is most profitably invested in the transportation system?

From decisions made concerning these and other questions should evolve the transportation policy of a school system. As the policy questions are resolved, operating rules, regulations, and procedures are developed. Periodic, systematic review of the transportation policy must be a part of the planning-implementation cycle, for as variables change, so must policy dealing with the variables. As policy shifts are made necessary by changing conditions and/or new educational goals, rules, regulations, and procedures for implementing policy must be modified. The overriding concern must always be to provide the best possible support and service to the learner and to the school system.

Contract versus District-Owned Equipment

One of the early planning decisions to be made is the resolution of the question of contract versus district-owned equipment. There are many advantages and disadvantages to either approach to pupil transportation, and the decision is often one of convenience rather than one based on careful planning and analysis of alternatives. There are a great many considerations to be assessed in reaching a decision on contract versus district-owned equipment, not the least of which is capital equipment expenditure. Rolling stock is not an inexpensive investment; the more elaborate and larger buses cost many thousands of dollars.

Convenience to the learner is another important criterion for deciding the contract versus district-owned issue. If, for example, there exists a well-developed public transportation system that has the capacity to service the needs of the school system while meeting the health, safety, and convenience criteria established for students, the decision to contract is relatively simple. But if use of the public transit system places an excessive burden on either the system or the clients, then other alternatives must be explored. In many instances the use of the public transit system provides for optimum use of that system while meeting the educational needs of the school district at the same time. In such cases it is to the advantage of both the school and the transit authority to enter into a cooperative effort to ensure that total utilization of community resources is being implemented.

In other locales there is no public transit system and the decision is more difficult. Contract opportunities with private carriers provide alternatives to district-owned equipment. Once again, health and safety needs, convenience, and cost benefits must be assessed before a decision is made. Among the advantages the private carrier offers to the school business administrator are:

- No large investment is required.
- A large administrative management task is eliminated.
- The school district is not in competition with private business.
- The enormous tasks of maintaining and operating a bus fleet are not the school district's.

- Transportation personnel are not added to the complement of school district employees.
- Many of the criticisms can be directed to the contractor rather than to the school administration.

Conversely, there are advantages inherent in school district–owned transportation systems. These include:

- Operating costs are usually less than with private contractors.
- Buses are available for use for other aspects of the school program.
- There is greater control over matters of health, safety, and convenience.
- The transportation program can be planned as an integral part of the total educational experience for the learner (as in the use of school buses for field trips).
- In many states, state subsidy is available to assist the local district in the capital expenditure.
- Transportation personnel can be selected and trained to ensure an appropriate level of both driving and educational competency. (Bus drivers are considered to have instructional roles as they can influence children in areas of citizenship, human relations, good manners, responsibility, cooperation, and so forth.)
- There is far greater flexibility inherent in a district-owned and operated transportation system.

While there are many contract agreements in operation across the country, well over 80 percent of the school transportation systems are district-owned and operated. Careful cost-benefit analysis of all options should lead to the best decision.

Routing and Scheduling

Without question, one of the more demanding and frustrating aspects of transportation system planning is the development of routes and schedules. Techniques range from maps identifying each student to be served (required by law in many states) to computer programming of routes and schedules, sometimes with questionable results. The difficulty of programming the variables of human behavior and the problems encountered when dealing with weather conditions and machinery make the development of routes and schedules additionally sensitive. Problems of routing and scheduling are compounded by population sparseness or density, traffic conditions, road quality and conditions, school schedules, and the variables of weather. Planning decisions on routes and schedules involve determinations as to appropriate roads to travel, what distance youngsters may walk to converge on a pick-up point, services provided the handicapped, effects on property owners of pupils congregating at a certain point, traffic flow and congestion, safety of pupils, time constraints, size of buses, geography of the route, and so on. Another important consideration is how to make the most efficient use of vehicles; that is, should routes be planned so that buses can make more than one trip, and if so, should age ranges of pupils play a major part in the route development?

As transportation systems become a more important component of the educational program, the problems of scheduling for educational use becomes more complex. Field trips of every description are valuable educational experiences, and the meshing of these activities with the primary home-to-school-to-home obligation presents severe logistical problems. The routing and scheduling of a fleet of buses to provide safe, economical transportation, as well as to support the variety of educational experiences possible with extended use of vehicles, requires thoughtful, resourceful, sensitive planning.

Recent developments in the use of computers to assist in scheduling have permitted much more efficient schedule development. Many districts have moved to a three-tier schedule whereby buses are utilized for three runs as opposed to two, giving a 50-percent increase in capacity. Computer scheduling permits a variety of options to be considered and will allow for many route configurations to be examined.

With the dramatic increase in fuel costs affecting all fleet operators, efficient scheduling becomes a must. The bus fleet must be utilized as effectively as possible in order to minimize the strain on the educational dollar. Careful examination of all bus usage is important in ensuring optimum program opportunity.

Inspection and Maintenance

School bus accidents, while very rare, are tragic specters for school personnel. Accidents due to mechanical failures are especially tragic and often involve negligence on the part of those responsible for transportation systems. When a school district commits itself to the purchase of a transportation fleet, it at the same time commits itself to a planned, systematic inspection of the maintenance program.

It is unfortunate that many maintenance programs are of an emergency nature, when the use of orderly, periodic inspection procedures can lead to a preventive maintenance program that will not only provide greater safety and service to users but also return savings to the school district. Typically, the school system finds itself with a growing fleet of school vehicles, but with little or no equipment to use in the care of these vehicles and with no trained personnel to assign to the maintenance of moving stock. The care of the transportation fleet is contracted to local garages and/or filling stations that attend to simple (e.g., gas and oil) needs on a regular basis and to other needs as they are requested. Because of the harsh reality of school budgets, vehicular maintenance is usually on an emergency basis and typically occurs only upon major breakdown of the vehicle. This is, in fact, false economy and leads to the inconvenience of the failure of transportation services. Occasionally, this method of operations leads to mechanical failures that result in tragic and avoidable accidents.

Regular inspection and planned maintenance of vehicles are crucial to the health and safety of users and permit the optimum utilization of the transportation system to the advantage of the educational program. Inspection and maintenance are closely interrelated and mutually dependent. Inspection is accomplished daily, weekly, monthly, quarterly, and annually, depending on the need of the vehicle. Maintenance, too, is accomplished according to a short- and long-term schedule. Inspection checklists filled out by the driver, mechanic, supervisor, and other personnel give information relative to maintenance needs. Daily inspections, usually performed by the vehicle driver, are mostly visual and are intended to act as safety checks on the vehicle. Examination of tires, testing of turn indicators, checking of braking power, testing of lights, engine warm-up, review of gauge reading, and examination of fuel levels are routine and perfunctory inspection tasks for the driver. Scheduled inspections by mechanics become more minute and intense as use time of the vehicle grows. Periodic lubrication efforts and minor engine tune-ups are performed on a regular basis. Annual inspections involve major repairs and replacement of worn and/or used parts. Certain maintenance tasks are the result of seasonal weather changes and may differ according to geographic location. Certainly in the northern regions, winterizing of vehicles must be planned and accomplished well in advance of winter weather conditions.

The realization of an adequate vehicular maintenance program is the result of careful planning and resource allocation. Equipment, space, and personnel must be provided for such a program to succeed. It is not unusual for school transportation fleets of from fifty to eighty vehicles to employ four to six full-time mechanics and to have garage facilities that will provide indoor workstations for at least six to ten buses. In addition, the stocking of sufficient parts, tires, tools, and equipment calls for an investment of thousands of dollars. It must be recognized that the typical fleet of fifty to one hundred buses represents an investment of from $500,000 to over $ 1,000,000 and an annual operating expenditure of significant size. If supply and equipment stocking is based on sensible prediction of need and the advantages inherent in volume purchase, great benefits can accrue to the school district. Most important, of course, is the savings involved with curtailment of vehicle downtime. While actual dollar savings cannot be computed in terms of downtime, the fact that the transportation system can meet its obligation in terms of service to the user is of tremendous importance. In addition, the dollars saved by district-performed maintenance will enable the expenditure for transportation to be a high-benefit expenditure.

An important part of the inspection and maintenance program is keeping adequate records on each vehicle. Routine and periodic maintenance operations depend on records. Records can also provide the basis for ordering equipment, parts, and supplies on an annual basis to encourage additional savings. Annual bids on fuel, oil, and other consumable materials can add to the savings. The annual bidding on fuel alone can result in enough savings to enable the costs of fuel pumps and storage tanks to be amortized over a very short time. Certain regional accommodations are also appropriate to realize optimum return on investments. For example, the use of antifreeze additives in fuel is desirable in northern climates. It can also be a direct savings if head bolt heaters are installed in subfreezing climates. Installation of such devices will guarantee cold morning starts and save countless hours of driver and mechanic time. One school district known to the authors calculated that the use of head bolt heaters on its fleet of eighty buses saved over $15,000 per year in driver and mechanic overtime, all for an initial expenditure of $2,700.

To conclude, if a school district determines that the transportation system should be school district–owned and operated, then plans for adequate inspection and maintenance procedures must also be formulated. Such a program must include adequate provision for regular inspection and preventive maintenance, conducted by trained personnel backed by appropriate equipment, space, and supplies. Such planning will not only provide safe, timely service, but will also be reflected in significant savings to the school system.

Staff Supervision and Training

The supervision and training of transportation personnel is another of the difficult tasks facing the school business administrator. Since the number of persons involved in the transportation system can range from very few to upwards of several hundred, general statements can be misleading. Generally, large bus fleets are under the direction of a director of transportation who is responsible to the chief school business administrator. In smaller systems the school business administrator assumes direct control of the transportation system, sometimes with the help of a supervisor or the head mechanic. However the system is organized, some office must assume training and supervisory responsibilities.

The training of drivers is an important and demanding task. Not only must school vehicle drivers have driving ability and the capacity to exercise good judgment; they must also have personal characteristics and qualities that make them positive influences on children. Qualities such as tolerance of noise, firmness, fairness, and love and understanding of children are as important as reaction time, driving ability, physical stamina, and good eyesight. The training of drivers must reflect the need for transportation personnel to relate well to young people. Many districts have developed concurrent programs that couple classroom instruction with on-the-road training with experienced drivers. Classroom instruction covers such items as child growth and development, safety, psychology, vehicular law, negligence, district demography and geography, and driving regulations. Aptitude and personality tests designed to measure adaptive capacity and stability are also used. Actual driving, first with the supervisor and/or mechanic, is used to develop appropriate driving habits and to learn the handling of large vehicles. As the neophyte gains in ability and confidence he/she is permitted to accompany other drivers on trips and to actually drive the loaded vehicle. After a series of such experiences, the novice is given certain ''short'' route responsibilities prior to assignment as a regular. Periodic ratings and test drives are part of the training sequence for drivers.

Many school systems encourage and even require transportation personnel to participate in periodic staff development programs in which safety procedures, driving techniques, child psychology, and so on are reviewed. In addition, periodic physical examinations are required for personnel to retain their positions.

While much rhetoric has been produced concerning the amount of court-ordered busing now being mandated, the reality is that the bulk of the pupil transportation provided is due to distance between home and school and not a court-ordered desegregation plan. In some instances mandated busing plans reduce time and distance for many pupils. ''Busing'' is, nonetheless, a negative term to many educators and parents, while ''pupil transportation'' carries a positive connotation. After a dramatic increase in federal court intervention on desegregation issues during the late 1960s and the decade of the 1970s, it appears that the political pendulum has swung to a posture of no longer requiring busing in such cases. The judicial process continues to be the focal point of the desegregation issue.

Utilization and Evaluation of Services

When examining school districts, one often finds beautifully developed auxiliary services divisions that are so underutilized that it is difficult to justify their existence. This is true in the case of many school-owned and -operated transportation systems. Vehicles are used for pupil transportation to school in the morning and home in the afternoon and then sit idle the remainder of the time. In addition, routes are often planned so that vehicles must cover an area a number of times to accomplish what could be done more efficiently in a single trip. Low utilization of transportation services not only makes its continuance questionable but, more importantly negates one of the more compelling rationales for the value of a highly developed vehicular capacity: the availability of buses for use as educational tools for the classroom teacher.

Highly skilled and creative curriculum developers plan cooperatively with the school transportation administrators to incorporate the use of the bus fleet into the continuing educational experience of the student. Regularly scheduled field trips, ranging from visits to the farm or dairy or fire station at the primary level, to high school–level visits to the museum or library or art institute and specialized visits to the university or architectural firm or machine shop, are important components of the program and cannot be left to individual whim or chance. Many sophisticated and innovative school systems provide a series of such trips at each grade level and, in addition, allow individual teachers the opportunity to plan further experiences calling for transportation.

In addition to field trips, appropriate uses for the transportation system include the movement of students between schools for particular programs to encourage optimum use of particular equipment and talent, e.g., a planetarium located in one school, an advanced math program, a technical offering. Also, the use of vehicles for extracurricular and cocurricular activities further optimizes the transportation system. It is important for the transportation division of the school system to recognize that as a service arm of the school it must stand ready to provide transportation services as the demands for such services are generated.

Although pupil transportation costs vary greatly from district to district depending on a great many factors, extended use of vehicles to provide additional educational benefits invariably reduces the pupil-mile cost ratio. This is because the added service provided is most efficient in terms of load factor and single destination. The gains in terms of educational enrichment are not as easily evaluated, but all indications point to greatly expanded opportunities for the learner.

Standards and Specifications

The setting of standards and specifications for school vehicles is closely related to the purposes and aims of the transportation program as well as the demography and geography of the school district. Minimal standards of safety and health are often prescribed by the state department of education. If not, one can call the U. S. Department of Education for assistance in determining such standards. Because of the minimal nature of the typical state and/or federal standards, many local school systems develop their own specifications to incorporate particular standards they deem necessary. Given the ease with which seemingly innocent specifications can eliminate desirable and reputable manufacturers of vehicles, great care must be exercised in their development.

National standards of safety must be made an important part of any specification, but beyond that there are a variety of considerations that must be faced. These include such items as:

- *What size vehicle is appropriate for the kind of use envisioned?* If basic uses involve transporting children short distances, and if density of population is such that large numbers of riders are gathered in a short time, then the larger-capacity vehicle is most appropriate. If, however, the travel distance is great and children are quite scattered, then a smaller vehicle might be more feasible.
- *What kinds of road conditions exist in the area to be served?* The type of vehicle to be specified must enable optimum satisfaction to the user. Excellent four-lane highways and fully developed, paved secondary roads warrant different usage than do gravel roads and rutted, ungraveled trails found in some locales.

- *What is the geography of the area?* Level, flat terrain calls for different vehicles than does uneven, mountainous territory. The type of bus, its engine, its capacity, and size will depend on the kind of terrain it must negotiate. Decisions on power equipment, engine capacity and horsepower, tires, gear system, and suspension system are all somewhat dependent on geography.
- *What is the climate of the area?* Heating and/or cooling capacity of the vehicle, types of extra equipment needed, engine size and power, and vehicle configuration are all related to weather conditions.

Answers to these concerns, coupled with strict attention to national safety standards, can lead to specifications suited to the needs of the particular school system. While it is important not to underestimate the need for a transportation system, it is equally important not to overestimate the need. Judgment and careful planning are crucial to the development of standards and specifications. Bidding procedures and specifications vary widely among states, ranging from state-developed and mandated procedures to state-approved procedures and specifications to complete local option.

Contracting Services

With continued increases in the cost of energy and the difficulty in providing transportation services at a cost-effective rate because of equally rapid increases in labor costs, many school systems are seriously examining the possible impact of contracted transportation services. Contracting for either the entire service or for the more highly specialized portions of the service, like special education and vocational education, can reduce the drain on local staff and budget in terms of logistics, capital replacement, labor contracts, and client pressures. A number of firms have become very large providers of transportation services throughout the country. These firms have excellent records and are capable of providing the amount of service requested. Additionally, the contract approach eliminates the need for the local education agency to get involved with all the details that are part of caring for full-time employees.

In a few cities the local education agency contracts with the local transit authority to provide transportation services. This seems to work well as long as the needed services fall along established routes and do not require too much deviation from those traditional patterns. However, because peak demand of normal ridership and the school system often coincide, the use of the public transit system is not as attractive as it might be. Still, many school systems utilize public transit for such special activities as field trips, athletic events, shuttle services, and other off–peak-demand opportunities.

The Energy Factor

The energy crisis is forcing careful rethinking and reordering of many of the plans developed in the past. It is possible that a number of previously discarded notions will be utilized to reduce the impact of the accelerating costs of energy. Such technological developments as cable television and data processing may provide activities that will help reduce the need for some transportation services. Some futurists predict that in the future, school–home audiovisual contact will become the norm rather than the exception.

The implications for the business office in the provision of the myriad of transportation services are great. Care in providing the best possible service at the lowest possible cost is an important charge.

Food Services

Another of the auxiliary services that is fast becoming one of the important support services of the school system is the food service operation. Realization that the hungry child has severe learning impediments, and that for many children the only balanced meal of the day is the school breakfast and/or lunch, has served to emphasize the importance of the food service program. Until recently federal support has grown steadily, from the provision of surplus foods at minimal (storage) costs to recent aid in the form of direct grants to provide hot meals to needy children. In many of our urban centers, one-third to one-half of the public school children qualify for the subsidized food program. Increasingly the pressures of an urbanized society, with its demands on the family and the continued expansion of the workforce to include more and more women, have generated greatly expanded demands for school food services. What was once a phenomenon unique to school districts serving consolidated schools that had to provide food services because of the distance traveled by the students has become a common service extending to many of the neighborhood schools of the country. Originally a means to utilize surplus foods, the food service program has become recognized as a most valuable component of the school system. Increasingly school systems are using the food service operation as an important sector of the educational program. Health, diet, consumer economics, ecology, nutrition, aesthetic development, chemistry, and an introduction to the service industry are all important contributions that the food service program can make to the curricular efforts of the school. However, the primary role of the food service operation is that of providing tasty, tempting, balanced meals at reasonable cost to the students.

Planning the food service operation is often a terrifying experience to the average school business official, who has little knowledge or appreciation of the complexity of such an effort. Often such planning is left to a local person who because of some culinary skills has been named head cook. While such people are experts in providing excellent meals for a family, the mass feeding of hundreds and even thousands of children requires skills far beyond those of persons responsible for food preparation in the home. The food service operation is as complex as that of the largest restaurant chain with split-second demands for service. Such an operation must be carefully planned and developed according to the food needs of the school system.

Decisions to be made include those related to contracted preparation versus local building-level food preparation and fixed menus versus flexible menus. Because food and labor costs continue to mount and because state/federal subsidies are being curtailed, more efficient delivery is essential.

Additionally, the need to dramatically reduce the waste being experienced in many lunch operations gives still another conflicting charge to the business office: how to serve food that meets type ''A'' requirements while still meeting student preferences so that the food is not wasted. Flexible menu planning to reflect prevailing student food preferences is but one of a variety of ways to address this issue. Ethnic preferences must also be considered as menu planning proceeds. The most successful food service operations provide choices for children, with such niceties as salad bars, soup and sandwich, and soup and salad, which are increasingly popular.

With reductions in commodities and in federal subsidies, contracted food services become more attractive. However, the local education agency (LEA) must recognize that complete control over menus, over variety of meats, and other issues is no longer possible and that the contractor can make decisions previously housed in the LEA. In many cases the contract service does provide food service at a lower unit cost because of the efficiencies of mass purchasing, mass production, and more effective use of trained manpower.

Increasingly school districts are going to the private sector to provide all food services to the schools. These national concerns, often operators of gigantic food service operations as well as hotels and restaurants, are superbly prepared for the task of planning and operating a food service program. They have been involved in mass feeding operations over the years and have specialized in producing low-cost meals that meet all requirements for quality, attractiveness, balance, and taste. Many of the concerns have operated food service operations for the universities and colleges of the country for decades and have just recently focused on public school systems as potential customers.

As with the use of the private sector in other auxiliary areas, the contracting of school food services imposes some restrictions on the local district. The contracts drawn for the provision of the service should explicate as many of the expectations as possible so that there are few surprises for either party down the road. For example, if the school expects the food service provider to provide services at extracurricular activities and PTA meetings, these must be stated in the bid document. Advantages in contracting with the private sector for the provision of food services are many. They include the obvious advantage of relieving the school system from the burden of providing fringe benefits and insurance benefits to a whole segment of their former workforce. With private sector contracts for food service, the problems associated with managing a workforce are no longer the primary responsibility of the business office, which in highly unionized areas can have a salutary effect. While there are few formal evaluations of private sector versus school-operated food service operations, consensus seems to be that it is worth careful consideration by the business office in the effort to provide the best possible service to the students of the school system.

Policies, Rules, Regulations, and Procedures

Policies established by the board of education become guidelines for the development of rules, regulations, and procedures for the operation of the food service program. Food service policies attempt to establish broad parameters for the operation and include determinations such as:

- Is the school food program to be available to all children or just to those who meet certain specified criteria?
- Is the school food service program to be a systemwide centralized operation, or is it to be a building-by-building procedure with each building principal, in effect, administering a lunch program?
- Is the program to be a hot foods program or a sack lunch?
- If the program is systemwide, should *a la carte* menus be available, or should all children be expected to participate in "type A" programs? What about snacks? What provisions are made for children who carry sack lunches?
- What provisions are to be made for feeding indigent children?
- Is food to be prepared at each building, or is central preparation with "hot cart" delivery more desirable?

- Shall the schools observe "open" or "closed" lunch periods? If closed, what about requests for children living close to school to be allowed to go home for lunch?
- Shall breakfast programs be initiated?
- What educational benefits can accrue from the food program?
- What is the line-staff relationship between food service personnel and building principals?

The development of rules, regulations, and procedures from policy statements leads to creation of an operating manual for day-to-day operations of the food service division. Standards and expectations for personnel and methods of operations are defined. Procedures for collection of monies, use of children as helpers, serving of food, dining room regulations, special food service capability, use of lunch facilities by outside groups, amortization and replacement of equipment, and so forth are important planning functions. Increasingly contracts with various school employee groups, i.e., teachers, clerks, custodians, and lunch personnel, become important in the development of rules and procedures. The use and effectiveness of the dining room as an educational resource depend on the availability of staff during the dining hours. Minimum standards of health, cleanliness, and decorum are important to the food service operation and must be well defined.

Because of the severe time constraints imposed by the school day, operating procedures have very real logistic implications. Delivery schedules, serving schedules, preparation schedules, and efficiency are very important for the food service program that must quickly accommodate large numbers of children during a short time span. Delays and confusion must be minimized in order to provide optimum service to children. Rules, regulations, and procedures must be explicit and direct while allowing sufficient flexibility to meet unique and unforeseen needs (for example, certain groups may periodically need picnic lunches provided, or may have to eat early or late on a particular day, or may invite a group from a different city for lunch).

Staffing and Supervision

Planning for the staffing and supervision of the food service operation requires that close attention be given to educational considerations as well as the culinary qualifications of applicants. Compatibility with children, health standards, temperament, adaptability, personal habits, energy level, and general appearance all contribute to the desirability of prospective staff members.

In districts numbering several thousand students housed in a number of buildings, it is desirable to engage a school food service director (and, if size and volume warrant, several persons) to administer and supervise the food service program. This person is generally trained as a dietician and/or mass-feeding specialist and brings a background in food service work to the school system. Sometimes a certified teacher trained in food service (home economics) is available and with appropriate support develops the capacity to administer the program. It is a great relief and benefit to the school business administrator to have such a person available to handle the day-to-day administration of the food service program.

The determination of the type and size of food service staff needed depends on a number of variables. Immediate concerns are:

- Is the program to use central food preparation, or is each building to have its own preparation capacity?
- What is the projected number of meals to be prepared either centrally or by building?
- Is the "type A" lunch to be the only meal served?
- Are silverware and dishes (plastic or china) used, or are throwaway utensils and dishes to be used?

If, for example, a centralized food preparation system is projected, with hot cart delivery to individual buildings, the preparation center is staffed very differently from the individual building preparation kitchens. In centralized preparation, specializations such as salad chef, meat chef, vegetable cook, baker, and dessert chef might be in order, while in decentralized preparation, categories such as head cook, assistant cook, and cook's helper are more common.

In-Service Training and Coordination with Educational Program

As in most school-related activities, there is a continuing need for staff training and development for food service employees, many of whom were homemakers before employment. These employees, while usually very fine family cooks, are not attuned to mass feeding and therefore must be encouraged to learn the techniques appropriate to such an endeavor. In addition, the use of the food service program as an important component of the educational program suggests other special talents that must be present and highly developed in food service personnel. The planning for, preparation, and serving of food to several hundred persons each meal is very different from the preparation of a family meal. Staff development activities include such items as recipe preparation and use, food display, health standards, reporting procedures, youth culture and preferences, actual preparation and seasoning of new recipes, ordering techniques, storage techniques, cleanliness standards and objectives, staff relations, student relations, and so on. Operating rules, regulations, and procedures are reviewed and adjusted to meet current needs and expectations. Objectives and goals of the food service program are emphasized as part of in-service activity.

Also related to staff development efforts is the coordination of the food service program with the educational program. There are certain constraints and time obligations that must be met if the food service program is to operate in schools. Children must eat at an appropriate time, and they must be fed quickly and efficiently so that the program of education is not unduly interrupted or disrupted. Additionally, the food service program has a great opportunity to become an important part of the educational program and can complement and support curricular efforts at every grade level. Health, safety, nutrition, food chemistry, economics, service vocations, and aesthetics are but a few of the potential areas to be supported by the food service division. Opportunities to provide such fringe services must be nurtured and expanded by making available the total food service resource to the educational staff.

Food Preparation Systems

Food service needs and the policies of the school system to meet these needs will dictate the specifications for food preparation areas. There are several alternative systems to serve individual situations. Among the alternatives are:

- The central kitchen
- Individual/independent kitchens
- Manufacturing kitchens
- Satellite kitchens[1]

Each system has strengths and weaknesses, advantages and disadvantages. Rationale as to which is most appropriate rests with individual districts and should be an outgrowth of local policy.

In centralized food service operations, provisions for trucking hot food on a very rigid time schedule are most important. Additionally, there must be personnel provided at the receiving schools to serve and distribute food, to handle the cleanup and dish return or disposal chore, and to supervise the dining room operation. While centralized food preparation is generally considered to be more efficient and while quality is more easily controlled in such a scheme, other considerations also enter into decisions on centralized versus decentralized food preparation. Obviously, quality control and administration are easiest in the central food preparation arrangement. Other advantages include savings in capital equipment and space costs and lower unit costs due to quantity preparations as well as potential for specialization in tasks. Still other advantages include the capacity to develop special foods production (such as baking, butchering, salads, and so forth), the capacity to accomplish long-range planning, and savings that accrue from volume purchasing and storage. However, certain disadvantages are also present. These include the loss of the food service operation as a component of the educational program, rigidity in terms of schedules and timing, loss of jobs for neighborhood people, loss of food service resources for community groups, dependence on transportation systems for delivery of foods, and limited capacity to meet local food service needs and tastes.

A difficulty that usually arises in decentralized food service operations is the conflict over who has line responsibility over kitchen personnel—the principal or the school lunch administrator. Generally, it is decided that although the food service administrator sets rules and procedures that pertain to food preparation, menus, distribution, and so forth, the principal has line responsibility as it pertains to the ongoing program of the school. In this sense the principal determines serving schedules, collection procedure, dining room expectations, and such. As a service to the teaching-learning process, the food program must meet the established overall educational needs of the school.

Menus, Prices, and Portion Control

School lunch menus are the result of careful long-range planning efforts. Seasonal harvests, market fluctuations, government surplus offerings, unique tastes, ethnic and racial group preferences, talents of preparation personnel, and regionality all play a part in menu planning. Most menu planning is based on cyclical rotation of a basic number of meals so that daily, weekly, and even monthly variety is provided. Past experience and records as to what meals are most accepted are also valuable planning tools. Generally menus are planned for the entire system, or at least subsystems of the total school district. If the basic lunch is "type A," there is little deviation from the menu. If, however, in addition to "type A" lunches there is to be provided an *a la carte* menu and perhaps snack or sandwich opportunities, the planning task is more complex. Usually such questions are resolved by insisting that the one-basic-meal menu be adhered to at the elementary school level, with variety and flexibility allowed at the secondary school.

Prices can and do vary greatly from area to area. The main objective of the food service program is to provide balanced, tasty meals at the lowest possible costs. Labor costs and food prices differ from place to place. Urban centers tend to reflect higher costs because of the highly unionized labor market and because fewer foods are grown locally. In spite of this, it is often possible to provide food at lower unit costs because of savings realized through mass production of foods.

It is important that the food service operation be a nonprofit operation in order to provide the greatest service at lowest possible costs to the user. It is equally important that the food service division consider such expenses as amortization of capital equipment, replacement of equipment, utility costs, custodial costs, and overhead when determining the real cost of the program in order to establish a price structure. If the board must subsidize the service, policy should provide for it.

Portion controls are usually established by regulation, and USDA minimum standards are used to determine the amount and variety of food to be served. Differences in age level should be reflected in both the size of the portion and in the price charged. Portion control is relatively easy in centralized operations that prepackage the meals. It becomes more difficult when food is served cafeteria style. Many systems use scales to weigh meat portions and sized serving utensils to determine vegetable portions. It is important that adequacy and consistency of portions be maintained.

Federal and state guidelines are used to determine qualifications for reduced and/or free food services. Each LEA provides the forms for parents to use in determining the validity of their request. Family income, number of family members, and local cost considerations are involved in the resolution of this serious problem. As costs increase, participation in the paid lunch program decreases and requests for reduced and/or free service increases.

Purchasing

Analysis of food purchasing practices among the school districts of the United States reveals a complete spectrum of purchasing practices. This spectrum covers a wide range, starting with the practice of the cook calling the corner grocer to place an order for the day's food needs, to very sophisticated bidding procedures that involve the cooperative efforts of forty to fifty school systems. The use of the corner grocer to supply all the food needs of the neighborhood school is fast becoming a thing of the past. Food service has simply become too big an operation to neglect the development of sophisticated purchasing procedures. For example, the medium-size school district that feeds an average of 10,000 students per day generates a total operating budget of from $600,000 to $700,000. This is apt to be the single largest departmental budget in the entire school system, which demands that careful planning be utilized in its expenditure. Since food costs, supply costs, and other purchases typically involve 50 to 75 percent of the total budget (depending on the current availability of federal surplus foods), and since there is a wide variety of different items needed in the food service operation, purchasing is fast becoming recognized as an important function in the administration of the food service program.

The purchasing procedure applicable for school food services is illustrated in Figure 14-1. It contains the essential elements of a general purchasing procedure, but it also highlights certain features relevant to school food service purchasing.

The development of bid procedures and of standards and specifications requirements for food service purchasing is a highly specialized task to be performed by someone well versed in mass feeding. Decisions as to canned foods versus fresh and/or frozen foods invoke such variables as freezer/refrigerator space, cold storage capacity, dry storage capacity, seasonal variance in food stuff availability, market conditions, and other difficult-to-predict conditions. In addition, the determination of quality standards, container and lot size, quality-control procedures, and delivery schedules has to be made by highly skilled food service personnel. Because savings of significant proportions can accrue to the school district through intelligent purchasing practices, the school business administrator must provide the support and talent needed to initiate such an effort. Examples of specific techniques include the purchase of paper goods in carload lots, the timing of bid requests to

FIGURE 14-1   Flow Chart for Purchases

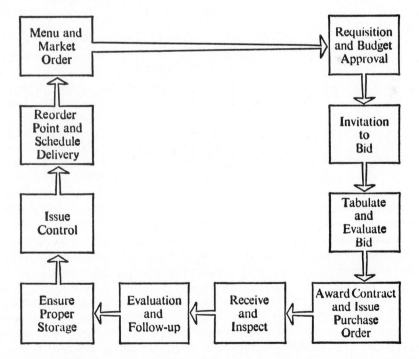

Source: From Thelma Flanagan, *School Food Purchasing Guide* (Evanston, IL: Association of School Business Officials, 1961), 120; reprinted with permission.

correspond to seasonal production of specific foods, realistic appraisal of quality (fancy labeled canned goods are premium priced and often not essential to high-quality food service), development of sufficient storage space to enable volume purchasing, contract purchasing of perishable foods to ensure price stability (milk products, baked goods, and so forth), group purchasing plans involving a number of school districts to provide volume, and many other creative and money-saving ideas.

Purchasing is an important component of the planning effort of the food service operation. Menu planning, projections of numbers to be serviced, and prediction of items needed all contribute to the purchasing process. Initiation of the purchase is only the start, however. Delivery schedules must be established to ensure that supplies and materials are available when needed. In addition, quality-control procedures must continue to ensure that standards and specifications are maintained at expected high levels. Skill in purchasing often determines how successful the food service operation will be, for the savings effected here will make possible the stabilization of costs to the user at a reasonable level.

Accounting, Reporting, and Cost Analysis

The amount of discretionary tolerance in terms of resource utilization is so slight in the food service operation that very careful and minute accounting, reporting, and cost-analysis procedures must be followed. Because in most school systems the food service operation is designed to be self-supporting, and because unit costs must be kept to a level that will encourage participation by all clients, the recordkeeping, planning, and implementation tasks are crucial to success.

Many states have well-established accounting manuals for the food service operation. Most recommend a modified encumbrance system that greatly assists in the planning effort. Because of the unique daily cash flow process found in the food service operation, daily income accounting procedures are desirable. Records showing number of meals served, income received, food and usable supplies consumed, worker-hours of labor required, and peripheral costs incurred are usually required for each cafeteria. Providing forms indicating these and other data, along with bank deposit slips and statements with the daily, weekly, and monthly report forms, is a task of utmost importance to the person charged with responsibility for the food service program. Encumbrance of wages, food costs, supplies, utilities, and so on will enable the reporting system to be meaningful and current. Because most income is on a cash basis (except for billing procedures for special functions and/or organizations) and because all expenditures are in the form of salary vouchers or payment of invoices submitted for goods and services, the use of daily records, purchase orders, and work orders is most important to the accounting process. Periodic audits, both internal performed by the business office and external by an audit firm, require accurate data. Responsible management also requires that recognized accounting practices be followed.

The use of daily, weekly, and monthly records and accounting practices to generate needed reports to a variety of persons is recommended. Reports indicating the overall status of the food service division along with building-by-building breakdowns are important information to be shared with personnel of the food service program as well as with principals and central office personnel. Data such as number of meals served, percentage of student participation, variance of participation with menu, special food services provided, and so forth are important items to be reported. Reports including these and additional interpretive cost data—for example, unit costs, labor charges, and food costs—are useful in the cost-analysis requirement and can provide valuable planning data. Many states require reports for participation in state and federal programs. Such reports can be the basis for generating a variety of in-house reports providing specific data of interest to specific groups. Certain informative data (participation, menu implications, labor and material use) should be reported on a daily basis, while other more interpretive reports can be made on a weekly and monthly cycle. It is also important (mandated by law and/or board policy in most districts) that an annual report and audit be submitted to the board of education.

Constant analysis of income and expenditures is most important to the continued health of the food service operations. Decisions and plans developed as a result of careful cost analysis will encourage optimization of the food service program. Given regional labor cost differences and the fluctuations in costs of foods and supplies, the analysis of food service operations must be a continuing effort to ensure maximum benefits for the user. Comparative cost data will help determine the most efficient and well-operated components of the food service division. If, for example, elementary school A is consistently averaging out to a ten cents per plate cost for labor as compared to fifteen cents per plate for elementary school B, and if the total number of meals served in each school is comparable and each school offers the same menu, then it is probable that school B needs some help in organizing its food service operation more efficiently. Similarly, cost data can provide information leading to reduction of waste or to improvement in menus, or give clues to deficiencies in certain units. Careful cost analysis should lead to increased benefits for the children of the school system in terms of tastier foods prepared in the most efficient, economical manner possible.

Remembering that the goal of the food service operation is to provide attractive, tasty, well-balanced meals to students at the most economical rate possible leads to full utilization of sophisticated accounting and reporting procedures as a means of generating data upon which to base cost analysis.

Security Services

The decade of the eighties saw a marked increase in the need for security services in all school systems. The dramatic rise in the number and intensity of youth gangs, the spread in the use of drugs, and the continued decline in the influence of the family and of social agencies and the church all contributed to the increase in violence in the schools. The general breakdown in society was coupled with pressures brought on by the education reforms of the eighties with their call for increased requirements and heightened standards without a corresponding requirement for viable alternatives to strict, inflexible standards. As a result, school became an impossible situation for many students, who then engage in deviant behavior to satisfy their need for recognition.

Statistics on juvenile crime rates show that while adult crime is leveling off and/or declining, the rate for youth is continuing to rise. Reasons for this are many and varied. Among the prime factors are the realities that the opportunity for gainful employment for youth not achieving a minimum of literacy has become virtually nil. The focus on high school completion as the minimum acceptable level for entry into the job market has served to place yet another burden on the school.

The drug culture and all that it implies is another factor in the dramatic increase in school-related crime. With the sharp increase in the availability of hard drugs at relatively low cost, the young people of America are increasingly trapped into dependence on drugs, and campuses have become places for conducting drug transactions. Drugs are no longer for just the affluent; young people of every economic level and ethnicity are involved in the activities related to drugs. Not only are the various drugs like cocaine, heroin, uppers, and downers actively marketed on many of the campuses of the country, but youth are increasingly turning to alcohol as an easily obtainable substance to abuse.

With the annual cost of vandalism now approaching one billion dollars, school systems have had to develop a number of ways to deal with the effects of and the causes of school vandalism. Approaches ranging from the use of dogs to sniff out the presence of drugs in lockers and cars to reward systems for classes and campuses that reduce vandalism to community patrols of the various campuses as a means of controlling possible trouble elements are being tried. Formal police patrols and even school system security forces in uniform and carrying firearms are being used in the effort to curb school crime rates. Elaborate security systems tied to local police stations are now common in most urban schools. The use of special forces to infiltrate the campus and pose as students is also becoming common.

Typically, responsibility for the establishment and conduct of a security system falls on the business office. It is crucial in planning for security services that the business official work cooperatively with the campus administrators to devise optimum plans for a particular campus. This will also create a more accepting posture on the part of the principal as plans for the protection of his/her campus are identified.

Approaches to Security Services

School districts across the United States use a variety of mechanisms to provide security services, ranging from large, internal security divisions to contracted services exclusively. Many provide security through some mixture of the two concepts, while others work closely with and depend on the local police department for the bulk of the service.

As school districts enter into the development of a school security force, a number of important issues arise. Included are those dealing with the type of persons to be employed, their training needs, their duties, and how the force is to be deployed. Typically the security function falls into several types of discrete activities. These include:

- Routine patrol activities that are carried out during nonschool hours and vacations. Building checks, routine site visits, and monitoring of devices to alert the staff when someone enters a building are part of this activity.
- Campus monitoring and patrol activities that are conducted during the school day and are intended to maintain order and ensure student and staff safety.
- Investigative activities that are conducted to resolve security issues and other crime-related concerns. Included here might be student-related concerns such as child abuse, excessive absence, and similar problems.
- Activities to ensure school safety, and student safety, which include OSHA concerns as well as traffic and vehicle-related matters.

- The ongoing task in every school system of monitoring drug and substance abuse concerns.
- School/police liaison activities that attempt to utilize the local police acting in concert with school staff to provide support services to schools, students, staff, and parents.

In addition, many variations of the above approaches are being utilized, including a number that call for volunteer and parent as well as student participation. It is generally accepted that uniformed police are used in situations where crowd control is necessary, for instance at interscholastic activities, concerts, and so forth.

Security Planning Considerations

Board of education policy generally begins with a statement of intent to provide educational services to all qualified students in an environment that protects individual rights while ensuring the safety of all participants. Protection of property and of persons involved is strongly suggested as a primary responsibility of the school system. Indeed, organization of staff and allocation of resources are often predicated on safety and security concerns.

Staffing and Supervision

As security concerns in recent years grew and became focused, specialized staff needs emerged and training activities became more visible. Indeed, a number of institutions of higher education now offer degree programs in school system security, while others incorporate such course offerings as part of the general law enforcement and criminal justice programs.

Many larger systems have developed sophisticated in-service efforts, often in cooperation with a local college or university. Generally, security staff is selected under a variety of criteria ranging from ability to relate to students to physical stature and strength. After a period of time, concerns about formal training in security skills arise, and efforts are mounted to provide a program for existing staff. Additionally, supervisory staff are recruited from various security agencies ranging from local police departments to graduates of formal degree programs in security.

Deployment of staff ranges from centrally controlled and assigned staff that responds to particular requests, to staff assigned permanently to specific units for overall security services. As staff becomes more sophisticated and better trained, specialties emerge and specific staff can be assigned these duties.

Relationship to Building Principal

Because most student-related security needs revolve around school buildings and/or school-related functions such as athletics, drama, and dances, the security personnel must be on a close working relationship with building principals and local staff. The principal, under site-based management concepts, has ultimate responsibility for security and safety. He/she must rely on the trained staff for advice, counsel, and support as particular concerns are addressed.

In matters requiring investigative procedures the principal can be invaluable to the security staff, for he/she knows the student body and its concerns and needs. The use of trained security persons to assist principals in investigative efforts is a major support service. Security staff assigned to the building report to the principal as do all others who are a part of the building staff.

Relationship to Students

The most successful security personnel are those who are respected and liked by the students they serve. Many act as quasi-counselors, with a firm grasp of prevailing value systems and student jargon and preferences.

As students develop trust and respect for security personnel, they tend to keep them informed of the nuances and rumors that spread around the campus. Additionally, students solicit the assistance of security personnel as potential difficulties arise.

An important planning consideration is the potential ability for the security applicant to relate to the various groups that make up the student body as well as to adult personnel who are part of the staff.

Under site-based management particularly the security person must observe dual reporting relationships. If assigned to a campus, the person is an integral part of the building staff and must respond to the principal, while at the same time being sensitive to districtwide needs as they arise. This, of course, implies a reporting relationship to the central security office as well.

Reporting not only encompasses the direct superordinate/subordinate relationships but also the gathering and sorting of statistical data related to security. Such data, when examined on both a campus-by-campus basis as well as a districtwide basis, can provide valuable planning information and assist in anticipating problems before they become serious confrontations and/or disturbances. In addition, data will assist in planning the total security operation with staff deployment and with preventive actions.

Other Auxiliary Services

Among other auxiliary services are the community use of school facilities, sale of specialized services, and sale of excess property and materials. The first of these, community use of school facilities, is probably an auxiliary service in the purest sense of the term. The others could be considered quasi-auxiliary in nature.

Community Use of School Facilities

Board of education policy must explicate the district's approach to community use of school facilities. Typically a fee schedule is developed by the business office for implementation. Fees are predicated on several factors, among them the type of group needing the activity, the type of activity planned, whether there is a profit motive involved, out-of-pocket expenses for personnel and utilities, and the definition of a school-related group.

Usually school-related groups are not charged a fee but in some instances are expected to cover the out-of-pocket expenses for utilities, cleaning, security, and so forth. School-related groups such as booster clubs, PTA, and such fall into the category of school organizations and are generally welcome to use facilities as the need arises.

Other community groups are generally charged a use fee depending on the plan for use of the facility. For example, a service club using a room for meeting purposes would be charged less than a private organization using an auditorium to present a program from which a profit is expected. Also, the size and type of the facility determines the fee. In setting a usage fee for special facilities such as swimming pools, gymnasiums, auditoriums, and cafeterias, one must consider the equipment and potential for damage. Some school districts require a bond to cover breakage as part of board policy.

Generally, community groups are encouraged to utilize facilities to the maximum and fees are kept at the lowest level possible. Because schools are public facilities and because citizens of a community are the people who pay for schools through the property tax, every effort should be extended to encourage community use of schools.

Included in these procedures and policies for community use of schools must be concerns related to scheduling and security. Additionally, priorities for facility use must be established, with definite guidelines to be used in scheduling. School groups have top priority. After this come community groups, and finally private parties. Scheduling is always a difficult task, and if there are no policy guidelines the process becomes very cumbersome and confused. Policies must be clear, concise, and definitive as to processes used. From these policies come procedures that establish fees, priorities, and scheduling directions.

Sale of School Services

Many school systems enter into contractual arrangements with other districts and other agencies for the provision of specific and specialized services. These can range from special programs, such as special education and vocational education, to data processing services to evaluation services to other activities such as tax appraisal. Obviously such interagency and multi–school district cooperation leads to more efficient use of scarce resources and provides an opportunity to share in the cost of highly specialized and expensive activities. It also enables the service costs to be spread over a wider area and extends sophisticated activities to more users of the particular services.

As an example, one district known to the authors provides data processing services to eighty school systems in a region of the state. This enables the operation of a most sophisticated data processing system with modern hardware and the capacity to develop software, as users request, yet provides the service at a modest per-pupil expenditure because the costs are distributed over such a broad base.

Summary

To summarize, auxiliary services are quite important to the success of the school system. While they are not directly involved in the teaching-learning process, their absence makes the educational process very difficult if not impossible. Auxiliary services are part of the board's scope of activities grouped under noninstructional services, without which the school system cannot exist. These services provide support to the instructional program in order to make possible the most effective delivery of instruction to student.

The presence of auxiliary services proceeding unobtrusively and unnoticed is probably an indication of the service being most effective and appropriate. As the directing force behind all noninstructional services, the business office can take great pride in the ongoing and important role auxiliary services play in the total operation of the school system.

The three auxiliary services most commonly under the direction of the business administrator, the transportation, food services, and security divisions of the school system, perform tasks very important to the primary teaching-learning task. Each of these divisions involves specialized activities requiring talented and highly trained personnel. The staffs of the three divisions must not only possess abilities in the specialized activities involved (e.g., vehicular or food service), but also need to have added talents and strengths in working with children. It is therefore very important that ongoing staff development programs be provided in each of these areas. Success in each of these areas rests upon the development of adequate policies leading to rules, regulations, and procedures governing the day-to-day activities of the three divisions. Supervision and administration of transportation, food service, and security often requires specialized personnel and is considered to be a full-time activity.

The school business administrator must adequately and carefully plan for auxiliary services. He/she will need to recruit well-trained supervisory personnel for the routine operating tasks involved, for each of the services described is a highly specialized, demanding activity. As the chief business planner, the school business administrator must have a working knowledge of each service, but he/she cannot hope to assume the actual operating responsibility of such diverse activities. Planning decisions, in order to be effective, must be made with some detachment from the ongoing operations of an activity.

Suggested Activities

1. Design a pupil transportation survey in a school having such a program. Try to find out such things as number of pupils transported, number of pupil miles traveled per day, number of miles traveled by each bus, the amount of driving time each day, and so forth.
2. Determine the state requirements regarding pupil transportation for your school system. To what extent are these requirements exceeded by local policy enacted by your school system?
3. Develop a plan for food services to meet the needs of your school system. Incorporate regional and/or ethnic needs that must be reflected in order to make the program successful.
4. Indicate the most severe security problems facing your school system. Develop a positive response to each of them.

Suggested Readings

Educational Facilities Laboratories. *Twenty Million for Lunch.* New York: Educational Facilities Laboratories, 1968.

Featherstone, E. Glenn, and John B. Murray. *State School Bus Standards.* Washington, DC: U.S. Department of Health, Education, and Welfare, 1962.

Neill, Shirley Boes. *Violence and Vandalism*. Arlington, VA: National Schools Public Relations Association, 1975.

Perryman, John H. *The School Administrator and the Food Service Program*. Washington, DC: National Association of Elementary School Principals, 1972.

Van Egmond-Pannel, Dorothy. *The Food Service Handbook: A Guide for School Administrators*. Reston, VA: ASBO, 1987.

Notes

1. William O'Donnell Miller, *Twenty Million for Lunch*. (New York: Educational Facilities Laboratories, 1968), 22–24.

15

School Business Administration Perspectives

A PERVASIVE THEME of this book is that planning is an important dimension of the school business administration function in contemporary school systems. Every attempt has been made to highlight the importance of school business administration to the total management team of the school system. Indeed, the role of the business administrator has been likened to that of the top aide to the chief executive officer, with identification such as Deputy Superintendent, Associate Superintendent, or Assistant Superintendent most common among the various titles assigned to the position. Explicit or implicit in this position is the responsibility of active participation in the planning function.

If planning is to be effective, one must have an image of the future. This image is an aggregation of many perspectives. Present and emerging societal as well as educational needs place increased emphasis and responsibility on the school business administration function. Conventional practices often impede instructional improvement. The school business administrator must respond to societal demands for reform and reconsider the school business administration function.

Some of the perspectives are complementary or interrelated; some are conflicting. In an uncertain present and facing an unclear future, all of these viewpoints must be considered. All in the education community must be aware of the new perspectives growing out of accelerated social change such as the recent events in China, East Berlin, the Balkan nations, the Baltic republics, Persian Gulf, and South Africa. Movements around the globe are likely to have powerful influences through the world and indirectly affect American educational institutions.

Significant national, state, and local changes have a more direct impact. Demographic changes in patterns of population shifts—in terms of numbers, regions, and age groups—are related to need and demand to change public policy and programs.[1] Technological breakthroughs create problems as well as opportunities. Philosophical and sociological movements or trends signal shifts in community and family relationships. Having a sensitivity to dramatic world events as well as continuing and emerging local, state, and national movements is essential to the planning function.

Fiscal and Economic Perspectives

International events and shifts in the international economy have impacted heavily on the American economy. The value of the American dollar, the flow of money and credit between nations, and the American market share in international enterprises have all impacted on the relative health of the American economy. The changes have had and will continue to have a dramatic impact on the size of the slice of pie going to education. Demographic changes and competing needs of other social agencies will no doubt exacerbate the problem of limited resources. This in turn will heighten the demand for economy and efficiency in educational programs. Parallel demands will likely be made to reduce administrative overhead and increase accountability in order to demonstrate that the scarce dollars are spent for the most effective and/or desirable educational programs.

The 1980s saw a variety of organized attacks on the public schools of the United States. A number of anti-tax groups focused in on the public schools as notable examples of waste in government. Anti-tax sentiment, coupled with the demographic reality that for the first time in our history there were more family units with no public school students in the household than those with students, made the passing of public school tax referenda a most difficult task. The result of these pressures is the need for careful, pragmatic planning of all school district activities, but especially those activities involving the expenditure of funds. The decade of the 1980s also saw, overall, a declining student population with only modest prospects for recovery in the 1990s. This decline in student enrollment has been accompanied by a dramatic rise in educational expenditures, such that the critics of public education level accusations of mismanagement and empire building against school administrators. The dilemma facing school business officials is a very complex one: For many districts, school officials must address the reality of decline instead of the historical pattern of growth that has been the rule. Indeed, not only must the school business administrator deal with a steadily decreasing student population; he/she must also face other serious problems: e.g., energy crises, tax-base erosion, increasing state/federal restrictions, and severe competition for the local tax dollar from a variety of municipal agencies. All these issues must be addressed in an economic climate that has produced a serious and constant inflationary spiral accompanied by a series of recessions that have severely inhibited the growth of the property tax base.

In the decades since the first great infusion of federal funds into local educational systems, via the National Defense Education Act of 1958, the increasing participation of the federal government in the support of education has become much more visible and important. Programs like the Elementary and Secondary Education Act of 1965 with all of its titles, the Bilingual and Migrant programs, various adult education programs, and several vocational education acts provide extensive federal support of local educational efforts. Accompanying this monetary support was a multitude of rules and regulations, some in contradiction with others. The result was a hodge-podge of regulations that severely hamstring the delivery of programs intended to serve specific pupils with special needs.

Because of concerns about inefficiency, program overlap, and the like, the Education Consolidation and Improvement Act (1981) converted many discrete programs into fewer block grants. At the same time, concerns about the increased federal deficit gave impetus to reducing or not increasing the funding of many federal programs. In the early 1980s the federal share of total revenue for public elementary and secondary schools was about 9 percent. By the 1989–90 school year it was estimated that the proportion has decreased to slightly over 6 percent.[2]

As the local tax base becomes more fiercely contested and as court decisions increase the pressure for equalization of resources across the various states, state revenues become a larger and more important segment of the total local education budget. Legally the state is the unit of government with total responsibility for education. Increasingly, as education consumes a larger amount of state revenues, the state legislatures and state boards of education are imposing program requirements and restrictions on local units. The American system of public education, which was historically based on local needs and local control (although the state has always had the legal capacity to control education), finds itself shifting to a state and perhaps a national system influenced by court decisions, laws, organized interest groups, and accrediting agencies.

Most recently, increasing pressures from the political right have further complicated the life of school business administrators. Sharp reductions in federal resources, serious attempts to subsidize nonpublic schools through tax credits, property tax revolts at the local levels, demands for educational and financial efficiencies, continued decline in enrollments, and continued inflationary pressures have made school budgeting a most complex and difficult task. At the same time the cries for educational reform, for expanded educational offerings, and for wider participation in the educational process continue to add increasing cost pressures.

Extraordinary measures taken during the 1980s to mitigate the pressures and deepening financial constraints include many innovative and creative actions to stretch decreasing educational resources. Such management tactics as cooperative purchasing activities, improved forecasting and investment practices, mothballing and selling of excess facilities, delaying of major capital investments, more effective planning and prioritizing of activities, energy conservation programs, increased use of technology to reduce manpower needs, and a variety of other responses have made the school districts of the United States some of the most efficiently managed and operated organizations in the country. Cost-control procedures utilized in the school systems of this country are usually fine and reflect the capacity of school business officials to protect the tax dollar as much as is humanly possible. Economies of scale and efficiencies already initiated make further savings even more difficult to come by. Because education is such a labor-intensive industry, further efficiencies will likely come through massive productivity increases. This, of course, means reductions in staff and increases in student–staff ratios.

It is a credit to the genius of school business administrators that although educational costs have sharply increased over the past decade, expenditures have been increasing at a lower rate than the inflationary spiral and at a rate below that of many other agencies and services.

In the immediate future the primary task for the school business administrator will be addressing the implications of the move toward increased autonomy at the building level. This move toward site-based management will require altering traditional business practices and procedures in order to accommodate the decentralization process.

The Centralization/Decentralization Dichotomy

A growing body of data suggests that one of the more powerful forces in the 1990s will be the move toward increased decentralization. During the past decade several models of decentralization have emerged as many school districts attempt to devise ways to effect a more responsive system.

Legitimate concerns over extreme centralization are appropriate and well taken. Bigness does lead to remoteness and impersonal responses. The past decade saw many of the largest school systems test a variety of organizational decentralization schemes. Many educational organization theorists including Cunningham, Campbell, Havighurst, Leu, Nystrand, and others have recommended such efforts.

As one reviews the work of a number of experts in addressing this issue, it becomes obvious that many of the decentralization efforts are doomed to failure because the implications were not carefully thought through. For example, it is the contention of the authors that it is not a question of centralization or decentralization but rather what activities are best performed on a highly centralized basis and what services are best delivered in a decentralized mode. It appears that in many instances decentralization efforts were responses to political pressures rather than efforts to create educational change to better serve clients of the system. In community after community, decentralization became very closely aligned with demands for community control, which are more political and not necessarily in the best interests of the client. An example of this is the 1989 Chicago experiment.

For the school business administrator, implications of decentralization can be traumatic. The business office must participate in developing the appropriate rationale for such organizational change. Preliminary decisions vis-a-vis decentralization are important and involve responses to two basic premises. First, the issue of what to decentralize and what to centralize must be resolved. The business administrator is key to this decision, for the functions that lend themselves to high levels of centralization are generally activities found in the business office. Those include such items as payroll, purchasing, data processing, maintenance, accounting, custodial services, and so forth, while such activities as program development and delivery, curriculum planning, services to students, and personnel selection are better accomplished at the building level. The school business administrator must assist in the development of procedures with which to develop decentralization activities. To do so, the pressures leading toward increased decentralization must be recognized and understood.

Increased State/Federal Control

As a countermovement to the decentralization movement, there has been a strong force for increased state/federal control. From the mid-1950s on, the gradual demise of local control and autonomy has continued, with increased state and federal participation in the educational process.

Increased federal participation, born of the scare generated by Sputnik, was greatly expanded with the National Defense Education Act of 1958. Subsequent legislation accelerated the role of the federal government in public education. The many Great Society programs of the 1960s—i.e., the Elementary and Secondary Education Act of 1965, the Civil Rights Act of 1964, the various vocational acts of the 1960s, and the Education of the Handicapped Act of 1975 (P.L. 94-142)—were indicative of the rising interest and participation on the part of the federal government. Various adult education acts and numerous education act amendments of the 1970s were largely categorical programs aimed at serving particular client groups who were denied certain educational opportunities. The guidelines and restrictions developed for each of these programs were intended both to protect the integrity of the program and to ensure that the program was delivered to the appropriate client.

Districts had to meet strict criteria for qualifying for a categorical program and even stricter guidelines to meet standards for compliance. Many local officials became disenchanted with and even hostile toward federal aid as a result of the voluminous paperwork and procedural requirements imposed on the local education agency (LEA). Indeed, LEA personnel often feel overburdened by the multitude of regulations accompanying federal aid. It is not unusual for local educators and citizens to hold different priorities than those addressed by a particular federal program. Yet, in order to receive the funds, the local education agency must provide the services specified in the act. Failure to do so would negate eligibility and would subject the local school district to judicial and/or agency action.

One of the more applauded developments of the 1980s was the move toward "block" grants or grants consolidation undertaken at the federal level. With the Education Consolidation and Improvement Act came dramatic decreases in federally required paperwork and much less fear of intervention. Local personnel have far greater flexibility in the application of federal resources with fewer restrictive rules and regulations. On the other hand, there is concern that the original intent of a particular grant—e.g., vocational education, bilingual education, education of the handicapped, and education of the poor—will be lost and the resource will become general aid to the LEA. This is a legitimate concern that is being debated in Congress as well as at the state and local levels.

Accompanying the grants consolidation effort is a dramatic reduction in federal aid to public education. This reflects a general move toward more conservative government with reduction of controls and regulations. While most local education agency personnel applaud the decreased regulations and intervention, the loss of resources has taken its toll on local school systems.

The issue of increasing state domination and control is more subtle yet immediate. The various states have the legal responsibility for education by virtue of the absence of reference to education in the federal constitution. The evolution of the schools of the United States is unique. Whereas most nations have a national school system, the United States has nearly 16,000 nearly autonomous school districts ranging in size from a mere handful of students to the 1,000,000 students in the New York City School District.

The movement to a highly centralized delivery system that encompasses larger LEAs created by consolidation of small districts, the increased state and federal mandates for specific actions, and the move toward unionization of public employees have all served to alienate students and patrons from the school system. The participatory model found in the one-room school has become a strictly professional affair that has served to close the school doors to parents and community. This failing has caused alienation, suspicion, and concern. Efforts to remediate this condition continue, but success has been elusive.

Parent/Student/Community Involvement

The 1980s saw increased demands for involvement on the part of parents and students. This was a reaction to the accelerating impersonalization of the public education systems. Many reasons are given for the aloofness and detachment of school systems from their constituency. Among them are:

- Bigness as a result of LEA consolidations
- The unionization movement, which is a centralizing force predicated on strong union/management negotiations
- Increased state control, which takes power from the local school and prescribes actions, courses, and procedures; the local board of education is an arm of state government and must represent state wishes
- Increased federal participation, with the courts imposing certain mandates as well as other federal agencies promulgating operating rules
- LEA aloofness, which results in alienation of patrons and community
- Instability of all public agencies, which creates schisms between patrons and the LEA
- State legislative responses to reform demands

Because the late 1960s and early 1970s saw the credibility of school systems reach a low point, many patrons, students, and educators began to press for involvement of all in the process of education. After all, the reasoning went, isn't public education supported by public taxes? Aren't LEAs owned by the citizens? Why then shouldn't citizens exercise their ownership by demanding the right to be a part of the decision-making process?

Starting in many of the major urban centers (New York, Detroit, and so forth) and spreading throughout the country, efforts were made to encourage and provide for community involvement. This press for involvement continues today, with many models of decentralization being implemented. Some are legislatively required, like the Detroit and New York regional plans. Others are locally inspired, as in Lansing, Michigan, Salt Lake City, Utah, and Chicago. Still other decentralization plans are required by state edict, like the California and Florida site plans. The essence of all these is that local patrons must be a part of the decision-making process in order for the educational system to serve them optimally, and such involvement calls for some form of decentralization.

Delivery of Educational Services

The primary task of the LEA is the delivery of educational services to its clients. As one considers the centralization/decentralization dichotomy, the differentiation of delivery becomes important. Certain services such as direct instructional services are only delivered where the students are located, at the building level. Others are not direct to students in nature and can be conducted at locations more remote from the students. These are categorized as noninstructional services and include the range of activities that are usually housed in the local school business office. These activities have been well identified in the text and need not be reiterated here other than to again emphasize their importance to the well-being of the system.

The noninstructional services are often unobtrusive and conducted at nonschool times and locations. The effectiveness and the quality of the LEA are often judged by the efficiency with which these services are accomplished. Indeed, the dispatch and quality of such activities often provide needed resources for the instructional program.

The delivery of educational services involves a multitude of activities ranging from such noninstructional tasks as cooking, purchasing, and construction to such primary tasks as teaching, tutoring, and testing. The dichotomy under discussion requires careful examination before solutions are posed. In the judgment of the authors, those activities that involve the direct teaching/learning act must be decentralized to the building or site at which they are conducted. Decisions relative to instruction and learning are ultimately dependent on the student, the parent or guardian, the principal, and the teacher. Everyone else is (or should be) considered as supportive of those persons who are primarily engaged in instructional activities at the site level.

While it is true that planning activities, curriculum development, materials production, and a myriad of actions take place at a locale removed from the site, the reality is that learning takes place where the students are located—at the building site. It is therefore important that decisions affecting the quality of learning and the delivery of services be made in conjunction with the personnel who must deliver the services to the students: the principal and the teacher in concert with the parents. Such decision making will require increased attention and assistance to the building principal or site manager.

Site-Based Management

Awareness of the importance of building-level activities to the learning growth of students has magnified during the past decade. Research data reported by Ron Edmonds, John Goodlad, and others has shown that the rate of academic achievement by pupils is directly related to the quality of the building-level staff and, more importantly, the caliber of the principal or site manager.

Emerging research reinforces what many educational statesmen have said for decades: that the building leader determines the quality of program provided to the students of that building. Historically, outstanding principals have provided exemplary leadership and have proven that all children can learn. These principals seem to function well in spite of, rather than because of, the system, and many take the posture that they will meet all mundane central office paperwork requirements and then proceed to run a good school without central involvement.

Other principals who have the potential to operate an effective school become so bogged down by the trivia that they spend all of their time producing reports and responding to surveys and requests. Still others hide behind procedures manuals to cover their own inadequacies. The authors estimate that upwards of 90 percent of the principals in the United States can, with proper training and support, become effective site-based managers.

The role of the school business administrator in this retraining effort is crucial. As the system moves toward site-based management (SBM), the principal assumes responsibility for a number of functions that were previously handled by others. The budget function is one that must be carefully orchestrated so that both the business office and the principal are involved and served. Assisting the site manager in budget control, purchasing, allocation development, personnel management, school operations, and building management are all activities that the school business administrator can help provide. Since many of these are routine, the competent principal can quickly assimilate the basic understanding and skills needed to become proficient. Moreover, the knowledge that the business official and his/her staff of specialists are on call as support staff makes the principal much more secure and willing to assume primary responsibility.

Support Services Needed in SBM Application

From the perspective of the school business office, a number of support services are crucial to the SBM concept. While these have been covered in other areas of this text, they bear repeating here as important considerations. They are: finance, noninstructional, reporting, auditing, and other support services.

Finance/Budget

The provision of financial resources and data at the building level is an important and difficult task for the business office. Whether the system has ten buildings or several hundred units, the decision to move toward SBM demands changed procedures on the part of the business office. In essence the SBM concept treats all units as ''mini'' school systems with amounts allocated to each site provided for in the budgeting and reporting process. As an example, staff groups are allocated by building with decisions as to how they are used made at the building. Thus, an allocation of twenty professional staff to an elementary building permits the allocation of those positions according to the educational plan of the building. They could be assigned on a strict pupil–teacher ratio, by need, by grade level, by discipline, or by specialty. That decision is part of SBM and could vary from unit to unit. What is constant is the equity of the original allocation. Similarly, allocations for supplies, equipment, and other personnel are equitably made, with both assignment and line distribution made at the building level. This does change the process considerably and causes refinements in the budgeting procedures. However, given the data-processing capability already available to most business offices, the capacity exists to surmount initial difficulties. The most difficult task is to change attitudes as to the propriety of the move toward SBM.

Noninstructional Services

The noninstructional services that are directly related to SBM include custodial-maintenance activities, food service, purchasing and distribution, transportation, and security. All or most of these are part of the domain of the school business administrator. Here, too, caution and discretion are urged. While noninstructional services are most efficiently provided on a highly centralized basis, one must meet flexible needs of local units. As an example, while custodial services are best performed during nonschool hours, coverage of emergencies during use periods is essential. Therefore, if a building is used from 8 AM to 9 PM, some regular staff must be available during that time and the cleaning schedule must be coordinated with the building use schedule. Additionally, all staff must recognize the line authority of the principal and respond to immediate and unique needs of the site.

In the purchasing area, economy of scale can be realized by mass purchasing. Cooperative definition of basic supplies and equipment will provide for meeting local unit needs as well as mass buying savings. Unique local requests and needs can be met on an ad hoc basis with all purchasing handled through one office. Other noninstructional services are also provided as flexibly as possible to enable local options and needs to be met.

Accounting/Reporting

The reporting of data, particularly financial data, becomes more complex and crucial. Periodic (weekly, biweekly, and monthly) financial status reports to each unit and department become essential. Because of the need for flexibility, the reporting system must allow for the shifting of resources from one line to another as the realities of needs emerge. Since allocations are largely ''block grant'' types of allocations, control is most essential in dealing with totals rather than at each line. Principals and budget center managers must have data available on request as the need arises.

Again, because of data-processing capacity available, this issue can be resolved with a minimum of difficulty. The major task will be the development of appropriate software. In addition, the desire (or reluctance) of the staff to implement SBM will hasten or delay success and/or failure.

Auditing

The auditing process becomes much more complex because many additional budget decision centers are generated as a result of SBM. Both internal as well as external audit trails will become more numerous, complex, and important. Auditing will have to be by site unit as well as in the aggregate, which will expand the auditing task somewhat.

Because of the serious nature of public fund use, the business office must assist in training site staff in appropriate business procedures and must provide a number of activities to enable the site personnel to understand what the audit process means. Among the tasks included are provision of proper forms and instructions on how to enter various activities, assistance in reviewing transactions and in assigning them to proper accounts, and provision of a system for keeping records that specifies which records to keep.

Other Support Services

Among other important support services to be provided site managers by the business administrator are insight and understanding of business procedures and an introduction to business terminology. Because business activities can be overwhelming to the uninitiated, the gradual immersion of staff into basic language is recommended. The important topic to stress is that there is no mystery or mystique to the business activities but that as public servants the staff must follow appropriate procedures. Indeed, it is a matter of self-protection that procedures be followed.

Personal Skills for School Business Administrators in the 1990s

The litany of competencies needed by chief school business administrators is best documented by a study published in 1980 by the Association of School Business Officials of the United States and Canada. The report, written by C. W. McGuffey,[3] examined a variety of sources of data and developed a list of competencies needed for the role of Chief School Business Administrator. The primary source of data was actual practitioners, who were grouped according to the district size. The study revealed the following findings and implications:

> *First, Chief School Business Administrators place high importance on fiscal tasks and less on other tasks that traditionally have been accepted as being their responsibility. These findings should be examined in light of other apparent phenomena, such as the development of specialists in facilities, personnel, public relations, and data processing.*
>
> *Second, this study pointed out possible differences in the way Chief School Business Administrators in small school districts perceive their roles as compared to the perceptions of Chief School Business Administrators in large school districts. . . .*
>
> *Third, implications for certification of Chief School Business Administrators are indicated. . . .*
>
> *Fourth, the complexities of school business administration are clearly indicated from the study. . . . Careful decisions must be made in the determination of the tasks to be assigned to the position.*
>
> *Fifth, implications for preparation programs are reasonably clear. The Chief School Business Administrator must be a trained generalist in the school business field. . . . He/she will need to know how to delegate, motivate, monitor and control specialists in some of the more specialized business fields.*[4]

The study further defined a list of twenty-eight work/task areas as noted by more than twenty authors in the field.[5] These were then examined by the practitioners and rank ordered as to importance. Table 15-1 reflects the manner in which the twenty-eight areas were rated.

The study also considered a number of school business administration functions along with the task areas to arrive at some 264 competency statements. These functions included organizing, staffing, influencing, controlling, decision making, evaluating, and planning. Additionally, a "behavior variable" was considered in the development of the 264 competencies.[6]

The conclusions arrived at in the study included the following:

> 1. *Two hundred and sixty-four competency statements in 28 task clusters were accepted as being important to the Chief School Business Administrator. . . .*
> 2. *The fiscal related competencies were ranked the highest in the competency list. . . .*
> 3. *Chief School Business Administrators do not have full responsibility for the competencies included in 12 of the 28 task clusters. Task clusters related to facilities planning and management, personnel management, data processing, grantsmanship, staff development, professional negotiations, and community relations have become highly specialized areas. Consequently, district organization patterns have removed many of these tasks from the school business responsibility. . . .*
> 4. *Chief School Business Administrators from smaller school districts perceive selected fiscal management competencies to be more important than other competencies on the list. . . .*
> 5. *Chief School Business Administrators in different size districts assume different levels of responsibility for activities related to the competency statements. Chief School Business Administrators in smaller school districts tend to "perform" more activities related to competencies . . . whereas Chief School Business Administrators in larger school districts tended to "delegate" more.*[7]

While recognizing the importance of the various competencies and tasks identified in the study, a number of general personal skills will also be crucial to success for chief school business administrators in the coming decades.

TABLE 15-1 Ranking of Task Clusters According to Importance Scores Assigned to Competency

Rank	Task Cluster	Importance Score
1	Financial Planning and Budgeting	7.94
2	Fiscal Accounting and Financial Reporting	7.47
3	Cash Management	7.34
4	Fiscal Audits and Reports	7.28
5	General Management	7.18
6	Payroll Management	6.76
7	Purchasing	6.52
8	Insurance and Risk Management	6.40
9	Capital Fund Management	6.35
10	Legal Control	6.28
11	Office Management	6.27
12	Educational Resource Management	6.05
13	Student Activity Funds	5.95
14	Classified Personnel Management	5.92
15	Plant Maintenance	5.80
16	Property Management	5.76
17	Plant Operations	5.69
18	Community Relations	5.66
19	Professional Negotiations	5.59
20	Plant Security and Property Protection	5.46
21	Data Processing	5.46
22	Transportation Services	5.45
23	Construction Management	5.25
24	Food Service	5.19
25	Staff Development	5.14
26	Grantsmanship	4.38
27	Educational Facilities Planning	4.30
28	Warehousing and Supplies Management	3.44

Source: C. W. McGuffey, *Competencies Needed by Chief School Business Administrators* (Park Ridge, IL: Association of School Business Officials of the United States and Canada, 1980), 39.

Planning Expertise

A planning point of view and some specific planning expertise rank at the top of the personal skills required for success as a chief school business administrator. Planning skills take on added importance when placed into the context of rapid and ongoing change that has become the rule rather than the exception.

As organizational changes proceed, as demographic patterns emerge and cause other changes, as educational needs change and demand that priorities be adjusted, as world conditions and local conditions make previous plans irrelevant and/or obsolete, as technology provides additional options and alternatives, then the chief school business administrator must utilize a planning perspective to adapt to emerging conditions. Further, the capacity to anticipate and adjust is an important planning skill that is mandatory for successful school business management.

It becomes crucial for the school business administrator to have planning skills in order to survive in an era when the notion of long-range planning has been reduced to a time span of three to five years, when mobility has risen to some 20 percent of the population per year, when traditional occupations and vocations are undergoing great change, when demographic patterns clearly portend a population shift to the Sun Belt, when technology is rapidly accelerating its impact on production and lifestyles, when traditional values and mores are undergoing modification, when political realities are having increasing impact on educational systems, and when the demands placed on the educational system continue to grow and diversify.

The top administrators of the school system—the administrative team—form the planning cadre for the organization. The chief school business administrator is a key member of that planning cadre because of the diverse yet related skills the office demands.

Financial Skills

The chief school business administrator must have financial expertise. Because of the complexity of school finance and because the financial picture is further complicated by the ongoing economic volatility under which the country operates, the fiscal acuity needed to continue to provide high-level services is a most important skill.

Since education is such a labor-intensive industry, some 80–85 percent of all education budgets is reflected in salary and wage-related costs. Approximately 6–9 percent of additional budget expenditures are fixed costs—i.e., energy, insurance, and so forth. The remaining 6–12 percent of budget could be considered discretionary, out of which all supplies, capital outlay, materials, and related expenses must come. Given the reality of collective negotiations on salaries and fringe benefits, the chief school business administrator must exercise great financial skill in stretching a minuscule portion of the budget to cover a multitude of needs.

Increasingly, in times of high interest rates, chief school business administrators are generating increased returns on investments through careful management of the school district investment portfolio. Care in minimizing bank balances, with all funds invested in highest-yield securities, can dramatically increase the return to the school system. Improved tax collection procedures and rapid pass-through of tax funds also increase investment return. Because the typical school budget year is on a July 1–June 30 calendar, having school tax collection in the summer will provide benefits in two ways. First, it will minimize borrowing needs, since money is collected early in the budget years, and, second, the availability of investment cash provides for a longer investment period.

Similarly, financial skills in cash management, in generating discounts for early payment, in anticipating cash flow, and in controlling staff positions with regard to turnover and replacement all contribute to more effective use of scarce education dollars.

The chief school business administrator can, through careful and prudent financial management, have a tremendous impact on the quality of organization and the delivery of services to students and community. Among the financial skills needed are those related to fiscal planning. The ability to project future implications of immediate decisions often causes danger signs to flash and permits the development of appropriate alternatives for consideration by decision makers.

Management Skills

In any organization that serves many thousands of clients, expends millions of tax dollars, and is among the largest employers in the area, management skills are crucial to the survival of top-level staff.

The school business administrator manages a number of very diverse activities and literally hundreds of persons who perform the many and varied noninstructional tasks involved. The ability to manage people, budgets, functions, and time deadlines is vital. Diverse management skills from labor negotiations and personnel management to contract development and budget control are included in the myriad of needed management skills.

Leadership and *management* are often synonymous; both require the ability to define problems and resolve them fairly, equitably, and in the best interest of the school system. The focal point of all management/leadership activities in public education is the delivery of educational services. The school business administrator must direct all of his/her efforts toward active support of the educational goals and objectives of the school system. Capable management of the noninstructional areas of the organization can contribute mightily to the overall effectiveness of the educational system.

Human Skills

Education is a human enterprise, and nowhere is that fact better exemplified than in the overt manifestation of human skills on the part of top management. The capacity to react and interact with diverse clients is an important human skill required of the school business administrator.

The school business administrator must deal not only with such professionals as bankers, corporate executives, and governmental leaders, but also with laborers, aliens, unemployed parents, and union officials. The ability to relate at the particular level of need is an important human skill. On the one hand, capacity to discuss investment portfolios, securities, bond sales, and contracts must be present, while, on the other hand, the understanding and appreciation of such basic human needs as shelter, food, and clothing is of equal importance.

Increasingly, public school systems reflect the most diverse and the broadest spectrum of citizens in the community. Each citizen has unique needs, desires, abilities, and interests. The district must respond to all in terms that they understand and appreciate. The school business administrator has an important role to play in the entire communications process. The actions, responses, and initiatives taken by the business division can help immeasurably in the development of a community support network for the educational program.

Energy and Commitment

It is perhaps redundant to dwell on the particular traits of energy and commitment needed by the successful school business administrator, as they have been addressed directly and also heavily implied throughout this book. However, it is important for the potential school business administrator to recognize the demands made on the office and the tremendous energy required to participate in the many activities of the position.

School business is big business, often the largest business in a community. It is also a public business, with the stockholders being all citizens of the district. Conducting public business in an increasingly public manner requires great commitment from the administrator, as every citizen has a vested interest in the school system and many do not hesitate to inform the school business administrator. The drain in terms of time, of pressures, and of diversity makes the position an exceedingly difficult one.

While school business administrators must provide a variety of services and make many decisions, and while certain technical and personal skills are required for success, few lists of skills required include a sense of humor and a capacity to enjoy situations as they arise. Yet the very best incumbents do in fact have a highly developed capacity to laugh, to enjoy, and to see the humor to be found in most situations. This ability often preserves sanity, relieves pressure, and enables the person to live and survive under a most difficult workload. It should also be noted that the intrinsic rewards of the position of school business administrator are very high and are important to those preparing for entry into the field.

Summary

The future is bright for those entering the school business administration field.

The positions to be filled in the school business arena are challenging and stimulating and will increase in their importance to the educational organization. Recent data suggest that a chief school administrator can command a top-level salary and enjoy significant stature and respect in the community. Indeed, recent breakthroughs in compensation of school personnel generally, and for school administrators particularly, make the field an attractive and rewarding professional challenge.

Increasingly, school districts are moving toward filling business office positions with personnel trained in specific areas such as accounting, data processing, institutional foods, mass transportation, and industrial engineering. The chief school business administrator should be a generalist with the capacity to understand and communicate in the various specialty areas.

As this book indicates, the contribution of the school business administrator to the management of the school district is of great importance. As a key member of the management team and as an important contributor to the planning process, the school business administrator occupies a most sensitive and important post in the administrative structure of the school district.

Suggested Activities

1. Develop a rationale for a site-based management plan for your district. Itemize those activities best decentralized and contrast them to those functions you would centralize.
2. List a number of emerging educational realities and explore the planning needed by the school business administrator to meet rising needs.
3. After reading the present chapter and related literature, interview a school business administrator in order to synthesize a job description for him/her. After completing it,

compare it with his/her present job description. Account for any major differences that seem to appear.

4. Given the job description developed above and the job expectations anticipated in the future, what are the implications for university-oriented preparation programs of the present and near future?

Suggested Readings

Astin, Alexander W., and Rita A. Scherrei. *Maximizing Leadership Effectiveness*. San Francisco: Jossey-Bass, 1980.

Hill, Frederick W. *The School Business Administration*. Chicago: Association of School Business Officials, 1970.

Jones, Thomas E. *Options for the Future*. New York: Praeger, 1980.

McGuffey, C. W. *Competencies Needed by Chief School Business Administrators*. Park Ridge, IL: Association of School Business Officials of the United States and Canada, 1980.

Notes

1. Joel D. Sherman, *Demographic Trends 1960–2000: Implications for School Finance* (Philadelphia: American Education Finance Association, 1982).

2. *Ranking of the States, 1989* (Washington: National Education Association, 1989).

3. C. W McGuffey, *Competencies Needed by Chief School Business Administrators* (Park Ridge, IL: Association of School Business Officials of the United States and Canada, 1980).

4. Ibid., 15.

5. Ibid.

6. Ibid., 18–19.

7. Ibid., 45–46.

GLOSSARY

Abatement   A reduction of a previously recorded expenditure or receipt item by such things as refunds, rebates, and collections for loss or damages to school property or resources.

Account   A descriptive heading under which are recorded financial transactions that are similar in terms of purpose, object, or source.

Accounting   The procedure of maintaining systematic records of events relating to persons, objects, or money and summarizing, analyzing, and interpreting the results thereof.

Accounting Period   A period at the end of which and for which financial statements are prepared; for example, July 1 to June 30.

Accounts Receivable   Amounts due an open account from private persons, firms, or corporations for goods and services they ordered.

Accrual Basis   The basis of accounting under which revenues are recorded when earned or when levies are made, and expenditures are recorded as soon as they result in liabilities, regardless of when the revenue is actually received or the payment is actually made.

Administration-Dominated Budget   A budgeting process that is monopolized by management, and more specifically, the central office.

Administrative Unit, Intermediate   A unit smaller than the state that exists primarily to provide consultative, advisory, or statistical services to local basic administrative units, or to exercise certain regulatory and inspection functions over local basic administrative units.

Ad Valorem Taxes   Taxes levied on the assessed valuation of real and personal property that, within legal limits, is the final authority in determining the amount to be raised for school purposes. Separate accounts may be maintained for real property and for personal property.

Advertising Sale   In selling bonds and in assuming passage of any school bond issue, a notice of sale is required by state statute. Bonds can be advertised in a newspaper with general district circulation.

Affirmative Action Practices   Require an employer to increase the employment and promotion of certain protected classes of people.

Amortization of Debt   Gradual payment of an amount owed according to a specified schedule of times and amounts.

Appraisal   The act of making an estimate of value, particularly of the value of property, by systematic procedures that include physical examination, pricing, and often engineering estimates.

Appropriation   An authorization granted by a legislative body to make expenditures and to incur obligations for specific purposes.

Appropriation Ledger   A ledger containing an account for each appropriation. Each account usually shows the amount originally appropriated, transfers to or from the appropriation, amounts charged against the appropriation, the encumbrances, the net balance, and other related information.

Appropriation, School   Money received out of funds set aside periodically by the appropriating body (district meeting, city council, or other governmental body) for school purposes; which funds have not been specifically collected as school taxes.

Arbitration   Mandatory settlement of a dispute between groups by an agent specified as a part of the negotiated agreement.

Assessment, Special   A compulsory levy made by a local government against certain properties to defray part or all of the cost of a specific improvement or service that is presumed to be of general benefit to the public and of special benefit to the owners of such properties.

Assets   The things of value a school system owns.

Audit   The examination of records and documents and the securing of other evidence for one or more of the following purposes: (a) determining the propriety of proposed or completed transactions, (b) ascertaining whether all transactions have been recorded, (c) determining whether transactions are accurately recorded in the accounts and in the statements drawn from the accounts.

Balance Sheet   A formal statement of assets, liabilities, and fund balance as of a specific date.

Benefit-Cost Analysis   An analytical approach to solving problems of choice that requires the definition of objectives and identification of alternatives, and that yields the greatest benefits for any given costs, or yields a required or determined amount of benefits for the least costs.

Bond Discount   The excess of the face value of a bond over the price for which it is acquired or sold. The price does not include accrued interest at the date of acquisition or sale.

Bonded Debt   The part of the school system debt that is covered by outstanding bonds of the school system.

Bond Premium   The excess of the price at which a bond is acquired or sold, over its face value. The price does not include accrued interest at the date of acquisition or sale.

Bond Rating   Dun and Bradstreet, Moody's, and Standard & Poor's are major raters of school bonds. A borrower who obtains an AAA rating has the best rating.

Books of Original Entry   The record in which the various transactions are formally recorded for the first time, such as the cash journal, check register, or general journal. Where mechanized bookkeeping methods are used, it may happen that one transaction is recorded simultaneously in several records, one of which may be regarded as the book of original entry.

Budget   A plan of financial operation incorporating an estimate of proposed expenditures for a given period or purpose, and the proposed means of financing them.

Budgetary Accounts   Those accounts necessary to reflect budget operations and conditions, such as estimated revenues, appropriations, and encumbrances, as distinguished from proprietary accounts.

Budgeting   Pertains to budget planning, formulation, administration, analysis, and evaluation.

Buying on Margin   *See* Leveraging.

Capital Outlay   An expenditure that results in the acquisition of fixed assets or additions to fixed assets that are presumed to have benefits for more than one year. It is an expenditure for land or existing buildings.

Capital Project Fund   A fund to account for all resources used for acquisition of capital facilities including real property.

Cash   Currency, checks, postal and express money orders, and bankers' drafts on hand or on deposit with an official or agent designated as custodian of cash; and bank deposits.

Cash Basis   The basis of accounting under which revenues are recorded only when actually received, and only cash disbursements are recorded as expenditures.

Cash Discounts   Allowances received or given by vendors for payment of invoices within a stated period of time.

Cash Flow   The cycles of revenue entering and expenditures leaving an account.

Categorical Aid   Educational support funds provided from higher governmental levels and specifically limited to a given purpose.

Cathode Ray Tube Terminal (CRT)   A device that contains a television-like screen for displaying data. Most CRT terminals have a typewriter-type keyboard.

Central Processing Unit (CPU)   Electric component that causes processing on a computer by interpreting instructions, performing calculations, moving data, and controlling the input/output operations. It consists of the arithmetical/logical unit and the control unit.

Centralized Budget   A budgeting process that treats all schools in a system alike. Though efficient in a sense, little consideration is permitted for differing needs among the various communities served under this type of process.

Certificate of Deposit (CD)   Issued by a bank or thrift, this is an interest-bearing term deposit that comes due at a specified future date.

Chart of Accounts   A list of accounts generally used in an individual accounting system. It includes the account title and an account number that has been assigned to each account.

Coding   Distinguishing among items and categories of information by assigning numbers or other symbolic designations so that the items and categories are readily identifiable.

Cohort Survival   A method of short-term enrollment projection utilizing the percent of change of cohorts within the immediate past.

Coinsurance   Insurer-provided coverage for the portion of a loss relative to the amount required to avoid penalty.

Compiler   A program that interprets computer statements in symbolic form and converts them into machine language instructions.

Comprehensive Planning   Planning usually done through a comprehensive survey that reveals future goals, needs, and resources.

Computer   A device that can perform computations, including arithmetic and logic operations, without intervention by a human being.

Concentration Account   An account that is the aggregation of all of an institution's other accounts for investment purposes.

Conditions   Provisions of a contract indicating areas and/or items with which compliance is essential to enforce the rights of the contract.

Contingency Fund   Assets or other resources set aside to provide for unforeseen expenditures or for anticipated expenditures of uncertain amount.

Continuous Budget   Under this concept of budgetary development, educational plans are conceived on a long-range basis and attempts are made to budget accordingly. Budget development is considered to be an integral part of daily operation.

Contracted Services   Services rendered by personnel who are not on the payroll, including all related expense covered by the contract.

Cost Accounting   A method of accounting that provides for the assembling and recording of all the elements of cost incurred to accomplish a purpose, to carry on an activity or operation, or to complete a unit of work or a specific job.

Cost Benefit   *See* Benefit-Cost Analysis.

Cost Center   The smallest segment of a program that is separately recognized in the records, accounts, and reports. Program-oriented budgeting, accounting, and reporting aspects of an information system are usually built upon the identification and use of a set of cost centers.

Cost-Effectiveness Analysis   Primarily a post-evaluation technique used to help determine program effectiveness, failures, and ways of improvement.

Cost Stream   Includes the costs associated with the researching, purchasing, financing, operating, and repairing of a system or piece of equipment.

Credit   Opposite of debit. An entry into the right side of an account reflecting a decrease in an asset or an increase in a liability or fund balance.

Critical Path Method (CPM)   A type of network analysis. Its analytical emphasis is to determine the programming strategy that will satisfy schedule requirements at minimum costs.

Current   The term refers to the fiscal year in progress.

Current Assets   Those assets that are available or can be made readily available to meet the cost of operations or to pay current liabilities. Some examples are cash, temporary investments, and taxes receivable that can be expected to be collected within one year.

Current Expense   Any expenditure except for capital outlay and debt service. Current expense includes total charges incurred, whether paid or unpaid.

Current Funds   Money received during the current fiscal year from revenue that can be used to pay obligations currently due, and surpluses reappropriated for the current fiscal year.

Current Liabilities   Debts that are payable within a relatively short period of time, usually no longer than a year.

Data Base   A comprehensive collection of data composed of files relating to specific areas of information such as pupils, staff, property, finance, instructional programs, and the community.

Data Processing   The activities of collecting and organizing data, sorting for future use, and preparing statistical reports.

Debit   Opposite of credit. An entry into the left side of an account reflecting an increase in an asset or a decrease in a liability or fund balance.

Debt Service   Expenditures for the retirement of debt and expenditures for interest on debt, except principal and interest of current loans.

Debt Service Fund   Used to finance and account for payment of interest and principal on all general obligation debt.

Decentralized Budget   A budgetary process that especially applies to large school systems. Each school in a system establishes individual budgets and establishes its own educational priorities within the parameters of the total system. The process fosters a high degree of participation by a wide variety of persons.

Delinquent Taxes   Taxes remaining unpaid on and after the date on which they become delinquent by statute.

Delphi Process   An intuitive methodology for eliciting, refining, and gaining consensus from individuals within an organization regarding a given issue.

Depreciation   Loss in value of service life of fixed assets because of wear and tear through use, elapse of time, inadequacy, or obsolescence.

Disbursements   Payments in cash.

Double Entry   A system of bookkeeping that requires for every entry made to the debit side of an account or accounts an entry be made for the corresponding amount or amounts to the credit side of another account or accounts.

Dynamic Programing   A technique used for solving multi-stage problems in which the output of one stage becomes input for another stage.

Educational Budget   The translation of educational needs into a financial plan that is interpreted to the public in such a way that, when formally adopted, it expresses the kind of educational program the community is willing to support for the budget period.

Emergency Maintenance   Plan for servicing equipment and/or facilities with no restrictions on number of calls, time, or costs.

Employee Assistance Programs   Established by organizations to help employees resolve personal problems (stress, chemical dependency, depression, financial, family, and so forth) that affect job performance by reducing absenteeism, turnover, tardiness, accidents, and medical claims.

Employee Benefits   Compensation, in addition to regular salary, provided to an employee. This may include such benefits as health insurance, life insurance, annual leave, sick leave, retirement, and social security.

Encumbrances   Purchase orders, contracts, and salary or other commitments that are chargeable to an appropriation and for which a part of the appropriation is reserved. They cease to be encumbrances when paid or when actual liability is set up.

Endorsements   Provisions added to a basic contract to increase or decrease the scope of the contract.

Endowment Fund   A fund from which the income may be expended, but whose principal must remain intact.

Entry   The record of a financial transaction in its appropriate book of accounts. Also the act of recording a transaction in the books of accounts.

Equipment   Any instrument, machine, apparatus, or set of articles that (a) retains its original shape and appearance with use and (b) is nonexpendable; that is, if the article is damaged or some of its parts are lost or worn out, it is usually more feasible to repair it than to replace it with an entirely new unit.

Equity   Equity is the mathematical excess of assets over liabilities. Generally this excess is called fund balance.

Exclusions   Areas, items, or actions causing insurance coverage to be omitted.

Expenditures   Charges incurred, whether paid or unpaid, that are presumed to benefit the current fiscal year.

Express Warranties   Explicit statements as to the quality, fitness, or performance of a product by a seller.

Fidelity Bond   A bond guaranteeing against losses resulting from the actions of the treasurer, employees, or other persons of the system.

Fiscal Period   Any period at the end of which a school system determines its financial condition and the results of its operation and closes its books. It is usually a year, though not necessarily a calendar year.

Fixed Assets   Land, buildings, machinery, furniture, and other equipment which the school system intends to hold or continue in use over a long period of time.

Fixed Charges   Charges of a generally recurrent nature that are not readily allocated to other expenditure categories. They consist of such charges as school board contributions to employee retirement, insurance and judgments, rental of land and buildings, and interest on current loans. They do not include payments to public school housing authorities or similar agencies.

Floppy Disk   A mylar-coated plastic disk about eight inches in diameter that can be used for magnetically storing data.

Flow Chart   A symbolic way of representing information about the relationships of discrete parts or steps in a process.

Flow Models   The generic term for models that lay out the facilities on the organizational chart and enable managers and administrators to see the flow of material, equipment, personnel, and information.

Food Services   Activities involved with the food services program that includes the preparation and serving of regular and incidental meals, lunches, or snacks in connection with school activities, and the delivery of food.

Formal Bids   Bids requiring public advertising, public opening, and award to lowest responsible bidder.

Friable Asbestos   Airborne asbestos that may have carcinogenic qualities.

Function   An action that contributes to a larger action of a person, living thing, or creating thing.

Functional Budget   A type of budgetary development that considers the educational objectives of a school district. The educational plan is translated into a budget for presentation to the community for reaction.

Functional Overlap   These modifications of flow models depict contacts that occur where specialized information is sought. Most typically these contacts happen when a specialist or intellectual leader expects influence without direct responsibility.

Fund   An independent accounting entity with its own assets, liabilities, and fund balances. Generally, funds are established to account for financing of specific activities of an agency's operations.

Fund Accounts   All accounts necessary to set forth the financial operations and financial condition of a fund.

Fund Balance   The excess of the assets of a fund over its liabilities and reserves, except in the case of funds subject to budgetary accounting where, prior to the end of a fiscal period, it represents the excess of the fund's assets and estimated revenues for the period over its liabilities, reserves, and appropriations for the period; also called equity.

Game Theory   A technique for analyzing choices between alternative strategies and competing decisions.

General Fund   Used to account for all transactions that do not have to be accounted for in another fund. Used to account for all ordinary operations of a school system.

General Ledger   A book, file, or other device in which accounts are kept to summarize the financial transactions of the school system. General ledger accounts may be kept for any group of items of receipts or expenditures on which an administrative officer wishes to maintain a close check.

Grants-In-Aid   Contributions made by a government unit and not related to specific revenue sources of the respective government, that is, general; or if related to specific revenue sources of the governmental unit, distributed on some flat grant or equalization basis. Grants-in-aid are made by intermediate governments, state governments, and the federal government.

Hardware, Computer   Physical equipment, as opposed to the program or method of use. For example, mechanical, magnetic, electrical, or electronic devices.

Implied Warranties   In the absence of express warranties, there is usually an implied warranty that the goods are reasonably fit for their purpose.

Improvements   Buildings, other structures, and other attachments or annexations to land that are intended to remain so attached or annexed, such as sidewalks, trees, drives, tunnels, drains, and sewers. Note: Sidewalks, curbing, sewers, and highways are sometimes referred to as *betterments* but the term *improvements* is preferred.

Informal Bids   A telephone quotation or a (preferred) written quotation whose dollar value is less than the statutory limit.

Input, Computer   Data to be processed by a computer.

Input-Output Analysis   A method for analyzing the consequences of alternate spending plans throughout a governmental unit. Educators can use it to help determine optimum levels of school financing within a city or community.

Insuring Agreements   Provisions distinguishing one contract from another.

Interfund Transfers   Money taken from one fund under the control of the board of education and added to another fund under the board's control. Interfund transfers are not receipts or expenditures of the school system.

Internal Auditing   Activities involved with evaluating the adequacy of the internal control system, verifying and safeguarding assets, reviewing the reliability of the accounting and reporting systems, and ascertaining compliance with established policies and procedures.

Inventory   A detailed list or record showing quantities, descriptions, values, and, frequently, units of measure and unit prices of property on hand at a given time.

Investments   Securities and real estate held for the production of income in the form of interest, dividends, rentals, or lease payments. The account does not include fixed assets.

Invoice   An itemized list of merchandise purchased from a particular vendor. The list includes quantity, description, price, terms, date, and the like.

Job Analysis   A study to determine the constructs underlying successful job performance and important or critical duties.

Job Description   A detailing of specific activities, responsibilities, and requirements of the position. These guidelines include necessary skills, types of responsibilities, and limitations imposed by the job.

Judgment   An amount to be paid or collected by the school system as a result of a court decision.

Journal   The accounting record in which the details of financial transactions are first recorded.

Land   A fixed asset account that reflects the acquisition value of land owned. If land is purchased, this account includes the purchase price and costs such as legal fees, filling and excavation costs, and other associated improvements costs that are incurred to put the land in condition for its intended use. If land is acquired by gift, the account reflects its appraised value at time of acquisition.

Least Cost Estimating and Scheduling (LESS)   A variation of CPM and PERT. LESS resolves the problem at what time and hour each and every job should be done in order to complete the project at minimum cost and within a specified time.

Ledger   Contains all the accounts of a particular fund or all those detail accounts that support a particular general ledger account.

Legal Opinion   (1) The opinion of an official authorized to render it, such as an attorney as to legality. (2) In the case of school bonds, the opinion of a specialized bond attorney as to the legality of a bond issue.

Leveraging   Using equity in one security or asset to buy an additional asset or security.

Levy   To impose taxes or special assets. The total of taxes or special assessments imposed by a governmental unit.

Liabilities   Debt or other legal obligations arising out of transactions in the past that are payable but not necessarily due. Encumbrances are not liabilities; they become liabilities when the services or materials for which the encumbrances were established have been rendered or received.

Liability Insurance   Expenditures for insurance coverage of the school system, or its officers, against losses resulting from judgments awarded against the system.

Linear Programming   An operations-research technique useful in specifying how to use limited resources or capacities to obtain particular objectives. It has been used to determine school transportation routes, location and number of warehouse and maintenance facilities, and the best location of schools.

Liquidity   Refers to the ease or difficulty of using assets that are invested.

Local Education Agency   Educational agency created by the state to carry out state policies and operate schools.

Long-Term Loan   A loan that extends for more than five years from the date the loan was obtained and is not secured by serial or term bonds.

Maintenance   Functions associated with repairs and/or replacements to ensure continuous usability of physical plant, equipment, and service facilities.

Maintenance Personnel   Personnel on the school payroll who are primarily engaged in the repairing and upkeep of grounds, buildings, and equipment.

Management by Objectives (MBO)   Process wherein management provides a structure of individuals and subsystems of the organization to relate their objectives to those of the larger system in a cooperative mode and to be evaluated on the achievement of the results.

Management Information System   A method for improving the quality of and access to information pertinent to an enterprise. The method consists of defining management decisions, explaining decision-making policies, determining the information needed to make decisions, and developing techniques for processing the information.

Mechanical Budget   Under this concept, budgeting is viewed as a revenue-and-expenditure operation—a bookkeeping chore required by law. This type of budgeting forces expenditures to fit income expectations and pays no attention to needs.

Mediation   Process for settling differences between groups by consent or agreement of both parties.

Microcomputer   A complete computer on a single miniature circuit board.

Minicomputer   A stored program computer, generally having less memory, and a smaller word size than larger machines.

Needs Assessment   A basic procedure for determining the quantitative and/or qualitative extent of the discrepancies between what is and what is required.

Negotiations   Processes for exchange between groups for the purpose of reaching mutually acceptable agreements.

Network Analysis   Generic term for a tool of analysis. Two basic types of managerial technique used in design, planning, and control are critical path method (CPM) and program evaluation and review techniques (PERT).

Notice to Bidders   Form that exists for the purpose of giving prior and proper notice to potential bidders. By means of the form bidders can record their prices for specifically described articles.

Object   The commodity or service obtained from a specific expenditure.

Object Classification   A category of goods or services purchased.

Obligations   Amounts that the school system will be required to meet out of its resources, including both liabilities and encumbrances.

Operation, Plant   Those activities that are concerned with keeping the physical plant open and ready for use. They include cleaning, disinfecting, heating, moving furniture, caring for grounds, operating telephone switchboards, and other such housekeeping activities. They do not include repairing.

OSHA   Occupational Safety and Health Act.

Output   Material generated by the computer on tape, paper, disc, and such for current or future use.

Participatory Budget   A budgetary process that attempts to involve school staff and lay public in the various levels of budget making. This process uses a combination of formal and informal methods to get persons involved.

Payroll   A list of individual employees entitled to wages or salaries, with the amounts due to each for personal services rendered. Payments are also made for such payroll associated costs as federal income tax withholdings, retirements, and social security.

Payroll Deductions and Withholding   Amounts deducted from employees' salaries for taxes required to be withheld and for other withholding purposes. Separate liability accounts may be used for each type of deduction.

Periodic Maintenance   Work on buildings and/or equipment scheduled at a specific time or specific number of times during a given period.

Petty Cash   A sum of money set aside for the purpose of paying small obligations for which the issuance of a formal voucher and check would be too expensive and time-consuming.

Planning   The selection or identification of the overall, long-range goals, priorities, and objectives of the organization, and the formulation of various courses of action to be followed in working toward achieving those goals, priorities, and objectives.

Planning, Programming, Budgeting, Evaluating System (PPBES)   A formal procedure for determining budgets. Some distinctive characteristics of this procedure are identification of the basic objectives of the enterprise, determination of future year implications and inclusion of all costs in budgetary considerations, and systematic analysis of alternatives with a view toward determining the relative benefits and costs.

Plant Security   Program for protecting each site against damages, vandalism, loss of keys, and so forth.

Posting   The act of transferring to an account in a ledger the detailed or summarized data contained in the cash receipts book, cash register, journal voucher, or similar books or documents of original entry.

Post-Sale Planning   Planning done after the sale of bonds is accomplished. Prompt payment of principal and interest, and the notification of bond owners, rating agencies, and underwriters about the financial status and progress of a school system are very important.

Premium on Bonds Sold   That portion of the sale price of bonds in excess of their par value. The premium represents an adjustment of the interest rate.

Preventive Maintenance   Program for servicing machines, systems, and structures devised to prevent a breakdown of the total system or any one of the component parts.

Principal   The amount of money that is invested.

Principal Systems and Priorities   The main systems of an information system in an educational enterprise might be student information system, materials information system, administrative and financial information system, and instructional system.

Privacy Act of 1974   Public Law 92-583, designed to protect citizens from unwarranted use of personal data.

Program   A plan of activities and procedures designed to accomplish a predetermined objective or set of allied objectives.

Program Evaluation and Review Technique (PERT)   A type of network analysis used in cases in which there is no established system for doing the task and therefore no exact basis for estimating the required time to complete each task.

Programming   Preparation of a logical sequence of operations to be performed by a computer in solving a problem or processing data; the preparation of coded instructions and data for such a sequence.

Programing Language   Sets of instructions or codes to communicate with a computer. Examples include FORTRAN (Formula Translation), COBOL (Common Business Oriented Language), and BASIC (Beginner's All-Purpose Symbolic Instruction Code).

Proprietary Accounts   Those accounts that show actual financial conditions and operations such as actual assets, liabilities, reserves, surplus, revenues, and expenditures, as distinguished from budgetary accounts.

Property Insurance   Expenditures for all forms of insurance covering the loss of, or damage to, property from fire, theft, storm, or any other cause. Also recorded here are costs for appraisals of property for insurance purposes.

Prorating   The allocation of parts of a single expenditure to two or more different accounts. The allocation is made in proportion to the benefits that the expenditure provides for the respective purposes or programs for which the accounts were established.

Pupil Accounting   A system for collecting, computing, and reporting information about pupils.

Pupil Activity Fund   Financial transactions related to school-sponsored pupil activities and interscholastic activities. These activities are supported in whole or in part by income from pupils, gate receipts, and other fund-raising activities. Support may be provided by local taxation.

Pupil Transportation   Consists of those activities involved with the conveyance of pupils to and from school activities, as provided by state law. This includes trips between home and school or trips to school activities.

Purchase Order   The document by which goods are procured. Every purchase order must include such information as name and address of school system, order number, date, name and address of vendor, description of materials, quantity, price, and signature of authorization.

Purchasing   Acquiring supplies, equipment, and materials.

Quadratic Programing   A technique having applications similar to those of linear programming. This technique is able to compute nonlinear relationships.

Queuing Theory (Waiting-Line Theory)   A mathematical technique for reducing lengths of waiting lines and for reducing time lost to waiting.

Real Estate   Land, improvements to site, and buildings; real property.

Rebates   Abatements or refunds.

Recurring Maintenance   Plan for servicing equipment and/or facilities regardless of the number of service calls needed and at the convenience of the contractor.

Redemption of Principal   Expenditures from current funds to retire serial bonds, long-term loans of more than five years, and short-term loans of less than five years.

Refund   A return of an overpayment or overcollection. The return may be either in the form of cash or a credit to an account.

Refunding Bonds   Bonds issued to pay off bonds already outstanding.

Register   A record for the consecutive entry of a certain class of events, documents, or transactions, with a proper notation of all of the required particulars.

Reimbursement   The return of an overpayment or overcollection in cash.

Remodeling   Any major permanent structural improvement to buildings. It includes changes of partitions, roof structure, or walls. Repairs are not included here but are included under maintenance.

Remote Entry   Ability to communicate with a data processing system from a location that is time, space, or electrically distant.

Rental-Purchase Agreement   A contractual agreement for the rental of property with the option to apply all or part of the rental monies toward the eventual purchase.

Repairs   The restoration of a given piece of equipment, a given building, or of grounds to original condition or completeness or efficiency from a worn, damaged, or deteriorated condition.

REPO (Repurchase Agreement)   Relatively short-term investments (even overnight or over a weekend) whereby the investor takes title to bank securities as collateral. Bank repurchases the securities at the end of the term, paying back principal plus interest.

Requisition   A written request to a purchasing officer for specified articles or services. It is a request from one school official to another school official, whereas a purchase order is from a school official (usually the purchasing officer) to a vendor.

Resource Allocation and Multi-Project Scheduling (RAMPS) A variation of CPM and PERT. By considering various restrictions and requirements, RAMPS is able to determine the schedule that satisfies various prescribed criteria and minimum costs.

Revenues Additions to assets that do not increase any liability, do not represent the recovery of an expenditure, and do not represent the cancellation of certain liabilities without a corresponding increase in other liabilities or a decrease in assets.

Revolving Fund A fund provided to carry out a cycle of operations. The amounts expended from the funds are restored by earnings from operations or by transfers from other funds so that it remains intact, either in the form of cash, receivables, inventory, or other assets. These funds are also known as reimbursable funds.

Riffing Derived from the term *reduction-in-force*.

School System All the schools and supporting services operated by the board of education, by a specified administrative unit, or by another organization that operates one or more schools.

Securities Bonds, notes, mortgages, or other forms of negotiable or nonnegotiable instruments.

Sequential Planning A family of techniques whose purpose is to sequence the various operations of an enterprise in order to reduce waste.

Serial Bonds Issues redeemable by installments, each of which is to be paid in full, ordinarily out of revenues of the fiscal year in which it matures or out of revenues of the preceding year.

Short-Term Loan A loan payable in five years or less, but not before the end of the current fiscal year.

Sinking Fund Money that has been set aside or invested for the definite purpose of meeting payments on debt at some future time. It is usually a fund set up for the purpose of accumulating money over a period of years in order to have money available for the redemption of long-term obligations at the date of maturity.

Site-Based Management Managerial decisions and processes carried out at the school site rather than at a higher organizational level.

Sociometric Overlap Modifications of flow models that describe relationships within the organization that are purely social. These may be positive or negative relationships.

Software Set of instructions for communicating with the computer. Also used to refer to all programs, whether locally produced or vendor supplied, for operating the computer system.

Staff Accounting Services rendered in connection with the systematic recording, filing, and storing of information related to staff members employed by the school system.

Stakeholders Individual and/or group representatives who share common interests in the educational process directed by a school district or building.

Statements (1) Used in a general sense, statements are all formal written presentations that set forth financial information. (2) In technical accounting usage, statements are presentations of financial data that show the financial position and the results of financial operations of a fund, a group of accounts, or an entire governmental unit for a particular accounting period.

Stock Insurance Company An insurance company owned by stockholders and managed by an elected board of directors. Company profits are shared among stockholders in the form of dividends.

Stores Supplies, materials, and equipment in storerooms and subject to requisition.

Student Activities   Direct and personal services for public school pupils, such as inter-scholastic athletics, entertainment, publications, clubs, band, and orchestra, that are managed or operated generally by the student body under the guidance and direction of adults or a staff member, and which are not part of the regular instructional program.

Supply   A material item of an expendable nature that is consumed, worn out, or deteriorated in use or loses its identity through fabrication for incorporation into a different or more complex unit of substance.

Supporting Services   Activities that provide administrative, technical, and logistical support to a program. Supporting services exist to sustain and enhance the fulfillment of the objectives of other major functions.

Surety Bond   A written promise to pay damages or to indemnify against losses caused by the party or parties named in the document, through nonperformance or through defalcation; for example, a surety bond given by a contractor or by an official handling cash or securities.

Surplus   The excess of the assets of a fund over its liabilities; or if the fund also has other resources and obligations, the excess of resources over obligations. The term should not be used without a properly descriptive adjective unless its meaning is apparent from the context.

Systems Analysis   Evaluation of alternatives that are relevant to defined objectives based on judgment, and wherever possible, on quantitative methods; the development of data processing procedures or application to electronic data processing equipment.

Tax Anticipation Notes   Notes issued in anticipation of collection of taxes usually retirable only from tax collections, and frequently only from the tax collections anticipated with their issuance. The proceeds of tax anticipation notes or warrants are treated as current loans if paid back from the tax collections anticipated with the issuance of the notes.

Taxes   Compulsory charges levied by a governmental unit for the purpose of financing services performed for the common benefit.

Taxes Receivable   The uncollected portion of taxes that a school system or governmental unit has levied and which has become due, including any interest or penalties that may be accrued. Separate accounts may be maintained on the basis of tax roll year and/or current and delinquent taxes.

Term Bonds   Bonds of the same issue, usually maturing all at one time and ordinarily to be retired from sinking funds.

Time-Sharing   A computing technique where several terminal devices utilize a central computer concurrently for input, processing, and output functions.

Title IX   Federal guidelines relating to sex discrimination in hiring practices.

Tort   A civil wrong (other than a breach of contract) for which an award of damages is appropriate.

Trial Balance   A list of the balances of the accounts in a ledger kept by double entry, with the debit and credit balances shown in separate columns. If the totals of the debit and credit columns are equal, or their net balance agrees with a controlling account, the ledger from which the figures are taken is said to be "in balance."

Unencumbered Balance   That portion of an appropriation or allotment not yet expended or encumbered; the balance remaining after deducting from the appropriation or allotment the accumulated expenditures and outstanding encumbrances.

Unit Cost   Expenditures for a function, activity, or service divided by the total number of units for which the function, activity, or service was provided.

Unit Record Equipment   Wired board–controlled machines without memory, basically used for accounting-type operations.

Valuation   Sound replacement cost of structures, equipment, and/or furnishings.

Voucher   A document that authorizes the payment of money and usually indicates the accounts to be charged.

Vouchers Payable   Liabilities for goods and services received as evidenced by vouchers that have been preaudited and approved for payment but which have not been paid.

Voucher System   A system that calls for the preparation of vouchers for transactions involving payments, and for the recording of such vouchers in a special book of original entry known as a voucher register in the order in which payment is approved.

Warrant   An order drawn by the school board to the school system treasurer ordering him/her to pay a specified amount to a payee named on the warrant. Once signed by the treasurer the warrant becomes a check payable by a bank named on the warrant by the treasurer.

Word Processing   The manipulation of certain types of data—words, sentences, reports, and so forth—to express ideas and distribute them in hard copy (paper) and/or visual copy (CRT screen).

Work Order   A written order authorizing and directing the performance of a certain task, issued to the person who is to direct the work. Among the information shown on the order are the nature and location of the job, specifications of the work to be performed, and a job number that is referred to in reporting the amount of labor, materials, and equipment used.

Yearly Budget   A type of budgeting process that is little more than a refinement of the mechanical type. The yearly budget forces quick decisions on expenditures and revenues with little effort made to evaluate the impact of these decisions.

Zero-Based Accounting   Implementing concept for developing the concentration account. Regular accounts are established as accounts payable. All carry a zero balance with all monies kept in the concentration account until needed for a particular account.

Zero-Base Budgeting (ZBB)   A process emphasizing management's responsibility to plan, budget, and evaluate. It provides for analysis of alternative methods of operation and various levels of effort. It places new programs on an equal footing with existing programs by requiring that program priorities be ranked, thereby providing a systematic basis for allocating resources.

INDEX

AASA (American Association of School Administrators), 51–52
Abatement, 357
Ability to pay theory of taxation, 37
Accommodation, in labor-management relations, 169
Account, 357
Accountability, 140
Accounting
  balancing the books, 158–159
  in contemporary practice, 152–160
  cycle, 149–152
  definition of, 141, 357
  emergence of system, 142–143
  equation, 143–147
  for food services, 334–335
  general ledger, 150–151, 158
  generally accepted procedures, 159–160
  objectives, 141–142
  period, 357
  process of, 144–148
  processing accounting data, 152
  public school vs. business, 142
  purchasing and, 211
  recording budgets and appropriations, 151–152
  recording transactions, 152
  tasks, 140
  terminology, 143–144
Accounts receivable, 357
Accrual basis, 150, 357
ACIR (Advisory Commission on Intergovernmental Relations), 39
Ad valorem taxes, 357
Administration-dominated budget, 113, 357
Administrative science, development phases of, 53
Administrative unit, intermediate, 357
Administrator
  accounting tasks of, 140
  auditing responsibilities, 161
  budgeting process and, 6, 27

centralization/decentralization dichotomy, 345–348
classified personnel and, 168
commitment of, 354–355
computer installation and, 90–92
conflict management, 170
contextual perspectives of, 8–9
conventional practice perspective, 9–10
educational obsolescence vs. physical obsolescence, 222
emerging challenges of, 10–13
energy of, 354–355
evaluation and, 72
federal-level influences, 22
financial skills of, 353
fiscal and economic perspectives, 343–344
functions of, 6–10, 17
future of, 355
hardware/software selection, 89–90
human skills of, 354
information generation and, 68–69
leadership, 51–52, 354
legal and judicial concepts for, 19, 21–30, 33
maintenance role, 219
management skills of, 354
money management and, 26
operational description of, 7
personal skills, 350–355
perspectives of, 342–355
planning and, 4, 6, 13–15, 352–353
as policy advocate, 35
principal and, 5
professional negotiations and, 187
responsibility areas of, 9–10
role levels of, 3–4
school reform implications and, 12–13
site-based management and, 5–6
state-level influences, 23–24
in superintendency team, 4–5
tasks of, 3
as tax policy advocate, 44

Administrator *(continued)*
  titles for, 3
  use of financial resources, 279
Advertising, for bids, 205
Advertising sale, 260, 357
Advisory Commission on Intergovernmental
  Relations (ACIR), 39
Affirmative action practices, 172–173, 357
Allocation models, linear programming, 64–65
American Association of School Administrators
  (AASA), 51–52
Amortization of debt, 357
Appraisals, 302, 357
Apprenticeship training, 174
Appropriations, 151–152, 358
Arbitrage, 291–292
Arbitration, 186–187, 358
Architect, 264–266, 269
Architectural planning, for new construction,
  263–268
Armed truce attitude, in labor-management
  relations, 169
Asbestos, 241–242, 308
Asbestos Hazards Emergency Response Act
  (AHERA), 20, 242
ASBO (Association of School Business
  Officials of the United States and
  Canada), 2, 9
Assessment, special, 358
Asset account, 150
Assets, 143–144, 358
Association of School Business Officials of the
  United States and Canada (ASBO), 2, 9
Assumptions, in forecasting, 69
Audit, 358
Auditing, 160–161, 350
Automation, of purchasing, 202
Auxiliary services
  community use of school facilities, 338–339
  definition of, 317, 339–340
  for food, 327–335
  planning, 317–318
  sale of school services, 339
  for security, 335–340
  for site-based management, 349–350
  for transportation, 318–326
Award, of bid, 206

Balance sheet, 358
Bargaining, 170
Barnard, Chester, 56
Behavioral science phase, 53, 54–55
Benchmark, 287, 289
Benefit-cost analysis, 358

Benefit theory of taxation, 37
Bids. *See* Competitive bids
Binding arbitration, 187
Block grants, 120, 346
Board of Election, minutes of, 25
Boles formula, 275
Bond attorney, retaining, 260
Bond discount, 358
Bond issues, 257, 260
Bond premium, 358
Bond rating, 260, 358
Bonded debt, 358
Books of original entry, 358
Budgetary accounts, 358
Budgeting, 26–27, 359
  administrator and, 6
  benefits of, 112
  components of, 35
  concepts of, 112–114
  fiscally dependent systems and, 27
  fiscally independent systems and, 27
  group involvement, 122
  personnel, 189–191
  site-based, 114–126
  statutory bases, 112
  zero-based, 130–133
Budget(s)
  administration-dominated, 113
  building, 125–126
  centralized, 113–114
  continuous, 134
  definition of, 111, 358
  development concepts, 133–136
  functional, 134
  mechanical, 112–113
  participatory, 134–135
  process, 136–138. *See* Budgeting
  rational/political/economic, 135–136
  recording, 15–152
  yearly, 113
Building design, energy conservation and,
  272–273
Building distribution, 121–122
Building funds, monitoring, 123–124
Building maintenance survey, 228
Burns, Arthur, 130
Bus drivers, supervision and training of, 323–324
Business, school system as, 1
Buying on margin, 359

CAFR (comprehensive annual financial report),
  159, 162–163
CAI (computer-aided instruction), 99
Capacity analysis, 255–256

Capital assets market, 311
Capital assets planning
  of construction, steps in, 262–268
  evaluation of existing facilities, 253–256
  quantitative aspect of need, 252–253
Capital assets planning and management,
    program analysis, 250–252
Capital expenditures, 256
Capital funding
  alternative, 261–262
  federal responsibility, 261
  local government responsibility, 257, 260
  state responsibility, 256–257, 261
Capital improvements decisions, 220
Capital outlay, 224, 359
Capital project fund, 359
Carryover, in autonomous fund budget process,
  124
Cash, 359
Cash basis, 359
Cash discounts, 203, 359
Cash flow, 359
Cash-flow analysis, 286, 292
Cash flow concept, 280–282
Cash for investment, nature of, 279–280
Cash management
  cash flow and, 280–282
  investment considerations, 282–292
  nature of cash investment and, 279–280
Cash management services, 289
Cash Position Report, 158
Castaldi formula, 275–276
Categorical funds or aid, 120, 359
Cathode ray tube terminal (CRT), 359
CD (certificate of deposit), 283, 284, 359
Census-based data, for demographic forecasting,
  70
Central Processing Unit (CPU), 359
Centralization, 344–348
  of budget, 113–114, 359
  of food service operations, 331
  of purchasing, 196
  of storage, 214–215
Certificate of deposit (CD), 283, 284, 359
Certification, 2–3, 52–53
Chandler, Alfred, 56
Chart of accounts, 359
Chemical analysis, of quality, 200
Choice. *See* Parent choice
CIPP model for evaluation, 70–72
Civil liberties premise, 22
Civil rights, 20
Civil Rights Act of 1964, 29, 31, 346
Civil service-union association, 187–188

Classical organization phase, 53–54
Classified personnel, 168
Clerk-of-the-works, 268
Closed system-rational actor era, 56
Closed system-social actor, 56
Coding, 359
Coding, of financial transaction, 153–155
Cohort survival, 70, 359
Coinsurance, 359
Collaboration, 170
Collective bargaining, 317
Collusion, in labor-management relations, 169
Commercial general liability (CGL), 307, 308
Commercial paper, 285
Commitment, of administrator, 354–355
Communication
  application of concepts, 80–81
  principles of, 78
  processes of, 78–80
Community
  in comprehensive strategic planning, 249
  involvement of, 122, 124–126, 347
  use of school facilities, 338–339
Competitive bids, 25–26, 205–207
  bidding process, 205–207
  on construction projects, 267
  for insurance acquisition, 299
  price quotations for, 202–204
  for procurement of furniture and equipment,
    269
Compiler, 359
Compliance, 31–32, 42
Comprehensive annual financial report (CAFR),
  159, 162–163
Comprehensive strategic planning, 140, 359
  educational goals, 251–252
  key participants, involvement of, 249–250
  steps, 248–249
Computer-aided instruction, 99
Computer-based information systems. *See*
  Information systems
Computer centers
  disaster recovery for, 106–107
  materials selection for, 107
Computer security, 94, 97–98
Computer viruses, 98–99
Computer(s)
  costs of, 105
  definition of, 102, 359
  effects on administrators, 90–92
  effects on staff system, 90
  functions of, relationships of, 104
  hardware development, 87
  hardware/software selection, 89–90

Computer(s) *(continued)*
inventory control and, 212–213
maintenance of, 105–106
in PPBES, 126–127
for scheduling, 322
software development, 87
system components, 102–103
systems. *See* Information systems
Concentration account, 289, 359
Conditions, in insurance contract, 302, 359
Conflict, in labor-management relations, 168, 170
Conflict of interest, 28
Constitutions, written, 22
Construction
architectural planning, 263–268
educational specifications, 262–263
multiple agency utilization, 263
planning, 266
progressive techniques, 268
review of plans and specifications, 266–267
Construction contract, awarding, 267
Construction contracts, 267
Construction management, 268
Context analysis, 250–251
Context evaluation, of CIPP model, 71–72
Contingent fund, 360
Continuous audits, 160
Continuous budget, 134, 360
Contract administration, 170
Contract agreement, fraud and, 198
Contract bonds, 313
Contract management, 317
Contract option, 105
Contracted services, 243, 326, 360
Contract(s), 25
awarding, 267
bidding on, 267
construction, 267
food service, 328
negotiated, 312
professional negotiations, 182–189
transportation, 320–321, 326
Contractual authority, of school districts, 25–26
Contractual employment arrangements, termination of, 181
Control information, 68
Coons, John E., 20
Cooperation, in labor-management relations, 169
Cooperative insurers, 307
Coordinate education, 251
Cost accounting, 360
Cost analysis, food services, 334–335
Cost benefit, 360

Cost center, 360
Cost-effectiveness analysis, 65–66, 232, 360
Cost stream, 220, 360
CPM (critical path method), 58–61, 268, 360
Credit, 145, 360
Crime, school-related, 335–336
Criminal noninsurability, 297
Critical path method (CPM), 58–61, 268, 360
Current, 360
Current assets, 360
Current expense, 360
Current funds, 360
Current liabilities, 360
Curriculum or program premise, 22
Custodial department, 233–240
analysis, 237
assignment, 236–238
duties of, 171, 235
equipment inventory, 231
reduction in force, 239–240
scheduling of services, 244–245
staff selection, 235–236
standards, 234
supervision of, 238–239
training of staff, 236
union agreements, 240
work time, 239

Data, 85
Data base, 360
Data-based management system, 85
Data collection, 88
Data flows, 8
Data processing, 360
cooperative centers for, 96–97
equipment for, 94–96
future of, 108
Data processing system, 93–94
Debit, 145, 360
Debt service, 360
Debt service fund, 360
Decentralization, 344–348
of budget, 361
of food service operations, 331
of operations, 236
of storage, 214–215
Declarations, in insurance contract, 301
Delinquent taxes, 361
Delivery of education services, 347–348
Delphi Process, 74–76, 361
Demographic analysis, 250
Demographic forecasting, 69–70
Depreciation, 361
Desegregation, 31, 319

Destruction, of obsolete equipment and materials, 213–214
Digital computing systems, 102–105
Disaster recovery, for computer centers, 106–107
Disbursements, 361
Disciplinary action, employee, 179–180
Discrimination, of race and/or sex, 29
Distribution systems, 214–217
District-owned transportation, 321
District use, of zero-based budgeting, 133
Diversification, 289
Division of labor and specialization, 53
Double-entry bookkeeping, 145, 147–148, 361
Drugs, 336
Due process, 29–30
Dynamic programming, 361

EAP (Employee Assistance Program), 190–191, 361
Edmonds, Ron, 11
Education Amendments of 1972, Title IX-Prohibition of Sex Discrimination in. *See* Title IX
Education Consolidation and Improvement Act of 1981, 22, 344, 346
Education of the Handicapped Act of 1975 (P.L. 94-142), 31–32, 254, 346
Educational administration, 7
Educational budget, 111, 361
Educational decisions, perspectives of, 7–8
Educational malpractice, 301
Educational obsolescence, vs. physical obsolescence, 222
Educational plan, 15–16, 35, 69, 136
Educational reform movement, 10, 17
Educational specifications, for new construction, 262–263
Educational vouchers, 20–21
Educators, purchasing and, 196–197
Effective ratio, 66
Effectiveness, 10–11
Electrostatic discharge, 241
Elementary and Secondary Education Act of 1965, 22, 343, 346
Elementary school, staff allotments, 117–118
Emergency maintenance, 227–228, 361
Employee Assistance Program (EAP), 190–191, 361
Employees. *See* Personnel
Encumbrances, 151, 361
Endorsements, 302, 361
Endowment fund, 361
Energy
    of administrator, 354–355

expenditures, for consumable supplies, 232
    management, 232–233
Energy audit, 232
Energy conservation, in facility planning, 272–273
Energy crisis, transportation systems and, 326
Energy-efficient construction, 220–221
Englehart, N.L., Sr., 2
Enrollment
    decline, 273–274, 275–276
Enrollment-based data, for demographic forecasting, 70
Enrollment forecasting, 252–253
Enrollments, future, 253
Entry, 361
Environment, of existing facility, evaluation of, 254–255
Environmental hazards, 241
Equalization programs, 46
Equipment, 361
    peripheral, 106
    types of, for information systems, 102–108
Equity, 11, 143–144, 145, 361
    taxation and, 39–40
Equity or fund balance accounts, 150
Estimated revenue summary, 151
Evaluation
    models, 70–72
    of purchasing, inventory and distribution systems, 216
    of staff, 177–178
Examination for the Certification of Educators in Texas (EXCET), 52
Excellence Movement, 11
Exclusions, 302, 361
Expenditure, in cash for investment equation, 279–280
Expenditure plan, budgeting and, 35
Expenditure summary, 151
Expenditures, 144, 361
Expenditures plan, in budget process, 136
Express warranties, 198, 362
External audits, 160
External reporting, 163–164

Facilities
    data, for PPBES, 128
    existing, evaluation of, 253–256
    private sector provision of, 262
    rental, 261
    sharing, 261
    upgrading, 275
Facility planner, in comprehensive strategic planning, 249

Faculty, in comprehensive strategic planning, 249
Fast tracking, 268
Federal Home Loan Mortgage Corporation
    (Freddie mAC), 284
Federal Impact Law 815, 256
Federal National Mortgage Association (Fannie
    Mae), 284
Federal Reserve Board, 287
Feedback, methods for obtaining, 78–80
Fidelity bond, 362
Fidelity bonds, 313
Field trips, 325
Finance office, 125
Finance support services, for site-based
    management, 349
Finance systems, constitutionality of, 20
Financial base decline, planning for, 274
Financial data, for planning, programming,
    budgeting, evaluation system, 128
Financial expertise, of administrator, 353
Financial resources
    analysis of, 256–262
    defining limits of dollars available, 125
Financial transactions, 150, 153–155
Fire and casualty insurers, 303–304
Fire insurance, 301
Fiscal accountability legislation, 20
Fiscal and economic perspectives, of
    administrator, 343–344
Fiscal forecast, cash flow, 280–282
Fiscal period, 362
Fiscal policy, control systems for, 26–27
Fixed assets, 362
Fixed charges, 362
Flat grant programs, 45, 47
Floppy disk, 362
Flow chart, 362
Flow models, 362
Food services, 362
    accounting, 334–335
    coordination with educational program, 330
    cost analysis, 334–335
    food preparation systems, 331
    in-service training, 330
    menu planning, 331–332
    planning, 327, 334
    policies of, 328–329
    portion control, 331–332
    prices, 331–332
    of private sector vs. contracted, 328
    purchasing, 332–334
    reporting, 334–335
    rules, regulations and procedures for, 329
    staff, 329–330

    supervision of, 329–330
    time constraints and, 329
    waste considerations, 327
Forecasting
    property tax, 43–44
Formal bids, 205, 362
Formal organization, 53
Foundation allotment, 120
Foundation programs, 45, 46
Fraud, 198
Friable asbestos, 362
Friedman, Milton, 11
Fringe benefits, 190, 312
Full state funded, 45, 47
Function, 362
Functional budget, 134, 362
Functional overlap, 362
Fund, 362
Fund accounting, steps, 148–149
Fund accounts, 362
Fund balance, 143–144, 145, 362
Furniture, procurement of, 269–270

Game theory, 362
General fund, 363
General ledger, 150–151, 158, 363
General liability insurance, 300, 307
Generally accepted accounting procedures
    (GAAP), 159–160
Governing boards, in comprehensive strategic
    planning, 249
Government National Mortgage Association
    (Ginnie Mae), 284
Governmental Accounting, Auditing and
    Financial Reporting, 159, 162
Grants, 120–121, 346
Grants-in-aid, 363
Grievance procedures, 188–189
Group negotiations
    with outside consultation, 185–186
    without outside consultation, 185
Group purchase/cooperative insurance, 305–307
Guaranteed tax yield/base model, 45, 46–47

Hardware, computer, 363
    backup provisions, 96
    costs of, 96
    need, selection process and, 94–95
    selection, administrator and, 89–90
Hawaii, 45, 47
Health evaluation, of existing facility, 254
Health maintenance organization (HMO), 310
Heating, ventilating, and air conditioning
    systems (HVAC), 232

Higher Education Act, 22
Hill, Frederick W., 2
Historical perspective, 1–2
HMO (health maintenance organization), 310
Homeowner insurance policies, riders for, 297
Housing, 251
Human interaction concepts, 76–77
Human relations, principles of, 76–77
Human relations phase, 53, 54
Human skills, of administrator, 354

Implied warranties, 198, 363
Improvements, 363
In loco parentis protection, 19
In-service training, 175, 270–271, 330
Income elasticity of yield, 39
Informal bids, 205, 363
Information, definition of, 85
Information flow, role and scope of, data-based
    management and, 88–94
Information generation, administrator's attitudes,
    68–69
Information systems
    computer installation, effect on staff, 90
    cooperative efforts in data processing,
        96–97
    equipment, types of, 102–108
    failure recovery, 87–88
    impact of, 69
    linguistics of, 85–86
    objectives of, 87
    office procedures operations, 108
    physical protection, 98
    recruitment/selection, 92–93
    selection process, 94–99
    standardization and maintenance procedures,
        100–102
    systems concept and, 86–87
    utilization of, 99–102
Input, computer, 363
Input evaluation, of CIPP model, 71–72
Input-output analysis, 363
Inspection, of transportation vehicles and
    equipment, 322–323
Inspections, safety, 240–241
Insurance
    acquisition, planning, 298–300
    definition of, 296
    for employees, 308–311
    no coverage, 305
    options, types of, 302–311
    planning, 295
    role of, 296–298
    vehicle, 313

Insurance agents, 299–300
Insurance brokers, 300
Insurance contracts, 300–302
Insurance coverage, 300
Insurance records, maintenance and protection
    of, 311–312
Insurance Service Office (ISO), 307–308
Insured, definition of, 296
Insurer, 296
    cooperative, 307
    fire and casualty, 303–304
Insuring agreements, 301, 363
Interfund transfers, 363
Interinsurance exchange, 304
Internal accountability, 140
Internal audits, 160, 363
Internal reporting, 164–165
Internships, 174
Inventory control, 212–214, 216, 231, 363
Investment pool, 289
Investment(s), 292, 363
    for cash management, 282–292
    instruments, 284–285
    opportunity, 292
    policy, 292
    returns on, 289
    selection of investment instrument, 286
    strategies, 285–290
    tactics, 290–292
Invoice, 363
Involvement, parent/student/community, 347

Job analysis, 171, 363
Job competence, 170
Job description, 363
Job descriptions, 171–172
Job obsolescence, 175
Job orientation, 173
Job training, 173–174
Journal, 150, 364
Journalizing, 155, 158
Judgment, 364
Junk bonds, 285
Jurisdiction, legal, 21–22
Just-in-time purchasing, 195

Keys, stolen, 244

Labor agreement, administration of, 186
Labor-management relations, personnel
    administration and, 168–169
Labor relations practices, alternative, 184
Laboratories, maintenance and operation of, 241
Land, 364

Law, 19–20
  administrative, 22
  data-processing records-keeping systems and, 93–94
  insurance contract requirements and, 300–301
  insurance contracts and, 300–301
  investments and, 283
  judge-made, 22
  legal opinion, 364
  levels and sources of, 22
  purchasing and, 197–198
  school personnel and, 137–138
Lawrence, Paul, 56
Leadership, 52, 354
Leadership in Educational Administration Development (LEAD), 53
Leadership training programs, 52–53
Learning, 7, 12
Leasing, salvage and, 213
Least cost estimating and scheduling (LESS), 60, 364
Ledger, 150–151, 364
Legislation, 20
LESS (least cost estimating and scheduling), 60, 364
Leveraging, 364
Levy, 364
Liabilities, 143–144, 364
Liability accounts, 150
Liability coverage, 294–295
Liability insurance, 307–308, 364
Lighting, existing, evaluation of, 254–255
Linear programming, 64–65, 364
Liquidity, 283, 292, 364
Litigation, precautionary plans, 298
Local education agency (LEA), 327–328, 346–348, 364
Long-term loan, 364
Lorsch, Jay, 56
Loss control program, 295–296
Loss fund, 306

Mainframes, 103
Mainstreaming, 319
Maintenance, 364
  budget considerations and, 222
  contracts, 105
  cost analysis, 224–225
  definition of, 219, 221
  emergency, 227–228
  of equipment and facilities, legal aspects of, 298
  organization of, 223–224
  periodic, 227

personnel, 364
personnel, selection and training of, 228–229
philosophy, 246
philosophy for, 221–222
preventive, 226–227
records, 229–230
recurring, 227
scheduling of services, 244–245
of transportation vehicles and equipment, 322–323
types of, 225–228
Management
  applications, 58–81. *See also specific applications*
  classical approach, 53–54
  concepts, nature of, 51–53
  private vs. public sector, 57–58
  school business administration as subset of, 58
  science, establishment of, 55–57
  umbrella concept of, 87
Management by objective (MBO), 55, 364
  goals, 73
  key features, 72–73
  mission, 73
  rewards, 74
  staff evaluation, 73–74, 177
Management information systems (MIS), 312, 364
  administrator's attitude and, 68–69
  analytical prerequisites, 67
  applications, 66–67
  development of, 67–68
  flow chart, 67
  impact of, 69
  informational requirements, 68
  purpose, 66
  reports, 88
  role and scope of information flow, 88–94
  systems concept and, 86–87
  utilization, 99
Management skills, of administrator, 354
Management theory, evolution of, 53
March, James, 56
Marketing, of municipal bonds, 260
Mastery learning, 12
Materials
  educational, distribution of, 214–215
  flow of, warehousing and, 211
Mayo, Elton, 56
McGregor, Douglas, 56
Mechanical budget, 112–113, 365
Mediation, 186, 365
Medical insurance, 310
Menus, for food services, 331–332

Microcomputer, 105, 365
Minicomputer, 104, 105, 365
Minutes of Board of Election, 25
MIS. *See* Management information systems
Modernization costs, 275–276
Modular construction, 268
Money management, 26, 27
Money market certificates, 285
Money Market Funds, 285
Mothballing, 276
Motivation, employee, 176
Multiple agency utilization, 263, 276
Multiple agent personnel, in comprehensive
    strategic planning, 249–250
Multiple control, 1
Mutual companies, 303

National Association of Public School Business
    Officials, 2
National Association of Secondary School
    Principals (NASSP), 51
National Defense Education Act of 1958, 22,
    343, 345
National Education Association and Council for
    Exceptional Children, 297
National Science Foundation Act, 22
Natural systems, 55
Needs assessment, 365
Negligence, 297–298, 313
Negotiated contracts, 312
Negotiations, 365
    individual, 184–185
    professional, 182–189
Network analysis, 365
    advantages of, 64
    critical path method (CPM), 58–61
    program evaluation and review technique
        (PERT), 58, 60–61
Nonbinding arbitration, 187
Noncompliance, 31
Noninstructional services. *See also* Auxiliary
    services
    for site-based management, 349–350
Nonrevenue monies, 26
Notice to bidders, 365
Numerical adequacy, 255–256

Object, 365
Object classification, 365
Objectives, establishing, by Delphi Process,
    75–76
Obligations, 365
Occupational Safety and Health Act (OSHA),
    254, 314, 365

Odd lots, 291
Office procedures operations, 108
Ohio accounting system, 152–154
On-the-job training, 174
Open system-rational actor era, 56
Open system-social actor, 56
Open systems, 55
Operating procedures, in-service training,
    270–271
Operation, plant, 230, 365
    asbestos management, 241–242
    cost reduction, 232
    custodial department, organization of, 233–240
    definition of, 219
    energy and resource conservation, 232–233
    environmental hazards, 241
    inspections, 240–241
    pest control, 242
    philosophy, 246
    philosophy of, 230
    scheduling of custodial and maintenance
        services, 244–245
    scheme for, 232
    security of, 243–244
Operational information, 68
Orientation, job, 173
Orientation and training programs, 270–271
OSHA, 254, 314, 365
Output, 365

Parent, involvement of, 347
Parent choice, 11, 20
Participatory budget, 134–135, 365
Passbook savings, 285
Passwords, 94
Payroll, 365
Payroll deductions and withholding, 365
PCB exposure, 241
Per-call basis maintenance contracts, 105
Percentage-equalization models, 45, 46, 47–48
Performance evaluation and review techniques
    (PERT), 55
Periodic maintenance, 227, 365
Perlman, Lewis J., 11–12
Personal interest, conflict of, 28
Personnel
    allocations, in school budget, 115–116
    allotments, 117–119
    benefits, 361
    in budget process, 137–138
    budgeting, 189–191
    classification, 168
    classified, noncertified, philosophy, 167
    in comprehensive strategic planning, 249

Personnel *(continued)*
  computer installation, effects of, 90
  data processing training, 93
  development of, 175–176
  discipline of, 179–180
  due process-related problems, 30
  evaluation of, 73–74, 177–178
  for food services, 329–330
  insurance for, 308–311
  involvement in site-based budgeting, 122,
    124–126
  maintenance, selection and training of,
    228–229
  motivation/career ladder, 176
  personal/professional liability policy,
    297
  planning and, 167
  promotion of, 179
  recruitment, 92–93
  renewal activities, 175–176
  retirements, 181–182
  riffing, 312
  for security service, 337
  selection, 92–93, 172–173
  staff accounting, 368
  termination, 180–181
  transportation, supervision and training of,
    323–324
  unemployment insurance, 311
  wellness programs, 310
Personnel administration
  challenges of, 167–170
  labor-management relations, 168–169
  orientation, training, development and
    motivation, 173–176
  planning and recruitment, 171–173
  professional negotiations, 182–189
  subordinator-subordinate relationships,
    169–170
Personnel data, for PPBES, 128
Personnel supervision, 176–182
PERT. *See* Program evaluation and review
  technique
Pest control, 242
Pesticides, 242
Petty cash, 365
Physical tests, of quality, 200–201
Planning, 365
  administrator and, 4, 6, 352–353
  of auxiliary services, 317–318
  benefits of, 112
  in budgetary process, 111. *See also* Budgeting
  of classified personnel, 167
  comprehensive strategic, steps in, 248–249

construction, 266
  of custodial and maintenance services,
    244–245
  for decline in enrollment, 273–274
  for financial base decline, 274
  food services, 334
  of food services, 327
  fund use, in site-based budgeting,
    122–123
  future perspective and, 342
  information, 68
  insurance, 295
  internal accountability and, 140
  legal aspects of, 20
  for local revenues, 43–44
  of menus, for food service, 331–332
  by one-person, 16
  by outside agency, 16
  participation in, 248
  personnel, 171–173
  security, 337–338
  in site-based budgeting, 114–115
  for state revenues, 45–48
  as strategy and process, 13–15
  transportation services, 319–324
  for vandalism control, 271–272
Planning, Programming, Budgeting, Evaluation
    System (PPBES), 15, 366
  accounting classification, 155, 156
  decision-making process, 126–127
  essential aspects of, 126
  evolution of, 126–130
  facilities data, 128
  financial data, 128
  personnel data, 128
  procedures, 128–130
  program data, 127
  pupil data, 127
Planning Programming Budgeting Evaluation
    System (PPBES), 15
Plant operation. *See* Operation
Plant security, 366
Pooling, insurance, 305
Portion control, for food services, 331–332
Post-audits, 160
Post-sale planning, 260, 366
Posting, 151, 366
Power bargaining, in labor-management
    relations, 169
PPBES (Planning Programming Budgeting
    Evaluation System), 15, 366
Pre-audits, 160
Premium on bonds sold, 366
Preventive maintenance, 226–227, 366

Price quotations, 202–204
Prices, for food services, 331–332
Principal, 366
  administrative responsibilities of, 6
  administrator and, 5
  fund use planning and, 122–123
  security service and, 337–338
  in site-based management, 348
Principal systems and priorities, 366
Privacy Act of 1974, 366
Private sector management, vs. public sector
    management, 57–58
Private sector provision of facilities, 262
Procedural due process, 30
Process evaluation, of CIPP model, 71–72
Procurement, of furniture and equipment,
    269–270
Product evaluation, of CIPP model, 71–72
Professional negotiations, 182–189
  civil service-union association, 187–188
  definition of, 182
  grievance procedures, 188–189
Professional standards, 297
Program, 366
Program adequacy, 255
Program budgeting, 127, 130
Program data, for planning, programming,
    budgeting, evaluation system, 127
Program evaluation and review technique
    (PERT), 58, 268, 366
  advantages, 64
  analysis example, 61–63
  charting the list of activities, 62
  diagram, 63
  estimation of time distribution, 62
  listing activities, 62
  PERT network, 60–61
  vs. critical path method, 60
Programming, 366
Programming language, 366
Promotion policies, employee, 179
Property insurance, 295, 300, 302–303, 366
Property-related rights, denial of, 30
Property taxes, 41–44
Proprietary accounts, 366
Prorating, 366
Protection, definition of, 296
Public finance officer, responsibilities of, 279
Public Law 92-318, 29
Public Law 94-142, 31–32, 254, 346
Public relations, for new construction, 270
Public transit system, 320
Pupil accounting, 367
Pupil activity fund, 367

Pupil data, for planning, programming,
    budgeting, evaluation system, 127
Pupil record file, characteristics of, 103
Purchase expediter, 210
Purchase order, 155–157, 198, 207, 209, 367
Purchasing, 194–195, 216–217, 367
  accounting and, 211
  automation of, 202
  bidding process, 205–207
  of computer software, 100
  educators and, 196–197
  evaluation of system, 216
  follow-up, 207–211
  for food services, 332–334
  of maintenance, 226
  objectives, 199
  powers and responsibilities, 195–196
  process, establishment of, 124
  quantities, 201–202
  quotations, 202–204
  relationship to other administrative divisions,
    199
  requisition, 199–200
  specifications, 200–201
Purchasing cooperatives or consortia, 207
Purchasing department, 124
Purchasing form, 124

Quadratic programming, 367
Qualitative aspects, of new construction, 263
Quality, definition and testing of, 200–201
Quantitative aspects, of new construction, 263
Queuing theory (Waiting-Line Theory), 367

Race discrimination, 29
Radon, 240–241
RAMPS (resource allocation and multi-project
    scheduling), 60
Rational/political/economic budget, 135–136
Rational systems, 55
Real estate, 367
Rebates, 367
Reciprocals, 304
Records
  maintenance, 323
Recreation, 251
Recurring maintenance, 227, 367
Recycling program, 232
Redemption of principal, 367
Reference manuals, 86
Refund, 367
Refunding bonds, 367
Register, 367
Rehabilitation, 275–276

Reimbursement, 367
Remodeling, 367
Remote entry, 367
Rental, of facilities, 261
Rental-purchase agreement, 367
Repairs, 367
REPO (repurchase agreement), 367
Reporting, 161–165
    external, 163–164
    food services, 334–335
    internal, 164–165
    nature of, 161
    for site-based management, 350
Repurchase agreements (REPOS), 284–285
Requisition, 208, 367
Requisitioner, 207
Resource allocation, budget process and, 138
Resource allocation and multi-project scheduling
    (RAMPS), 60, 368
Resource and fiscal decisions, 36
Retirement, early, 312
Retirements, 181–182
Revenue plan, 35, 136
Revenue summary, 151
Revenue(s), 26, 144, 368
    balanced and diversified sources, 41–42
    forecasting, 280
    local, planning for, 43–44
    sources of, 36
    taxation and, 40–42
Revolving fund, 368
Riding the yield curve, 290
Riffing, 312, 368
Risk
    analysis of, in computer center disasters,
        106–107
    definition of, 294
    exposure to, elimination of, 297
    insurable, 296–297
    investments and, 283
Risk management
    aggressive program, 296
    alternative financing, 311
    components of, 295
    insurance role, 296–298
    personnel and contractor concerns,
        312–313
Round lots, 291
Routing, 214, 321–322

Safety inspections, 240–241, 254
Safety standards, for transportation system,
    325–326
Salary increase policy, 189–190

Salvage, 213–214
Scheduling, 321–322
    of custodial and maintenance services,
        244–245
    of preventive maintenance, 227
    by request, 214
    routing, 214
School budget, 111
    composition of, 115–116
    nonstaff components, 116
School business administration, management
    and, 58
School capital outlay, sources of support,
    258–259
School districts, 23, 346
    contractual authority of, 25–26
    responsibilities of, 24
    state-delegated responsibilities of, 24
School leaders, performance goals for, 51
School monies, classification of, 26
School prayer decisions, 31
School reform, 11–13
School system, 368
"Schools of choice" legislation, 319
Secondary schools, staff allotments, 118–119
Securities, 368
Securities and Exchange Commission, 282
Security
    computer, 94, 97–98
    of physical plant and equipment, 243–244
Security requirements, for bid deposits, 206
Security services, 335–338
    approaches to, 336–337
    need for, 335–336
    planning, 271–272, 337–338
    principal and, 337–338
    staffing, 337
    students and, 338
    supervision, 337
    vandalism control, 271–272
Self-insurance, 295, 304–305
Selling, of surplus, 213
Selznick, Philip, 56
Sequential planning, 368
Serial bonds, 368
Service, definition of, 296
Service-center concept, for data-processing
    equipment, 96
Sex discrimination, 29
Sharing of facilities, 261
Short-term loan, 368
Short-term rollovers and matching, 291
Simplex method, 64
Sinking fund, 368

Site-based budgeting, 114–126
  building allocation procedures, 117–119
  community and staff involvement, 122,
      124–126
  components of, 115–117
  control procedures, 121–124
  process of, 114–115
  using allocation model, 119–121
Site-based management, 17, 141, 149, 368
  administrator and, 5–6
  auditing, 350
  auditing for, 350
  labor-relations conflicts, 169
  management information systems and, 88–89
  operations practices and, 230
  purchasing, 197, 207
  purpose of, 4
  reporting, 350
  security personnel and, 337, 338
  support services for, 349–350
Sociometric overlap, 368
Software, computer, 368
  development of, 99–100
  need, selection process and, 94–95
  purchase of, 100
  selection, administrator and, 89–90
  standardization of formats, 102
Sound replacement cost, 302–303
Sovereign immunity concept, 27–28
Span of control, 53
Spreads, 291
Staff. *See* Personnel
Stakeholders, 368
Standardization of tasks, 53
State
  aid programs, classification of, 45–48
  capital funding responsibility, 256–257, 261
  compliance requirements, 32
  full state-funded status, 43
  funding, interaction with local funding,
      44–45
  increased control, movement for, 345–346
  local school district responsibilities, delegation
      of, 24
  mandated purchasing responsibilities, 195
  public school fund accounting systems and,
      142–143
  qualifications for subsidized food programs,
      332
  responsibility and authority of, bases for,
      23–24
  revenue forecasting, 47–48
  as revenue source, 36
  revenues, planning for, 45–48

school capital outlay sources, 258–259
statutory bases for budgeting, 112
transportation mandates, 319
State insurance, 304
Statements, 368
States, accounting systems for school districts
    and, 152
Statutes, legal, 22
Statutory due process, 30
Stock insurance company, 368
Stock life insurance companies, 303
Storage, central vs. decentralized, 214–215
Storeroom layout, 212
Stores, 368
Strike contingency planning, 189
Students, 249, 347, 369
Subsidized food programs, 327, 332
Substantive rights, 29–30
Sugarman, Stephen D., 20
Superintendency team, organizational context
    of, 4–6
Superintendent, 1, 4
  business administration function of, 3
  planning and, 15
  state, 23
Supervision
  of food services, 329–330
  of personnel, 176–182
  of security service, 337
Supplies
  consumable, for computer center, 107
  materials and equipment, resource allocations
      for, 120
  nonconsumable, for computer center, 107
  recycling program, 232
Supply, 369
Support services, for site-based management,
    350
Supporting services, 369
Surety bond, 369
Surety bonds, 313
Surplus, 213–214, 369
Swaps, 291
Systems analysis, 369

T accounts, 145, 146, 152
Tax, 369
  ability-based, 37
  adequacy of, 40–41
  benefit-based, 37
  components of, 37
  definition of, 36–37
  elasticity, 41
  flexibility of, 41

Tax *(continued)*
  stability of, 41
  yield, 39
Tax anticipation notes, 369
Tax elasticity, 38–39
Tax impact, 38
Tax Reform Act of 1986, 292
Tax shifting, 37–38
Taxation, 48–49
  administrative feasibility and, 42–43
  criteria, 39–43
  distributive aspects, 38
Taxation theories, 37
Taxes receivable, 369
Taylor, Frederick W., 53, 56, 168
Teacher empowerment policies, 10–11
Teaching, administration and, 7
Term bonds, 369
Termination, of personnel, 180–181
Texas Education Agency, leadership training
    program, 52
Textbooks, selection of, 7
Theory X, 56
Theory Y, 56
Time and motion studies, 53
Time distribution, estimation of, 62
Time sharing, of data-processing equipment,
    96
Time-sharing, 369
Title IX, 29, 172–173, 236, 254, 369
Tort, 301, 369
Tort liability, 27–28, 297
Training, of custodial staff, 236
Transportation services, 32, 318, 367
  contract vs. district-owned equipment,
      320–321
  contracting, 326
  energy crisis and, 326
  evaluation of, 324–325
  planning, 319–324
  routing and scheduling, 321–322
  safety standards for system, 325–326
  specifications for system, 325–326
  supervision and training of personnel,
      323–324
  utilization of, 324–325
  vehicle summary, 225
Treasury bills or notes, 289
Trial balance, 148, 369
Tuition tax credits, 20
Tutorials, 86

Unemployment insurance, 311
Unencumbered balance, 369

Union agreements, 182–183, 240
Unions, grievance procedures, 188–189
Uniqueness of function, 53
Unit control, 1
Unit cost, 370
Unit record equipment, 370
United States
  capital funding, 261
  federal aid, 36
  federal deficit of, 343–344
  federal responsibility and authority, bases of,
      22
  increased control, movement for, 345–346
  mandated purchasing powers, 195
  as revenue source, 36
  subsidized food programs, 332
United States Department of Education,
    325
Unity of command, 53
University of Texas, training program for
    educational administrators, 52
U.S. Government Agency bonds, 284
U.S. Treasury bills, bonds and notes, 284
User's manuals, 86

Valuation, 302–303, 370
Vandalism control, planning for, 271–272
Vandalism prevention, 244
Vehicle(s)
  inspection of, 322–323
  insurance for, 313
  liability, 307
  log, for mail and distribution, 215
  maintenance of, 322–323
Vendor evaluation, for bidding, 206
Vendor notification, of purchasing department
    rejections, 200
Vendor performance, evaluation of, 203–204
Vestibule training, 174
Vocational Education Act of 1963, 22
Voucher, 150, 370
Vouchers payable, 370

Warehousing, 216–217
  inventory control and, 211–214
  storeroom layout, 212
Warrant, 370
Warranties, 198
Weber, Max, 56
Weick, Karl, 56
Wellness programs, 310
Word processing, 370
Work order, 370
Work schedules, 229

Workers' compensation, 307, 309–310
Working budget, 137

Yearly budget, 113, 370
Yield curve, 286–287, 290

Yield on investment, 283, 286–288
Yield rates, 282

Zero balance accounting, 289–290, 370
Zero-based budgeting, 130–133, 370